# SECESSION FROM A MEMBER STATE AND WITHDRAWAL FROM THE EUROPEAN UNION

This is the first book to jointly scrutinise two existential issues for the EU: withdrawal of a member state (i.e. Brexit) and territorial secession (affecting Scotland, Catalonia and beyond). The book applies normative and empirical analysis, explores new approaches and discusses the deep theoretical problems unleashed by these processes. Featuring a superb constellation of legal and political science scholars, the book combines specific legal analysis and considers the political dynamics behind the processes. It provides extensive coverage and sophisticated analysis of the interpretation of Article 50 and the possible consequences it may have. The implications of withdrawal and secession on EU citizenship are discussed in depth and there is an overview of the evolving nature of the relationship between the regions and the EU. Finally, there is an engaging normative discussion on the deeper meaning of these two processes with respect to the objective of European integration.

CARLOS CLOSA is Professor of Political Science at the Institute of Public Goods and Policies, Consejo Superior de Investigaciones Científicas, Madrid and Program Associate at the Robert Schuman Centre for Advanced Studies at the European University Institute, Florence.

# SECESSION FROM A MEMBER STATE AND WITHDRAWAL FROM THE EUROPEAN UNION

## Troubled Membership

Edited by

CARLOS CLOSA

*Institute for Public Goods and Policies, IPP*
*Spanish National Research Council, CSIC, Madrid*

**CAMBRIDGE**
**UNIVERSITY PRESS**

University Printing House, Cambridge CB2 8BS, United Kingdom

One Liberty Plaza, 20th Floor, New York, NY 10006, USA

477 Williamstown Road, Port Melbourne, VIC 3207, Australia

4843/24, 2nd Floor, Ansari Road, Daryaganj, Delhi – 110002, India

79 Anson Road, #06–04/06, Singapore 079906

Cambridge University Press is part of the University of Cambridge.

It furthers the University's mission by disseminating knowledge in the pursuit of education, learning, and research at the highest international levels of excellence.

www.cambridge.org
Information on this title: www.cambridge.org/9781107172197
DOI: 10.1017/9781316771464



First published 2017

Printed in the United States of America by Sheridan Books, Inc.

*A catalogue record for this publication is available from the British Library.*

ISBN 978-1-107-17219-7 Hardback
ISBN 978-1-316-62336-7 Paperback

# CONTENTS

*List of Figures and Tables* page vii
*List of Contributors* viii
*Acknowledgements* xiii
*Table of Cases* xiv
*Legislation* xviii
*List of Abbreviations* xxiii

1 Troubled Membership: Secession and Withdrawal 1
CARLOS CLOSA

2 Secessionism and Its Discontents 12
JHH WEILER

3 Internal Enlargement in the European Union: Beyond Legalism and Political Expediency 32
NEIL WALKER

4 Secession and the Ambiguous Place of Regions Under EU Law 48
CRISTINA FASONE

5 Political and Legal Aspects of Recent Regional Secessionist Trends in some EU Member States (I) 69
JEAN-CLAUDE PIRIS

6 Political and Legal Aspects of Recent Regional Secessionist Trends in some EU Member States (II) 88
JEAN-CLAUDE PIRIS

7 The Reach and Resources of European Law in the Scottish Independence Referendum 106
KENNETH A. ARMSTRONG

8 The Political Rights of EU Citizens and the Right of Secession 134
MANUEL MEDINA ORTEGA

9 Unions and Citizens: Membership Status and Political Rights in Scotland, the UK and the EU 153
JO SHAW

10 Interpreting Article 50: Exit, Voice and ... What about Loyalty? 187
CARLOS CLOSA

11 This Way, Please! A Legal Appraisal of the EU Withdrawal Clause 215
CHRISTOPHE HILLION

12 Be Careful What You Wish for: Procedural Parameters of EU Withdrawal 234
ADAM ŁAZOWSKI

13 EU Citizenship and Withdrawals from the Union: How Inevitable Is the Radical Downgrading of Rights? 257
DIMITRY KOCHENOV

*Index* 287

# FIGURES AND TABLES

## Table

9.1 Scottish Government comparison between status quo and hypothetical Scottish citizenship *page* 166

## Figure

13.1 The value of UK citizenship 282

# CONTRIBUTORS

The Editor:

CARLOS CLOSA is Professor of Political Science, Institute of Public Goods and Policies (IPP), CSIC (Madrid) and previously Director of the Research Area European, transnational and global governance at the Global Governance Program (GGP) of the RSCAS-EUI. He has been Deputy Director of the Centro de Estudios Políticos y Constitucionales (CEPC, Ministry of the President of the Spanish Government) and member of the Venice Commission for Democracy through Law (Council of Europe). He was formerly professor at the Universities of Zaragoza and Complutense (Madrid) and at the Instituto Universitario Ortega y Gasset, in Madrid. He was also Visiting Fellow at the Minda de Gunzburg Centre of Harvard University, Jean Monnet Fellow and Salvador de Madariaga Fellow at the EUI and, between 2010 and 2011, Emile Noël Fellow at the Jean Monnet Centre, NYU. He is currently co-editor of the *European Political Science Review* (EPSR). He has published on EU citizenship, the EU's constitutional structure, Europeanization and the relationship between the EU and member states. His latest monographs are *The Politics of EU Treaty Ratification* (Routledge; 2013) and *Models of Supranational Legal Integration: Comparative Toolbox from the Universe of International and Regional Organizations* (CUP, 2016) with Lorenzo Cassini and he has co-edited *The Future of Europe: Democracy, Legitimacy and Justice after the Euro Crisis* (Rowan and Littlefield, 2014) with Miguel Maduro, Danniel Innenarity and Serge Champeau and he is co-editor with Dimitry Kochenov of *Reinforcing Rule of Law Oversight in the European Union* (CUP, 2016).

The Contributors:

KENNETH A. ARMSTRONG, University of Cambridge

Kenneth A. Armstrong is Professor of European Law at the University of Cambridge. He was previously Professor of EU law at Queen Mary,

University of London. He has also held positions at Keele University and the University of Manchester. He has held visiting positions at Edinburgh University, the European University Institute and at New York University School of Law. He is a Fellow of Sidney Sussex College. He has written extensively in the field of European Union law and policy, with a particular focus on the evolving governance and institutional structures of the EU. His book *Governing Social Inclusion: Europeanization through Policy Coordination* was published by Oxford University Press in 2010 and won the 2011 UACES Best Book Prize. His most recent book is *Brexit Time: Leaving the EU - Why, How and When?* published by Cambridge University Press.

CRISTINA FASONE, LUISS Guido Carli University, Rome

Cristina Fasone is Assistant Professor of Comparative Public Law, Department of Political Science, LUISS Guido Carli University, Rome. She is holder of a Jean Monnet Module on Parliamentary accountability and technical expertise: budgetary powers, information and communication technologies and elections (PATEU) (2017–2019) within the Summer School on 'Parliamentary Democracy in Europe' at LUISS School of Government. She has been Max Weber Postdoctoral Fellow (2013–2015), European University Institute and has held visiting positions at Georgetown University Law Center, Washington DC, Victoria University of Wellington, European University Institute and Uppsala University. Her research focuses on parliaments and Constitutional Courts in the EU and in the Eurozone crisis, parliamentary committee systems and forms of government (*Sistemi di commissioni parlamentari e forme di governo* is the title of her monograph, Cedam, 2012), and national and EU budgetary powers with procedures. Her last co-edited book, with Nicola Lupo, is titled Interparliamentary Cooperation in the Composite European Constitution (Hart, 2016).

CHRISTOPHE HILLION, Leiden University, Faculty of Law, SIEPS, Stockholm

Christophe Hillion is Professor of European Law at the Universities of Leiden and Gothenburg, Research Professor at the Norwegian Institute of International studies (NUPI) and Centre for European Law in Oslo, and Senior Researcher at the Swedish Institute for European Policy Studies (SIEPS) in Stockholm. He has published on external relations, enlargement and constitutional law of the European Union.

DIMITRY KOCHENOV, University of Groningen

Dimitry Kochenov is Professor of EU Constitutional Law in Groningen and Fellow of the Institute of Global and European Studies, Basel. He has held numerous fellowships and visiting professorships worldwide, including, most importantly, at Princeton (Crane Fellowship in Law and Public Affairs, Woodrow Wilson School), NYU Law School (Émile Noël Fellowship), Osaka Graduate School of Law, University of Turin (Italy) and College of Europe (Natolin) and numerous others. Professor Kochenov has advised international institutions and governments, including the governments of the Netherlands and Malta, and has published widely in the areas of EU constitutional law and citizenship. His latest edited volumes include *EU Citizenship and Federalism: The Role of Rights* (Cambridge 2017), *The Enforcement of EU Law and Values* (with A Jakab, Oxford, 2017), and *Reinforcing Rule of Law Oversight in the EU*'(with C Closa, Cambridge, 2016).

ADAM ŁAZOWSKI, University of Westminster

Adam Łazowski is Professor of Law in the School of Law at the University of Westminster (London). He obtained a Master's Degree in 1999 and a PhD in 2001 from the Faculty of Law at the University of Warsaw. Between 1999 and 2003, he lectured at the University of Warsaw. During the next two years, he worked as a senior researcher in European law at the T.M.C. Asser Institute (The Hague). His research interests include the law of the European Union as well as public international law. His research has so far led to a number of books, articles, contributions to edited volumes and conference papers. Adam publishes in English and Polish. His book on the preliminary ruling procedure was translated into Bulgarian and Estonian. His work is often cited by Polish courts, including the Supreme Court and the Supreme Administrative Court.

MANUEL MEDINA ORTEGA, Former Member of the European Parliament

Manuel Medina Ortega was a Member of the European Parliament (1986–2009) and Member of the Spanish Parliament (1982–87). He was Professor of International Law and International Relations at Complutense University of Madrid (1959–1975), Professor at the University of Redlands, California (1969–70), Dean of the Faculty of Political Science and Sociology at Complutense University of Madrid (1975), Professor of International Law at the Universidad de La Laguna

(1975–78), Vice-Rector at the Universidad de La Laguna (1976–78) and Professor of International Relations at Complutense University of Madrid (1978–82). He is a member of the Spanish Association of Professors of International Law and International Relations.

JEAN-CLAUDE PIRIS, Former Director-General of the Legal Service of the European Council and of the European Union Council

Jean-Claude Piris is a leading architect of, and authority on, the EU's treaties, institutions, policies, law and procedures. He is CEO of Piris Consulting, a consulting firm on EU and international public law, advising private entities and governments. Mr Piris was the Legal Counsel of the European Council and Director General of the EU Council's Legal Service from 1988 to 2010. During this period, he participated in all important decisions on EU treaties (from Maastricht to Lisbon), on EU legislation and external relations and on economic and monetary union. He also acted as the Council's advocate in the Court of Justice of the EU. He is an honorary French Conseiller d'Etat and a former French diplomat to the UN, as well as the former Director of Legal Affairs of the OECD. An ENA alumni, he has written many articles and a number of books, including *The Lisbon Treaty: a legal and political analysis* (Cambridge University Press, 2010, foreword by Angela Merkel). Most recently he has published extensively on Brexit.

JO SHAW, University of Edinburgh

Jo Shaw holds the Salvesen Chair of European Institutions and is the Director of the Institute for Advanced Studies in the Humanities at the University of Edinburgh. She previously held Jean Monnet Chairs at the Universities of Manchester and Leeds. Her interests lie in EU law in its politico-legal context, with an emphasis on citizenship and constitutionalism, and in other aspects of citizenship. She is Co-Director of the EUDO Citizenship Observatory. She tweets @joshaw.

NEIL WALKER, University of Edinburgh

Neil Walker holds the Regius Chair of Public Law and the Law of Nature and Nations at the University of Edinburgh. His main area of expertise is constitutional theory. He has published extensively on the constitutional dimension of legal order at sub-state, state, supranational and global levels. He has also published at length on the relationship between security, legal order and political community. He maintains a more general interest in broader questions of legal theory as well as in various substantive dimensions of UK and EU public law. Previously he was Professor of Legal and Constitutional Theory at the University of Aberdeen (1996–2000), and Professor of European Law at the European University Institute in Florence (2000–8), where he was also the first Dean of Studies (2002–5). He has also held various visiting appointments – including the Eugene Einaudi Chair of European Studies, University of Cornell (2007), Distinguished Visiting Professor of Law, University of Toronto (2007), Global Professor of Law, New York University (2011–12) and Sidley Austin-Robert D. McLean Visiting Professor of Law, Yale University (2014–5). His most recent books are Intimations of Global Law (Cambridge, 2015) and The Scottish Independence Referendum: Constitutional and Political Implications (co-editor, Oxford, 2016)

J H H WEILER, Professor, New York University

Professor J H H Weiler is University Professor and Director of the Jean Monnet Centre at the NYU School of Law. He also serves as Senior Fellow at the Centre for European Studies at Harvard. He has recently served as President of the European University, Florence. Weiler is Editor-in-Chief of the European Journal of International Law and ICON – The International Journal of Constitutional Law.

# ACKNOWLEDGEMENTS

This book originates in a seminar held at the European University Institute (EUI) in Florence on July 2014 within the Global Governance Program (GGP) at the time I was co-director of the Research Strand on European, Transnational and Global Governance in that program. I am deeply indebted to Brigid Laffan, program director and also director of the Robert Schuman Centre for Advanced Studies (RSCAS), who enthusiastically supported the project. Several participants in the seminar fed into the discussions and the final drafts of the authors and their input deserves full credit: Graham Avery, Alan Boyle, Paul Craig, Ignacio Molina, Andreu Olesti Rayo, Paolo Ponzano, Richard Rose, Andrew Scott, Antonello Tancredi and Bruno de Witte.

Alastair Maciver provided invaluable research assistantship in the preparation of the seminar, the elaboration of the summary paper which followed and the preparation of the book proposal. This summary paper was published in the EUI Working Paper Series. Harry Panagopulos carefully prepared the edition of this manuscript before sending it to press.

The idea for this book derives from conversations with Christophe Hillion, who first signalled the interest of treating the two processes jointly, although full responsibility for any shortcomings here remains totally mine.

# TABLE OF CASES

### European Union Case Law

Case C-62/14, *Gauweiler and Others* v. *Deutscher Bundestag*, ECLI:EU:C:2015

Case C-650/13, *Delvigne* v. *Commune de Lesparre Médoc and Préfet de la Gironde*, ECLI:EU:C:2015:648

Case C-156/13, *Digibet Ltd and Gert Albers v Westdeutsche Lotterie GmbH & Co. OHG.* ECLI:EU:C:2014:1756

Opinion 2/13 of 18 December 2014, ECLI:EU:C:2014:2454

Case C-399/11, *Stefano Melloni* v. *Ministerio fiscal*, ECLI:EU:C:2013:107

Case C-75/11, *Commission of the European Communities* v. *Austria*, ECLI:EU:C:2012:605

Case C-364/10, *Hungary* v. *Slovak Republic*, ECLI:EU:C:2012:630

Case C-434/09, *McCarthy*, EU:C:2011:277

Case C-34/09, *Gerardo Ruiz Zambrano v Office national de l'emploi (ONEm)*, EU:C:2011:124

Case C-135/08, *Janko Rottman v Freistaat Bayern*, EU:C:2010:104

Case C-103/08, *Arthur Gottwald v Bezirkshauptmannschaft Bregenz*, ECLI:EU:C:2009:597

Case C-192/05, K. Tas-Hagen and R. A. Tas v Raadskamer WUBO van de Pensioen- en Uitkeringsraad. ECLI:EU:C:2006:676

Case C-300/04, *M. G. Eman and O. B. Sevinger v College van burgemeester en wethouders van Den Haag*, ECLI:EU:C:2006:545

Case C-403/03, *Egon Schempp v Finanzamt München V.*, ECLI:EU:C:2005:446

Case C-145/04, *Kingdom of Spain v United Kingdom of Great Britain and Northern Ireland.*, ECLI:EU:C:2006:543

Case C-265/03, *Igor Simutenkov* v. *Ministerio de Educaciri y Cultura and Real Federacil Espaaaci de Fde Fa*, ECLI:EU:C:2005:213

Case C-209/03, The Queen, on the application of Dany Bidar v London Borough of Ealing and Secretary of State for Education and Skills, ECLI:EU:C:2005:169

Case C-148/02, Carlos Garcia Avello v Belgian State, ECLI:EU:C:2003:539

Case C-338/01, *Commission of the European Communities* v *Council of the European Union* [2004], ECLI:EU:C:2004:253

Case C-253/00, *Antonio Muton y Cia SA and Superior Fruiticola SA* v. *Frumar Ltd and Redbridge Produce Marketing Ltd.*, ECLI:EU:C:2002:497

Case C-413/99, *Baumbast and R v Secretary of State for the Home Department*, ECLI: EU:C:2002:493

Case C-192/99, *The Queen v Secretary of State for the Home Department ex parte Manjit Kaur*, EU:C:2001:106

Case C-184/99, *Grzelczyk*, ECLI:EU:C:2001:458

Case C-63/99, *The Queen* v. *Secretary of State for the Home Department, ex parte Wiesław Gloszczuk and Elżbieta Gloszczuk*, ECLI:EU:C:2001:488;

Case C-224/98, *d'Hoop*, ECLI:EU:C:2002:432

Joined cases T-32 and T-41/98, *Nederlandse Antillen, Nederlandse Antillen* v. *Commission of the European Communities* [2000], ECR II-201

Case C-180/97, *Regione Toscana v Commission of the European Communities* ECLI:EU: C:1997:451

Case C-95/97, *Region Wallonne* v. *Commission* ECLI:EU:C:1997:184

Case T-609/97, *Regione Puglia* v. *Commission of the European Communities and Kingdom of Spain* [1998], ECLI:EU:T:1998:249

Case T-238/97, *Comunidad Autónoma de Cantabria* v. *Council of the European Union* [1998], ECLI:EU:T:1998:126,

Case T-70/97, *Region Wallonne* v. *Commission of the European Communities*, Order of 29 September 1997 [1997], ECR II-1513

Case T-214/95, *Vlaamse Gewest* v. *Commission of the European Communities* [1998], ECLI:EU:T:1998:77

Case C-214/94, Ingrid Boukhalfa v Bundesrepublik Deutschland[ 1996], ECLI:EU: C:1996:174 Opinion 1/91, Opinion of the Court of 14 December 1991. - Opinion delivered pursuant to the second subparagraph of Article 228 (1) of the Treaty. - Draft agreement between the Community, on the one hand, and the countries of the European Free Trade Association, on the other, relating to the creation of the European Economic Area. [1991], ECLI:EU:C:1991:490

Case C-2/90, *Commission of the European Communities v. Kingdom of Belgium* [1992], ECLI:EU:C:1992:310

Case C-192/89, *S. Z. Sevince* v. *Staatssecretaris van Justitie*, ECLI:EU:C:1990:322;

Case C-407/85, *Drei Glocken GmbH and Gertraud Kritzinger v. USL Centro-SUD and Provincia autonoma di Bolzano* [1988], ECLI:EU:C:1988:401 Case C-197/84, *Steinhauser v. City of Biarritz* [1985], ECLI:EU:C:1985:260

Joined cases 35 and 36/82, Elestina Esselina Christina Morson v State of the Netherlands and Head of the Plaatselijke Politie within the meaning of the Vreemdelingenwet; Sweradjie Jhanjan v State of the Netherlands. [1982], ECLI:EU:C:1982:368

Case 104/81, *Hauptzollamt Mainz* v. *C.A. Kupferberg & Cie KG a.A.*, ECLI:EU: C:1982:362

Case 21/74, *Jeanne Airola* v *Commission of the European Communities* [1975], ECLI: EU:C:1975:24

Case 26/62, *NV Algemene Transport- en Expeditie Onderneming van Gend & Loos* v. *Netherlands Inland Revenue Administration*, ECLI:EU:C:1963:1

## European Court of Human Rights

*Jeunesse* v. *The Netherlands* (App. No. 12738/10), ECtHR 3 October, 2014
*KURIĆ and others* v. *Slovenia* (App. No. 26828/06), ECtHR 26 June, 2012
*Matthews* v. UK [GC] (App. No. 24833/99), ECtHR 18 February, 1999
*Beldjoudi* v. *France* (App. No. 12083/86), ECtHR 26 March, 1992

## Other International Courts

*Accordance with International Law of the Unilateral Declaration of Independence in Respect of Kosovo*, Advisory Opinion of 22 July 2010 [2010] *International Court of Justice, Reports of Judgments, Advisory Opinions and Order*

## National Courts

Canada
Supreme Court of Canada, Reference, *re Secession of Quebec* [1998] 2 S.C. 217
Czech Republic
Czech Republic Constitutional Court Judgment Pl. ÚS 19/08: *Treaty of Lisbon* I 2008/11/26
Germany
*BVerfG, Judgement of the Second Senate of 12 October 1993, BVerfGE 89* Cases 2 BvR 2134/92, 2 BvR 2159/92 *Re Maastricht Treaty* [BVerfG 89,155]
BVerfG, Judgment of the Second Senate of 30 June 2009 in joint cases 2 BvE 2/08, 2BvE 5/08, 2 BvR 1010/08, 2BvR 1022/08, 2 BvR 1259/08 and 2 BvR 182/09 (Lisbon Treaty) - paras. (1–421)
Poland
Constitutional Tribunal, 11 May 2005, Case K 18/04 (re Conformity of the Accession Treaty 2003 with the Polish Constitution) OTK Z.U. 2005/5A/49
Spain
Spanish Constitutional Court, Judgment of 2 December 2015, no. 259/2015. Impugnación de disposiciones autonómicas 6330-2015. Impugnación de disposiciones autonómicas 6330-2015. Formulada por el Gobierno de la Nación respecto de la resolución del Parlamento de Cataluña 1/XI, de 9 de noviembre de 2015, sobre el inicio del proceso político en Cataluña como consecuencia de los resultados electorales del 27 de septiembre de 2015
Spanish Constitutional Court, judgment of 11 June 2015, No. 138/2015, Boletín Oficial del Estado, Nº 138, 6 July 2015 Impugnación de disposiciones autonómicas 6540-2014. Formulada por el Gobierno de la Nación respecto de las actuaciones de la Generalitat de Cataluña relativas a la convocatoria a los catalanes, las catalanas y las

personas residentes en Cataluña para que manifiesten su opinión sobre el futuro político de Cataluña el día 9 de noviembre de 2014

Spanish Constitutional Court Judgment 32/2015 l, 23 February 2015, Boletín Oficial del Estado, Nº 64, 16 March 2015, Section TC Impugnación de disposiciones autonómicas 5830-2014. Formulada por el Gobierno de la Nación en relación con el Decreto del Presidente de la Generalitat de Cataluña 129/2014, de 27 de septiembre, así como de sus anexos, de convocatoria de la consulta no referendaria sobre el futuro político de Cataluña.

Spanish Constitutional Court, judgment 42/2014, 25 March 2014, Boletín Oficial del Estado, Nº 87, 10 April 2014, Section TC Impugnación de disposiciones autonómicas 1389-2013. Formulada por el Gobierno de la Nación respecto de la Resolución del Parlamento de Cataluña 5/X, de 23 de enero de 2013, por la que se aprueba la Declaración de soberanía y del derecho a decidir del pueblo de Cataluña.

Spanish Constitutional Court, Judgment 31/2010, 28 June 2010 Recurso de inconstitucionalidad 8045-2006. Interpuesto por noventa y nueve Diputados del Grupo Parlamentario Popular del Congreso en relación con diversos preceptos de la Ley Orgánica 6/2006, de 19 de julio, de reforma del Estatuto de Autonomía de Cataluña.

Spanish Constitutional Court Judgment 103/2008, 11 September 2008, *Boletín Oficial del Estado*, Nº 245, 10 October 2008, Supplement Recurso de inconstitucionalidad 5707-2008. Interpuesto por el Presidente del Gobierno contra la Ley del Parlamento Vasco 9/2008, de 27 de junio, de convocatoria y regulación de una consulta popular al objeto de recabar la opinión ciudadana en la Comunidad Autónoma del País Vasco sobre la apertura de un proceso de negociación para alcanzar la paz y la normalización política.

United Kingdom

Supreme Court, *R (on the application of Miller and Dos Santos) v Secretary of State for Exiting the European Union and associated references* [2017] UKSC 5, 24th January 2017.

Supreme Court *Shindler and Maclennan* v. *Chancellor of the Duchy of Lancaster and Secretary of State for Foreign and Commonwealth Affairs* [2016], EWHC 957 (Admin) UKSC 2016/0105

Supreme Court *Moohan and Another* v. *Lord Advocate* [2014], UKSC 67

Court of Appeal *R (Preston)* v. *Wandsworth London Borough Council* [2013], QB 687

United States

Supreme Court, *Texas* v. *White*, 74 (1869), US 700

# LEGISLATION

## Primary EU Legislation

Articles 1, 4, 5, 16, 48, 49, 50, 52, 53, 55 Treaty on European Union
Articles 167, 174, 176, 217, 218, 263, 267, 355, 356 Treaty on the Functioning of the European Union
Protocol (No. 2) on the application of certain aspects of Article 26 of the Treaty on the Functioning of the European Union to the United Kingdom and to Ireland
Protocol (No. 15) on certain provisions relating to the United Kingdom of Great Britain and Northern Ireland
Protocol (No. 20) on the application of certain aspects of Article 26 of the Treaty on the Functioning of the European Union to the United Kingdom and to Ireland
Protocol (No. 21) on the position of the United Kingdom and Ireland in respect of the area of freedom, security and justice
Protocol (No. 30) on the application of the Charter of Fundamental Rights of the European Union to Poland and to the United Kingdom.
Article I-5 of the Constitutional Treaty
Article I-59 Draft Constitutional Treaty
Articles 263 and 265 Treaty establishing the European Community, now 305 and 307 TFEU respectively
Article 240 of the Treaty of Rome

## Other Primary Legislative Sources with Respect to EU Law

Treaty between the Kingdom of Belgium, the Kingdom of Denmark, the Federal Republic of Germany, the Hellenic Republic, the Kingdom of Spain, the French Republic, Ireland, the Italian Republic, the Grand Duchy of Luxembourg, the Kingdom of the Netherlands, the Republic of Austria, the Portuguese Republic, the Republic of Finland, the Kingdom of Sweden, the United Kingdom of Great Britain and Northern Ireland (Member States of the European Union) and the Czech Republic, the Republic of Estonia, the Republic of Cyprus, the Republic of Latvia, the Republic of Lithuania, the Republic of Hungary, the Republic of Malta, the Republic of Poland, the Republic of Slovenia, the Slovak Republic, concerning the accession of the Czech Republic, the Republic of Estonia, the Republic of Cyprus, the Republic of

Latvia, the Republic of Lithuania, the Republic of Hungary, the Republic of Malta, the Republic of Poland, the Republic of Slovenia and the Slovak Republic to the European Union [2003] OJ L236/17

Treaty amending, with regard to Greenland, the Treaties establishing the European Communities [1985] OJ L 29/1

Documents Concerning the Accession to the European Communities of the Kingdom of Denmark, Ireland, the Kingdom of Norway and the United Kingdom of Great Britain and Northern Ireland, Protocol No. 3, 27 March, 1972 [1972] OJ L 73/164

Article 4, Protocol No. 2 to the Act of Accession, Relating to Færoe Islands [1972] OJ L 73/163

Overeenkomst tot wijziging van het Verdrag tot oprichting van de Europese Economische Gemeenschap ten einde de bijzondere associeatieregeling van het vierde deel van het Verdrag op de Nederlandse Antillen te doen zijn of 13 November 1962 [1964] OJ 2413/64

## External Agreements Between the EU and Third Countries

Agreement between the European Community and the Swiss Confederation concerning the criteria and mechanisms for establishing the State responsible for examining a request for asylum lodged in a Member State or in Switzerland [2008] OJ L53/5

Agreement between the European Union, the European Community and the Swiss Confederation on the Swiss Confederation's association with the implementation, application and development of Schengen acquis, [2008] OJ L53/52

Agreement on scientific and technological co-operation between the European Community and the European Atomic Energy Community, of the one part, and the Swiss Confederation, of the other part [2007] OJ L189/26.

Agreement between the European Community and the Swiss Confederation concerning the participation of Switzerland in the European Environment Agency and the European Environment Information and Observation Network [2006] OJ L90/37

Agreement between the European Community and the Swiss Confederation in the audiovisual field, establishing the terms and conditions for the participation of the Swiss Confederation in the Community Programmes Media Plus and Media Training [2006] OJ L90/23

Agreement between the European Community and the Swiss Confederation on co-operation in the field of statistics [2006] OJ L90/2

Agreement between the European Community and the Swiss Confederation amending the Agreement between the European Economic Community and the Swiss Confederation of July 22, 1972 as regards the provisions applicable to processed agricultural products [2005] OJ L23/19

Agreement between the European Community and the Swiss Confederation providing for measures equivalent to those laid down in Council Directive 2003/48 on taxation of savings income in the form of interest payments [2004] OJ L385/30

Agreement between the European Community and its Member States, of the one part, and the Swiss Confederation, of the other, on the free movement of persons [2002] OJ L114/6

Agreement between the European Community and the Swiss Confederation on Air Transport [2002] OJ L114/73

Agreement between the European Community and the Swiss Confederation on the Carriage of Goods and Passengers by Rail and Road [2002] OJ L114/91

Agreement between the European Community and the Swiss Confederation on trade in agricultural products [2002] OJ L114/132

Agreement between the European Community and the Swiss Confederation on mutual recognition in relation to conformity assessment [2002] OJ L114/369

Agreement between the European Community and the Swiss Confederation on certain aspects of government procurement [2002] OJ L114/430

Agreement between the European Community and the Republic of Iceland and the Kingdom of Norway concerning the criteria and mechanisms for establishing the State responsible for examining a request for asylum lodged in a Member State or in Iceland or Norway [2001] OJ L93/40

Agreement concluded by the Council of the European Union and the Republic of Iceland and the Kingdom of Norway concerning the latter the EEA countries to facilitate with the implementation, application and development of the Schengen acquis [1999] OJ L176/36

Agreement between the EFTA States on the Establishment of a Surveillance Authority and a Court of Justice [1994] OJ L344/1

Agreement between the European Economic Community and the Kingdom of Norway [1973] OJ L171/2

Agreement between the European Economic Community and the Republic of Iceland, [1972] OJ L301/2

Association Agreement between the European Union, the European Atomic Energy Community and their Member States, of the one part, and Ukraine, of the other part [2014] OJ L161

Association Agreement between the European Union and the European Atomic Energy Community and their Member States, of the one part, and Georgia, of the other part [2014] OJ L261

Association Agreement between the European Union and the European Atomic Energy Community and their Member States, of the one part, and the Republic of Moldova, of the other part [2014] OJ L260

Co-operation Agreement between the European Community and its Member States, of the one part, and the Swiss Confederation, of the other part, to counter fraud and all other illegal activities to the detriment of their financial interests [2009] OJ L46/8

Europe Agreement establishing an association between the European Communities and their Member States, of the one part, and the Republic of Poland, of the other part [1993] OJ L348/2

Interim Agreement on trade and trade-related matters between the European Community, of the one part, and the Republic of Serbia, of the other part [2010] OJ L28/2

Stabilisation and Association Agreement between the European Communities and their Member States, of the one part, and the Republic of Albania, of the other part [2009] OJ L107/166

## Secondary EU Legislation

Council Decision 2014/295/EU of 17 March 2014 on the signing, on behalf of the European Union, and provisional application of the Association Agreement between the European Union and the European Atomic Energy Community and their Member States, of the one part, and Ukraine, of the other part, as regards the Preamble, Article 1, and Titles I, II and VII thereof [2014] OJ L161

Council Decision 2014/494/EU of 16 June 2014 on the signing, on behalf of the European Union, and provisional application of the Association Agreement between the European Union and the European Atomic Energy Community and their Member States, of the one part, and Georgia, of the other part [2014] OJ L261

Council Decision 2014/493/Euratom of 16 June 2014 on the signing, on behalf of the European Union, and provisional application of the Association Agreement between the European Union and the European Atomic Energy Community and their Member States, of the one part, and the Republic of Moldova, of the other part [2014] OJ L260

Council Regulation (EEC) 1911/91 of 26 June 1991 on the application of the provisions of Community law to the Canary Islands [1991] OJ L 171/1

## Other International Agreements

Article 128 European Economic Area Agreement (OJ 1997 L1/1)

Articles 54, 56, 62 Vienna Convention on the Law of Treaties 1969

Article 3, Protocol 1 European Convention on Human Rights 1953

Treaty Establishing a European Political Community 1952

Article 2(7) Charter of the United Nations 1945

## National Legislation Canada

An Act to give effect to the requirement for clarity as set out in the opinion of the Supreme Court of Canada in the Quebec Secession Reference 1999, 2nd session, 36th Parliament

## National Legislation – Spain

Article 168 Spanish Constitution

Organic Law 15/2015 of 16 October, amending Organic Law 2/1979 of 3 October of the Constitutional Court, for the purpose of enforcing the resolutions of the Constitutional Court as a guarantee of the rule of law, *Boletín Oficial del Estado*, No. 249, Saturday 17 October 2015, Section I

Resolution 5/X approving the Declaration on sovereignty and the right to decide of the people of Catalonia, 250–00059/10 and 250–00060/10, DSPC-P 4, *Butlletí Oficial del Parlament de Catalunya* 7, *Diari de Sessions del Parlament de Catalunya*, P.4, 23 de enero de 2013, pp. 60–61

## National Legislation – United Kingdom

European Union Referendum Act 2015
Scottish Independence Referendum Act 2013
Scottish Independence Referendum (Franchise) Act 2013
European Union Act 2011
Section 18(1)(b) Electoral Administration Act 2006
Political Parties, Elections and Referendum Act 2000
Section 6(3)(e) Representation of People Act 2000
Section 30 and Schedule 5 Scotland Act 1998
Referendums (Scotland and Wales) Act 1997
Representation of the People Act 1983

# ABBREVIATIONS

| | |
|---|---|
| ALDE | Alliance of European Liberals and Democrats (Group at the EP) |
| CoE | Council of Europe |
| CMLRev | Common Market Law Review |
| CSCE | Conference on Security and Co-operation in Europe |
| EC | European Communities |
| ECHR | European Convention of Human Rights |
| ECtHR | European Court of Human Rights |
| EEA | European Economic Area |
| EEC | European Economic Communities |
| EFARev | European Foreign Affairs Review |
| EFTA | European Free Trade Association |
| ELRev | European Law Review |
| EP | European Parliament |
| EPP | European People's Party |
| EU | European Union |
| EuConst | European Constitutional Law Review |
| IACHR | Inter-American Court of Human Rights |
| ICCPR | International Covenant on Civil and Political Rights |
| ICLQ | International & Comparative Law Quarterly |
| IGC | Inter-Governmental Conference |
| IMF | International Monetary Fund |
| ITO | International Trade Organization |
| ITU | International Telecommunication Union |
| KENDO | Korean Peninsula Energy Development Organization |
| MEP | Member of the European Parliament |
| OAS | Organization of American States |
| OECS | Organization for Eastern Caribbean States |
| OPCW | Organization for the Prohibition of Chemical Weapons |
| SEA | Single European Act |
| SNP | Scottish National Party |
| S&D | Socialists and Democrats (Group at the EP) |
| TCE | Treaty establishing a Constitution for Europe |
| UK | United Kingdom |

| | |
|---|---|
| UKCLA | UK Constitutional Law Association Blog |
| UKIP | United Kingdom Independence Party |
| UNGA | United Nations General Assembly |
| UPU | Universal Postal Union |
| VCLT | Vienna Convention on the Law of Treaties |
| WTO | World Trade Organization |

1

# Troubled Membership: Secession and Withdrawal

CARLOS CLOSA

This book was planned in 2014, before the Scottish referendum on independence from the UK.[1] At that time, the possibility of an UK withdrawal from the EU, even taking into account the British Government's commitment to hold a referendum on the issue, seemed a remote possibility. Contrary to expectations, the remote possibility has become a reality and the results of the 23 June 2016 referendum on EU membership in the UK shook not only that country but the whole of the EU, affecting the European project to its very foundations. Partly, this shock results from the unexpected outcome, but it also comes because, following the line of argument of JHH Weiler in relation to secession in Chapter 2 of this book, the results underline the reliance on the basis of a kind of atavistic community which has survived the rationalising effects of membership in an organisation whose main virtue is precisely the management of complex interdependences through constitutional tolerance[2] and based on a clear distinction between European integration and nation-building.[3] Few expected the 'leave' result, probably because few believed in the ability of a cause often appealing to pejorative, derogatory and aggressive views to attract the support of rational voters. But this happened and it rendered even more compelling the comparison of cases of troubled membership: that is, when a territory seeks to exit a EU Member State and when a state seeks to leave the EU.

[1] See the summary of the original seminar behind this project in C. Closa, 'Troubled Membership: Dealing with secession from a Member State and withdrawal from the EU' (2014) EUI Working Paper *RSCAS* 2014/91 http://cadmus.eui.eu/bitstream/handle/1814/32651/RSCAS_2014_91rev.pdf.

[2] J. H. H. Weiler, 'Federalism Without Constitutionalism: Europe's Sonderweg', in Kalypso Nicolaidis and Robert Howse (eds.), *The Federal Vision: Legitimacy and Levels of Governance in the United States and the European Union* (Oxford: OUP, 2001).

[3] J. H. H. Weiler, 'To be a European citizen – Eros and civilization', *Journal of European Public Policy*, 4(4)(1997)

## I Differences and Similarities Between Seeking Exit in Withdrawal and Secession

The project did not aim to scrutinize specific events, although the referendum in Scotland, the Catalan process and the prospects of Brexit inevitably inform the arguments behind the various contributions. Rather, it aims at discussing from a long-term perspective the kind of issues involved and unleashed when the perception of a traumatic belonging (the notion of troubled membership which gives the title to this book) reaches the point of staking membership itself as the only way forward. The logic of withdrawal from the EU and secession from a Member State share some similarities. To start with, both processes happen within the exercise of reconfiguration of power and authority in the EU which has been labelled multilevel governance.[4] The EU plays a central role in the logics triggering both processes (although with different value in each of these): withdrawal is a reaction to the Union while secession from a Member State is based on the assumption of retaining EU membership. Both cases illustrate how efforts to accommodate territories and/or states within larger unions through mechanisms such as derogations (in the EU) or devolution (in cases of multinational states such as the UK or Spain) have not generated stable outcomes satisfying all parties. The most extreme exit option becomes credible and even valuable for these unsatisfied constituencies. In the EU partial exits (opt-outs), mechanisms of voluntary participation (such as enhanced cooperation), derogations and policy exceptions fulfilled the function of alleviating tensions within the membership. At the state level, several forms of devolution in countries such as UK or Spain have expanded greatly the margin for self-government but some actors still perceive these forms as insufficient and they sought the extreme exit option (i.e. independence). In a way, this represents an irony of destiny: the expectation in the 1980s and 1990s was that the increased involvement of regions in the EU (as illustrated by Fasone in this volume) would constrain demands for independence (a thesis sustained by Walker also in this volume).

Actors making claims for withdrawal from the EU or independence from a Member State loudly voiced their dissatisfaction with the state/organisation which they felt could not deliver and preferred an alternative

[4] Marks and Hooghe first coined this concept in the 1990s. Marks, G. and Hooghe, L. (1996) "European Integration from the 1980s: State-Centric v. Multi-level Governance". *Journal of Common Market Studies*, Vol.34, No. 3, 341-378

(yet unknown) situation outside the Union/state to the *status quo*. Significantly, in both cases, these actors aim at retaining some (or all!) of the conditions of the previous status quo, such as access to markets and the status of citizenship. In the case of secessionist territories, pro-independence actors coincide in assuming that it only makes sense if they retain full EU membership. In the case of withdrawal, actors face a much more complex landscape since the range of possible future scenarios[5] is quite wide and uncertainty of the outcome prevails.

Both processes become meaningful alternatives to membership once the real or imagined results of the sum of the costs and benefits of staying or leaving the Union become positive. However, it could be wrong to perceive these exercises as purely instrumental calculations. Rather, to some extent, secession and withdrawal represents a failure of the rationalist project of sharing a polity out of rational choice, and the will of doing so, and by rationally constructing links of allegiance, mutual respect and trust. Displacing sober utilitarian/rational considerations, identity seems to have played an important role in the quest for independence in Scotland and drive the secessionist process in Catalonia.[6] In the case of Brexit, scholarly interpretations of the origins of the vote are still pending, although the worries and even fears of significant sectors of the population, which perceive themselves as deprived, appears to have played an important role in an expressive result which seems to include a significant element of feelings of exclusion.[7] Brexit gives reason to these that warned about the post-functionalist phase of European integration with the end of the permissive consensus on European integration and its politization in domestic electoral processes.[8]

Even though a combination of ontological and instrumental considerations inspires decisions to withdraw or secede, the concern of this

[5] Jean Claude Piris outlined no less than seven options. See Jean Claude Piris, 'Brexit or Britain: is it really colder outside?' (26 October 2015) Robert Schuman European Foundation Issue No. 369, <http://www.robert-schuman.eu/en/doc/questions-d-europe/qe-355-bis-en.pdf>, accessed 27 February 2017.

[6] Muñoz and Tormos have shown that identity remains the main predictor for pro-independence moves in Catalonia and economic motivations are more relevant for citizens with ambivalent identity positions and for those that have no party identification, or are partisans of parties with less clear-cut stances on the issue. Jordi Muñoz and Raül Tormos, 'Economic expectations and support for secession in Catalonia: between causality and rationalization', *European Political Science Review*, 7(2) (2015), 315–341.

[7] John Lanchester, 'Brexit Blues', *London Review of Books*, 38(15) (2016), 3–6.

[8] Hooghe, L. and Marks, G. (2009) 'A Postfunctionalist Theory of European Integration: From Permissive Consensus to Constraining Dissensus', *British Journal of Political Science*, 39(1), pp. 1–23

project is more located in the former: the perceived limited capacity to construct political projects able to deliver the goods that increased interdependence possesses when those projects are subject to large expectations and demands. This represents a (limited) failure of rational-instrumental projects and the parallel verification that the lack of pre-political components of communities still seems enough as to compromise their stability and, lately, their success.

Outlining similarities must not mask the evident differences between withdrawal from the Union and secession from a Member State. The first and main difference refers to the degree of unilaterality involved in both options. In withdrawal processes, respect for requirements such as the Rule of Law and domestic constitutional requirements is mainly a matter for domestic concern and the EU does not have a substantial say in the decision (although allegedly, a withdrawal process which undermines the values in Article 2 could lead to activation of Article 7). In secession, however, unilaterality simply does not legally and legitimately exist within the EU: it is dubious whether the declaration of independence of a given territory could occur against the background of the explicit opposition of an existing Member State (and it is equally dubious that the EU would support a unilateral declaration of independence in ordinary circumstances).

Both processes concern the EU but the EU is by and large a passive, bystanding actor. This neutral position results from both the set of rules at play and the practical considerations at stake: actors involved in both secession and withdrawal processes demand that the Union does not interfere (although pro-independence Catalan politicians have eagerly sought the involvement of EU institutions backing their demands vis-à-vis the Spanish central authorities). In legal terms, withdrawal is a totally unilateral decision in which the EU does not play a role in the assertion of the right. However, the EU retains a strong bargaining position for negotiating the withdrawal settlement. In relation to secession, EU neutrality refers not only to the absence of explicit treaty provisions Walker and Fasone in Chapters 3 and 4 advocate introducing such a provision but also to the silent attitude which its authorities largely maintained in the processes in Scotland and Catalonia.

The differences in the institutional design of the rules for dealing with withdrawal and secession also convey deep understandings of the nature of the community. The model of EU norms (Article 50 for withdrawal, absence of regulation on secession) underlines the notion of sovereign statehood. The accuracy of claims made to justify exit does not matter since being members of a sovereign state, citizens have a legitimate right to express their view on whether they want to remain a full member or to exit. However, this assumption of sovereign statehood fits with increasing unease with the pragmatic and normative assumptions on which the EU stands. On the pragmatic front, being the EU a community of interdependence, decisions on either secession/withdrawal would affect others beyond those taking the decision. In secession, it has been said that this amounts to little: reconfiguration of the institutions of the EU, in particular, and redistribution of seats and votes although a more careful and detained exam shows that these effects have a deeper impact and create a normative case of a larger EU engagement with the issue.[9] In withdrawal processes, the effects are felt in a much deeper sense: it will have an impact on power balances, policy priorities and institutional balances. But much more importantly, it will affect EU citizens and their rights in both the withdrawing state and the remaining Union. This leads to the normative dimension in which basically the EU has increasingly become a community defined by all-affectness. This thick interdependence means that a democratic decision taken within one jurisdiction affects all other jurisdictions. The normative corollary is that in a community of interdependence, all affected have an entitlement to propose to limit the externalities created by the functioning of national democratic policymaking.[10] Decisions on either secession from a Member State or withdrawal from the Union affect others beyond those (democratically) adopting the decision and hence a legitimate question is whether the EU should have a more explicit role. At a minimum and even though the Treaties do not create explicitly these requirements for these processes, they should fulfil certain unavoidable conditions: respect for the Rule of Law and the constitutional principles. Much of this remained unexplored

[9] C. Closa, 'Secession from a Member State and EU Membership: The View from the Union', *European Constitutional Law Review*, 12 (2016), 240–264

[10] J. Neyer and C. Joerges, 'From Intergovernmental Bargaining to Deliberative Political Processes: The Constitutionalisation of Comitology', *ELJ*, 3(3) (1997), 273 (who argue that national democracies are burdened with a grave deficiency which makes them systematically predisposed to disregard the interest of these who, in spite of being affected by their operation, remain in a disenfranchised state); and Somek, 'The Argument from Transnational Effects I: Representing Outsiders through Freedom of Movement', *ELJ*, 16(3) (2010), 315 (who makes the argument that supranational forms of integration are desirable on account of democracy itself: national democracies are forced to confront and to internalise the externalization effects which they may cause for one another. The argument favours normative limitation of national political processes).

but the Brexit process has triggered the need for prospective thinking on these issues.

## II When Withdrawal Meets Secession

The concretisation of withdrawal after the June 2016 referendum in the UK forces us to reflect on an unknown and unexplored situation for which there is little preparedness in the EU. Beyond Article 50 procedural mechanisms, the question is what the EU's attitude should be towards a withdrawing state? Is this just a matter of law, i.e. of a strict interpretation of Article 50? In the absence of clearly defined principles and guidelines, there is little doubt that the logic of bargaining and negotiation will determine the result and, indirectly, shape the principles for which the EU must stand for in this situation. This refers not to preventing any spillover effects, contagion or domino effects, but rather reasserting the nature of the project of European integration when facing an instance of disintegration. And the proper way to reassert that nature is to root the EU position on its own principles, such as fairness, non-discrimination, sincere cooperation, even if the logic of negotiation and bargaining may subvert them. These principles apply not only to EU Member States and their citizens but also, as much as possible, to the UK and its citizens. Whenever possible, the EU should aim at protecting equally the interests of EU and UK citizens although it seems evident that, in cases of conflict, EU citizens' interest should prevail. Equally, the settlement should not seek freely to impose costs upon the citizens of the withdrawing state, since the EU integration project is essentially one of domesticating externalities and not oppressing strangers. But EU citizens should also not unnecessarily nor disproportionately bear the costs of withdrawal. For the UK, this could be understood as accepting that the costs of a democratic decision cannot be externalised upon third parties.

The result of the 2016 UK referendum has suddenly created the conditions for the emergence of the scenario that the title of this book implies, simultaneous withdrawal from the Union of a Member State and the parallel secession of a territory of that Member State which wishes to remain a part of the EU. There is now a real and distinct possibility that this could happen simultaneously: after the results of the UK referendum, the Scottish First Minister and others argued that a second independence referendum could be held if Brexit ultimately occurs. Therefore, there is evidence that Scotland could renew its bid for independence precisely because of UK withdrawal from the EU.[11] Doctrinal debates have revolved on a different situation (i.e. secession from a Member State which retains EU membership). Against that background, the dominant interpretation from the EU perspective[12] has to be that the accession of a seceding territory once it becomes an independent state should occur under Article 49; that is, the normal accession procedure. A seamless transition or internal enlargement routes seem closed in this scenario. Normative and prudential reasons suggest this path.

The change in the background conditions also implies a reappraisal of this thesis. While the formal arguments remain unchanged, the normative standpoint is somehow modified. It is certainly telling that a territory would be willing to secede from its original state as the only way to remain part of the EU. Because this decision happens in the context of the reassertion of the national identity of the withdrawing state, the parallel move of the seceding territory acquires a different meaning. It implies the sanctioning of the non-ethnic and non-identity-driven nature of the EU project and, in parallel, an endorsement of its rationalistic character. In the critical juncture created by withdrawal, opting for EU membership over continuation of state bonds means granting a superior value to rational logic behind accession over traditional identity bonds.[13]

Alternatively, some authors[14] have advanced the proposal of a non-independent Scotland retaining EU membership and this applies, *caeteribus paribus*, to Northern Ireland and Gibraltar. In reality, these three territories define very different cases. Both for Northern Ireland and Gibraltar, the UK's EU membership has a net value by creating

[11] The Scottish Government argued that the rationale for a second independence referendum was to be found in the "significant and material change in the circumstances that prevailed in 2014, such as Scotland being taken out of the EU against our will". Scottish Government will intervene in Article 50 legal case http://news.gov.scot/news/scottish-government-will-intervene-in-article-50-legal-case 08/11/16, accessed 27 February 2017

[12] See a summary of the discussion in Closa (note 9).

[13] See an outline of the different possibilities in Carlos Closa Changing EU internal borders through democratic means *Journal of European Integration* Vol.39, No.5 http://dx.doi.org/10.1080/07036337.2017.1327525

[14] Chalmers and Menon have outlined a kind of special status for Scotland (which seeks to preserve UK union by maintaining EU access): if Scotland wants a tighter relationship with the European Union, there could be a commitment not to repeal any EU laws insofar as they affect Scotland. Scotland would, of course, have to apply all EU laws as EU law, including free movement of persons and fisheries, and contribute to the EU Budget. This is of course constitutionally possible. Damian Chalmers and Anand Menon, 'Getting out quick and playing the long game', *Open Europe Briefing*, (2016) <http://openeurope.org.uk/wp-content/uploads/2016/07/OE_Chalmers_Menon_July_2016.pdf>.

a valuable framework for compromise on the status quo. For Northern Ireland, the border with the Republic of Ireland and the relevance of EU membership of the UK as a contribution to the peace process should be taken into account and be the main driving force behind any consideration. In the case of Gibraltar, EU's membership of Spain and the UK could redirect and nuance the sovereignty's claims of the former. In both cases (North Ireland and Gibraltar), the existence of a third party which is also an EU member sets the basic conditions for settling any future agreement. However, Scotland does not share a land border with any other EU member and thus poses the question in its purest form. Leaving aside the political issues concerning Northern Ireland and Gibraltar, there are a significant number of practical issues involved such as, for instance, the border regime between each of these territories and with the remaining UK. This scenario goes beyond the traditional question of Scotland retaining membership by means of a seamless transition towards EU membership to encompass ontological questions on whether is it possible for a territory of a non-Member State to remain part of the EU. The statist twist inserted in the Lisbon Treaty (Article 1 speaking of High Contracting Parties, and Articles 48 and 49 referring to states as the actors of accession and withdrawal) severely limit this option on legal grounds. Leaving aside whether legal engineering could find a way to circumvent these limits, practical difficulties involving issues such as territorial representation and assumption raise a paradox: these being state prerogatives, the withdrawing state, the UK, would have to accept, in the last instance, responsibility and representation. Hence, whether Scotland moves towards independence or opts to remain within the UK, the effects in terms of its future relationship with the EU are unforeseen at this stage.

## III The Contents of This Volume

Most contributors addressed the two issues gathered under the notion of troubled membership separately. However, JHH Weiler opens the book with Chapter 2, in which he presents a dual reading of the dynamics of secession and withdrawal: a pessimistic one emphasising the denial of the very foundations of the European project; and a positive reading where he points to the shortcomings in terms of democratic quality of that project as the cause for these tendencies – owing to the failure to create a community of fate which could transcend nation states – though concluding that the drama of the EU is in its not being able to generate the same sense of community of fate among European citizens.

The first part of the volume discusses secession with the Scottish and Catalan cases in mind. In Chapter 3, arguing explicitly against Weiler's thesis, Walker declares that a subjective, collective aspiration for independence and EU membership should not be summarily dismissed. He proposes that the EU should adopt a policy of neutrality as far as accession of newly independent territories is concerned: it should influence the debate by its mere presence rather than by any strategy of active intervention. He concludes that the existence of the EU changes the expressive significance of national sovereignty and its alternatives by supplying a new level of political identity (including a new form of citizenship) and a new point of reference for interpreting national identity. This is precisely the paradox elaborated by Cristina Fasone in Chapter 4 of this book. She details the evolution of the EU's attitude towards the regions from regional blindness to a more encompassing role. This evolution has not meant, however, the contention of claims for simultaneous independence and EU membership. She concludes by proposing a more explicit provision regulating the possibility of secession from an existing Member State.

In Chapters 5 and 6, Jean Claude Piris constructs an elaborated case which starts with the observation that secession with simultaneous accession to the EU cannot be legally discarded. Piris reviews the events and discussions behind the Scottish and Catalan bids for secession underlying their similarities but also their differences. Piris contends, in line with several other contributions in this volume, that the proper avenue for accession is that of Article 49 (instead of the seamless transition via Article 48 favoured by pro-independence forces in Scotland and Catalonia). In Chapter 6, Piris provides a very sceptical view of whether the secession of a territory from a Member State and its simultaneous accession to the EU is likely. Chapters 5 and 6 were written before the 2016 UK referendum. Piris concludes that enlargement as consequence of internal secession in a Member State will be totally detrimental to the EU, bringing no benefit and many costs.

In Chapter 7, Kenneth A. Armstrong looks closer to the Scottish debate in 2014 and before, to argue that economic, political and social actors have instrumentalised EU law in order to articulate and contest claims in the referendum on Scotland's independence from the UK. He shows that the use of EU law did not trump domestic politics but became a useful resource to inform, to direct or to amplify domestic narratives, choices and claims. In Chapter 8, Medina uses international and constitutional law to distinguish the situations of Scotland and Catalonia. He forcefully argues that the political rights of the EU citizens do not include a right to secession of a part of the territory of a Member State. Under international law, the right to secession is subject to the provisions of the national constitutions. Where, as in the case of the UK, the Constitution is flexible, an act of Parliament could provide an adequate legal basis for the secession of a part of its territory. In Chapter 9, Jo Shaw discusses the relations between boundaries and citizenship when confronting decisions on secession and withdrawal. She discusses the delimitation of the electorate entitled to vote in both the Scottish and UK referendums, unveiling the underlying notions of the community behind those. She finally discusses the challenges of creating a new citizenship regime in the case of secession.

The second part of the book addresses withdrawal and centres on the EU institutional design driving this process. In Chapter 10, Closa argues that the introduction of an explicit withdrawal clause in Article 50 TEU has transformed the classical interpretation of the mechanisms of voice and exit that JHH Weiler outlined in his *Transformation of Europe*. Withdrawal provisions create a unilateral and unconditional (although no necessarily immediate) right for Member States that modifies the conditions for its exercise under public international law. This provision incentivises strategic behaviour, and thus the movement of voice mechanisms from securing control of political decisions via veto, to the possibility of unilaterally seeking to derogate selectively from the EU *acquis* by threats of exercising the option. Hillion explores the subtleties of the withdrawal procedure and makes a very compelling case in Chapter 11 interpreting that Article 50 may not be compatible with the spirit of the aim of achieving an ever-closer Union. He however argues somehow paradoxically that the withdrawal provision may make further integrative steps easier, since it allows a state to opt out rather than to hold up changes. Next, Adam Łazowski provides an authoritative account of the complex procedures of Article 50. Very little was known about the working of this procedure and Łazowski warns of the need to consider not only the procedural traps but also to deal with the hypothetical alternatives to full membership. Anticipating discussions in the post-Brexit environment, Chapter 12 demonstrates that a plethora of procedural and institutional matters need to be considered the early stages of the withdrawal process. Last but not least, in Chapter 13 Dimitry Kochenov offers a pessimistic outlook on the challenge faced by the citizens of the withdrawing state. He also predicts a severe downgrading in the quality of the nationality of the withdrawing state compared to how it was as a member of the Union because of the loss of some rights. Kochenov, however, does not explore the implications for the citizens of third Member States residing in the withdrawing state.

# 2

# Secessionism and Its Discontents

JHH WEILER

## I Introduction

There are currently two trends in Europe sweeping across and within the EU Member States which, at first glance, appear contradictory.

The first trend is the turn to secessionism within Member States, the two most visible but certainly not unique, instances being Catalonia and Scotland. Interestingly, in the internal discourse of secessionism, European integration is considered favourably and the European Union is viewed as the safe haven within which the newly independent State would be firmly anchored. Take away that safe haven and the appetite for secession would be considerably diminished.

The second trend is the normalisation and mainstreaming of Euroscepticism in various forms. From being a sideline show usually associated with the lunatic fringes of established politics, Euroscepticism now enjoys considerable support, is an official part of the platform of established parties and has made considerable electoral gains. On some counts, at least seven out of the twenty-eight *governments* of the Member States in 2016 could be counted as Eurosceptic to one degree or another.

The Brexit referendum – regardless of its outcome – is a manifestation of both these trends whereby it is widely assumed that the exit of the UK from the European Union (the second trend) would be accompanied by the exit of Scotland from the United Kingdom, the ostensible trigger being the unacceptability in Scotland of an English majority taking Scotland out of the Union.

In fact – or at least such is my argument – though the superficial language of the two trends seems to be contradictory (internal secessionism as Europhilic and external secession as an extreme manifestation of Euroscepticism), the deep structure of both discourses draws from the same well: the turn, or return, to national identity as a potent mobilising and coalescing factor in social and political life. Note that the turn, or return, is to a national identity which ruptures the usual assumption that Member State identity equals national identity. This turn to identity is, in almost all places, associated with dissatisfaction with the functioning of democracy either within the State or within the Union, and in some well-known instances is associated with an attraction of what is not euphemistically called, illiberal democracy. Whether an illiberal regime is consistent with a modern understanding of democracy may or may not be just a question of definition, but the sanctifying power of the word 'democracy' helps make this particular political pig kosher.

What complicates the picture even further is the frequent intermingling of these two issues with the problems associated with mass immigration, the refugee crisis and the growing xenophobia associated with this. We note, for example, that the debate in the UK, which has been largely shielded from the mass immigration of those forcibly expelled because of strife in the Middle East, internal EU free movement is conflated with 'migration' and instrumentalised as such.

I want to offer two contrasting normative readings to the phenomenon underlying the two trends – secessionism and Euroscepticism; one antipathetic and the other sympathetic. I do this purposefully because I think neither trend can be dismissed simply by painting it black or white.

The demand for secession from the Union – Brexit as an extreme manifestation of Euroscepticism – or from within a State is often couched in moral terms. The moral argument is typically understood in its negative manifestation: that it would be immoral (and illegal) to deny such independence to distinct nations such as the Scots or the Catalans. At its most powerful, the moral argument is linked to some form of democratic claim. At its starkest this could be expressed by the proposition that majoritarian democracy is predicated on the majority and minority being part of the same demos, and that by contrast, the absence of independence in effect enshrines the rule of one demos or some demoi over another. This would be true as regards both types of secession discourses. It is the precise point at which the vocabulary of sovereignty meets the vocabulary of democracy.

One difference lies in the legal dimension: no one calls into question the legal right of the UK to secede from the Union, whereas the legal right of, say, Catalonia to secede from Spain is hotly disputed. But other elements of this type of argument seem to be of the same cloth.

The alleged legal difference, as regards the right to secession between the two narratives, is of little concern to me in this essay. Though I take the view that under international law neither Catalonia nor Scotland enjoy a *right* to secede,[1] I do not give much moral weight to the international legal position as a valid proxy for a real moral argument. The international legal position was articulated most cogently in the 1960s Declaration on Friendly Relations[2] and it is clear to me that it was affected by quite a cynical political position by States which had won independence in the post-Second World War decolonisation process and were eager not to give legal space to the partition of their newly won independent territories. I do not, as a result, believe that the legal position as such enjoys even a presumption of being a proxy for a comprehensive moral position.[3]

Indeed, for this reason I applaud the political maturity of both the UK and Canada which allowed a referendum on the exit of Scotland and Quebec respectively, whilst holding to the position that neither one nor the other enjoyed a legal right to secede. It is an open and vexed question whether in those cases (and the case of Catalonia) such a referendum should have included the citizens of the entire union or of the sub-unit alone. It is understandable why in Spain, a much younger modern democracy, there is far greater reluctance to allow Catalonia alone to decide on the breakup of the kingdom.

Beyond legality, at a deeper level the nexus between the two secession discourses is that they represent, reflect and reinforce a general trend in Europe which has two characteristics.

[1] The matter was in my view expressed quite convincingly and conclusively in the decision of the Canadian Supreme Court in the Reference by the Governor in Council concerning certain questions relating to the secession of Quebec from Canada, as set out in Order in Council P.C. 1996–1497, dated 30 September 1996. Full decision <http://scc-csc.lexum.com/scc-csc/scc-csc/en/item/1643/index.do>, accessed 3 June 2017.

[2] Declaration on Principles of International Law Concerning Friendly Relations and Cooperation among States in Accordance with the Charter of the United Nations (United Nations [UN]) UN Doc A/RES/2625(XXV).

[3] Principle 5 in the declaration provides that 'all peoples have the right freely to determine, without external interference, their political status and to pursue their economic, social and cultural development, and every State has the duty to respect this right in accordance with the provisions of the Charter'. But, what Paul giveth, Peter taketh as we find just a few lines after: 'Nothing in the foregoing paragraphs shall be construed as authorizing or encouraging any action which would dismember or impair, totally or in part, the territorial integrity or political unity of sovereign and independent States conducting themselves in compliance with the principle of equal rights and self-determination of peoples as described above and thus possessed of a government representing the whole people belonging to the territory without distinction as to race, creed or color'.

The first is a turn away from one of the fundamental moral drivers of the post-Second World War European circumstance: a turn to a politics which views with abhorrence some of the ills of nationalism and seeks a politics (and a polity) which transcends this and places the individual, in his or her full humanity, at the centre.

The second, even more worrying, and particularly manifest in certain strands of Eurosceptic speak, is a fatigue with the humdrum greyness of post-Second World War democracy itself, which is concerned with the day-to-day business of economic management and individual and collective welfare and safety.

Mark Mazower, in his brilliant and original history and historiography of twentieth-century Europe,[4] insightfully describes a cyclical pattern of the rise and demise of democracy and messianic narratives in twentieth century Europe. The Europe of monarchs and emperors which entered the First World War was often rooted in a political messianic narrative in various states (in Germany, Italy and Russia, and even Britain and France). It then oscillated after the war towards new democratic orders, which then oscillated back into new forms of political messianism in fascism and communism. As the tale is usually told, after the Second World War, the Europe of the West was said to oscillate back to democracy shorn of messianic dreams as expressed in its Member States old and new. The fear is that we are now at the moment of the cyclical return again. It is noticeable how frequently Eurosceptic discourse not only reemploys national and even nationalist images, but how notions of 'destiny', 'masters of our own fate', power, and some form of promise of a better 'kingdom to come' creep into this imagery; the staples of messianic politics replacing democratic processes.

The ground is fertile for such imagery when our inevitably imperfect democracies fail to deliver the goods, as has been the perception for close to a decade now in both economic and security terms, or when it fails to distribute its benefits equitably, which has been the case for even longer.

Fatigue sets in and the scene is set for yet another European turn to narratives such as those which appeared in the interwar period. The writing is clearly on the wall in bold graffiti in Hungary, Poland, the Netherlands, Denmark and Sweden, but the ascendance of these temptations is present elsewhere both in the East and in the West.

Some readers might be bristling at the way I have indicated a nexus between some of these ugly manifestations of Euroscepticism, illiberal

[4] M. Mazower, *Dark Continent: Europe's Twentieth Century* (London: Allen Lane, 1998).

democracy and re-emergence of messianic political imagery with the secession movements in, say, Scotland and Catalonia, which intend to become independent States, normal imperfect democracies as all democracies are. It is precisely this allusion to the previous European cycles in the wake of the First World War which justify, in my view, the claim of such a nexus.

So how may we regard the drive for an independent Scotland or Catalonia at least in some way as cut from the same cloth as the uglier features of Euroscepticism?

## II Siren Claims for Secession

The claims of Catalonia, Scotland and the like eerily recall that exact period in the early twentieth century after the First World War and the then prevailing understanding of the building blocks of national democracy. It was a period when self-determination as an operational and legal concept was invented (or rediscovered) and at that time appeared, indeed in some respects was, a progressive idea associated as it was with the breakup of empires and the domination of one people over another. It re-emerged, with even greater moral force and legal solidity in the post-Second World War with the decolonisation process. The post-First World War Statutes of Minorities were an expression of that form of progressiveness and were motivated by the same impulse to limiting domination.[5] However, the mere fact that those special regimes for the protection of minorities was the supposed solution to the idea that a single 'nation state' had to be just that: a single-nation state, and that encompassing more than one nationality within the nation state was a problem which required a 'progressive' solution – hence the special treaties on minorities which abounded in the breakup of the Ottoman and the Austro-Hungarian Empires. These arrangements, perhaps representing progress in their time, also eventually embodied a very dark side – let us not shy away from the ugly facts – feeding and leading to that poisonous logic of national purity and ethnic cleansing. Make no mistake: I am not suggesting for a minute that anyone in Catalonia or Scotland or anywhere else is an ethnic cleanser. I am suggesting that the 'go-it-alone' mindset is associated with that kind of mentality.

[5] A useful synoptic view can be found in David Engel, 'Minority Treaties' *YIVO Encyclopedia of Jews in Eastern Europe*, <www.yivoencyclopedia.org/article.aspx/Minorities_Treaties> accessed 3 June 2017.

The secession movements represent a turn away from the double shift which occurred in the post-colonial era in the latter half of the twentieth century: a more inclusive notion of the nation itself and of the State to allow for the possibility of uniting, under a single citizenship, more than one nationality. At its simplest, this part of my claim is that the secessionist movement is a turning of one's back on these more inclusive and tolerant mindsets and a revival of earlier, more purist, but normatively less compelling notions of State, nation and national sovereignty. There is some poetic political irony that, in all likelihood, the exit of the UK from the European Union will also bring about the breakup of the Union of the UK – everyone happily purer and basking in their national sovereignty.

Fuelling the reversion are the revival and reconstruction of historical narratives of grievance and oppression. Yes, Catalans and Basques suffered serious historical wrongs in the pre-democracy era in Spain. (It takes a Braveheart to ascribe the same to *modern* Scotland). And I have huge, truly huge, empathy and sympathy for Catalans who want to live and vindicate their cultural and distinct political identity. For thousands, perhaps the majority, this is really all it is about. But to play, say, the 'Franco card' as a justification for secession is but a fig leaf not only for an outdated sense of the collective self but for seriously misdirected social and economic egoism, cultural and national hubris and often the naked ambition of local politicians.

It is in this light that one can read the zeal of internal secessionists from the European Union. It is not only, as I argued above, that it provides a safe haven of political and economic comfort but also the supposed moral legitimacy of being 'good Europeans.'

However, in my view it actually runs diametrically contrary to the historical ethos of European integration. The commanding moral authority of the Founding Fathers of European integration – Schumann, Adenauer, De Gaspari and Jean Monnet himself – was a result of their rootedness in the Christian ethic of forgiveness coupled with an enlightened political wisdom which understood that it is better to look forward to a future of reconciliation and integration rather than wallow in a past, which was infinitely worse than the worst excesses of, say, the execrable Franco. It inevitably has a general spillover effect to all 'foreigners' feeding at its worst an atavistic xenophobia. We cannot but notice in this context the speed with which the UK, in the run up to the Brexit referendum, announced that it will not be part of any resettlement of Syrian refugees deal worked out with Turkey.

Should we celebrate, encourage or morally validate every distinct national, cultural and linguistic 'minority' in Europe to hold a referendum about secession and independence? Dig deep enough and far enough in the past and grievances galore could be found. The Corsicans? The Bretons? The Welsh? The German speakers of the Alto Adige? The list is endless given the wonderful cultural richness of Europe. I would argue that it is only under conditions of actual political and cultural repression that a case for regional secession can convincingly be made. With its extensive (even if deeply flawed) Statute of Autonomy it is simply laughable and impossible to take for instance Catalan arguments for independence seriously, arguments which cheapen and insult meritorious – if inconclusive – cases such as the Chechens'.

The very ethos of European integration should, in my view, discourage the Union as such from welcoming these movements and encouraging them by the promise of easy accession. In part the argument here is utilitarian too. The Union is struggling today with a decisional structure which is already overloaded by twenty-eight Member States. But more importantly with a sociopolitical reality which makes it difficult to persuade a Dutch or a Finn or a German that they have a human and economic stake in the welfare of a Greek or a Portuguese or, yes, a Spaniard. Why would there be an interest in accepting into the Union a polity such as an independent Catalonia predicated on such a regressive and outmoded nationalist ethos which apparently cannot stomach the discipline of loyalty and solidarity which one would expect it would owe to its fellow citizens in Spain? Or to the UK? Or Italy? Or France? To take Catalonia again as an example, the very demand for independence from Spain, an independence from the need to work out political, social, cultural and economic differences within the Spanish polity, independence from the need to work through and transcend history, arguably morally and politically disqualify Catalonia, and the like, as future Member States of the European Union.

On this antipathetic reading, Europe should not appear as a Nirvana for that form of irredentist Euro-tribalism which contradicts the deep values and needs, not only of the Union as a political institution, but of Europe's noble attempt to move away from its sanguinary past. It would be hugely ironic, this time with no poetic tinge, if the prospect of Membership in the European Union ended up providing an incentive for an ethos of political disintegration. There really is a fundamental difference to the welcoming into the Union of a Spain or a Portugal or a Greece emerging from ugly and repressive dictatorships and a Catalonia or Scotland, which are part of functioning democracies which are at this very moment in need of the deepest expression of internal and external solidarity. In seeking separation, the secessionists are betraying the very ideals of solidarity and human integration for which the European construct stands.

## III What Then Would a Sympathetic Reading Look Like?

First there is the circumstance of Europe itself, and in particular the circumstance of European democracy. Europe itself bears considerable responsibility for the turn against itself.

This is an interesting time to be reflecting on European democracy, given the overall nadir of the European construct which one cannot remember for many decades. To many, the issue of democracy had been definitively solved with the Lisbon Treaty.[6] The surface manifestations of crisis are with us every day on the front pages: the euro crisis[7] and the migration crisis being the most current. Beneath this surface at the structural level, lurk more profound and long-term signs of enduring challenge and even dysfunction and malaise. Let us refract them through the lens of democratic legitimacy.[8] For Lisbon notwithstanding, there is a persistent, chronic, troubling democratic deficit, which cannot be talked away.

[6] See, for example, Plenary session of the European Parliament in Strasbourg on the Treaty of Lisbon (20 February 2008), which includes various statements from the members of the European Parliament, Janez Lenarcic, President of the Council and Margot Wallstrde, Vice-President of the European Commission, as well as European Parliament resolution of 20 February 2008 on the Treaty of Lisbon (2007/2286(INI)); 'Brussels European Council 14 December 2007' (14 February 2008) 16616/1/07 REV 1, including the EU declaration on globalisation; European Commission, *Your Guide to the Lisbon Treaty* (Luxembourg: Publications Office of the European Union, 2010); President Buzek, President Jerzy Buzek's speech at commemorative event marking the entry into force of the Treaty of Lisbon - 1 December 2009 http://www.europarl.europa.eu/former_ep_presidents/president-buzek/en/press/speeches/sp-2009/sp-2009-November/speeches-2009-November-7.html;jsessionid=64801F5437F77F33BF0CA992331D2F1C accessed 3 June 2017 J. M. Durao Barroso, President of the European Commission, 'The European Union after the Lisbon Treaty' (4 December, 2007) 4th Joint Parliamentary meeting on the Future of Europe, Brussels, SPEECH/07/793, 7 December 2007.

[7] D. Dinan, 'Governance and Institutions: Implementing the Lisbon Treaty in the Shadow of the Euro Crisis', *Journal of Common Market Studies*, 49(S1) (2011), 103.

[8] The literature is rich. Here is a partial sample of some truly helpful studies: Jacques Thomassen (ed.), *The Legitimacy of the European Union after Enlargement* (Oxford: OUP, 2009); J. Thomassen and H. Schmitt, 'Introduction: Political Legitimacy and Representation in the European Union', in H. Schmitt and J. Thomassen (eds.), *Political Representation and Legitimacy in the European Union* (New York and Oxford: OUP, 1999), pp. 3–21; D. Beetham and C. Lord, *Legitimacy and the European Union*, (London/New York:

First, although the 'no demos' thesis seems to have receded in recent discourse, its relevance is suddenly more acute than ever. The difficulties of, say, constructing some form of 'fiscal union'-type solutions for the euro crisis are explicable in no small measure as the result of 'no demos' – a lack of transcendent responsibility for the lot of one's fellow citizens and nationals. Germans and Dutch and Finns are not saying: 'a bailout is the wrong policy'. They are saying, 'Why should we, Germans, or Dutch, or Finns, help those lazy Italians or Portuguese or Greeks?' A very visible manifestation of the no-demos thesis of Europe's crisis of democracy.

Second, there are failures of democracy which simply make it difficult to speak of governance 'by and of' the people. The historical error was the belief that simply by granting extensive powers to the European Parliament – a necessary step – would be a sufficient step to close the deficit. The essence of the problem is the inability of the Union to develop structures and processes which adequately replicate or 'translate'[9] at the Union level even the imperfect habits of governmental control, parliamentary accountability and administrative responsibility as practised with different modalities in the various Member States. Make no mistake: it is perfectly understood that the Union is not a State. But it is in the business of governance and has taken over extensive areas previously in the hands of the Member States. In some critical areas, such as the interface of the Union with the international trading system, the competences of the Union are exclusive. In others, they are dominant. Democracy is not about States. Democracy is about the exercise of public power – and the Union exercises a huge amount of public power. We live by the credo that any exercise of public power has to be legitimated democratically and it is exactly here that process legitimacy fails.

And yet two primordial features of any functioning democracy are missing – the grand principles of accountability[10] and representation.[11]

Longman, 1998); M. Haller, 'Is the European Union legitimate? To what extent?', *International Social Science Journal*, 60(2009), 223; A. Moravcsik, 'Reassessing Legitimacy in the European Union', *Journal of Common Market Studies*, 40 (2002), 6030; B. Guastaferro and M. Moschella, 'The EU, the IMF, and the Representative Turn: Addressing the Challenge of Legitimacy', *Swiss Political Science Review*, 18 (2012), 199–219

[9] N. Walker, 'Postnational Constitutionalism and the Problem of Translation', in J. H. H. Weiler and M. Wind (eds.), *European Constitutionalism Beyond the State* (Cambridge: CUP, 2003), p. 29.

[10] A. Przeworski, S. C. Stokes and B. Manin (eds.), *Democracy, accountability and representation*, (Cambridge: CUP, 1999); P. C. Schmitter and T. L. Karl, 'What democracy is . . . and is not', *Journal of Democracy* (Summer 1991), 67.

[11] P. Mair, 'Popular Democracy and the European Union Policy', *European Governance Papers*, (EUROGOV) No C-05-03, (2003), 4.

As regards accountability,[12] even the basic condition of representative democracy which at election time the citizens 'can throw the scoundrels out'[13] – that is, replace the government – does not operate in Europe.[14] The *Spitzenkandidaten* exercise was a hugely important step in the right direction but it will take several cycles to transform the political culture. The overtly political stance of the Junker Commission gives some hope for the future.

This form of European governance[15] – governance without government – is and will remain for a considerable time, perhaps forever, such that there is no 'Government' to throw out. Dismissing the Commission by Parliament (or approving the appointment of the Commission President) is not quite the same, not even remotely so.

Startlingly but unsurprisingly, political accountability of Europe is remarkably weak. There have been some spectacular political failures of European governance. The embarrassing Copenhagen climate fiasco;[16] the weak (at best) realisation of the much-touted Lisbon Agenda (aka the Lisbon Strategy or Lisbon Process);[17] the very story of the defunct 'Constitution',[18] to mention but three. It is hard to point in these instances to any measure of political accountability, of someone paying a political price as would be the case in national politics. In fact, it is difficult to point to a single instance of accountability for political failure as distinct from personal accountability for misconduct in the annals of

[12] C. Harlow, *Accountability in the European Union* (Oxford: OUP, 2003).

[13] I. Shapiro, *Democracy's place* (Ithaca: Cornell University Press, 1996), p. 96; J. H. H. Weiler, 'To be a European citizen: Eros and civilization', in *The Constitution of Europe 'Do the New Clothes Have an Emperor?' and Other Essays on European Integration* (Massachusetts: Harvard University Press, 1999), p. 329.

[14] R. Dehousse, 'Constitutional Reform in the EC', in J. Hayward (ed.), *The crisis of Representation in Europe* (Abigdon: Frank Cass, 1995), pp. 118, 123.

[15] P. Allott, 'European Governance and the re-branding of democracy', *European Law Review*, 27(1) (2002), 60.

[16] See European Parliament Resolution of 10 February 2010 on the outcome of the Copenhagen Conference on Climate Change (COP 15) (10 February, 2010) P78TA (2010)0019, especially points 5–6.

[17] I. Begg, 'Is there a Convincing Rationale for the Lisbon Strategy', *Journal of Common Market Studies*, 43(1) (2008), 427; Report from the High-Level Group chaired by Wim Kok 'Facing the challenge. The Lisbon strategy for growth and employment', (2004) https://ec.europa.eu/research/evaluations/pdf/archive/fp6-evidence-base/evaluation_studies_and_reports/evaluation_studies_and_reports_2004/the_lisbon_strategy_for_growth_and_employment__report_from_the_high_level_group.pdf accessed 3 June 2017

[18] I. Ward, 'Bill and the Fall of the Constitutional Treaty', *European Public Law*, 13(3) (2007), 461; Editorial Comments, 'What should replace the Constitutional Treaty?' *CMLRev*, 44(2007), 561.

European integration. This is not, decidedly not, a story of corruption or malfeasance.[19] My argument is that this failure is rooted in the very structure of European governance. It is not designed for political accountability. In a similar vein, it is impossible to link the results of elections to the European Parliament in any systematically meaningful way to the performance of the political groups within the preceding parliamentary session, in the way that this is part of the mainstay of political accountability within the Member States.[20] Structurally, dissatisfaction with 'Europe' when it exists has no channel to affect, at the European level, the agents of European governance. Depressingly, Parliament has reverted to its 'rotation exercise' among the two big centre-left, centre-right blocs, and the European Council has made its dissatisfaction with the *Spitzenkandidaten* exercise quite clear with a determination not to allow a repetition of the exercise.

Likewise, at the most primitive level of democracy, there is simply no moment in the civic calendar of Europe where the citizen can influence directly the outcome of any policy choice facing the Community and Union in the way that citizens can when choosing between parties which offer sharply distinct programmes at the national level. The political colour of the European Parliament gets only very weakly translated into the legislative and administrative output of the Union.[21]

This political deficit, to use the felicitous phrase of Renaud Dehousse[22] is at the core of the democratic deficit. The Commission, by its self-understanding linked to its very ontology, cannot be 'partisan' in a right-left sense, neither can the Council, by virtue of the haphazard political nature of its composition. Democracy must normally have some meaningful mechanism for the expression of voter

[19] On this aspect, see V. Mehde, 'Responsibility and Accountability in the European Commission', *CMLRev*, 40 (2003), 423.

[20] J. Priestley, 'European political parties: the missing link', *Notre Europe, Policy Paper*, 41 (2010); F. Roa Bastos, 'Des partis politiques au niveau européen? Etat des lieux à la veille des élections européennes de juin 2009', *Etudes et Recherches*, 71 (2009); O. Audeoud, 'Les partis politiques au niveau européen. Fédérations de partis nationaux', Les cahiers du GERSE: Nancy (February 1999).

[21] V. Bogdanor, 'Legitimacy, Accountability and Democracy in the European Union', *A Federal Trust Report*, (2007), 7–8; A. Follesdal and S. Hix, 'Why There is a Democratic Deficit in the EU: A Response to Majone and Moravcsik', *Journal of Common Market Studies*, 44(3) (2006), 545.

[22] R. Dehousse, 'Constitutional Reform in the EC', in J. Hayward, (ed.), *The Crisis of Representation in Europe* (London: Frank Cass, 1995), p. 124. See also, J.-M. Ferry and P. Thibaud, *Discussion sur l'Europe* (Paris: Calmann-Lévy, 1992).

preference predicated on choice among options, typically informed by stronger or weaker ideological orientation.[23] That is an indispensable component of politics. Democracy without politics is an oxymoron;[24] and yet that is not only Europe, but it is a feature of Europe – the 'non-partisan' nature of the Commission – which is celebrated. The stock phrase found in endless student textbooks and the like, that the Supranational Commission vindicates the European Interest, whereas the intergovernmental Council is a clearing house for Member State interest, is naïve at best. Does the 'European Interest' not necessarily involve political and ideological choices? At times explicit, but always implicit? Again, the formidable Mr. Junker has only been able marginally or in a Machiavellian way (I use this term in the best sense of the word) to redress this problem in the selection of his Commission. He could allocate portfolios with imagination but could not choose the candidates of Member States based on programmatic commitment.

Thus the two most primordial norms of democracy, the principle of accountability and the principle of representation are compromised in the very structure and process of the Union.

This structural argument is consistent with the noticeable paradox of the extraordinary decline in voter participation in elections for the European Parliament. The rate of participation in Europe as a whole is below 45 per cent, with several countries, notably in the East, with a rate below 30 per cent. The correct comparison is, of course, with political elections to national parliaments where the numbers are considerably higher.[25] What is striking about these figures is that the decline coincides with a continuous shift in powers to the European Parliament, which today is a veritable colegislator with the Council. The more powers the European Parliament, supposedly the *Vox Populi*, has gained, the greater the popular indifference to it seems to have developed.[26] The last

[23] Hix, 'Why There is a Democratic Deficit in the EU' (note 21), 545.

[24] See P. Manent, *La raison des nations, ralso, J.-Msur la démocratie en Europe* (Paris: Gallimard, 2006), p. 59.

[25] A. Menon and J. Peet, 'Beyond the European Parliament: Rethinking the EU's democratic legitimacy', *Center for European Reform Essays* (2010); P. Magnette, 'European Governance and Civic Participation: Can the European Union be politicised', *Jean Monnet Working Paper*, 6/01 (2001).

[26] J. Buzek, 'State of the Union: Three Cheers for the Lisbon Treaty and Two Warnings for Political Parties', *Journal of Common Market Studies*, 49(7) (2011), pp. 7, 15; see also, J. H. H. Weiler, *The Constitution of Europe 'Do the New Clothes Have anEmperor?'* (note 13), p. 266.

elections saw the lowest turnout of voters in the history of direct elections and in all likelihood it would have been even lower but for the Eurosceptic mobilisation. It is sobering but unsurprising to note the relative absence of the European Parliament as a major player in the current crisis.

The critique of the democratic deficit of the Union has itself been subjected to two types of arguments. The first has simply contested the reality of the democratic deficit by essentially claiming that wrong criteria have been applied to the Union.[27] The lines of debate are well known.[28] For what it is worth, I have staked my position above. However, I am more interested in the second type of critique which is an implicit invocation of Result or Output legitimacy. Since the Union, not being a state, cannot replicate or adequately translate the habits and practices of statal democratic governance, its legitimacy may be found elsewhere.[29]

In analysing the legitimacy (and the mobilising force) of the European Union, in particular against the background of its persistent democratic deficit, political and social science has indeed long used the distinction between process legitimacy and outcome legitimacy (aka input/output, process/result, etc.).[30] The legitimacy of the Union more generally and the Commission more specifically, even if suffering from deficiencies in the democratic state sense, are said to rest on the results achieved in the economic, social and ultimately political realms.[31] The idea hearkens back to the most classic functionalist and neo-functionalist theories.[32]

[27] J. H. H. Weiler, 'Does Europe Need a Constitution? Demos, Telos and the German Maastricht Decision', *ELJ*, 1(3) (1995), 219, especially 225 *et seq.*

[28] P. Craig, 'The Nature of the Community: Integration, Democracy, and Legitimacy', in P. Craig and G. de Búrca (eds.), *The Evolution of EU Law* (Oxford: OUP, 1999), p. 25.

[29] N. MacCormick, 'Democracy, Subsidiarity, and Citizenship in the "European Commonwealth"', *Law and Philosophy*, 16(1997), 331–356.

[30] See, for example, C. R. Beitz, *Political equality: an essay in democratic theory* (Princeton: Princeton University Press, 1990), chapters 2 and 4; R. A. Dahl, *Democracy and its critics* (New Haven: Yale University Press, 1991), p. 163. See also more specifically, G. Majone (ed.), *Regulating Europe* (London: Routledge, 1996); F. W. Scharpf, *Governing in Europe: Effective and Democratic?* (Oxford: Oxford University Press, 1999), p. 7 *et seq.*

[31] K. Featherstone, 'Jean Monnet and the Democratic Deficit in the European Union', *Journal of Common Market Studies*, 32(2) (1994), 149, 150.

[32] Ibid., p. 155; C. Pentland, 'Political Theories of European Integration: Between Science and Ideology', in D. Lasok and P. Soldatos (eds.), *The European Communities in Action* (Brussels: Bruylant, 1981), pp. 545, 550 *et seq.*; B. Rosamond, *Theories of European Integration* (New York: Palgrave Macmillan, 2000), p. 20 *et seq.*; D. Mitrany, *A Working Peace System* (Chicago: Quadrangle Books, 1966); E. B. Haas, *The Uniting of Europe* (Stanford: Stanford University Press, 1958); E. B. Haas, 'Turbulent Fields and the Theory

I do not want to take issue with the implied normativity of this position – a latter-day *Panem et circenses* approach to democracy, which at some level at least could be considered quite troubling. It is with its empirical reality that I want to take some issue. I do not think that outcome legitimacy explains all, or perhaps even most, of the mobilising force of the European construct. But whatever role it played, it is dependent on the *Panem*. Rightly or wrongly, the economic woes of Europe, which are manifest in the euro crisis, are attributed to the European construct. So, when there suddenly is no bread, and certainly no cake, we are treated to a different kind of circus where the citizens' growing indifference becomes hostility and the ability of Europe to act as a political mobilising force seems not only spent, but even reversed. The worst way to legitimate a war is to lose it, and Europe is suddenly seen not as an icon of success but as an emblem of austerity, thus in terms of its promise of prosperity, failure. And now, the migration crisis too is scandalously but persistently associated with 'Europe'.

If success breeds legitimacy, failure – even if wrongly allocated – yields the opposite. The abject failure of Europe and its Member States (with the usual finger-pointing) to deal adequately with the migration/refugee crisis adds oil to the conflagration.

This brings us back to the phenomenon of secessionism, internal and external, which are the extreme manifestation of the seemingly contagious spread of 'anti-Europeanism' in national politics.[33] What was once the preserve of fringe parties on the far right and left has inched its way into more central political forces. The 'Question of Europe' as a central issue in political discourse was for long regarded as an 'English disease'. There is a growing contagion in the Member States in North and South, East and West, where political capital is to be made in non-fringe parties by anti-European advocacy.[34] The spillover effect of this phenomenon is the mainstream parties' shift in this direction as a way of countering the gains of others at their flanks. If we are surprised by this it is only because we seem to have airbrushed out of our historical consciousness

of Regional Integration', *International Organization*, 30 (1976), 173; L. N. Lindberg, *The Political Dynamics of European Economic Integration* (Stanford: Stanford University Press, 1963); L. N. Lindberg and S. A. Scheingold (eds.), *Regional Integration: Theory and Research* (Cambridge: CUP, 1971).

33 C. Leconte, *Understanding Euroscepticism* (Palgrave Macmillan, 2010).

34 R. Harmsen and M. Spiering (eds.), *Euroscepticism: Party Politics, National Identity and European Integration* (Amsterdam: Rodopi, 2005), p. 13; A. Szczerbiak, P. A. Taggart, *Opposing Europe* (Oxford: OUP, 2008) vols. I and II.

the rejection of the so-called European Constitution, an understandable amnesia since it represented a defeat of the collective political class in Europe by the *vox populi*,[35] albeit not speaking through but rather giving a slap in the face to the European construct itself.[36] I had earlier stated that internal secessionist trends such as Scotland and Catalonia see a safe haven in the European Union. This however does not contradict my argument that the failures of European democracy are a catalyst in undermining democracy itself which is one of the feeders of secessionism.

## IV The Mobilising Force

In the antipathetic reading of 'secessionism' I described this turn to national identity as a lamentable regression towards post-First World War notions of nation, state, nation state and democracy which deserved at least some measure of normative contempt.

Nationalism, however, may also be viewed as a response, surely not the only one, rooted deeply in the human condition, namely an existential yearning for life-meaning, one expression of which is given (and often abused) by a sense of collective belongingness. It is easy to see the appeal of such meaning in more than one way. The (national) collective transcends the life of any individual – and thus automatically bestows, on each and every one to whom it belongs, both a past and a future. National identity often breeds distinct forms of creativity – and what is important are both elements of the equation: creativity and distinctiveness, since it is those which respond to the yearning for meaning. The distinctiveness can be in all forms of culture from obvious linguistic distinctiveness and its derivatives in narratives, literature, poetry, etc., to the kitchen and the wardrobe. But it is the belongingness in and of itself which is the most intriguing. Herder's Community of Fate was, notoriously, an idea abused by National Socialism. But read through the eyes of, say, Isaiah Berlin, one understands the appeal that the Community of Fate holds – in its sense of mutual responsibility, its demands of a certain measure of selflessness and not least one of the powerful antidotes to an existential sense of individual loneliness which itself is part of the human condition.

[35] N. Fligstein, *Euroclash. The EU, European Identity, and the Future of Europe* (Oxford: OUP, 2008).

[36] For former examples, see J. H. H. Weiler, U. R. Haltern and F. C. Mayer, 'European Democracy and Its Critique', in J. Hayward (ed.), *The Crisis of Representation in Europe* (Abigdon: Frank Cass, 1995), p. 4.

In the community of fate everyone has some form of a family. One finds manifestations of such in the most interesting of contexts, such as in the fans of football clubs, especially those who hardly ever win.

The European Union aspired at its inception in its aspiration to an ever-closer union among the distinct peoples of Europe, to be such a community of fate.

This was a compelling vision which animated at least three generations of European idealists where the 'ever closer union among the people of Europe', with peace and prosperity as the icing on the cake, constituted the beckoning of a promised land.[37]

It is worth exploring further the mobilising force of this new plan for Europe. At the level of the surface language it is a straightforward pragmatic objective of consolidating peace and reconstructing European prosperity. There is much more within the deep structure of the plan, however.

Peace, at all times an attractive desideratum, would have had its appeal in purely utilitarian terms. But it is readily apparent that in the historical context in which the Schuman Plan was put forward, the notion of peace as an ideal probes a far deeper stratum than simply beating Swords into Ploughshares, sitting under one's Vines and Fig Trees, the Lambs laying with the Wolves – the classic Biblical metaphor for peace. The dilemma posed was an acute example of the alleged tension between Grace and Justice which has taxed philosophers and theologians through the ages – from William of Ockham (pre-modern), Friedrich Nietzsche (modernist) and the repugnant but profound Martin Heidegger (post-modern).

These were, after all, the early fifties, with the horrors of war still fresh in the mind and the memory of the unspeakable savagery of German occupation, in particular. It would take many years for the hatred in countries such as the Netherlands, Denmark or France to subside fully. The idea, then, in 1950 of a Community of Equals to provide the structural underpinning for long-term peace among yesterday's enemies, represented more than the wise counsel of experienced statesmen.

[37] F. Piodi, 'From the Schuman Declaration to the Birth of the ECSC: the Role of Jean Monnet', (May 2010) European Parliament, Directorate-General for the Presidency, Archive and Documentation Centre, *CARDOC Journals* No 6; T. Hoerber, 'The Nature of the Beast: the past and future purpose of European integration', *L'Europe en formation*, 1 (2006), 17; 'Introduction: We will do, and hearken', in J. H. H. Weiler, *The Constitution of Europe 'Do the New Clothes Have an Emperor?'*, (note 13), p. 8.

It was, first, a 'peace of the brave', requiring courage and audacity. At a deeper level, it managed to tap into the two civilisational pillars of Europe: The Enlightenment and the heritage of the French Revolution and the European Christian tradition.[38]

Liberty had already been achieved with the defeat of Nazi Germany – and Germans (like their Austrian brethren-in-crime) embraced with zeal the notion that they too were liberated from National Socialism. But here was a project, encapsulated in the Schuman Declaration, which added to the transnational level both Equality and Fraternity. The post-First World War Versailles version of peace was to take yesterday's enemy, diminish him and keep his neck firmly under one's heel, with disastrous results of course. Here instead was a vision in which yesteryear's enemy was regarded as an equal – Germany was to be treated as a full and equal partner in the venture – and engaged in a fraternal interdependent lock which indeed would make the thought of war to resolve future disputes unthinkable.[39] This was in fact the project of the enlightenment taken to the international level, as the Kant himself had dreamt. To embrace the Schuman Plan was to tap into one of the most powerful idealistic seams in Europe's civilisational mines.

The Schuman Plan was also a call for forgiveness, a challenge to overcome an understandable hatred. In that particular historical context the Schumanian notion of peace resonated with, was evocative of, the distinct teaching, imagery and values of the Christian call for forgiving one's enemies, for Love, for Grace – values so recently consecrated in their wholesale breach. The Schuman plan was in this sense evocative of both Confession and Expiation, and redolent with the Christian belief in the power of repentance and renewal and the ultimate goodness of humankind. This evocation is not particularly astonishing given the personal backgrounds of the Founding

[38] See, for example, J. Habermas and J. Derrida, 'February 15, or, What Binds Europeans Together: Plea for a Common Foreign Policy Beginning in Core Europe', in D. Levy, et al., *Old Europe, New Europe, Core Europe: Transatlantic Relations after the Iraq War* (London: Verso, 2005) pp. 5, 10–12; A. Finkielkraut, *La défaite de la pensée* (Paris: Gallimard, 1987); J. H. H. Weiler, *L'Europe chrétienne: Une excursion* (Paris: Editions du Cerf, 2007); J. M. Ferry, *La république crépusculaire. Comprendre le projet européen in sensu cosmopolitico* (Paris: Editions du Cerf, 2010); R. Schuman, *Pour l'Europe* (Paris: Editions Nagel Briquet, 1963), p. 55 *et seq.*

[39] A. Muñoz, 'L'engagement européen de Robert Schuman', in S. Schirmann, (ed.), *Robert Schuman et les pères de l'Europe: cultures politiques et années de formation* (Brussels: Peter Lang, 2008) pp. 39, 44.

Fathers – Adenauer, De Gaspari, Schuman and Monnet himself – all seriously committed Catholics.[40]

The mobilising force, especially among elites, the political classes who felt more directly responsible for the calamities from which Europe was just exiting, is not surprising given the remarkable subterranean appeal to the two most potent visions of the idyllic 'Kingdom' – the humanist and religious combined in one project.[41] This also explains how for the most part, both Right and Left, conservative and progressive, could embrace the project.

It is the model which explains (in part) why for so long the Union could operate without a veritable commitment to the principles it demanded of its aspiring members – democracy and human rights.

[40] A. Fimister, 'Integral Humanism and the Re-unification of Europe', in S. Schirmann (ed.), *Robert Schuman et les pères de l'Europe: cultures politiques et années de formation* (Brussels: Peter Lang, 2008), p. 25; '*Schuman was an ardent Roman Catholic, and his views about the desirability of political unity in Western Europe owed much to the idea that it was above all the continent's Christian heritage which gave consistence and meaning to the identity of European civilization. And the Europe he knew and loved best was the Carolingian Europe that accorded with his religious faith and his experience of French and German cultures*'; M. Sutton, 'Chapter 1: Before the Schuman Plan', in *France and the Construction of Europe, 1944–2007: The Geopolitical Imperative* (New York and Oxford: Berghan Books, 2007), p. 34; 'It is with deep faith in our cause that I speak to you, and I am confident that through the will of our free peoples, with your support and with God's help, a new era for Europe will soon begin': extracts from a speech by Alcide De Gasperi at the Consultative Assembly of the Council of Europe in Strasbourg on 16 September 1952 *Official Reports of Debates of the Consultative Assembly of the Council of Europe*, 3 (1952).

[41] One should add that the transnational reach of the Schuman plan served, as one would expect, a powerful internal interest the discussion of which even today meets with resistance. The challenge of 'fraternity' and the need for forgiveness, love and grace was even more pressing internally than internationally. For each one of the original Member States was seriously compromised internally. In post-war Germany, to put it bluntly, neither State nor society could function if all those complicit in National Socialism were to be excluded. In the other five, though ostensibly and in a real sense victims of German aggression, important social forces had been complicit and were morally compromised. This was obviously true of Fascist Italy and Vichy France. But even little Luxembourg contributed one of the most criminally notorious units to the German army and Belgium distinguished itself as the country with the highest number of indigenous volunteers to the occupying German forces. The betrayal of Anna Frank and her family by their good Dutch neighbours was not an exception but emblematic of a Dutch society and government who tidily handed over their entire Jewish citizenry for deportation and death. All these societies had a serious interest in 'moving on' and putting that compromised past behind them. If one were to forgive and embrace the external enemy, to turn one's back to the past and put one's faith in a better future, how much more so, how much easier, to do the same within one's own nation, society and even family.

Aspirant States had to become members of the European Convention of Human Rights, but the Union itself did not. They had to prove their democratic credentials, but the Union itself did not – two anomalies which hardly raised eyebrows.

It was a 'Lets-Just-Do-It' type of programme animated by great idealism (and a goodly measure of good old state interest, as a whole generation of historians such as Alan Milward[42] and Charles Maier[43] have demonstrated).

The European double helix has from its inception been Commission and Council: an international, (supposedly) apolitical transnational administration/executive (the Commission) collaborating not, as we habitually say, with the Member States (Council) but with the governments, the executive branch of the Member States, which for years and years had a forum which escaped in day-to-day matters the scrutiny of any parliament, European or national. Democracy is simply not part of the original vision of European integration.[44]

This observation is hardly shocking or even radical. Is it altogether fanciful to tell the narrative of Europe as one in which 'doers and believers' (notably the most original of its institutions, the Commission, coupled with an empowered executive branch of the Member States in the guise of the Council and COREPER), an elitist (if well-paid) vanguard, were the self-appointed leaders from whom grudgingly, over decades, power had to be wrested by the European Parliament? And even the European Parliament has been a strange *vox populi*, for has it not been for most of its existence a champion of European integration, so that to the extent that when the Union and European integration inevitably inspired fear and caution among citizens (only natural in such a radical transformation of European politics), the European Parliament did not feel like the place citizens would go to express those fears and concerns?

This narrative produced a culture of praxis, achievement and ever-expanding agendas. Given the noble dimensions of European integration, one ought to see and acknowledge their virtuous facets.

42 A. Milward, *The European Rescue of the Nation State* (2nd edition, London and New York: Routledge, 2000).

43 C. S. Maier and G. Bischof (eds.), *The Marshall Plan and Germany: West German Development within the Framework of the European Recovery Program* (Providence: Berg Press, 1991).

44 Featherstone, 'Jean Monnet and the Democratic Deficit in the European Union', (note 31), p. 150; J. Delors, *Independent*, 26 July 1993.

But that is only part of the story. They also explain some of the story of decline in European legitimacy and the mobilising pull which is so obvious in the current situation. *Part of the very phenomenology of political vision is that it always collapses as a mechanism for mobilisation and legitimation.* It obviously collapses when the project fails – when the revolution does not come. But interestingly, and more germane to the narrative of European Integration, even when successful it sows the seeds of its collapse. At one level the collapse is inevitable, part of the very phenomenology of any such project. Reality is always more complicated, challenging, banal and ultimately less satisfying than the dream which preceded it. The result is not only an absence of mobilisation and legitimation, but actual rancour.

Europe became a victim of its success in two ways. First, its stupendous achievement in making war unthinkable as a means for resolving differences has been so compelling that to new generations acculturated within this culture of peace, the sense of achievement has disappeared: it is taken for granted, and we should not lament this. Since, as I outlined above, the project progressed with a deep-seated structural democratic deficit, its legitimation was increasingly based on results, on outputs. The point I am making is not the obvious one that as results falter, the legitimacy that comes with them falters too. It is the deeper point that result discourse displaced the original ideal discourse. It displaced the sense of mutual responsibility, the sense of polity and community. In 'selling' European citizenship the vocabulary was always one of rights, never duties. One of benefits, never sacrifice or selflessness. The deep tragedy of the European construct has been its failure to engrain itself, implant itself in the social and political consciousness as a community of fate.

It is this void of meaning which is now occupied increasingly by the two different but interconnected strands of secessionism, including their regressive atavistic appeals.

Europe's tragedy is however also its future potential promise, since in an increasingly complex world, the economic, security and population challenges are such that they simply cannot be solved by any single state offering the potential of revival of that transcendent responsibility – both within its Member States and among them.

3

# Internal Enlargement in the European Union: Beyond Legalism and Political Expediency

NEIL WALKER

## I Introduction

This paper proceeds in three stages. I begin by criticising the tendency in recent debates on substate nationalism in Europe to avoid the deeper questions of political morality concerning the entitlement (or otherwise) of these substate nations which are ceding from existing Member States to assume membership of the European Union. I then raise these deeper questions and argue, against Joseph Weiler in particular, that the correct attitude for the EU to adopt is one of considered neutrality rather than strong endorsement either of the case for accession or of the case against accession, by new internal states. In the final part of my argument I consider what role, if any, the EU has to play in the absence of such a directorial mandate. I examine, and dismiss as unlikely though attractive, a more modest procedural role. I conclude by arguing that the EU nonetheless influences the debate over the sovereign aspirations of substate nations simply by existing, and thereby, changes the balance of political incentives in a way which is more accommodating of forms of autonomy short of independence.

## II Avoiding the Question

A famous thesis on the European Union holds that its original motivation and ongoing legitimating purpose has been 'the rescue of the nation state'.[1] Today, sixty years on, it remains the case that the most critical political and public examinations of the EU are often framed in nation state-centred terms, typically triggered by events which pose profound problems for particular members or groups of members. Whether

[1] A. Milward, *The European Rescue of the Nation State* (2nd ed., London: Routledge, 1999).

addressing the Greek economic crisis or the prospect of mass migratory movement into the states at the Union's Southern and Eastern borders, existential challenge to the Union itself tends to be closely bound up in an existential challenge to one or more of its component nations.

Does the question of internal division and separation of Member States conform to this pattern? Certainly, substate independence has begun to acquire the status of a serious existential threat *within* those Member States most immediately affected in recent years, but compared to other prominent continental events, it was slow to be identified as a problem in which the EU itself was closely implicated. Yet all that began to change with the Scottish independence referendum. The Scottish campaign was an exceptionally long one, stretching from early 2012 until the fateful decision of 18 September 2014 to remain part of the UK. One widely canvassed justification for such an extended process was precisely that it would allow a number of difficult questions concerning an independent Scotland's relationship to the wider international community to be addressed in advance. And among the most important of such questions was the matter of an independent Scotland's membership of the European Union.

Should an independent Scotland follow the ordinary Treaty amendment procedure for existing Member States under Article 48 TEU in seeking to secure the continuing membership of its citizens? Or, as always seemed more plausible, should it follow the conventional accession route for aspiring Member States under Article 49 TEU? Whichever route it followed, would that route imply the certainty of success, or at least its strong expectation, and better still for the supporters of independence, would it entail a rapid and seamless acknowledgement of Scotland's seat at the European table? Did the Treaty's horizontal obligations of sincere cooperation and solidarity between Member States, along with the vertical framework of rights and responsibilities connecting the EU with its citizens, ground a legal duty on all parties to negotiate Scotland's accession in good faith?[2] Or should Scotland simply take its place at the end of a long queue of candidate states, with no legal basis for special treatment or consideration, and no guarantee or even legitimate expectation of eventual success? And tied to these threshold questions, on what

[2] On which, see, for example, David Edward, 'Scotland and the European Union', (December 2012) *Scottish Constitutional Futures Forum Blog* <www.scottishconstitutionalfutures.org/OpinionandAnalysis/ViewBlogPost/tabid/1767/articleType/ArticleView/articleId/852/David-Edward-Scotland-and-the-European-Union.aspx>, accessed 7 July 2015.

terms could Scotland expect to negotiate entry? Could it seek to rely on UK opt-outs on Schengen or the Euro – the latter particularly important in light of the pro-independence campaign's tenacious commitment, against the opposition of the UK Government, to stick with sterling?[3]

Clarity on these matters would have allowed for a more informed assessment ahead of 'D' day by all involved in the drawn out constitutional drama – a more considered appraisal of the risks to EU membership attendant upon the choice for an independent Scotland. But clarity was not in fact forthcoming. Instead, the emergence before the vote of a clear and precise legal picture of the membership prospects of an independent Scotland was probably always a naive hope. There are, after all, no precedents for 'internal enlargement' of the EU following the separation of an existing Member State, no Treaty provisions directly in point, and no obvious forum outside of the political process where a definitive statement of the relevant law can be supplied or enforced.[4] And even if we were to reach agreement on the best understanding of the relevant law, or at least to acknowledge some legal positions as more persuasive and widely supported than others, and even if we were to assume there was a forum in which the most persuasive version could be definitively pronounced, it is not clear how far that would take us. For most plausible interpretations of the relevant law seem in any case only to fill in some of the background and leave much to the discretion, negotiating position and even the conformity strategy of the relevant parties. So, for example, the majority of informed opinion may favour the Article 49 TEU route – the bespoke accession clause – over Article 48 TEU,[5] but whichever is chosen, much is left in the way of timing and terms to the negotiation of the Member States and various supranational institutions. Similarly, we may agree that as a new Member State, an independent Scotland would,

[3] See, for example, The Scottish Government's independence manifesto *Scotland's Future: Your Guide to an Independent Scotland* (2013) Chapter 3, <www.gov.scot/resource/0043/00439021.pdf>, accessed 7 February 2016.

[4] See, for example, S. Douglas-Scott, 'Why the EU should Welcome an independent Scotland', (August 2014) *Scottish Constitutional Futures Forum Blog*, <www.scottishconstitutionalfutures.org/OpinionandAnalysis/ViewBlogPost/tabid/1767/articleType/ArticleView/articleId/4041/Sionaidh-Douglas-Scott-Why-the-EU-Should-Welcome-an-Independent-Scotland.aspx>, accessed 7 February 2016.

[5] See, for example, Richard Hoyle, 'Scottish Independence and EU Membership, Part II', (September 2014) EJIL *Talk!*, <www.ejiltalk.org/12126/>, accessed 7 February 2016. See also De Witte, 'Towards Partial EU Membership of the United Kingdom?', in this volume.

under present Treaty rules, be required to commit in principle to membership of the Euro, but as membership is conditional on meeting various convergence criteria which are under the at least partial control of the states themselves, that still leaves a significant margin for manoeuvre to the new state in the post-accession phase.[6] In a nutshell, then, even if *legal clarity* had been forthcoming, that would not have produced *legal certainty of outcome*, since the relevant law is concerned much more with process and conditional requirements than with final outcomes.

If we add to the mix the unsurprising tendency of both sides in the referendum debate to exploit this uncertainty by talking up those arguments which best serve their cause, with the nationalists arguing for easy access and the Unionists maintaining the opposite, as well as the reluctance of European institutions to be drawn into the struggle by pronouncing on the correct approach – of which we will say more in due course – it is no surprise that the legal case for new or continued Scottish membership remained unresolved throughout the campaign. And, of course, given the eventual Scottish 'no' vote, and the failure even to reach the stage of a constitutionally recognised referendum on independence in the other prominent contemporaneous 'internal enlargement' theatre of Catalonia and Spain,[7] the legal issues remain moot today. The answers are as incomplete and uncertain as they ever were, just as the questions threaten to go 'live' again. An early second independence referendum for Scotland became a tangible prospect following the unprecedented gains of the Scottish National Party in the post-referendum UK general election of May 2015,[8] and this prospect was reinforced after the seismic shock caused by the UK Brexit

[6] See, for example, Andrew Scott, 'An Independent Scotland Could not be required to adopt the Euro as its Currency', (November 2012) *Scottish Constitutional Futures Forum Blog*, <www.scottishconstitutionalfutures.org/OpinionandAnalysis/ViewBlogPost/tabid/1767/articleType/ArticleView/articleId/480/Drew-Scott-An-Independent-Scotland-Could-Not-be-Required-to-Adopt-the-Euro-as-its-Currency.aspx>, accessed 7 February 2016.

[7] On the Catalan case, see Medina Ortega in this volume. On the Spanish Constitutional Court's refusal to recognise the constitutionality of a referendum in 2014, see Victor Ferreres Comella, 'The Spanish Constitutional Court Confronts Catalonia's "Right to Decide" (Comment on the Judgment 42/2014)', *European Constitutional Law Review*, 10 (2014), 571–590; see also Javier García Oliva, 'Catalonia in Spain: The Significance of the 25th September 2015 Elections', (July 2015) *UK Constitutional Law association Blog*, <http://ukconstitutionallaw.org/2015/07/24/javier-garcia-oliva-catalonia-in-spain-the-significance-of-the-25th-september-2015-elections/>, accessed 7 February 2016.

[8] The Scottish National Party won fifty-six out of fifty-nine Scottish seats in the general election, based on 50 per cent of the popular vote.

referendum vote of June 2016 (which, if in due course followed by UK withdrawal from the EU under Art. 50 TEU, will reframe the question of continuing membership of a pro-EU independent Scotland as one of 'internal contraction' rather than 'internal enlargement' – though many of the same questions will arise). For its part, the Spanish situation has been similarly unsettled by the renewed (if qualified) success of parties with an independence mandate in the Catalonian regional elections in September 2015.[9]

The search for advance clarity has not merely proven fruitless, however. Worse than that, it has tended to deflect attention from the deeper questions of political morality at play – just as it might do so again in the case of a second Scottish referendum or a similar event in Catalonia or elsewhere – for the climate of debate has tended to swing between the two poles we have identified: on the one hand, an earnest but frustrated legalism which can never substantiate its own claim to authoritative resolution, and on the other hand, a strategically measured – some might say cynical – political opportunism (on all sides) that seeks to follow the line of most convenience. As each approach supplies the reinforcing condition of the others, little space exists for serious reflection on the compatibility of internal secession with the fundamental purposes of the EU.

## III Secession Through a European Lens

Against this backdrop, Joseph Weiler's interventions, most notably in the last days of the Scottish referendum campaign, have been refreshing, at least at one level.[10] He observed no technical legal impediment to an independent Scotland joining the EU, and he did not seek to contrive

[9] The pro-independence parties won 72 out of 135 seats in the regional election of 25 September 2015, which had been presented by them as a 'de facto' plebiscite (a 'de jure' plebiscite having been forbidden under the ruling of the Spanish Constitutional Court [note 7 above]). The result, however, was far from an unambiguous success for the independence camp, as they won only 47.7 per cent of the popular vote. See, for example, D. Gardner, 'Catalonia's election leaves Spain with a constitutional crisis' (2 October 2015) *Financial Times*, <www.ft.com/cms/s/0/7633bc6e-66b5-11e5-97d0-1456a776a4f5.html#axzz3nOdKaCGb>, accessed 6 February 2016. See also Garcia Oliva, (note 7) above.

[10] 'Scotland and the EU: A Comment' (September 2015) *Verfassungsblog*, <www.verfassungsblog.de/scotland-eu-comment-joseph-h-h-weiler/#.VgJnup1waUk>. This piece sparked wider debate on the blog in the week before the Scottish referendum. For my own contribution, on which the present piece builds, see N. Walker, 'Scotland and the EU: A Comment' (September 2015) *Verfassungsblog*, <www.verfassungsblog.de/scotland-eu-comment-neil-walker/#.Vg5BIvlVhBc>, accessed 5 February 2016.

such an impediment. Nor was he concerned to make a definitive moral judgment against any and all secession claims in Europe considered on their own terms. Rather, to the extent that he did take seriously the concerns of other states – Spain, France, Italy, Belgium and elsewhere – from whom secession is threatened or is a more distant possibility, he did so, not in terms of a critique of their narrow strategic self-interest, but on account of the disadvantage to all of a 'domino effect' of ever more strident nationalist claims across the continent and beyond.

But Weiler's main argument, building upon an earlier comment he had made on the situation in Catalonia,[11] is located in a more EU-specific strain of public reason. He begins by noting that just as national minorities in existing Member States who presently enjoy extensive forms of individual and collective freedom have no automatic right to secede as a matter of general international law, so too should the EU, in its accession and general membership policy, not be expected to indulge the independence claims of these unoppressed substate nations. On the contrary, the very ethos of integration, reconciliation and continental solidarity which has fed the European project from its post-war beginnings should cause the EU and all those who endorse the best understanding of its foundations, to take a dim view of any separatist impulse that seems to betray these founding virtues. From this perspective, therefore, far from having a stronger claim than those external candidates who have benefited from the EU's extensive post-cold war enlargement, those nations already comfortably nested inside the EU's Western European heartland should be refused a supranational haven if they continue to insist on the path to independence.

The candour of Weiler's argument, and his refusal to conceal his preferences behind either the law's false certainties or the strategically hostile motives of some European politicians apprehensive about independence movements in their own backyard,[12] is welcome. Yet I join

[11] J. H. H. Weiler, 'Catalonian Independence and the European Union' *European Journal of International Law*, 23 (2012), 909–913

[12] As was Barroso's repeated tendency when President of the Commission. His warning of the possible negative reactions of some Member States and the dangers this posed to the accession process, was most explicitly stated on UK nationwide television in the BBC's Andrew Marr show on February 17th 2014, sparking a very lively reaction. For comment, see N. Walker, 'Hijacking the Debate' (February 2015) *Scottish Constitutional Futures Forum Blog*, <www.scottishconstitutionalfutures.org/OpinionandAnalysis/ViewBlogPost/tabid/1767/articleType/ArticleView/articleId/3068/Neil-Walker-Hijacking-the-Debate.aspx>, accessed 5 February 2016. The Commission's stance was somewhat

others in finding his approach too stringent.[13] To begin with, it is in danger of not taking a people's own view of its preferred collective future seriously enough. Whether we are dealing with the Scottish or the Catalan case or that of any other national minority, surely more store than Weiler allows should be set by an aspiring nation's founding virtues and its own sense of what is the constitutionally adequate vindication of its desire for collective autonomy. If nothing short of independence is deemed sufficient from the perspective of the constituency in question as an affirmation of shared political identity, it is difficult to see why such a subjective collective aspiration should be summarily dismissed in favour of a supposedly objective standard of adequate individual and collective freedom – one that, incidentally, always leaves in successful place another and a prior, but far from necessarily, morally superior claim to nation-statehood.

Granted, as already noted, international law, with its high threshold of a 'right' to self-determination might appear to be of little help in grounding this alternative perspective, since its establishment-biased concern has always been with the minimum necessary disturbance of the existing international distribution of sovereign authority, rather than the fairest and fullest accommodation of self-determination claims. Yet international law today is more fluid on this matter than first impressions suggest. There are in fact competing philosophies bubbling under its doctrinal surface.[14] The present position tends to reflect the Remedial Right or Just Cause theory, according to which secession is only justified if some basic injustice is present and uncorrected, such as a historically unconsented annexation, a continuing lack of protection of basic rights and security or the economic interests of a region, a pattern of systematic group discrimination, or a breach of an existing agreement for autonomous self-government or for the

softened later in the year when the then President Elect, Jean-Claude Juncker, remarked that as an internal applicant a newly independent Scotland, having completed a constitutionally recognised secession from the UK, would be deemed already to meet 'core-EU requirements' and so, to that very limited extent, would be treated as a special and separate case, http://www.scotsman.com/news/politics/independence-juncker-sympathetic-to-scots-eu-bid-1-3482266

[13] See, for example, various contributions to the *Verfassungsblog* debate on Weiler, (note 10) above.

[14] See, for example, S. Mancini, 'Secession and Self-Determination', in M. Rosenfeld and A. Sajo (eds.), *The Oxford Handbook of Comparative Constitutional Law* (Oxford: OUP, 2012), pp. 481–500, at 483–487; A. Patten, 'Democratic Secession from a Multinational State', *Ethics*, 112 (2002), 558–586.

protection of distinct collective rights.[15] But in a postcolonial age in which international law has gradually come to recognise and support the democratic tide in matters of state formation, this approach is increasingly being challenged by a more generous Primary Right or Choice theory according to which any community which views itself as a distinct national community and which has a special association with a particular territory possesses a claim to sovereign self-determination.[16] Moreover, in practice, there is evidence of a creeping convergence of these positions in the relevant jurisprudence. Since the landmark *Quebec Secession*[17] decision of the Canadian Supreme Court, some jurists have begun to proceduralise the right to self-determination into something like the right of a national group 'to be taken seriously'[18] in its efforts to secede from an existing state. That is to say, even though there continues to be no automatic entitlement absent a standing injustice, the articulation of a desire for independence on the part of a substate national group, ideally through the mechanism of a referendum, should be sufficient to trigger a requirement on the part of the existing state to negotiate in good faith with the substate nation over their aspirations for independence.

But even if, notwithstanding these shifts in general international law and in the conventional morality of international relations, a special case for the EU as an entity possessing and pursuing a unique historical mission to make internal secession unnecessary and unacceptable can be persuasively advanced along the lines advocated by Weiler, it seems unduly dogmatic to use this to justify a rigid policy against continued

[15] See, for example, the many works of Allen Buchanan, including *Justice, Legitimacy and self-determination* (Oxford: OUP, 2004); see also W. Norman, *Negotiating Nationalism; Nation Building, Federalism and Secession in the Multinational State* (Oxford: OUP, 2006).

[16] See, for example, Daniel Philpott, 'In Defense of Self-Determination', *Ethics*, 105 (1995), 352–385, and 'Self-Determination in Practice', in Margaret Moore (ed.), *National Self-Determination and Secession* (Oxford: OUP, 1998), pp. 79–102; Christopher Wellman, 'A Defense of Secession and Political Self-Determination', *Philosophy & Public Affairs* 24 (1995), 142–71; Harry Beran, 'A Democratic Theory of Political Self-Determination for a New World Order', in Percy Lehning (ed.), *Theories of Secession* (London: Routledge, 1998), pp. 32–59;

[17] *Reference re Secession of Quebec*, SCR 2 (1998), 217. The emphasis here is again on clarity rather than on certainty of outcome, to revert to a distinction drawn earlier in the text.

[18] See, in particular, J. Klabbers, 'The Right to be Taken Seriously: Self-Determination in International Law', *Human Rights Quarterly* 28 (2006), 186–206; see also C. Bell, 'What we talk about when we talk about international constitutional law', *Transnational Legal Theory* 5(2014), 241–284.

membership of new internal states. There are, after all, other and rival views of the deeper purpose and distinct regional mission of the European Union. The priority given in the Preamble to the TEU to the principle of subsidiarity offers one different strand, just as the deepening significance of EU citizenship as a horizontal relationship among persons as Europeans rather than state nationals offers another. These strands, and other forms of recognition of substate identity through the Committee of the Regions and various mechanisms of regionally sensitive distribution of supranational funds, reflect an alternative and more autonomy-friendly perspective. In the face of these competing narratives, the EU's public policy on accession should surely remain more agnostic.

Yet would such agnosticism, and a consequential refusal neither to oppose Scottish membership nor to concede everything to its fast-track aspirations, not simply involve an extension of the failure to take seriously the deeper questions of political morality at stake which we have already found – and criticised – in the preoccupation with the odd couple of 'pure' legalism and 'impure' political expediency? My answer to that questions is a mixed one.

On the one hand, to the extent that the EU has in practice taken an agnostic approach, this *in fact* appears to be a product of weakness rather than strength. The Commission (mainly through its Presidency) alone among the European institutions has been prepared to speak on the matter, but in so doing, has said as little as possible.[19] Its attitude has been to avoid controversy and deflect responsibility by stressing the need to cleave to the existing framework of legal rules *and* political practice as a template of disinterested and deferential process. That is to say, its stance has been one of 'legalism *plus*' gesturing to the procedural rules but also to the leeway for the exercise of political discretion these rules permit as together supplying the appropriate decision pathway, and in so doing excluding itself from any active influence over, and absolving itself of, any responsibility for that decision. The policy position which emerges from Brussels' attitude of prudential minimalism I have described elsewhere as 'conservative neutrality',[20] in which the state-protective orientation of domestic constitutional norms on secession, and the equally state-centred slant of its own European procedures on

[19] See (note 12) above. For a fuller discussion, see N. Walker, 'Beyond Secession? Law in the Framing of the National Polity', in S. Tierney (ed.), *Nationalism and Globalisation* (Oxford: Hart Publishing, 2015), pp. 155–184.

[20] Walker, (note 19) above, pp. 168–177.

accession is emphasised and their close adherence promised. From this perspective, the EU institutions, already uncomfortable under the heavy contemporary burden of unavoidable political judgment in matters as controversial as the sovereign debt crisis and, more recently, on mass immigration, instead defer in the self-determination context to a process which inevitably re-empowers the Member States themselves individually and collectively.

One ironic consequence of this is that, as substance need not follow form, the EU's formal deference to domestic constitutional norms permits substantively different outcomes. Scotland, from this perspective, has benefited from an increasingly permissive constitutional culture in the UK in which the Union state has come to accept the continuing right of it parts to self-determine their own future, whereas the Spanish federal constitution has remained firmly locked against the politically powerful claims for a referendum from its Catalan part. The EU's acquiescence in the national constitutional position on secession in each case implies an acceptance of quite different answers to the plebiscitary aspirations of two substate nations.[21]

On the other hand, however, neutrality *could* amount to more than this pragmatic reflex. There is a big difference between merely avoiding the question of principle for fear of courting political controversy, which seems to have characterised the EU's actual approach, and answering the question of principle through a position of *considered neutrality* in which, as set out above, the existence of reasonable alternative interpretations of the public philosophy of the EU means that it would be unwarranted for the EU to take a categorical stance one way or the other. What is more, and what is crucial, in any case the EU can contribute and should be understood as contributing something other to the Scottish debate, and to that of the sovereign aspirations of any substate nation, than the role of ethical gatekeeper whose authority is dubious and, if exercised, liable to breed resentment and bring the authority of the EU itself into disrepute. Considered neutrality, in short, need not imply an absence of influence.

## IV Reframing the European Secession Debate

The Union's influence on the debate might instead be more indirect, but also more telling. Two possibilities may be pursued here, both of which

[21] Ibid. pp.168–177

involve the EU in a form of 'reframing' of the internal secession question. In the first less likely and purely hypothetical case, the reframing would be of a procedural character. In the second and more likely case, the reframing concerns alterations already underway in our very understanding and imagination of political community in the European domain. Let us look at each of these in turn.

### A. *Reframing of Procedures*

To begin with, regardless of the substantive merits of the arguments for and against the accommodation of new internal Member States, and regardless of the EU's own highly doubtful credentials as a strong voice in that debate, there might in principle be merit in the development of a new Treaty or otherwise 'constitutional' provision of a purely procedural character designed to regulate relations between the EU and separating internal territories. There are a number of reasons for this, each referring back to points discussed above.

First, there is the argument from public reason. The EU is notorious for possessing a 'constitution without constitutionalism'[22] – the hardware of institutional design without the software of a public philosophy to make sense of, and breathe life into, that institutional design. This can leave the EU badly exposed in circumstances where some kind of coherent and confident expression of a historically sensitive constitutional culture is required. As we have seen in the instant case, the EU institutions may instead be minded either to avoid the issue or to resort merely to the strategic preferences of the day with little sense of the distinction between polity and government – between the long-term constitutional integrity of the entity as a whole and the balance of short-term institutional preferences.[23] The danger, however, is that the EU is damned both ways, either for presumptive interference or for dereliction of constitutional responsibility. The development of a new procedure-centred Treaty provision might find a route between these two hazards.

[22] See, for example, J. H. H. Weiler, 'Does Europe Need a Constitution? Demos, Telos and The German Maastricht Decision' *European Law Journal* 1(1995), 219.

[23] Another recent example was the controversy over the strategic positioning of various actors in the choice of a new President of the Commission following Treaty changes seeking to increase the responsibility of the Commission to Parliament in the making of that choice; see, for example, M. Kumm, 'Why the Council is Under a Legal Duty to Propose Juncker as a Commission President' (June 2014) *Verfassungsblog*, <www.verfassungsblog.de/en/der-europaeische-rat-ist-verpflichtet-juncker-vorzuschlagen/#.Vg5j4_lVhBc>, accessed 5 February 2016.

It would require the issue of new internal states and its attendant controversies to be addressed, reasoned and defended in public, prior to and aside from the exigencies of any particular case. Constitutional policy could be made openly and consultatively by the relevant constitutional actors, rather than by academics and institutional players of the day compensating for the conspicuous silence or the backstage rumours and whispers of these same constitutional actors.[24]

Secondly, despite appearances to the contrary, a general procedure-centred Treaty provision would be much better equipped to discriminate between very different scenarios than the treatment of individual cases on an ad hoc basis as they arise. In the latter case, the temptation is to treat all cases of new internal membership as identical in principle, in order to avoid claims of discrimination and to assert the appearance of neutrality. Yet there may be important distinctions to draw. We have already mentioned the *arguably* significant difference between Member States, such as the United Kingdom, which have gradually come to recognise the legitimacy of internal secession in their own constitutional terms, and those like Spain, which do not. Another potential difference lies between States where the internal separation can persuasively be characterised as one of 'secession' – with one part voluntarily departing and leaving the entity as a whole reduced but intact (as most commentators would view the Scottish situation) and 'voluntary disassociation', in which all the parties seek divorce (as in Czechoslovakia) or other forms of 'dissolution' (including the pertinent example of Belgium, where Flanders would be the likely instigators of any separation, but as the dominant region economically and population-wise could hardly be argued to have 'seceded' from a continuing Belgian Member State). In the case of these and other key variables – such as the one that has become urgently relevant in the case of Brexit, in which only one part (in Scotland's case, the smaller part) of an internally separating state wishes to remain within the EU – a general and wide-ranging procedural provision offers the opportunity to work out the basis on which different types of internal separation may be treated similarly or differently. To revert again to our key example, this may or may not involve discriminating between Scotland and Catalonia in terms of their basic standing even to be considered as the subjects of an accession process, but a general provision would at least expose the arguments either way and provide a publicly reasoned and predictable resolution.

[24] See Walker, (note 19) and (note 12) above, 'Hijacking the Debate'.

Thirdly and finally, while it would not permit the EU to assume the position of sovereign regulator of the internal composition of the Member States, a general provision would allow it to impose certain procedural requirements consistent with a developing public philosophy regarding its own composition. For example, for logistical reasons the EU might wish to impose a timescale for processing new or continuous membership, just as it presently does in the context of withdrawals under Article 50 TEU (and all the more so, as in the Brexit scenario, where the withdrawal of the Member State as a whole coincides with the desire of one of its parts to remain or accede).[25] More ambitiously, if, as suggested above, it was acknowledged as a matter of the EU's substantive neutrality that internal separation should not entirely preclude the possibility of accelerated facilitation of new or continuous internal membership, a key procedural prerequisite consistent with the principle of democracy might be an explicit referendum vote affirming the desire of the majority of the seceding state to remain within the EU. The question of Scottish membership might have appeared significantly less vexed to the EU institutions and the other twenty-seven member states if the referendum on independence on 18 September 2014 had been required, as a matter of EU law, to include a second question on EU membership. An affirmative answer to that second question could then have been treated as a precondition of the newly emergent state's acceptance as a candidate within the accession process.

For all these potential advantages, however, we must conclude on a highly sceptical note. At a time when the consensus necessary to achieve *any* Treaty reform in the EU post-Lisbon remains a distant prospect,

[25] Article 50 was introduced by the Treaty of Lisbon 2009, and is evidence of how the Union, even in the recent past, has been able to mobilise constitutional reform around the sensitive question of its own composition.

Sir David Edward, the former CJEU Judge, has also suggested the need for such a systematic Treaty-based procedural approach to ensure, so far as is possible and consistent with the need for detailed accession negotiations and the requirement for consent of all Member States, a relatively smooth and pre-planned transition in membership status in the case of a new internal Member State. Such an approach would of course have to resolve the prior choice between an Article 48 or Article 49 Treaty amendment route for internal accessions, or alternatively propose an entirely new procedural 'third way'. See Edward's evidence to the Scottish Parliament's European and External Relations Committee of 23 January 2014, http://www.parliament.scot/S4_EuropeanandExternalRelationsCommittee/Meeting%20Papers/Public_papers_23_Jan_2014.pdf. As noted in the main text, such a procedural rationalisation would be at an even greater premium in a Brexit-type situation.

intervention in an area such as this will likely win little support. Indeed, given the national sensitivities involved, even the most modest procedural proposal will likely be summarily dismissed as a form of unwanted encouragement to the forces of disorderly nationalism. And so, even though continued *ad hoc* actions may expose the EU just as painfully, the veto points in EU decision-making are just too many, and the forces of political inertia too formidable, for us to contemplate such a change in the foreseeable future.

### *B. Reframing of the Political Imagination*

If the EU's hands are tied in terms of what it *does*, what it *is* nevertheless has significance for the secession debate. For crucially, in ways which are little remarked on but broadly experienced, its very existence alters the stakes of political nationalism. First, and in material terms, by pooling significant sovereign powers above the state, the EU demonstrates that the choice between national independence and continued incorporation in another state is far from being an all-or-nothing affair, and by providing various economic and social rights and measures of non-discrimination it offers the kind of cosmopolitan freedom which guarantees against the systematic ill-treatment of minority nations and nationalism within existing state forms. Secondly, and in symbolic terms, by supplying a new level of political identity (including a new form of citizenship) and a new point of reference for interpreting national identity, the EU surely also changes the expressive significance of national sovereignty and its alternatives. Just as 'independence in Europe', as in the pro-EU Scottish nationalists' long-standing slogan, conveys a very different meaning and sense of collective identity than would the 'separatism outside Europe's Northern edge' of an unattached Scotland, so too 'Britain in Europe' is much less isolationist than without its qualifier (whose elimination is promised if the Brexit referendum result is pursued to its Article 50 TEU conclusion),[26] and 'Scotland-in-Britain-in-Europe' suggests a much less subordinate Scottish native identity than merely 'Scotland in Britain'.

[26] See, for example, S. Douglas-Scott, 'British Withdrawal from the EU: An existential threat to the United Kingdom?' (October 2014) *Scottish Constitutional Futures Forum Blog*, <www.scottishconstitutionalfutures.org/OpinionandAnalysis/ViewBlogPost/tabid/1767/articleType/ArticleView/articleId/4411/Sionaidh-Douglas-Scott-British-Withdrawal-from-the-EU-an-Existential-Threat-to-the-United-Kingdom.aspx>, accessed 5 February 2016.

As the examples imply, the argument here cuts both ways. The protective presence of the EU certainly offers a spur to new national sovereignty projects. Yet it also supplies a set of considerations which makes the project of new statehood less consequential, and in the instant case – provided we could trust in *continuing* UK membership of a *continuing* EU (both of which statuses need careful attention, and the first of which is now in mortal danger) – less relevant, arguably unnecessary, and in the eyes of some substate nationalists at least, ultimately redundant. The sense that the EU has been materially and symbolically adept at securing the kinds of guarantees and forms of individual dignity and collective recognition whose presence are generously accommodating of various species of substate nationalism, and whose absence might otherwise fuel and justify independentist claims, is crucial here. Doubtless, it lies behind Weiler's insistence that the EU should also be explicitly and concretely resistant to new claims to legal and political identity which are divisive of existing Member States. But in my view these new claims should be allowed to stand or fall on its own merits. The EU, as we have seen, simply lacks the legitimising presence to play a robust directorial role in treating the internal secession question, but its background work of 'stage redesign', so to speak, and therefore, of reframing how we see and experience the goods of political community in ways which are highly relevant to that same question, has nevertheless been profound.

The 'carrot' of current EU membership, in sum, should be its own incentive, without the 'stick' represented by the raw threat of future exclusion. As we face the prospects of further and more intense pressure from European national movements, the supranational case for the accommodation of these substate nations within the existing pattern of statehood remains better served, and served with less prospect of collateral damage to the supranational project itself, by emphasising the space for the expression and realisation of national political interests which Europe offers in the here and now, rather than by dire warnings of privations to come for those who might opt otherwise.

## V Conclusion

For some, the conclusion that the EU should influence the debate by its presence rather than any strategy of active intervention might seem disappointingly modest. To them I would simply reiterate that any more active approach is fraught with the kind of existential danger to the EU to which reference was made in the opening section. The EU cannot afford to overstep its authority in this area in a political age in which it has no option but to make inevitably deeply controversial choices in other areas associated with its economic and physical security. If instead we continue to believe that the EU has succeeded at least in some measure in one of its founding missions, of taming the more unattractive forces and consequences of nationalism, we may have to accept that whichever way the challenges of Scotland, Catalonia, Flanders and the rest are resolved, at least the reasonable prospect of their continuation within the cover of the EU would ensure that these resolutions do not present themselves as zero-sum outcomes to most of the populations involved. The hope is that this consideration should in the final analysis persuade the Member States, without any steer from the European institutions, to adopt a more generously welcoming approach to the prospect of an internal separation, even if they might regret the particular outcome.

# 4

# Secession and the Ambiguous Place of Regions Under EU Law

CRISTINA FASONE*

## I Introduction: On the Myth of 'Regional Blindness' and Secession

The European Union (EU) has been traditionally neutral towards the internal constitutional structure of its Member States and has usually dealt with them as if they were 'monoliths'. Indeed, in 1957 the only federal state in the European Community (EC) was Germany. Gradually, with the accession of federal or regional Member States (Austria and Spain), and the federalisation of the existing ones (Belgium and Italy), the then EC has increasingly paid attention to the subnational dimension. This process has occurred while preserving the European construction against fragmentation and inefficiency.

This oversimplified image of the existing relationships among levels of government within the EC and now the EU – often described as EU 'regional blindness'[1] – has been instrumental in protecting the functioning of the EU legal system. For example, it has permitted attributing clear responsibility for violations of EU law to the states,

* Assistant Professor of Comparative Public Law, Department of Political Science, LUISS Guido Carli University, Rome.

1 This notion was coined by H. P. Ipsen, 'Al Bundesstaat in der Gemeinschaft', in E. Von Caemerer and W. Hallstein (eds.), *Probleme des Europäischen Recht. Festschrift für Walter Hallstein zu seinem 65. Geburstag* (Frankfurt am Main: Verlag Vittorio Klostermann, 1966), pp. 248–256. More recently, in particular after the experience of the Convention on the Future of Europe, scholars such as S. Weatherill, 'The Challenge of the Regional Dimension in the European Union', in S. Weatherill and U. Bernitz (eds.), *The Role of Regions and Sub-National Actors in Europe* (Oxford: Hart Publishing, 2005), pp. 3–6; and M. Olivetti, 'The Regions in the EU Decision-Making Processes', in M. Cartabia, N. Lupo and A. Simoncini (eds.), *Democracy and Subsidiarity in the EU. National Parliaments, Regions and Civil Society in the Decision-Making Process* (Bologna: Il Mulino, 2013), pp. 326–329, argue that the idea of EU 'regional blindness' is no longer realistic and accurate.

regardless of their unitary, regional or federal structure, and has avoided the difficulties which would certainly arise should the EU decide to manage its relationship simultaneously with the seventy-four European regions endowed with legislative powers in addition to the twenty-eight Member States. Nonetheless, the European Social Fund and the cohesion policy have taken the regional dimension into account for decades. Although the cohesion policy acknowledges that regions do exist in the EU, it also aims to foster an ever-closer Union as the paramount objective of the process of European integration (Article 1 TEU). Aiming 'at reducing disparities between the levels of development of the various regions and the backwardness of the least favoured regions' (Preamble TFEU and Article 174 TFEU), cohesion policy fosters the equalisation of regional territories.

In other words, the EU does not have any interest in furthering differentiation and asymmetries within its Member States. The more homogeneous the regions are, the better it is for the EU. Unfortunately, the cohesion process and the objective of an ever-closer Union have not eliminated the centrifugal forces which endanger the integrity of some Member States from within (Italy, Spain and the UK).[2] The secession claims that are spreading in Europe with a domino effect from Member State to Member State are a clear example of this.[3]

Interestingly, when regions like Scotland, Catalonia and Veneto make their official claim for secession and independence, the EU is always invoked and one of the first actions that the prospective seceding territory

[2] Despite the frequent attempts to reform the federal system (the sixth reform of the State constitutes the last example) and the results of the 2014 elections, the situation is different in Belgium. The EU and the status of Brussels as the capital of the Federation and headquarter of most EU institutions provide a constraint against the threat of a partition of Belgium. See V. Laborderie, 'La fin de la Belgique et ses impossibilities: L'hypothèse d'une independence flamande à l'épreuve des faits', *Outre-Terre. Revue européenne de géopolitique*, 3(2014), pp. 114–123; and P. Popelier and K. Lemmens, *The Constitution of Belgium. A Contextual Analysis* (Oxford: Hart Publishing, 2015).

[3] See, in particular, the secessionist attempts underway in Scotland, discussed in depth in the aftermath of the Brexit referendum of 23 June 2016 – although the Scottish referendum of 18 September 2014 gave a negative response; in Catalonia, also following the elections of 27 September 2015, which increased the representation of independentist parties in the regional Parliament, and the approval by the Catalan Parliament of several Resolutions defining a roadmap for the secession, Resolution 1/XI of 9 November 2015 declared unconstitutional on 2 December 2015 (Sentencia del Tribunal Constitucional [Ruling of the Constitutional Tribunal] 259/2015) and Resolution 306/XI of 6 October 2016 declared unconstitutional on 14 February 2017 by the Spanish Constitutional Court (S.T.C. 215/2016. See also Auto 24/2017, on the enforcement of the rule of law); and in Italy, where the regional Council of Veneto approved a law, No. 16/2014, calling for a referendum on independence, which was declared unconstitutional by the Italian Constitutional Court (judgment No. 118/2015).

invariably commits to take is to regulate its relationship with the EU and its membership.[4] Of course, joining the EU is a very attractive prospect for the regions which want to secede in terms of the power and autonomy they can gain.

In addition to the strategic incentives seceding regions see in joining the EU as independent states, has the EU seconded, perhaps unintentionally, such a dangerous trend in any way and what can be done in the present context? Could the EU, once hailed as the rescuer and servant of the interests of the Nation States,[5] now be held responsible for their disintegration? This contribution argues that in the last few years the EU has sent contrasting signals to regions within the Member States, in particular those with legislative powers. The EU 'dogma' of treating the state–region relationship as being relevant only to domestic constitutional law and as falling beyond the domain of EU law has been at least partially challenged (Section II). Some Treaty provisions now offer a different account, for example Article 5(3) TEU on the principle of subsidiarity, as well as Protocol No 2.[6] The attempts of secession in some EU countries by regions which found themselves in asymmetric positions in their states and which had already sought unsuccessfully to gain more autonomy at a domestic level can be triggered also by the EU's acknowledgment of an European enhanced role for regions and the increasing attention the EU institutions are devoting to the territorial organisation

[4] See in the case of Spain and Catalonia, Resolución 742/IX del Parlamento de Cataluña, sobre la orientación política general del Gobierno de la Generalidad, 27 September 2012, which contains an *ad hoc* section on foreign policy and international projection (V.1.1.), where the development of relationships between Catalan institutions and the European Commission and the European Parliament is considered a priority; the same holds true in the case of the UK and Scotland, as shown by the Scottish Government, *Scotland's Future. Your Guide to an Independent Scotland* (Edinburgh: November 2013), pp.216–224, available at scotreferendum.com, and, even more so, by the Scottish Parliament's Report on Determining Scotland's future relationship with the European Union (Edinburgh, March 2017), pp. 20–57. when Article 50 TUE was about to be triggered by the British Government. See also in Italy, Article 3, regional law of Veneto, No. 16/2014, providing for a consultative referendum on the independence of Veneto that urges the regional authorities to establish institutional relationships with the EU institutions and the United Nations.

[5] According to A. S. Milward, *The European Rescue of the Nation-State* (London: Routledge, 2000).

[6] See Committee of the Regions, *The Subsidiarity Early Warning System of the Lisbon Treaty – the role of regional parliaments with legislative powers and other subnational authorities*. This report was prepared by the Leuven Centre for Global Governance Studies (Pierre Schmitt, Tom Ruys and Axel Marx) in consultation with the Edinburgh Institute of Governance (Charlie Jeffery, Wilfried Swenden, Niccole Pamphilis and Barbara Gaweda) European Union, November 2013, pp. 1–7.

of the Member States. Although there are differences among the current attempts to secede in procedural terms and as for what is allowed by national Constitutions, it is maintained that a set of common principles can be identified among the Member States in order for a secession to be lawful under EU law and, as a consequence, for a seceding territory to be accepted as an EU Member State (Section III).[7] The next section provocatively argues that as long as the provisions of EU treaties take the territorial organisation of the Member States into account in European policymaking and strengthen regions with legislative powers, the EU should consistently include an *ad hoc* provision regarding the monitoring of secession processes in the Member States, which may in turn bring with it significant advantages before and after a secession takes place.

## II Ambiguous Signals from the EU on the Relevance of the Territorial Organisation of Member States

### A. *Neutrality of the EU: The Traditional View*

On the one hand, the EU confirms the above-mentioned 'dogma'. Immediately after recalling the principle of conferral in Article 4(1) TEU as a limit to the Union's competence, Article 4(2) sets another limit. The EU cannot interfere with the national identity of the Member States. The fact that in the English version of the Treaty 'identities' is plural does not appear to lead to the conclusion that several national identities within a single Member State are acknowledged and respected by the EU. The other linguistic versions of the article speak in

[7] The analysis of the appropriate procedure and legal basis for a new independent entity seceding from an EU Member State to regulate its relationship with the EU is beyond the scope of this chapter and is dealt with by other chapters in this volume: see, for example, Chapter 5, J.-C. Piris, 'Political and Legal Aspects of Recent Regional Secessionist Trends in some EU Member States(I)'. By the same token, the problems arising also in terms of the status of the European citizens living in the seceding territory remains outside the focus of this chapter: on this point, see Chapter 9, J. Shaw, 'Unions and Citizens: Membership Status and Political Rights in Scotland, the UK and the EU'; Chapter 3, N. Walker, 'Internal Enlargement of the European Union: Beyond Legalism and Political Expediency'; and Chapter 7, K. Armstrong, 'The Reach and Resources of European Law in the Scottish Independence Referendum'; all in this volume.

This chapter instead considers first what the position of the regions is under EU law, in particular those with legislative powers, and after arguing that the EU is not really neutral towards them, supports the idea of finding minimum requirements for a secession within an EU Member State to be considered as legitimate under EU law as a precondition for a future EU accession of that new entity.

the singular as only one national identity is to be recognised by the EU: that of the State concerned. Article 4(2) TEU clarifies that national identity (singular) comprises the 'fundamental structures, political and constitutional, *inclusive of regional and local self-government* [emphasis added]'. It follows that regional and local self-government, being part of the national identity, is not something for the EU to take into consideration and to regulate. Indeed, in a decision dealing with a potential restriction to the freedom to provide services – in particular on offers of gambling games via the internet – by a federal legislation, which had however not been applied for a certain period by the German Land Schleswig-Holstein, the EU Court of Justice stated that:

> In the present case, the division of competences between the *Länder* cannot be called into question, since it benefits from the protection conferred by Article 4(2) TEU.[8]

Moreover, the EU 'shall respect their [Member States] essential State functions, including ensuring the territorial integrity', which can be put under attack either from outside, for example a foreign invasion, or from within the State, such as a secession. Therefore, the territorial integrity of a Member State and the potential secession of a part thereof are in principle to be managed and regulated by the State itself. At the time that Article I-5 of the Constitutional Treaty – which the current Article 4(2) TEU reproduces – was drafted within the Convention on the Future of Europe, the European Parliament made it clear that it considered 'internal territorial organisation and the division of competences within each Member State to be matters to be decided upon by the Member States alone'.[9]

Other provisions in the Treaties which mention the regions also point towards creating again an ever-closer Union without encroaching upon the domestic relationship between State and Regions: for example, by promoting the balanced development of the regions (Articles 174 and 176 TFEU) and by balancing national and regional diversity while 'at the same time bringing the common cultural heritage to the fore' (Article 167(1) TFEU).

However, a clear example of the ambiguous approach of the EU towards regions, in particular those with legislative powers, which have

[8] Case C-156/13, *Digibet Ltd*, ECLI:EU:C:2014:1756, para. 34.

[9] See the Report of the Committee on Constitutional Affairs of the European Parliament *on the division of competences between the European Union and the Member States*, A5-0133/2002 final, 24 April 2002, § 34.

been directly affected by the extensive exercise of EU competences, is found in the position of regions when looking, on the one hand, at the case law of the Court of Justice of the EU and, on the other hand, at their *locus standi* before this Court. In matters of free movement of goods, workers and services the Court of Justice has always confirmed that regions are bound, as any other authority of the State exercising public powers is, to apply EU law.[10] It follows that regions, likewise state authorities, are responsible for the compliance of domestic law with the *acquis communautaire*. However, at a European level it is the State, i.e. the national government, which is required to respond to a violation of EU law by a region, while at a domestic level the State can proceed against regional authorities seeking compensation for the damage caused. By the same token, although a region can be injured in its powers and competence by an *ultra vires* action of the EU institutions, the region at stake is considered neither as a privileged applicant, like the Member States and the EU institutions, nor as a semi-privileged applicant, like the Committee of the Regions after the Treaty of Lisbon.[11] The regions concerned would stand before the Court of Justice as any other natural or legal person subject to the strictest *locus standi* conditions. Both before and after the Treaty of Lisbon and with the partial exception of state aid policy, regions have very narrow avenues as individual actors to reach the Court of Justice and to see their actions declared at least admissible.[12] In order to have direct access to the Court, a region must prove that it has a direct and individual concern deriving from the challenged EU measure. Nor does the indirect access of regions to the Court of Justice, either through preliminary ruling proceedings or through annulment actions

[10] See Case C-2/90, *Commission* v. *Belgium* [1992] ECR I-4431; Case C-103/88, *Fratelli Costanzo* [1989] ECR 1839; Case C-407/85, *Drei Glocken GmbH and Gertraud Kritzinger* v. *USL Centro-SUD and Provincia autonoma di Bolzano* [1988] ECR 4233; Case C-197/84, *Steinhauser* v. *City of Biarritz* [1985] ECR 1819. S.Weatherill, 'The Challenge for the Regional Dimension in the European Union', (note 1) above, pp. 4–5.

[11] See Case C-95/97, *Region Wallonne* v. *Commission*; Case T-70/97, *Region Wallonne* v. *Commission*, Order of 29 September 1997 [1997] ECR II-1513; Case C-180/97, *Regione Toscana*; Case T-214/95, *Vlaamse Gewest* v. *Commission* [1998] ECR II-717; Case T-238/97, *Comunidad Autonoma de Cantabria* v. *Council* [1998] ECR II-2271; Case T-609/97, *Regione Puglia* v. *Commission and Spain* [1998] ECR II-4051; Joined cases T-32 and T-41/98, *Nederlandse Antillen, Nederlandse Antillen* v. *Commission* [2000] ECR II-201. C. Evans, 'Regional Dimensions to European Governance', *International Comparative Law Quarterly* 52 (2003), pp. 21–42; and A. Thies, 'The Locus Standi of the Regions Before EU Courts', in C. Panara and A. De Becker (eds.), *The Role of the Regions in EU Governance* (Berlin: Springer, 2011), pp.45–48, at 27.

[12] A. Thies, 'The Locus Standi of the Regions Before EU Courts', (note 11) above, pp. 28–40.

brought by States on behalf of the regions – as provided for in Austria, Belgium and Germany – contribute to countering their unbalanced position.[13] This is why the traditional account of the position of the regions in the EU considers that the EU 'imposes substantial obligations on the regions while allowing them little access to policy-formulation or judicial control'.[14]

### *B. A Regionally Oriented EU? Emerging Developments from Maastricht to Lisbon*

Not only is the EU attractive to regions seeking more autonomy by spontaneously offering them opportunities for visibility and economic incentives, the EU has to some extent actively promoted the integration of regions into EU decision-making, although not always with enough conviction and success.[15] In this regard, the EU can be seen as a destabilising force on relationships between Member States and their internal components.

A turning point, also in the inclusion of regions in EU procedures, was the Treaty of Maastricht. The Committee of the Regions was established as an advisory body composed of representatives of Member States' regional and local authorities directly elected by the people or accountable before an elected assembly (Article 263 TEC, now 305 TFEU). This Committee is consulted by the European Parliament, the Council and the Commission where provided by the Treaties and in all other cases they deem it appropriate (Article 265 TEC, now 307 TFEU). Moreover, an amendment was introduced through the Treaty of Maastricht allowing for representation of regional ministers in the Council. According to the new formula adopted and still valid today (Article 16 TEU), the Council 'shall consist of a representative of each Member State at ministerial level' without further specification of the domestic level of government being referred to. As a consequence, some Member States – such as Germany, Italy and Spain – have amended their national legislation to allow regional executives to participate in the Council's meetings when

[13] Ibid., pp. 41–44.

[14] S. Weatherill, (note 1) above, p. 6

[15] For example, the outcome of the Convention on the Future of Europe, where the Committee of the Regions participated with observer status, although enhancing the position of the regions in the EU, has certainly been not revolutionary for them, according to C.Jeffrey, 'Regions and the European Union: Letting Them In, and Leaving Them Alone', in S. Weatherill and U. Bernitz (eds.), (note 1) above, pp. 39–41.

a regional legislative competence is concerned. The involvement of regional ministers has worked quite well in Germany,[16] while it has not proved particularly well suited to Spain because of the asymmetric regionalism, and has never been applied in Italy. The new provisions on the Committee of the Regions and the composition of the Council responded to the enlargement of the pool of competences conferred to the EU and, in prospect, presupposed that regions with legislative powers would otherwise be sidelined from their respective domains. In other words, the Treaty of Maastricht has triggered a process of true Europeanisation of the regions.[17]

At the turn of the twenty-first century the new attitude of the EC towards regions has been made explicit, with a few *revirements* from time to time. Being aware of the need to consult the regions widely before putting forward its legislative proposals, as this is crucial for their subsequent implementation, the European Commission has appraised the contribution of the regions to European policymaking in a variety of documents, starting with the White Paper on European Governance and continuing to two Communications of 2002 and 2003 on the partnership needed between the Community, States and regional and local authorities for the formulation of European policies.[18]

In 2002, the European Parliament noticed that the regions, particularly those with legislative competence, were playing an increasing role in the implementation of Union policies and encouraged proposals from the Member States 'to ensure that their respective territorial entities are more closely involved in drawing up and, where appropriate, transposing

[16] See P.-C.Müller-Graff, 'The German Länder: Involvement in EC/EU Law and Policy Making', in S. Weatherill and U. Bernitz (eds.), (note 1) above, pp. 103–117.

[17] See T. A. Börzel, *States and Regions in the European Union: Institutional Adaptation in Germany and Spain* (Cambridge: Cambridge University Press, 2001), pp. 45–150, P. Zuddas, *L'influenza del diritto dell'Unione europea sul riparto di competenze legislative tra Stato e Regioni* (Padova: Cedam, 2010), pp.3–164 and G. Martinico, 'The Impact of "Regional Blindness" on the Italian Regional State', in I. Cloots, G. De Baere and S. Sottiaux (eds.), *Federalism in the European Union* (Oxford: Hart Publishing, 2012), pp.362–380.

[18] See European Commission, Communication on *European Governance: A White Paper*, COM (2001) 428 final, 25 July 2001; Communication on *A framework for target-based tripartite contracts and agreements between the Community, the States and regional and local authorities*, COM (2002) 709 final, 11 December 2002; Communication on *Dialogue with associations of regional and local authorities on the formulation of European Union policy*, COM (2003) 811 final, 19 December 2003.

EU rules, provided that the individual Member States' constitutions are not infringed'.[19]

The message conveyed by the European Parliament and the Commission signalled that the regional dimension had become crucial for the EU. The willingness of the regions to cooperate with the EU institutions, in spite of the legal responsibility falling solely on the State in the case of a lack of compliance, was perceived as fundamental for the enforcement of the structural principles of EU law, like primacy. Indeed, a few years later in its Guidelines for the application and monitoring of the subsidiarity and proportionality principles adopted on 16 November 2005, the Committee of the Regions stated that 'the local and regional level is responsible for implementing more than 70 per cent of EU legislative acts'.

The EU has also taken significant steps forward in the direction of acknowledging regional diversities within the EU. It is not by chance that next to the 24 official languages of the EU, 'some regional languages, such as Catalan and Welsh, have gained a status as co-official languages of the European Union'.[20]

After the entry into force of the Treaty of Lisbon, also from a legal point of view, the attitude of the EU towards regions has remarkably changed. In the ordinary operation of the EU institutions lawmaking at a subnational level is taken into consideration. For example, compared to the Maastricht version of the article,[21] the new Article 5(3) TEU, on the principle of subsidiarity, requests that in order to assess which level of government is best suited to act and to achieve the EU objectives the local, the regional, the state and the EU level must be taken equally into account, starting first from the level which is closest to citizens. In other words, the option is not just between the EU and the national level as a whole but also the ability of local authorities and regions to reach the

[19] See the Report of the Committee on Constitutional Affairs of the European Parliament *on the division of competences between the European Union and the Member States*, (2001/2024(INI)), 24 April 2002, § 34 and 35. Even more explicit on the need to enhance the role of the regions with legislative powers in the EU, both in terms of locus standi before the Court of Justice and direct participation in the European Parliament's Committee on regional policy, transport and tourism, was the Report of the Committee on Constitutional Affairs on *the role of regional and local authorities in European integration*, (2002/141(INI)), 4 December 2002, § 3 to 8.

[20] See http://ec.europa.eu/education/policy/linguistic-diversity/official-languages-eu_en, accessed 20 May 2017.

[21] See R. Schütze, 'Subsidiarity After Lisbon: Reinforcing the Safeguards of Federalism?', *Cambridge Law Journal*, 68(3)(2009), pp. 525–536.

objectives is assessed. This implies that the EU institutions and, in particular, the Commission must look at what happens within the Member States, at regional administrations and legislation, before they take action. Article 5(3) TEU thus acknowledges that Member States can have different constitutional structures and that this can count as applying for the principle of subsidiarity. By the same token Article 2, protocol No. 2 on the application of the principle of subsidiarity and proportionality, asks the Commission to consult widely before a draft legislative act is presented and such consultations shall 'take into account the local and the regional dimension of the action envisaged'.[22] Article 5 of Protocol No. 2 is along the same line and imposes on the Commission a duty to include in the detailed statement justifying a draft directive, on the grounds of subsidiarity and proportionality, its implications for national rules including, where necessary,[23] regional legislation.

Article 6 of the same Protocol goes one step further. It allows the regions to participate in the early warning system through consultation of the national parliament and, most importantly, detects which institution at the regional level must be consulted, where appropriate: 'regional parliaments with legislative powers'.[24] This provision, which affects only the eight Member States which endow all or some of their regions with legislative powers,[25] appears finally to overturn the dogma of 'regional blindness' which so far has characterised the EU approach towards the constitutional architecture of the Member States.

[22] See H.-J. Blanke et al., 'Comment on Protocol No. 2, on the Application of the Principle of Subsidiarity and Proportionality in the European Union Annexed to the Treaty of Lisbon', in H.-J. Blanke and S. Mangiameli (eds.), *The Treaty on European Union (TEU)* (Vienna-New York: Springer, 2013), pp. 1635–1736.

[23] 'Where necessary' means that when the subject matter at the national level falls within the legislative competence of regions the point of reference for the Commission is the regional legislation, not the national, i.e. state-federal.

[24] See A-L. Högenauer and V. Arribas, 'Legislative Regions After Lisbon: A New Role for Regional Assemblies?', in C Hefftler et al. (eds.), *The Palgrave Handbook of National Parliaments and the European Union* (New York: Palgrave Macmillan, 2015), pp. 133–152. The involvement of regional parliaments with legislative powers in the early warning system had already been devised by Art. 6 Protocol No. 2, through the application of the principles of subsidiarity and proportionality annexed to the Constitutional Treaty. See P. Kiiver (ed.), *National and Regional Parliaments in the European Constitutional Order* (Groningen: Europa Law Publishing, 2006).

[25] These Member States are: Austria, Belgium, Finland, Italy, Germany, Portugal, Spain and the UK.

The aim of Article 6 Protocol No. 2 is a positive one: to enhance the democratic legitimacy of EU lawmaking by fostering the participation in the early warning system of the elected assemblies with legislative powers which are closest to the citizens. The same goes for the other provisions of Article 5 TEU and Protocol No 2. They give the regions the opportunity to voice their concerns at the EU's legislative activity, on the merits and opportunity for EU legislative proposals, before they are adopted.[26]

Even if the EU treaties and protocols intervene for good reasons in this sphere, such as to assign new functions to a particular type of subnational institution – regional parliaments with legislative powers – and to design new relationships at the national level between national and regional parliaments, it is this type of intervention which has normally been precluded from EU competence. New procedures have thus been created in the eight Member States which are particularly significant for those countries which lack constitutional mechanisms for representation of the regions in the second chamber of their national parliaments. The participation of regional parliaments in the early warning system, especially in Italy, Spain and the UK, has become the main avenue for building up a relationship between national and regional legislatures which was lacking – entirely or partially – before the Treaty of Lisbon and which, even if it existed at all, had been devised exclusively by the national constitutions.[27]

In contrast, where the role assigned to regional legislatures by national constitutional law is more prominent than the one reserved by Protocol No. 2, as in Belgium, a formal declaration attached to the Treaties (No. 51) has been adopted to clarify the position of the regional legislatures in the constitutional system. Regional legislatures in Belgium are not simply consulted by the national parliament; rather,

[26] See K. Borońska-Hryniewiecka, 'Subnational parliaments in EU policy control: explaining the variations across Europe', *EUI Working Papers* RSCAS 2013/38, pp. 9–23; and C. Fasone, 'Regional legislatures in the early warning mechanism. When the national (constitutional) identity affects the cooperation among parliaments in EU affairs', *Federalismi.it*, 2(2015) 28 January 2015.

[27] K. Borońska-Hryniewiecka, 'Democratising the European Multi-Level Polity? A (re-)assessment of the Early Warning System', *Yearbook of Polish European Studies*, 16(2013), pp. 167–187 and D. Fromage, 'Regional Parliaments and the Early Warning System: An Assessment and Some Suggestions for Reform', in A. Jonsson Cornell and M. Goldoni (eds.), *National and Regional Parliaments in the EU Legislative Procedure Post-Lisbon: The Impact of the Early Warning Mechanism* (Oxford: Hart Publishing, 2017), pp. 117–136.

depending on the legislative competence concerned, they are also able to send reasoned opinions to the Commission on the ground of subsidiarity on their own, without any filter by the national parliament.[28] However, regional parliaments in other Member States, in particular some German *Landtages* such as that of Baden-Württemberg, have also started to do so with the support of the European Commission, which responds to these regional opinions. This practice is expected to be strengthened in the future.[29] Therefore, regional parliaments with legislative powers in the eight Member States now enjoy a power at a national and EU level which directly derives from the Treaty of Lisbon.

Finally, this Treaty has empowered the Committee of the Regions – not the individual regions, which remain non-privileged applicants – to bring actions for annulment in defence of its own prerogatives and for a violation of the principle of subsidiarity by legislative acts when the Treaties provide for its mandatory consultation.[30] This second type of action, which has not yet been used, links the role of the Committee of the Regions to monitoring compliance with the principle of subsidiarity, although in this case the delivery of a prior negative opinion by the Committee is not a requirement.

The Treaty of Lisbon has granted regions new tools for participating in EU decision-making, directly or through national parliaments and governments. Although the new regional powers in the EU have not yet been fully exploited, now that the European Treaties have opened this Pandora's box by acknowledging an enhanced role for regions in the EU through which they can make themselves heard,[31] then it should come as no surprise that the problem of secession has suddenly come to the fore in the national and European debate in several Member States at the same time. In other words, the expanded leeway for regions to 'voice' their

[28] Cf P. Popelier and V. Wandebruwaene, 'The Subsidiarity Mechanism as a Tool for Inter-Level Dialogue in Belgium: On "Regional Blindness and Cooperative Flaws"', *European Constitutional Law Review*, 7(2) (2011), 204–228; and M. Romaniello, 'Beyond the Constitutional "Bicameral Blueprint": Europeanisation and National Identities in Belgium', in M. Cartabia, N. Lupo and A. Simoncini (eds.), (note 1) above, pp. 281 ff.

[29] See the Declaration adopted by the Conference of the Presidents of the Länder in June 2014, p. 3; and D.Fromage, 'Regional parliaments and the Early Warning System', (note 27) above.

[30] See A. Thies, 'The Locus Standi of the Regions Before EU Courts', (note 12) above, pp. 45–48 and S. Piattoni and J. Schonlau, *Shaping EU Policy from Below: EU Democracy and the Committee of the Regions* (Cheltenham: Edward Elgar Publishing, 2015), pp. 57–104.

[31] See A. Cygan, 'Regional Governance, Subsidiarity and Accountability within the EU's Multi-Level Polity', *European Public Law*, 19(1)(2013), 188.

concerns and channel their claims for more autonomy in the EU has favoured the construction of a new 'loyalty' towards the EU which competes with that of the Member State and increases the appeal of the 'exit option' from the existing state authority.[32]

The EU should adopt a consistent stance on the matter. Either it ignores how the state–regions relationship is shaped nationally, and thus leaves itself easily able to overlook the voices of regions at the EU level; or if the EU intervenes in that relationship and in the role of subnational institutions, it follows that it cannot neglect the territorial organisation of the state, the powers of its regions, and their asymmetric positions and claims.

## III Not All Secessions are Alike from the EU Perspective

By affecting the domestic division of competences between regions and states, and by allowing regions to participate directly in EU policy-making-also in competition with the state level of government and up to the point of identifying the regional institution to be involved, as in Protocol No. 2-, it is clear that the EU is able to exert a strong influence over the territorial structure of its Member States. As long as the EU conditions by law the sustainability of the domestic federal or regional organisation, it cannot remain indifferent and neutral towards secession attempts.

While on the international scene the EU has often taken a negative stance towards secession attempts, for instance in the Former Yugoslavia,[33] it has made general claims of neutrality towards regional secession attempts from within an EU country. However, this is less true in practice. Regarding both the Scottish and Catalonian secession attempts, the then Presidents of the European Commission, José Manuel Barroso, and the European Council, Herman van Rompuy,

[32] To this end, the classical analysis by A. O. Hirschman, *Exit, Voice and Loyalty. Responses to Decline in Firms, Organizations, and States* (Harvard: Harvard University Press, 1970) has been adapted to the circumstance of the secession of a region from an EU Member State in the post-Lisbon context.

[33] See V. Constantinescu, 'La politique de l'Union européenne face au pehénomène de la fragmentation des États: de l'ex-Yougoslavie aux Balkans occidentaux', in S. Perre-Caps and J. D. Mouton (eds.), *États fragmentés* (Nancy: PUN, 2012), pp. 143–164. The EU, in contrast, has supported Montenegro's independence or has subsequently revised its position towards secession processes from skepticism to pragmatism, once independence is achieved de facto: see, for example, K. Friis, 'The Referendum in Montenegro: The EU's "Postmodern Diplomacy"', *European Foreign Affairs Review*, 12(1) (2007), pp. 67–88.

respectively stated in 2012 and 2013, that a new independent sovereign entity seceding from an existing EU Member State becomes a third country where the Treaties no longer apply. Nevertheless, the new state can apply for accession under Article 49 TEU, provided that it complies with the principles set out in Article 2 TEU.[34] These are statements which certainly do not encourage secession and do not foresee a special shortcut for the accession of former EU regions, where EU law was applied until the very last moment before secession.[35] In that case, what should be done with a new independent territory seceding from a Member State?

The EU's response to such an outcome – it is argued here – should depend on how the secession is achieved, in particular if it is pursued in compliance with the fundamental values of the EU, such as democracy and the Rule of Law (Article 2 TEU)[36] and, as a consequence, if it complies with the constitutional procedures of the Member State concerned and with the constitutional traditions common to the Member States (Article 6(3) TEU). In other words, the compliance with Article 2 TEU and the common constitutional traditions by a seceding territory cannot be assessed only with regard to the

[34] See the Letter of 10 October 2012 sent by José Manuel Barroso to the UK House of Lords in the framework of the inquiry into 'The Economic Implications for the United Kingdom of Scottish Independence', available from www.parliament.uk, the Statement of Herman van Rompuy on a potential unilateral declaration of independence by Catalonia at the press conference of 13 December 2013 and available at *EurActiv.es*, and M. Campins Eritja, 'The European Union and the Secession of a Territory from a EU Member State', *Diritto pubblico comparato ed europeo*, 2 (2015), pp. 492–493.

[35] It remains to be seen, however, what will happen in the event of a new (likely) attempt by Scotland to secede from the UK during the negotiations for the UK withdrawal from the EU or in the aftermath of the withdrawal.

[36] Although D. Kochenov and M. van den Brink, 'Secessions from EU Member States: The Imperative of Union's Neutrality', *University of Edinburgh School of Law Research Paper Series*, 6(2016), p. 1 claim that the EU's neutral position towards secession is crucial, the authors' underlying assumption is that 'the process of the territorial reframing of statehood is taking place in a nonviolent fashion and in full conformity with the law'. However, as it is shown below, the compliance with national constitutional law and Article 2 TEU of the secession of Catalonia and Veneto can hardly be confirmed. See also J.-W. Müller, 'Should the EU Protect Democracy and the Rule of Law inside Member States?', *European Law Journal*, 21(2)(2015), pp. 141–160; C. Closa, D. Kochenov and J. H. H. Weiler, 'Reinforcing Rule of Law Oversight in the European Union', *EUI Working Papers*, RSCAS 2014/25; A. von Bogdandy and M. Ioannidis, 'Systemic Deficiency in the Rule of Law: What It Is, What Has Been Done, What Can Be Done', *Common Market Law Review*, 51(1)(2014), pp. 59–96. Although the Article 7 TEU procedure does not apply in this particular context, these authors recall the problems with the enforcement of Article 2 TEU in the Member States.

democratic functioning of the institutions within it and their respect of the Rule of Law; in order for it to accede to the EU, the whole process leading to secession on the part of the seceding territory must be accomplished according to the principles enshrined in Article 2 TEU and derived from Article 6(3) TEU,[37] under the conditions pointed out below.

Not all secessions are alike, as was clearly highlighted by the Canadian Supreme Court's landmark decision on the secession of Québec.[38] According to this Court, 'a clear majority vote in Québec on a clear question in favour of secession would confer democratic legitimacy on the secession initiative which all the other participants in Confederation would have to recognise'.[39] The application for secession by a province triggers a process of negotiation among the province in question, the other provinces and the federal government, but this could also lead to disagreement rather than consensus. A by-no-means lawful secession would happen in Canada as the result of a unilateral act by a province, even if it was supported by the majority of the *Québécois*.[40]

With respect to secessions within EU Member States, in the UK a constitutional 'agreement' was reached between the seceding territory – Scotland – and the Central Government on how to manage secession and on what can be considered a legitimate secession from a constitutional perspective, despite the UK lacking a codified constitution and thus a formal procedure to amend it. This 'constitutional compromise' is entrenched in the Edinburgh Agreement of 2012.[41]

In Catalonia, the unilateral attempt to declare the region as a sovereign state, which originated in the *Declaración de soberanía y del derecho*

[37] C. Closa 'Secession from a Member State and EU Membership: the View from the Union', *European Constitutional Law Review* 12 (2016), pp. 240–264

[38] *Reference re Secession of Québec*,[1998] 2 SCR 217. S. Mancini, 'Secession and Self-Determination', in M. Rosenfeld and A. Sajó (eds.), *Oxford Handbook of Comparative Constitutional Law* (Oxford, Oxford University Press, 2012), pp. 497–501 and D. Haljan, *Constitutionalising Secession* (Oxford, Hart Publishing, 2014), pp. 309–312.

[39] *Reference re Secession of Québec*, para. 150.

[40] Interestingly, the Supreme Court did not prescribe following one of the specific constitutional amendment procedures provided for by the *Constitution Act 1982* (Sections 38 to 49) for the secession of Quebec. R. Albert, 'The Difficulty of Constitutional Amendment in Canada', *Alberta Law Review*, 53 (2015), pp. 85–113, highlights that the path traced by the Supreme Court in this case and the subsequent *Clarity Act* constituted a derogation to the Canadian written constitutional amendments' rules.

[41] N. Walker, (note 7) above. See *Agreement between the United Kingdom Government and the Scottish Government on a referendum on independence for Scotland*, Edinburgh, 15 October 2012, <www.gov.scot/Resource/0040/00404789.pdf> accessed 20 May 2017.

*a decidir del pueblo de Cataluña*, passed by the Catalan Parliament on 23 January 2013,[42] was found unconstitutional by the Spanish Constitutional Court (S.T.C. 42/2014) as they were the subsequent Resolutions of the Catalan Parliament of 9 November 2015 and of 6 October 2016 defining a roadmap for Catalonia's independence (S.T.C. 259/2015 S.T.C. 215/2016). Therefore, if Catalonia secedes under the conditions set out in the Declaration and in the Resolutions, by no means could this be considered a new legitimate state by the EU and the other Member States. The Constitutional Court recognised that a 'right to decide' does exist for the Catalan people but it has to be exercised in such a way as to activate the procedure for amending the Spanish Constitution under its Article 168 and then eventually to call for a referendum on Catalonia's independence.[43] Just calling a popular consultation in the region is not enough. By the same token, arguing that the Catalan people hold, by reason of democratic legitimacy, legal and political sovereignty is in breach of the Constitution: only the people of Spain as a whole are sovereign.

The decision of the Italian Constitutional Court, No. 118/2015, on the regional law of Veneto No. 16/2014 which established a procedure to call a referendum on the independence of the region reflects the more *tranchant* position of the Italian Constitution and constitutional case law on the point of the constitutional sustainability of secession.[44] Regional law No. 16/2014 amounts to an *extra ordinem* initiative of Veneto which violates Articles 5 and 139 of the Italian Constitution and in particular the principles of the unity and indivisibility of the Italian Republic which stand as unamendable principles of the Constitution. In other words, not even a constitutional

[42] This Declaration is just a parliamentary resolution paving the way to a procedure which could lead to calling a 'popular consultation' in Catalonia on its independence. This consultation was finally held on 9 November 2014 as the Spanish Constitution does not allow regions to provide for and call referendums despite the case law of the Spanish Constitutional Court. Of those who voted, –41 per cent of the Catalan population – 81 said 'yes' to independence.

[43] The Catalan Parliament can initiate such a constitutional amendment bill before the Spanish Parliament, but of course there are no guarantees that it will be adopted (Art. 87(2) and 166 Spanish Constitution). See J. M. Castellà Andreu, 'The Proposal for Catalan Secession and the Crisis of the Spanish Autonomous State', *Diritto pubblico comparato ed europeo*, 2 (2015), pp. 429–488.

[44] D. Tega, 'Venezia non è Barcellona. Una via italiana per le rivendicazioni di autonomia?', *Le Regioni*, 5–6 (2015), pp. 1141–1155 and C. Fasone, 'Una, indivisibile, ma garantista dell'autonomia (differenziata): la Repubblica italiana in una recente pronuncia della Corte costituzionale sulle leggi regionali venete nn. 15 e 16 del 2014, *Revista catalana de dret públic* – (Blog post) 15 September 2015, <http://blocs.gencat.cat/blocs/AppPHP/eapc-rcdp/>, accessed 20 May 2017.

amendment could provide a legal basis for secession. Indeed, by contrast to Spain, in Italy there is no constitutional clause like Article 168 of the Spanish Constitution allowing even the total revision of the Constitution without substantive and explicit limits.

The legitimate solutions pointed to by the Spanish and Italian Constitutional Courts are thus rather different from the one adopted in Scotland (as well as the one of the Canadian Supreme Court), but this is inevitable as national constitutional law provides for different conditions in terms of the democratic procedures applicable to secession. Even if there are differences among EU Member States, there are nonetheless principles shared among most EU countries which permit the definition of what a lawful secession process would look like in the EU, according to the common constitutional traditions of its Member States. The procedure:

a) cannot be unilateral on the part of the seceding territory without the involvement of the Central Government and the procedure itself (whether it leads to a formal constitutional amendment or not) must be agreed among the parties, regardless of its outcomes;
b) must comply with democratic principles through the involvement of the people by means of a national or a regional referendum or both, and with the Rule of Law;
c) must comply with the relevant national constitutional law.

## IV How Should the EU Deal with These Secession Attempts? Some Provocative Thoughts

In the light of the EU's foundation on the values of democracy and the Rule of Law, common national constitutional traditions and, at the same time, respect of the national identity (singular) of the Member States, it does not appear legally feasible that the EU could allow regions which unilaterally secede in breach of national constitutional rules to enter the EU. The same logic would apply to the Member States, which of course would be asked to agree to such accession (Article 49 TEU) or Treaty revision, if the path of Article 48 TEU and a fast-track procedure are followed.[45]

[45] See P. Athanassiou, 'EU Accession from Within? – An Introduction', *Yearbook of European Law*, (2014), pp.1–50 and M. Chamon and G. Van der Loo, 'The Temporal Paradox of Regions in the EU Seeking Independence: Contraction and Fragmentation versus Widening and Deepening', *European Law Journal*, 20 (5) (2014), pp.613–629.

Nor could those principles of democracy and the Rule of Law be invoked by the seceding territories against 'their' Member States in the name of self-determination, at least if we agree with the interpretation of this notion provided by the Supreme Court of Canada in the *Secession Reference* (and by international law).[46] No region within the EU Member States is definitely in the exceptional situation of oppression, violation of human rights, or colonisation which could allow a seceding territory to struggle for its self-determination.

Although this is certainly a provocative thought in challenging, to some extent, the autonomy of the Member States and the present limits of EU competence, in the future the EU could set out in a new *ad hoc* provision in the Treaty the minimum requirements an aspiring seceding territory should have to meet in order to apply for EU accession afterwards. This would appear desirable to protect the fundamental values of the Union, including its unity, and to make the transition from secession to new EU membership smooth, which might be appropriate particularly in the case of Scotland and in light of the UK's withdrawal from the EU.[47] A seceding region, indeed, is not precisely in the same position as a third country, where no EU law is applied and where no EU citizenship is acknowledged.[48] On the other hand, the peaceful and harmonious development of the EU integration process could be undermined if a seceding territory is admitted to join the EU as a new Member regardless of the lawfulness of the secession procedure and the relationship with the Member State affected by secession.

[46] The position of international law is however nuanced in that it neither forbids nor expressly authorises secessions: see A. Cassese, *International Law* (Oxford, Oxford University Press, 2001), p. 108; and A. Tancredi, 'Neither authorized nor prohibited? Secession and international law after Kosovo, South Ossetia and Abkhazia' *Italian Yearbook of International Law* (2008),pp. 37–62.

[47] See the chapters 9, 10, 11, 12 and 13 of this volume. It is worth recalling that in the Brexit referendum, 62 per cent of the voters in Scotland voted to remain in the EU and, in the wake of the national results of the referendum, the Scottish First Minister Nicola Sturgeon hinted at holding a second referendum on independence from the UK; a 'commitment' that has been subsequently confirmed, following the judgment of the UK Supreme Court of 24 January 2017 (*R (on the application of Miller and Dos Santos) v Secretary of State for Exiting the European Union and associated references*, [2017] UKSC 5), which has not considered the involvement of the devolved legislatures a requirement for triggering Article 50 TEU.

[48] See J. Shaw, (note 7) above.

These requirements could be:

1) the compliance of secession with the constitutional traditions common to the Member States (Article 6(3) TEU), meaning that a unilateral secession avoiding negotiations and procedural agreement with the national government will not be recognised by the EU. None of the EU Member States appear to include a right to self-determination and secession in their constitutions (as in Ethiopia, the USSR and Yugoslavia);[49]
2) respect for a procedure which requires the Member State potentially affected by secession and the seceding territory immediately to submit to the European Commission all relevant documents, updates and outcomes on their negotiations and to wait for a certain number of years before independence is finally gained by the seceding territory, in particular for the purpose of protecting citizens' rights.

Such a clause could have three beneficial effects. First, it could allow the EU to monitor if, and to what extent, its founding values of democracy and the Rule of Law are respected throughout the secession process, and eventually to inform the Member State that there is no ground to accept the seceding territory as a new member of the Union. As a consequence, the seceding territory can decide what to do, bearing in mind the EU's position. If it becomes independent, it could try to arrange its relationship with the EU differently, for instance by means of an association agreement.

Secondly, an *ad hoc* clause on seceding territories could limit the problem of leaving a seceding region and its citizens in a sort of 'limbo', where they do not know if, and when, they could become EU members. If the secession complies with the minimum EU requirements, then a legitimate expectation to become a new Member State should be protected and this would also protect the uncertain situation of the region's citizens in terms of continuity of EU citizenship. It is preferable to perform a pre-assessment of the suitability of a seceding territory to become a Member State rather than doing it *ex post*, with no way back except for the withdrawal procedure (Article 50 TEU).

Thirdly, the need to embark on a procedure which is monitored by the EU could lead the parties to take a more faithful and cooperative approach and even to create a disincentive against the most groundless attempts to secede.[50]

[49] See D. Haljan, (note 38) above, pp. 249–251.

[50] J. H. H. Weiler, 'Editorial', *European Journal of International Law*, 23(4)(2012), pp. 910–912.

## V Conclusions

Is the EU today able to 'rescue' Member States from internal disintegration and should it play any role in this regard? Since the Treaty of Maastricht, a process has begun leading to the gradual recognition of a role and place for the regions in the EU, in particular those with legislative powers, which is no longer 'regionally blind' and whose legal impact on the territorial organisation of the EU's Member States, even on regional forms of government, is a reality.

Not only are the regions aware of these legal changes, but particularly those claiming greater autonomy, if not independence, view EU membership as a constant point of reference. Secession initiatives in Italy, Spain and the UK tried immediately to establish a link between their demands and EU membership. A European Citizens' Initiative, one that the European Commission refused to register, requested Catalonia's automatic accession to the EU and for the continued citizenship of its nationals, in the event that it declared independence.[51] Furthermore EU membership is indeed a contentious issue when it comes to Scottish secession and a major point of controversy between the UK, now in the process to withdraw from the EU, and Scotland, which convincingly voted for the 'remain' at the Brexit referendum (62 per cent of the voters).

By impacting on the national division of competence between State and regions, on their institutional design, and on the way these institutional actors participate in EU policymaking, the EU cannot claim to remain neutral and indifferent to secession within its Member States, although it does not enjoy a specific competence in this field. In other words, the EU bears part of the responsibility for these developments and after the Treaty of Lisbon it has acted as if it were regionally oriented.

Despite there being constitutional differences among the EU Member States regarding the conditions and procedures for allowing the secession of a region, it is felt that a set of minimum requirements can be identified from the constitutional traditions common to these countries in order to characterise a lawful secession from an EU perspective. In particular, the prohibition of unilateral declarations of independence, respect for the principles of democracy and the Rule of Law and compliance with

[51] See European Commission, Response to the application to register a citizens' initiative on the 'Fortalecimento de la partecipación ciudadana en la toma de decisions sobre la soberanía colectiva', COM(2012) 3689 final, 30 May 2012.

national constitutional rules are conditions that the EU and its Member States should take into account when evaluating requests for accession by seceding territories.

Moreover, it is argued that EU law in prospect should contemplate introducing a procedure for monitoring ongoing secession processes by the European Commission under a substantive (compliance with common constitutional traditions and Article 2 TEU values) and procedural (exchange of information and delivery of progress reports) perspective. This monitoring procedure would permit channelling secession into a path which is acknowledged as feasible and legally sustainable, more transparent and predictable, also for the many parties concerned, and finally it would discourage regions from seeking secession lightly or, when they do so, the European monitoring procedure would enhance the prospects of cooperation between the seceding territory and the Member State in question.

5

# Political and Legal Aspects of Recent Regional Secessionist Trends in some EU Member States (I)

JEAN-CLAUDE PIRIS

After the Second World War, the terms 'secessionism', 'partition' and 'modification of borders' became taboo in Europe. During the 1970s and 1980s, diplomatic life was dominated by the Cold War. Discussions among international lawyers and deliberations at diplomatic conferences were centred around the development of Principles of International law, such as 'Friendly Relations',[1] 'Non-Aggression'[2] or the 'Intangibility of Borders'.[3] This was more particularly the case in Europe, where the period was marked by the adoption, in Helsinki in 1975, of the Final Act of the Conference on Security and Co-operation in Europe (CSCE). Among the most important Principles adopted by the thirty-five signatory States, thirty-three of them being European,[4] were 'Inviolability of Borders',[5] 'Territorial Integrity of States'[6] and 'Non-Intervention in Internal Affairs'.[7]

## I Partition of States Is Not Rare in International Life

The fall of the Berlin Wall in 1989 and the break-up of the USSR, which followed in 1991, were certainly helped by that diplomatic work, especially the work done on the basis or within the framework of the CSCE.

1 Declaration 2625 XXV adopted by the United Nations General Assembly (UNGA) on 24 October 1970, on Principles of International Law concerning Friendly Relations and Co-operation among States in accordance with the Charter of the United Nations.

2 Definition of Aggression: Resolution 3314 XXIX, adopted by the UNGA on 14 December 1974.

3 These Principles were not meant to apply to decolonisation.

4 The two other ones were Canada and the United States.

5 Principle Three.

6 Principle Four.

7 Principle Six.

Since then, history has confirmed that in international law, the splitting up of a State is still possible.

To begin with the USSR, its dissolution gave birth to no less than fifteen independent States. The successor State of the USSR was the Federation of Russia. Three of the 'new' States,[8] the Baltic States, later became, in 2004, members of the European Union (EU): Estonia, Latvia and Lithuania. The dissolution of the Federation of Czechoslovakia in 1993 gave birth to two new States, the Czech Republic and Slovakia, which also became EU members in 2004. The dissolution of the Federation of Yugoslavia was less peaceful. After political turmoil and armed conflicts during the early 1990s, six new States were created.[9] Two of them have become EU members, Slovenia in 2004 and Croatia in 2013. Others would also like to become EU members, but they do not yet fulfil the necessary conditions in a number of respects. In international practice, it is therefore obvious that the partition of States, giving birth to new States, is well known, even excluding decolonisation. The number of States which are members of the United Nations has grown from 51 in 1945 to 113 in 1962, and it has continued to grow to 193 (since 2011).

## II Movements of Secession in Some EU Member States

The population of some of these new States born from schism from a pre-existing State is small. This is also the case for new Member States of the EU. Of the thirteen States which have acceded to the EU since 2004, seven have less than five million inhabitants, and two less than one million: Cyprus (0.8 m) and Malta (0.4 m). This could not remain unnoticed by the movements for secession which existed in some regions of the 'older' Member States. These movements stress that the number of inhabitants in Catalonia and in Scotland are respectively 7.5 and 5.3 million, respectively more than Bulgaria and Ireland. They also note that EU Member States are now accepting some secessions, not only in Asia (Timor-Leste) or in Africa (South Sudan) but also in Europe (Kosovo).[10] They may consider that there is now, in Europe, a willingness to accept or tolerate secessions. Some people noted that the 1975 Helsinki Conference also

[8] The three Baltic States were not actually new, as they were independent States before their invasion and annexation by the USSR in 1940.

[9] A seventh, Kosovo, was established later.

[10] However, Spain, as well as four other EU Member States, are refusing to recognise Kosovo as an independent State.

adopted the 'Principle of Equal Rights and Self-Determination of Peoples'.[11] However, this trend to secessionism has never been tested within the borders of the fifteen 'older' EU Member States (i.e. the six founding members and the nine others having acceded to the Union before 2004).

The novelty is that now, the partisans of secession in some regions of the EU hope that their region could become an independent State while 'staying secure within the big EU family'. That has boosted the separatist movements. As Brian Beary wrote in 2010:

> Ironically, such questions about secession and partition were supposed to have been answered by the example of the European Union, where a process of gradual integration and ceding of national sovereignty was structured in order to reduce the importance of national borders. That vision has largely succeeded in the sense of eliminating the risk of war between EU Member States and promoting a 'globalizing' era in which national borders matter less and less to the lives and livelihoods of citizens in the Member States.[12]

## III Catalonia and Scotland

In Spain, there are mainly two regions in which separatist movements have existed for a long period: the Basque Country and Catalonia. They both have, since the entry into force of the Spanish Constitution in 1978, a status of Autonomous Communities. Despite the fact that they have never been independent States[13] in the past, their identity is strong. This is symbolised by their local official languages, Catalan and Basque ('Euskera'), distinct from Spanish ('Castellano'), as well as their own culture and specific traditions and customs. The Basque country's long running independentist movements, went down the path of terrorism in the twentieth century. Their armed branch 'ETA',[14] founded in 1959,

[11] Principle Eight.

[12] Brian Beary, 'EU and US Show Gingerly Interest in Partition and Secession to Settle Conflict', article published by The European Institute Washington, 2010. See the book by the same author: *Separatist Movements: A Global Reference* (Washington: CQPress, 2011).

[13] Although this is disputed by some, according to most historians Catalonia was not an independent State before becoming part of Spain, as it was part of the Crown of Aragon. As for the Basque country, it has known long periods of autonomy, but it also appears to be agreed that it was never independent. See further Medina, 'The Political Rights of EU Citizens and the Right of Secession', Chapter 8 in this volume.

[14] Euskadi Ta Askatasuna.

committed numerous terrorist acts, causing the death of hundreds of people. In Catalonia, a separatist movement also existed a long time ago, but has developed quickly recently and with peaceful means.[15] This movement is mainly focused on economic interests. Its arguments are that there is a fiscal imbalance in favour of the Central Government, and unjustified transfers from Catalonia to the rest of the Kingdom. This was further encouraged by the current Spanish economic and financial crisis. As observed by Christopher K. Connolly[16] in his excellent study:

> Catalan nationalists have capitalized on the eurozone crisis by arguing that a Catalonia freed from the shackles of the Spanish economy would take its place among the wealthier and more stable States of the European 'north'.

Separatist movements existed in Scotland well before the beginning of the European project. Scotland was actually an independent State until the early eighteenth century (1707). There too, the economic crisis and the arguments that Scottish taxpayers pay too much into the British budget and do not receive enough from it are at the centre of the arguments of the secessionist political party.[17]

The reactions from the governments of the two States directly concerned, Spain and the UK, were completely different. Of course, the Spanish Constitution is very clear about the issue, while the UK does not have a written constitution as such. The UK Government decided to give the Scots the right to decide, by referendum, whether they wanted Scotland to become an independent State. There was no UK constitutional or legal impediment to that decision. In Spain, where the Constitution is 'based on the indissoluble unity of the Spanish nation' (Article 2), the government refused any discussion which could imply a possible route towards independence. That position was politically supported not only by its own

[15] The two biggest nationalist parties in Catalonia are *Convergencia* de Catalunya (CIU) and *Esquerra* Republicana de Catalunya (ERC).

[16] Christopher K. Connolly, 'Independence in Europe: Secession, Sovereignty, and the European Union', *Duke Journal of Comparative and International Law*, 24(2013), 51–105.

[17] The major secessionist political party is the Scottish National Party (SNP), led until after the 2014 referendum by Mr Alex Salmond. At the time of writing, it is led by Ms Nicola Sturgeon. The SNP became the largest party in the Scottish Parliament in 2007 and obtained an overall majority in 2011, Mr Salmond becoming the First Minister. Ms Sturgeon succeeded him in late 2014. In the most recent UK national elections, on 8 May 2015, the SNP obtained fifty-six out of the fifty-nine seats representing the Scottish electors in the House of Commons.

majority, but also by the main national opposition party, as well as by a strong majority in the national Parliament.[18] This view was also legally shared by the Constitutional Tribunal,[19] which judged that a partition of Spain is excluded by the Constitution.[20]

### A. *The September/November 2014 Events in Scotland and Catalonia*

On 18 September 2014, Scottish voters were asked at referendum: 'Should Scotland become an independent country?' A majority of 55.3 per cent (2,001,926 votes), against 44.7 per cent (1,617,989 votes), decided that Scotland would remain part of the United Kingdom. The participation rate was extremely high: 84.6 per cent. That referendum was organised with the agreement of the British authorities, which had made a legal commitment to implement its results.[21] Despite these results, many political observers consider the question of more or less autonomy for Scotland within the UK, or even of independence, could come back in the medium or long term. This view was strengthened by the strong increase in the votes for the SNP in the subsequent national elections to the House of Commons in May 2015.

On 9 November 2014, the Catalonian Government organised an informal 'advisory vote' on the possible independence of Catalonia from the Kingdom of Spain, despite the Spanish Government's opposition. The Spanish authorities, both political and judicial, had found that a regional referendum on the issue would be contrary to the Constitution.[22] This is why the Catalan Government presented the vote not as a referendum, but as an informal consultation which would

[18] In April 2014, by 299 votes against forty-seven.

[19] In March 2014, the Constitutional Tribunal found that it would be contrary to the Constitution for an autonomous Community to organise a referendum on self-determination.

[20] The Spanish Constitution of 27 December 1978 was adopted by referendum on 6 December 1978 by 91.8 per cent of the votes, with a participation rate of 67.1 per cent. (These figures were 90.5 per cent. and 67.4 per cent respectively in Catalonia). See footnote 22 below on the pertinent provisions of the Constitution.

[21] 'Agreement between the United Kingdom Government and the Scottish Government on a referendum on independence for Scotland', signed in Edinburgh on 15 October 2012 by David Cameron, Prime Minister of the United Kingdom of Great Britain and Northern Ireland, and Mr Alex Salmond, First Minister of Scotland.

[22] Article 2 of the 1978 Constitution provides:

> 'The Constitution is based on the indissoluble unity of the Spanish nation, the common and indivisible country of all Spaniards; it recognises and

have no legal value. Seized by the government, the Constitutional Tribunal declared that the consultation would be illegal and invalid in any event.[23] Both the Spanish Parliament and the Spanish Government considered this vote contrary to the Constitution and consequently, as null and void.

The consultation consisted of two questions:

1. 'Do you want Catalonia to become a State?'
2. 'If so, do you want this State to be independent?'

All residents in Catalonia aged sixteen or over were allowed to vote. Catalans residing elsewhere, including in other Spanish regions, could not vote. Residents of Catalonia could vote, even if they were originally from another part of Spain. Residents who were nationals of another EU State were also allowed to vote, at least in principle. In the absence of an electoral roll, as the consultation was not organised by the Spanish State, identity cards indicating residential address were used for the polling, which excluded all foreigners *de facto*. No neutral body monitored the conduct of the vote, either of the vote itself or of the vote count.

The results showed 2,305,290 votes counted, thus a participation rate of less than 40 per cent. A number of voters may have chosen to abstain, given that the consultation was legally invalid. The votes in favour of independence (yes to both questions) were 1,861,753 or 80.76 per cent[24] of the votes cast: this was not an increase compared to the results of previous regional elections.[25]

guarantees the right to autonomy of the nationalities and regions of which it is composed, and the solidarity amongst them all.'

According to Article 149 of the Constitution:

*1. The State holds exclusive competence over the following matters:*
'[. . .] (xxxii) authorisation for popular consultations through the holding of referendums.'

[23] On 3 November 2014.

[24] The other votes were as follows: Yes to the first question and No to the second: 232,182 or 10.07 per cent; Yes and blank: 22,466 or 0.97 per cent; No: 104,772 or 4.54 per cent; blank: 12,986 or 0.56 per cent; Other: 71,131 or 3.09 per cent.

[25] Daniel Silva, *Agence France Presse*, 10 November 2014: 'The total number of votes in favour of independence was less than the votes cast in the last regional elections in 2012 for the four Catalan nationalist parties which called the referendum'. According to figures published in the newspaper 'La Vanguardia', there were more than two million votes in favour of these four Catalan political parties in the 2012 regional elections. As for the elections to the European Parliament of May 2014, the independentists political parties got approximately 55 per cent of the votes ('NAXIS Flash', 29 August 2014).

### B. *The Regional Elections in Catalonia on 27 September 2015*

The Prime Minister of Catalonia, Artur Mas, then decided to have a snap regional election on 27 September 2015, and thus dissolved the Catalonian Parliament. He declared that, given the national government's refusal to grant Catalonians the possibility of having a referendum, the regional elections should be interpreted as a vote for independence. The three traditional separatist political parties, all in favour of EU membership, decided to run together in the elections on a single list, '*Junts pel Sí*' (the 'JxS list': 'Together for Yes'). Initially, they claimed they would transform the vote into a referendum, but would in that case have needed a majority of votes to declare a victory. They later said that, should they have an absolute majority of seats in the regional Parliament, they would consider that a victory which would enable them to prepare for the adoption of a unilateral declaration of independence. A 'victory' could thus be obtained with less than a majority of the votes cast. They also later said that they would prepare a draft Constitution for a future independent State of Catalonia.

The participation rate was 77.12 per cent, about 10 per cent higher than in the 2012 regional elections. As foreseen, the List JxS came first. However, it only got 39.34 per cent of the votes and sixty-two seats out of 135, far from an absolute majority of the votes cast and close, but not quite, a majority of seats. The List was thus obliged to look for an alliance with the other independentist party, the radical left separatist CUP (the People's Unity List, which got 7.95 per cent of the votes and ten seats). Together, they had less than 48 per cent of the votes, thus less than a majority, but a majority of seats (seventy-two out of 135). On that basis, the leaders of both JxS and CUP made triumphal statements of victory and announced a renewed push for independence. They remain however quite divided: CUP is in favour of exiting the EU and NATO, and does not support Mr Mas and his economic policy. Moreover, in some statements made after the vote, the CUP, while advocating a 'rupture' with Spain, excluded the unilateral declaration of independence promoted by Mr Mas and the JxS List. At the time of writing, it is not clear whether Mr Mas's candidacy for re-election as the Head of the Catalan Government will be supported by the CUP.

We can well understand why both camps proclaimed a victory, both in favour of independence and against it. The truth is, first, that a regional election cannot be assimilated into a referendum. Whatever its results, such an election is regional and cannot provide a legal mandate for independence. Second, the percentage of votes in favour of independence did not increase from 2012 to 2015. It remained at a high level, between 47 and 48 per cent of voters, not far, but crucially below the 50 per cent threshold. Therefore, even if the vote was regarded politically as a 'plebiscite' on the independence question (*quod non*), as Mr Mas claimed before the vote, the independentists would have lost it, despite their *heteroclit* coalition. The political situation has thus not been clarified.

Regions other than Catalonia and Scotland are also experiencing secessionist trends in some EU Member States, such as Northern Belgium (Flanders), Northern Italy (Lega Norte, Veneto) or in Spain again, the Basque Country. A contagious flare up of this issue could affect them, or other regions in other Member States. Moreover, in Spain, the current Constitution devolves more powers to some regions (Catalonia, the Basque Country or Navarra) and less to others. This asymmetry could create problems in the longer term, as regional identities are strong in Spain, and that there are separatists everywhere, whether in Andalucia, Galicia or Valencia.

### C. *The EU is Partly, Even if Involuntarily, 'Responsible' for the Recent Resurgence of Separatist Trends within Some of Its Member States*

There are good reasons why these separatists trends should not be seen only from a national perspective, but also from a European one. Many legal and institutional issues need to be considered, although the issue is primarily political, including for the EU itself. It is actually arguable that the EU is partly 'responsible' for this resurgence of separatist trends, because it is seen as able to carry out tasks which cannot be accomplished as well by small entities. These entities can envisage independence more securely, if they were certain of remaining under the protection of the EU umbrella.

The success of the EU has thus favoured a resurgence of separatist movements in some of its Member States. As expressed by Professor JHH Weiler: 'Feeding this frenzy for secession and independence in Europe is the premise that all these new States will somehow find a safe haven as Member States of the EU. Absent that assumption, appetite for independence would be significantly muted, the rough seas of "going it alone" far more threatening'.[26]

[26] Professor JHH Weiler wrote this in an Editorial of the European Journal of International Law (Vol. 23/4) published in December 2012.

This is why one of the major arguments put forward by the proponents of independence was the same in Catalonia and in Scotland, and it was stressed with insistence. After independence, the 'preservation' of 'being' an EU member State would be 'guaranteed' for the new State born of the secession. This 'preservation' was initially presented as 'automatic': the newborn State would 'remain' an EU member. There was neither a need for a treaty revising the European Treaties nor for any international agreement requiring the consent of the present Member States.[27]

According to that legal thesis, the economic operators of the newborn State would continue to have access to the EU's internal market, and to benefit from its common trade policy. The citizens of the newborn State might hold the nationality of their new State, but they would nevertheless retain their EU citizenship and the rights attached to it. The supporters of independence did not consider those views as a legal thesis which needed to be argued and demonstrated, but as evident per se: 'We are IN, we will stay IN'. They pretended to be 'horrified' when specialised EU lawyers dared oppose their views. The arguments of these 'opponents' were seen as politically biased, and as an attempt to 'expel' the future new State from the EU, to 'deprive' its citizens of their EU citizenship, to 'strip them' of their rights, etc. [28] Almost all pamphlets issued by the Scottish National Party since 1989 have taken Scotland's continued EU membership after becoming an independent State for granted.

The EU is thus objectively one of the causes, albeit indirect and unintended, of the recent resurgence of separatist movements in some of its Member States. The assumption that the new State, freshly born from a secession, would at its birth 'remain' an EU member, part of 'the

[27] See C. K. Connolly, (previously cited), which quotes both: Nicola Sturgeon, then the Scottish deputy First Minister and today the First Minister of Scotland: '[w]e would automatically be members of the EU' (quoted from Stephen Castle, 'Scots' Referendum Raises a Slew of Legal Issues' (New York Times, 13 February, 2012); and the Catalan nationalist Oriol Junqueras: 'Catalonia should become an independent State and automatically a member State of the EU' (same source). The current President of Catalonia, Artur Mas, has also argued for automatic Catalan membership of the EU in a speech in Brussels on 7 November, 2012. Various leaflets issued by the separatist political parties both in Scotland and in Catalonia, have often repeated this legal affirmation, without providing any argumentation.

[28] See, for example, David Scheffer, Professor of Law at the Northwestern University School of Law (Illinois, USA), in the Scottish Independence Insta-Symposium: The Legal Terrain Following a Yes Vote for Scottish Independence: 'Caustic and unsubstantiated statements by EU officials and Westminster politicians in the past that relegate Scotland to new applicant status shorn of any existing rights under EU law have been narrow-minded expressions of insecurity'.

EU family', played a crucial role in reassuring the people concerned. This was demonstrated by polls conducted in Catalonia, where different answers were given, in the case of an independent Catalonia to 'remaining' or not in the EU.

## IV A Political and Moral Paradox

Other factors, historical, cultural and political, probably play a greater role in the minds of the people concerned. Furthermore, the economic crisis is also exacerbating populism, nationalism and regional egoism. It is no accident that secessionist trends appear in the richest regions: Flanders, Scotland, Catalonia, South Tyrol or the Veneto. This is a classic trend, as D. L. Horowitz demonstrated in a general sense. Richer regions try to avoid solidarity with the poorer parts of the State to which they belong, to keep control of their revenues and not subsidise the poorer regions.[29]

In that context, the fact that the success of the EU is objectively an encouraging factor to these recent outbreaks of secessionism is a political and moral paradox. In fact, the historical goal of the European project is 'the end of the division of the European continent'. The EU aims to continue the 'process of creating an ever closer union among the peoples of Europe' and to advance 'European integration', as this is enshrined in the EU Treaties. The European ideal tends towards more solidarity between European peoples, while the key objective of Catalan and Scottish independentists is less solidarity with the rest of the State to which they belong.[30] Their values appear, in this respect, to be different from the EU's.

The partition of an EU member State would be unprecedented. The case of Algeria[31] and Greenland[32] were obviously different and involved exits from the EU. The reunification of Germany did involve the

[29] D. L. Horowitz, *Ethnic Groups in Conflict* (Berkeley: University of California Press, 2001).

[30] JHH Weiler, 'Scotland and the EU', Verfassungblog, 8 September 2014, <http://verfassungsblog.de/scotland-eu-comment-joseph-h-h-weiler-2/>, accessed 5 July 2015: 'I watched the televised debates. Most of the sparring was utilitarian: will we better off, especially economically. More employment, yes or no. Better social network, yes or no, etc., etc. So this is what will ultimately decide things. This runs diametrically contrary to the historical ethos of European integration'.

[31] The territory of Algeria, as part of France, was expressly subject to the European Economic Community (EEC) Treaty. When it became independent in 1962, it automatically ceased to be so, while France continued as the successor State. See A. Ortega and J. De Areilza, 'Escisión y permanencia en la Unión Europea. Aproximación a un marco teórico sin precedentes', *Claves de Razón Práctica*, 100 (2000).

[32] Treaty amending, with regard to Greenland, the Treaties establishing the European Communities of March 1984, OJ L29, 1 February 1985. See Weerts: 'L'évolution du

'enlargement' of the EU, but it was different too: it can be argued that the 'Eastern Lander' were intended ultimately to gain automatic access to the EU, from the beginning of the European Economic Community.[33] As for Czechoslovakia, it had dissolved before the accession of the Czech Republic and Slovakia to the EU in 2004.

## V The EU Treaties Neither Foresee Nor Prohibit the Partition of a Member State

If the partition of an EU State were to arise in the future, a number of constitutional and legal questions would be raised concerning the relationship to be established between the new State and the EU. These questions have been deliberately obscured by political passions in recent years. The debate needs to be cleared up, in case such outbreaks of secessionism reappear in the future, especially given the contagion risks.[34]

The first question would be to clarify whether the EU Treaties forbid or authorise partitions of the EU Member States. The possibility of a partition of a Member State is not mentioned in the EU Treaties. This is understandable, as Member States are, according to the famous formula of the German Federal Constitutional Court, 'the masters of the EU Treaties'. Would any State seek to encourage its own partition, by stating in an international treaty that such a partition is legally possible and go as far as to provide a 'user manual' on how to do it?

The partisans for independence, in both Catalonia and Scotland, stressed the 'neutrality' of the EU Treaties on this point. They also thought that if their region was to become an independent State, it could either 'remain' or quickly become an EU member. First, it is true that were this to happen, in observance of the Rule of Law the EU Treaties would be neutral on the partition of a Member State. Second, it is equally true that were such a partition to occur in observance of the Rule of Law, the EU Treaties would even provide a procedure for dealing with the admission of the new State.

droit de retrait de l'Union européenne et sa résonance sur l'intégration européenne', *Cahiers de Droit européen*, 2 (2012).

[33] See attached to the 1957 EEC Treaty, the 'Protocol on German Internal Trade and Connected Problems'. See J.-P. Jacqué, 'L'unification de l'Allemagne et la Communauté européenne', *Revue générale de Droit international public*, 94 (4) (1990); and Arnold, *La unificación alemana. Estudios sobre derecho alemán y europeo*, (Madrid: Civitas, 1993).

[34] JHH Weiler, (previously cited): 'Scottish independence coupled with simultaneous, or close to simultaneous, membership of the Union, will provoke a domino effect'.

### A. *The EU Treaties Provide a Legal Procedure to Admit New States, Which Could be Applied to the Case of a State Born from the Partition of a Current Member State*

What would happen in legal terms if such an event occurred, and the newborn non-successor State applied to become a candidate for accession to the EU? What would be the correct legal procedure to follow to examine the candidacy of that State?

To the extent that the new State would be recognised by all EU Member States and that it would consider itself able to fulfil the conditions of Articles 49 and 2 TFEU,[35] it could apply to become a member of the EU. Early in their respective campaigns, the supporters of the secession of Catalonia and of Scotland claimed that the new State 'would automatically remain' an EU member. They were later obliged to admit that some kind of procedure could not be avoided.

### B. *In Case of a Candidacy to the EU of a New State, Born from the Partition of a Member State, Article 48 TEU Could Not Be Used as the Legal Basis for the Admission Procedure*

The Scottish independentists claimed that an Accession Treaty, adopted by the EU in accordance with the procedure provided by Article 49 TEU, would not be necessary. They argued that instead, Article 48, which is the legal basis for adopting revisions to the EU Treaties, would provide the right and sufficient legal basis. They argued that an Article 48 procedure would deliver quicker results than an Article 49 procedure. However, this was by no means guaranteed, given that first, Article 48 provides for an additional stage, a 'Convention' to work on the issues in question before an Inter-Governmental Conference (IGC) can be convened. Such a Convention would take time, as the Convention on the 'Constitutional

[35] The conditions to which the 'Criteria of Eligibility' referred to in Article 49 TEU, generally referred to as 'The Copenhagen Criteria', have to be added. These criteria were approved by the European Council, meeting in Copenhagen, on 21–22 June 1993, <www.consilium.europa.eu/en/european-council/conclusions/pdf-1993–2003/presidency-conclusions_-copenhagen-european-council_-21-and-22-june-1993/>, accessed 5 July 2015: 'Membership requires that the candidate country has achieved stability of institutions guaranteeing democracy, the rule of law, human rights, respect for and protection of minorities, the existence of a functioning market economy as well as the capacity to cope with competitive pressure and market forces within the Union. Membership presupposes the candidate's ability to take on the obligations of membership including adherence to the aims of political, economic and monetary union'.

Treaty for Europe' demonstrated.[36] However, the European Council may decide, 'after obtaining the consent of the European Parliament', not to convene a Convention, if the extent of the proposed amendments 'does not justify it'. But would the admission of a twenty-ninth member State be considered as a secondary issue by the Parliament, especially when that institution is largely represented in a Convention and is not represented in an IGC, other than by a few observers?

Second, Article 49 limits the issues which may be addressed by an Accession Treaty to the conditions of admission of the applicant State and to the adjustments of the Treaties which this admission entails. On the contrary, Article 48 allows the Parliament, the Commission and any Member State to 'submit to the Council proposals for the amendment of the Treaties'. This could open a Pandora's Box, especially at a time when the Parliament favours significant Treaty change. Finally, the applicant State could not participate in the negotiations in an IGC based on Article 48.

The common agreement of all Member States would be needed for both procedures, as well as their ratifications in accordance with their national constitutional requirements, which all involve the authority to ratify being granted either by a vote in Parliament[37] or by referendum.

According to the advocates for secessions, a revising Treaty (Article 48) is legally appropriate to achieve an 'enlargement from within'.[38] The only basis for this argument is that the newborn State is 'already member of the EU', even if it is admitted that it did not exist as a State. Therefore, according to this argument, there would be no legal need to admit the new state into the EU, as 'it was there already'. This view continues to be promoted, despite official replies to questions from Members of the European Parliament from three successive Presidents of the Commission,

[36] The Convention started in February 2002 and finished its work a year and a half later, in July 2003. Its work served as the basis for the IGC, which begun work in October 2003 and reached agreement in June 2004. However, the 'Constitutional Treaty for Europe', signed in Rome in October 2004, never entered into force. It was abandoned after two negative referendums in France and the Netherlands in 2005. While the substantive provisions of the Lisbon Treaty, which entered into force in December 2009, were based on the text of the failed Constitutional treaty, its political significance was however quite different from the political aims of that failed treaty.

[37] Seven different Parliaments in the case of Belgium. See in general, C. Closa, *The Politics of Ratification of EU Treaties* (London: Routledge, 2013).

[38] This terminology was used in 2004, probably for the first time, by Professor Neil MacCormick (1941–2009), a member of the Scottish National Party, in 'The European Constitutional Convention and the Stateless Nations', *International Relations*, (2004), 331.

Romano Prodi, José Manuel Barroso and Jean-Claude Juncker.[39] It must be stressed that written answers to Members of the European Parliament by the President of the Commission are not given in a personal capacity, as the independentists pretend, but on behalf of the European Commission. The President of the European Council, Herman Van Rompuy, took exactly the same position:

> The European Union has been established by the relevant Treaties among the Member States. The Treaties apply to the Member States. If a part of the territory of a member State ceases to be part of that State because that territory becomes a new independent State, the Treaties will no longer apply to that territory. In other words, a new independent State would, by the fact of its independence, become a third country with respect to the Union and the Treaties would from the date of its independence, not apply anymore on its territory.[40]

## C. *Article 49 TEU Would Provide the Only Correct Legal Basis, Both for Reasons of Substance and Procedure*

Arguing for use of Article 48 instead of Article 49 TEU is indeed legally wrong, both in terms of substance and procedure. Regarding the question

[39] Firstly, Romano Prodi, President of the Commission, on 1 March 2004: 'When a part of the territory of a member State ceases to be a part of that State, i.e. because that territory becomes an independent state, the Treaties no longer apply to that territory. In other words, a newly independent region would, by the fact of its independence, become a third country with respect to the Union and the Treaties would, from the day of its independence, not apply anymore on its territory' OJ C84 E/422, 3 April 2004. Secondly, the same answers were given by José Manuel Barroso, President of the Commission, eight years later, on behalf of another College of Commissioners. These answers were also published in the Official Journal, on 3 December 2012 and on 1 February 2013. Thirdly, exactly the same answer was given by Jean-Claude Juncker, President of the Commission, as recently as in September 2015. See also the letter sent by Viviane Reding, Vice-President of the Commission, on 4 October 2012 to the Spanish Secretary of State for European Affairs, Iñigo Méndez de Vigo (available from <www.asktheeu.org, www.asktheeu.org/en/request/251/response/698/attach/html/2/MENDEZ%20DE%20VIGO%20reply%20pdf.pdf.html>, accessed 5 July 2015); and her letter to the Scottish Parliament on 20 March 2014 (<www.scottish.parliament.uk/S4_EuropeanandExternalRelationsCommittee/Inquiries/Letter_from_Viviane_Reding_Vice_President_of_the_European_Commission_dated_20_March_2014__pdf.pdf.>, accessed 5 July 2015). Finally, see the written evidence to the Scottish Parliament (at its request) of Jean-Claude Piris, the former Legal Counsel of the European Council and Director General of the Legal Services of the Council of the EU, on 12 January 2014 (<http://www.parliament.scot/S4_EuropeanandExternalRelationsCommittee/Inquiries/Jean-Claude_Piris_written_evidence.pdf.>, accessed 5 July 2015).

[40] Council of the EU, '*Remarks by the President of the European Council on Catalonia*', 12 December 2013, EUCO 267/13, PRESS 576.

of substance, the substantive meaning of the procedure provided by Article 49 is threefold:

i) to check if all the criteria for admission are respected by the candidate country;
ii) to negotiate a treaty to agree on the specific conditions of admission; and
iii) to adopt the necessary adjustments to the EU Treaties entailed by the admission.

To address the first point, the first purpose of the admission process is to check whether a candidate State meets all the conditions required to become an EU Member State. These conditions include respect for the EU's values, the acceptance and ability to implement and to control the correct application of all the 'chapters' of the *acquis communautaire* in the territory under its jurisdiction, etc. The independentists argue, with some supported from a few, but eminent, lawyers,[41] that this meticulous procedure should not be followed when the candidate State results from the partition of an existing EU Member State. They do not base their thesis on textual legal arguments. They argue that this would be a 're-application', while the entity in question 'is already member of the EU', and that it would be an unnecessary verification, as this entity is already fulfilling the necessary conditions and is implementing the *acquis communautaire*.

This is neither legally nor practically correct. If it were, it would mean that any fraction of a Member State which became independent would necessarily be regarded as satisfying by definition, all the necessary political, economic, judicial and administrative conditions. A few theoretical examples can be considered to show that this is absurd: what about Sicily or Corsica or one or several Balearic, Greek or Swedish islands? Is there really no need to verify whether such new States fulfil all the necessary conditions?

[41] See Professor B. de Witte, 'Seamless Transition? Scottish Membership of the EU by Means of Treaty Revision Rather than Accession', (2014), Paper presented at the Workshop Trouble membership: secession from a Member State and withdrawal from the Union, EUI Florence 14 July 2014, as well as a former ECJ Judge, Sir D. Edward, 'EU Law and the Separation of Member States', (2013) 36 *Fordham Int'l LJ* 1151; and S. Douglas-Scott 'How Easily Could an Independent Scotland Join the EU?', (July 2014) *University of Oxford Legal Research Papers*. The opposite position was generally taken by lawyers, for example by Professors J. Crawford and A. Boyle in an Annex (*Referendum on the Independence of Scotland: International Law Aspects*) to the official Report of the UK Government, *Scotland Analysis: Devolution and the implications of Scottish Independence*, February 2013.

In any case, this is not a question of fact, it is a legal question of principle. Legally, the fact that Catalonia and Scotland might both be able rapidly to fulfil the necessary conditions to become EU Member State could help accelerate the procedure, but could not dispense with following it.

What matters legally is that a new State is at issue. A new State born from a partition of an existing State would obviously be a different entity from the State of which it was part. It would not have the same Constitution as the predecessor State, neither the same political system, nor the same administrative apparatus, nor the same judicial organisation, nor the same financial and technical means, nor the same human resources, which are needed to be able to respect its obligations, for example 'the capacity to cope with competitive pressure and market forces within the Union' (one of the 'Copenhagen Criteria of Eligibility'). And who would guarantee that the new Member State would be able to fulfil all the commitments made previously by the successor State (e.g. either the UK or Spain) in areas where the new State (e.g. either Scotland or Catalonia) had not the necessary legal powers before its independence.

A new State is a new State. Nothing can establish that 'by definition' a new State would be founded with the same values, have the same capabilities and be able to fulfil the necessary conditions to become a Member State of the EU in its own right.

To address the second point, the accession procedure under Article 49 must lead to the adoption of a treaty containing 'the conditions of admission': according to this Article, these conditions 'shall be the subject of an agreement between the Member States and the applicant State.' Legally, these conditions cannot be adopted on the basis of Article 48. Therefore, on which legal basis could they be agreed? In the absence of the Accession Treaty foreseen in Article 49 to adopt these conditions, in which instrument could they be enumerated, knowing that it would need to be an instrument which is binding both on the new Member State and on the current ones? It is stressed that Article 49 provides for this Accession Treaty to be ratified by the applicant country and by the twenty-eight current Member States, because the agreement should contain all the necessary conditions of substance, including:

> the legal commitment of the new Member State to adopt and implement the *acquis communautaire*, which includes the commitment to adopt the euro as its currency when the necessary conditions are met

(Article 119(2) TFEU), as well as to become a member of the Schengen area once the relevant conditions for that are met: see Article 7 of Protocol No 19 'on the Schengen acquis integrated into the framework of the European Union', which is particularly clear on this obligation;[42]

The possible adoption of transition periods, and/or of derogations, and/or of adaptations, and/or of safeguard clauses: it is legally clear that, contrary to the claims of proponents of independence in Scotland, all opt-outs and derogations obtained by the UK over the years constitute exceptions to normal EU law – they would thus not be applicable *ipso* faco to Scotland, unless formally agreed by the current twenty-eight Member States; and

The adoption of conditions for the participation in the financing of the EU budget: the idea of getting a 'rebate' similar to the UK was suggested by the Scottish independentists but has been ruled out by statements from the authorities of several Member States.

Certainly, the fact that the EU law was already being applied in a territory which is becoming a new Member State (or that it has been applied there for many years until a point in the recent past) would significantly facilitate and accelerate the accession negotiations. However, there must be legal clarity: there is no magic trick which could dispense with negotiating and concluding replacement treaty.

To address the third point, these substantial conditions are additional to the amendments of the Treaty: these necessary amendments should also, according to the EU Treaties, be adopted in accordance with Article 49 in case of an admission.

Regarding the question of procedure, in its consistent case law the Court of Justice of the EU has ruled that the legal bases established by the EU Treaty cannot be used by the EU institutions as these institutions politically wish or see fit: 'The choice of a legal basis for a Community measure must rest on objective factors amenable to judicial review, which include in particular the aim and content of the measure'.[43] The two main rules which have to be respected when EU institutions choose which

[42] 'Article 7: For the purposes of the negotiations for the admission of new Member States into the European Union, the Schengen *acquis* and further measures taken by the institutions within its scope shall be regarded as an *acquis* which must be accepted in full by all States candidates for admission'.

[43] For an example, see Case C-338/01 *Commission* v *Council* [2004] ECLI:EU:C:2004:253.

article or articles of the EU Treaties will constitute the legal base of an EU act are:

- The legal basis of any EU legal act must be determined by reference to its aim and content.
- Specific Articles of the Treaties have priority over general articles (*lex specialis*).

In that context, it is a fact that Article 48 TEU does not deal specifically with the admission of a State to the EU, but with the revision of the Treaties. It does not allow conditions for admission of a new Member State to be set. The aim and content of the Agreement to be adopted in the case in question would be precisely the accession of a new Member State of the EU, to be listed in Article 52(1) TEU, and to determine the conditions of accession of that State. Article 49 TEU is the only specific article in the EU Treaties dealing with accession to the EU: it allows for the adoption, in the same agreement, of the two sets of arrangements necessary for the EU to admit a new Member State. According to Article 49, the same Agreement must contain both necessary elements:

✓ 'the conditions of admission'; and
✓ 'the adjustments to the Treaties on which the Union is founded, which such admission entails'.

Therefore, Article 49 is the only correct, necessary and sufficient basis.

In addition, the procedures for the EU institutions when acting on the basis of Article 48 and 49 TEU are not the same. Article 49 requires not only unanimity in the Council but also 'the consent of the European Parliament, which shall act by a majority of its component members'. This voting rule is exceptional. It is not normally required by Article 48, for ordinary Treaty revision.[44] It means that since the EP counts 751 members with its President,[45] the majority required by Article 49 in such a case would at least be of 376 positive votes, while most amendments to the EU Treaties based on Article 48 (except for the first and second sub-paragraphs of its paragraph 7) require a simple majority of those members of the EP who are present and voting. Use Article 48 instead of 49 for the admission of a new Member State would also therefore be incorrect for that reason.

[44] This is required only for a case of 'simplified' revision of the Treaty in accordance with Article 48(7), first and second sub-paragraphs, and where no Convention and no Inter-Governmental Conference need be convened.

[45] See Article 14(2) TEU.

As is the case for a revising Treaty based on Article 48, the ratification of a Treaty of accession by the twenty-eight Member States would also be required. We should stress that, in the case of France, the Constitution provides that the ratification of an Accession Treaty[46] must in principle be approved by a referendum,[47] which is not required by the French Constitution for a Treaty revising the EU Treaties.

## VI Conclusion

We cannot say that the partition of a State, followed by the admission of the newborn non-successor State to the EU, would be legally impossible if it were allowed by the Constitution of the EU Member State in question. This is not forbidden, neither by international law nor by European Union law.

Is that likely to happen in the real world? That is the question which will be examined in Chapter 6.

[46] After the last one, on the accession of Croatia, in 2013.

[47] See Article 88-5 and Article 89, third sub-paragraph, Constitution of the French Republic. A derogation to this procedure is legally possible but requires a positive vote of both Chambers of the French Parliament.

6

# Political and Legal Aspects of Recent Regional Secessionist Trends in some EU Member States (II)

JEAN-CLAUDE PIRIS

The partition of an EU Member State and the accession to the EU of the new State born from that partition is not likely to happen. Even if there are legal ways of achieving this while completely respecting international law, EU law and the Constitution of the EU Member State concerned, the political and legal obstacles on the road would be huge. This makes it an unlikely scenario.

## I International Law Does Not Recognise a General Right to Self-Determination for Substate Entities

In Catalonia the independentists argued that, in international law, there is a 'right to self- determination' which they called '*el derecho de decidir*' (the right to decide), and that this right is available for an entity like Catalonia. This is not legally correct.

The 'Quebec' judgment of the Supreme Court of Canada[1] is the best description thus far of the meaning and limits of the right to self-determination in international law. At paragraphs 138, 151 and 154 in particular, the Supreme Court demonstrates that in international law, the right to self-determination exists only when certain conditions are fulfilled. This right does not exist *ipso facto* for any substate entity and under all circumstances. In particular, as a matter of principle, it does not exist in a democratic State. This is the case when such a State's institutions respect the Rule of Law, constitutional structures and human rights, including the rights of persons belonging to minorities. In that case, such

[1] 20 August 1998. Renvoi relatif à la sécession du Québec, Recueil (1998) 2 RCS 217.

a right may exist only in accordance with the conditions and procedures foreseen by the Constitution of the State concerned.[2]

We could also point to the Advisory Opinion of the International Court of Justice on the Unilateral Declaration of Independence of Kosovo.[3] The Opinion of the International Court of Justice deals exclusively with the possibility of making a unilateral declaration and not the issue of recognition. The Opinion is about international law only. It does not refer to the conformity of a unilateral declaration of independence with the applicable constitutional law. In any case, it does not contradict the fact that a unilateral declaration of independence, not backed by recognition from the international community, would remain a dead letter.

Article 4(2) TEU confirms that it is the sole responsibility of each Member State to decide its fundamental political and constitutional structures, including regional and local self-government. *A fortiori* this would be the same for a split into two or more independent States. The same Article 4(2) adds that the EU, regarding its Member States, 'shall respect their essential State functions, including ensuring the territorial integrity of the State'. This sentence is particularly important in the context of the present study. In my opinion, it legally implies that the other Member States would not be legally free to recognise, as a State, an entity constitutionally under the jurisdiction of a Member State, if such an entity were unilaterally to declare its independence in violation of the Constitution of the Member State concerned. In that case, the other Member States would be legally obliged to refuse to recognise it. The consequence would be that the entity in question, which would not be recognised as a State by any Member State of the EU, would not even be able to legally apply to become a member of the EU.

In fact, from the perspective of Catalonia's possible candidacy to become a Member State of the EU, what would the legal effects be of the adoption, by the Catalonian Parliament, of a 'declaration of independence'?

[2] See also the judgment of the Spanish Constitutional Court of 25 March 2014 (STC 47/2014); A. Buchanan, 'Self-Determination and the Right to secede', *Journal of International Affairs*, 45 (2) (1992); J. de Miguel Barcena, 'El derecho a decidir y sus aporias democráticas', *Cuadernos de Alzate, Revista Vasca de la Cultura y las Ideas*, (2013) pp. 46–47 and J. Rodriguez-Zapata Pérez, 'Sobre el Derecho de autodeterminación y su compatilidad con la Constitución', *Teoría y Realidad Constitucional*, 3 (1) (1999), 103–124.

[3] 22 July 2010, <www.icj-cij.org/docket/index.php?p1=3&p2=4&case=141&p3=4>, accessed 5 July 2015. See the criticism of this Opinion in *Revista Española de Derecho Internacional*, Vol. 63.

Pursuant to EU law, if, after such a unilateral declaration, Catalonia were to invoke Article 49 TEU to 'apply to become a member of the Union', that application could only be accepted – thus allowing the commencement of a negotiation procedure – if all three conditions set out in Article 49 were met:

1) being a 'European State';
2) respecting 'the values mentioned in Article 2' (of the same TEU);
3) taking into account 'the conditions of eligibility agreed upon by the European Council': these are known as 'the Copenhagen criteria' because they were adopted by the European Council in that city in 1993.

In order to be a European State, you first need to be a State. In international law, a State is an entity which comprises three fundamental constitutive elements (population, territory and government), and which is recognised as a sovereign State by the international community. In the case of Catalonia, it would need at the very least to be recognised as a State by all twenty-eight EU Member States. This would be necessary because, according to Article 49 TEU, the representatives of the twenty-eight Member States in the EU Council have to act 'unanimously' in the preliminary phase of the application process. In the event that the Member States were called upon to decide on an application of an entity which has not yet been recognised by them as a State, they would probably decide, as explained above, that they cannot for legal reasons grant recognition. In other words, they would not accept that Catalonia is an independent State capable of making an application to accede. The legal reason is that according to Article 4(2) TEU, the Union 'shall respect [essential] State functions, including ensuring the territorial integrity of the State'. An entity failing to be recognised as a State by the twenty-eight EU Member States could not apply for membership of the EU.

In addition, there are two other conditions set out in the same Article 49 TEU which would not have been respected by the unilateral declaration of independence either. That article refers to the Copenhagen criteria, which specify that the admission of a new Member State 'requires that the candidate country has achieved stability of institutions guaranteeing democracy, the rule of law, human rights, respect for and protection of minorities'. Article 49 also requires respect by the applicant country of the 'values referred to in Article 2', which also include 'the rule of law'. An entity which declares unilateral independence, violating the law, and most particularly the national constitution it must uphold, will be in flagrant violation of these basic requirements. This would be the case for Catalonia, so long as the current Spanish Constitution remains unchanged. According to Article 2 of the Preliminary Part of the Spanish Constitution of 27 December 1978: 'The Constitution is based on the indissoluble unity of the Spanish Nation, the common and indivisible homeland of all Spaniards. It recognizes and guarantees the right to self-government of the nationalities and regions of which it is composed and the solidarity among them'. Moreover, according to Article 149 (1.32) of the Constitution, the Spanish State has an exclusive competence to authorise popular consultations by means of a referendum.

## II What Would Be the Consequences of a Splitting-Up of an EU Member State? The Difficult Issue of the Succession of States

Were a secession to be conducted in conformity with the law (national, European and international), the new entity would become a legal entity distinct from its State of origin, as from the date of its independence.[4] At that point, each EU Member State would be legally able, in the same way as any other State in the world, unilaterally to decide to recognise this entity as an independent State, without being legally obliged to do so.[5] If the new State were to be recognised, and unless an EU accession Treaty or another treaty providing for interim provisions were to come into force at the same time, the relationship between the newborn State and the EU would be terminated as from the moment of its independence from its 'mother' successor State.[6] In that case, while the 'successor State' would remain an EU Member State, the newborn State would not, *ipso*

[4] See Ignacio Molina, 'Independentismo e integración europea: la imposible adhesión automática a la UE de un territorio secesionado' *ARI Real Instituto Elcano* (2012), <www.realinstitutoelcano.org/wps/portal/rielcano/contenido?WCM_GLOBAL_CONTEXT=/elcano/elcano_es/zonas_es/europa/ari80-molina_ue_escocia_catalunya>, accessed 25 July 2016.

[5] The decision to recognise a State does not fall within the competences of the EU, but the competences of its Member States. The example of Kosovo deserves emphasis: five EU Member States out of the twenty-eight have not recognised Kosovo as an independent State: Cyprus, Greece, Romania, Slovakia and Spain. The political reasons behind this non-recognition are obviously linked to their domestic issues with secessionist movements.

[6] See M. I. Torres Cazorla, *La Sucesión de estados y sus Efectos sobre la Nacionalidad de las Personas Físicas* (Málaga: Universidad de Málaga, 2011); and A. M. Martin, 'La Secesión de Territorios en un Estado miembro: efectos en el Derecho de la Unión Europea', *Revista de Derecho de la Unión Europea*, 47(2013).

*facto* become a member of the EU. It would be a third State vis-à-vis the EU.

The idea has been defended, albeit seldom, that both States (the rump Spanish state and Catalonia, the rump UK and Scotland) could legally become successor States and that the four of them could 'remain' EU Member States. However, such a thesis is legally incorrect, both in international law and in EU law,[7] and it would not solve the issue of the 'conditions of accession' to the EU.

The remainder of the State from which the new entity would have separated would legally become, in accordance with international law, 'the successor State',[8] at least in the two examples of Catalonia and Scotland.[9] In international law, determination of the 'successor State' (or 'continuing State') is done on the basis of objective criteria: share of the territory, of the population and of the GNP, location of the political and administrative capital and of the armed forces, etc. The successor State remains bound by treaties concluded by the preceding State and remains a member of international intergovernmental organisations of which the original State was a member. It does so under the same conditions (e.g. as a permanent member of the Security Council of the United Nations in the case of the UK) and with the same rights,

[7] See S. Tierney, 'Legal Issues Surrounding the Referendum on Independence for Scotland' (2013) *University of Edinburgh School of Law Research Paper Series* No. 2013/34, at p. 23: 'But the dual succession argument does not address the following issues that must be settled for Scotland to accede to membership: on what terms would Scotland find itself a member of the EU? Would it be required to adopt the Euro or not? Would it "succeed" with or without existing UK Treaty opt-outs? How many seats in the European Parliament would it have, how many votes in the Council, etc.? These cannot be matters of succession but inevitably of accession, which the EU by the unanimous consent of its members would require to agree upon'.

[8] The problems raised by the succession of States are among the most difficult problems in international law. Two Conventions have been negotiated under the aegis of the United Nations, but without great success:

1) in 1978 the Convention on Succession of States in Respect of Treaties finally entered into force in 1996, which still has only twenty-two Parties, and neither Spain nor the UK; and
2) the Convention on Succession of States in Respect of State Property, Archives and Debt was concluded in 1983 but never entered into force (only seven States actually concluded it).

Questions must thus be solved on a case-by-case basis: see A. Sáenz de Santamaría, 'Problemas actuales de la sucesión de Estados', in *Curso de Derecho Internacional* (Bizkaia: Universidad del País Vasco, 1995).

[9] When the Republic of Ireland separated from the UK, the remainder of the UK was the successor State.

conditions and duties (whether in the United Nations, the European Union or NATO, etc.). This is not the case for the newborn State established by the secession, which would have to introduce its candidacy to those international organisations and negotiate new treaties with third States and organisations.[10]

The successor State would thus remain a Member State of the EU, in accordance with the pre-existing specific conditions: participation or non-participation in the Schengen area, use or not of the euro as its currency, possible exemptions from EU law or a rebate for the financing of the EU budget, etc. The number of members of the European Parliament elected on its territory, and the weight of its vote in the Council, would be adjusted in accordance with the rules in force, as well as other pertinent figures.[11]

## III What Would Happen to the Citizens of a Newborn State after the Splitting-Up of an EU Member State?

The citizens of the successor State, as continuing nationals of an EU Member State, would remain citizens of the Union, with all the rights and duties attached to that citizenship.[12] Alongside them, the citizens of the new State born from the partition would lose their previous nationality and acquire the nationality of the newborn State. By the same token, as they will cease to be nationals of a Member State of the EU, they would no longer be EU citizens.[13] Contrary to what has sometimes been said elsewhere, EU law does not provide for 'acquired rights' for former EU citizens, and does not establish a 'principle of continuity' of EU citizenship in this respect. Article 20(1) TFEU is clear: 'Every person holding the nationality of a Member State shall be a citizen of the Union. Citizenship

[10] See Bühler, *State succession and membership in international organisations. Legal theories versus political pragmatism* (The Hague: Kluwer Law International, 2001).

[11] The modalities of participation in the budget of the EU (Article 310 TFEU), the number of members of the Committee of the Regions (Article 301 TFEU) and of the Economic and Social Committee (Article 305 TFEU), subscription to the capital of the European Investment Bank (Article 5 of Protocol 5 to the EU Treaties), participation in various European funds, etc.

[12] Articles 20 to 25 TFEU.

[13] See, C. Brölmann and T. Vandamme (eds.), *Secession within the EU-Intersection Points of International Law and European Law* (Amsterdam: Amsterdam Centre for European Law and Governance, 2014). See in particular P. Garcia Andrade, 'State Succession and EU Citizenship', Ibid.: ('The loss of the nationality of a Member State implies the loss of EU citizenship'); and A. Schrauwen, 'Secession and the Loss of Rights for EU Citizens', Ibid.

of the Union shall be additional and not replace national citizenship'. This means that no one may be an EU citizen without having the nationality of an EU Member State.[14]

It would be inconceivable that this rule could be circumvented by another Member State, which would decide to grant its nationality to all citizens of a State which is not within its jurisdiction. Trying to allow citizens of a State which is not an EU Member State to enjoy the rights described in Articles 20 to 25 TFEU would be contrary to the EU Treaties.[15] These rights comprise the right to move, to work and to reside freely within the EU, to vote and to stand as candidates in elections to the European Parliament and in the municipal elections of their Member State of residence, to benefit from the protection of diplomatic and consular protection of all Member States when travelling abroad, etc. The opposite legal thesis would mean for example that were the UK to one day withdraw from the EU, one of the Member States might take the unilateral decision to grant its own nationality to the 65 million British citizens! This, on top of being contrary to the Treaties, would lead to absurdities, for example, on the right to vote in political elections.

For Spain, some observers stressed that, according to Article 11(2) of the Constitution, no Spanish citizen can be deprived of his nationality. However, it would appear obvious that if the Spanish State were to be partitioned, the change to its Constitution, which would in any case necessarily precede the partition, would at the same time, provide that the new nationality of the citizens of the newborn State would preclude Spanish nationality. This has been the consistent practice in international relations so far.

Therefore, from the date of Scottish independence, Scottish citizens would, in the absence of a new treaty providing for interim measures, lose their EU citizenship and the rights attached to it. However, this does not necessarily mean that Scottish people would be expelled from the EU State where they live and work. The European Court of Human Rights (ECtHR) decided in 2012[16] that already acquired permanent residence rights remain valid for individuals even after they lose the nationality which had provided them with those rights. This judgment

[14] For another opinion, though legally weak, see A. O'Neill: 'A Quarrel in a Faraway Country? Scotland, Independence and the EU' (14 November 2011) *Eutopia law blog*, <http://eutopialaw.com/2011/11/14/685/>, accessed 23 July 2015.

[15] And probably also contrary to the applicable national constitutional rules.

[16] *KURIĆ and others* v. *Slovenia* (App. No. 26828/06) ECtHR 26 June, 2012.

is not based on the EU Treaties: the ECtHR based it on Article 8 of the ECHR.[17] The same would equally be valid for EU citizens living in Scotland at the date of independence. However, this would be based on the application of the European Convention and not on EU law and on a continuation of EU citizenship.

## IV Difficult Problems Would Be Raised by the Candidacy to the EU of a Newborn State

If it fulfilled the necessary conditions, the newborn non-successor State could decide to apply to become a member of the EU, according to the procedure provided for in Article 49 TEU. This would raise difficult problems given the *negative effects* for the EU. Were an EU Member State to split, and then the EU to accept the accession of the non-successor State, it would not only constitute a major political change for the newborn State. It would also weaken one of the most powerful Member States of the EU (in the cases under consideration, Spain or the UK) and also politically weaken the EU as such,[18] along with its institutions.

The composition and balance of all the institutions of the EU would be negatively affected:

- The composition of the European Parliament: each accession of a sparsely populated State shifts the EU further from the democratic principle of 'one person, one vote'.[19]
- The increased number of Commissioners, who are already too many, would further complicate the functioning of the Commission, aggravating the relative weakening this institution has experienced since the mid1990s.
- In the European Council and the Council, the number of cases where a veto could be used would increase, in an EU where the most delicate and important decisions must be taken unanimously or by common

[17] Signed in Rome on 4 November 1950.

[18] Other international organisations, such as NATO, might also be affected.

[19] See the case law of the German Federal Constitutional Court, in particular its judgment of 30 June 2009 on the Lisbon Treaty, at para. 276 et seq., especially at para. 284: 'the weight of the vote of a citizen from a Member State with a low number of inhabitants may be about twelve times the weight of the votes of a citizen from a Member State with a large number of inhabitants' (translation in English provided on the Court's website: <www.bundesverfassungsgericht.de/SharedDocs/Entscheidungen/EN/2009/06/es20090630_2bve000208en.html>, accessed 5 July 2015).

agreement.[20] Moreover, the number of people around the table would increase, thus making discussions and negotiations more difficult.[21]

This, obviously, would not be a reason for not enlarging the EU, given the benefits of actual EU enlargements for everybody. However, no 'enlargement' would happen in that case. It would only entail negative effects for the EU, without any of the positive political and economic benefits of a enlargement. Political stability, democratic principles, the Rule of Law and good economic governance would be extended neither to a new geographic area nor to new individuals. No one in Europe would benefit from it. The reality is that the result of the partition of an EU Member State, followed by the accession to the EU of the part of that State which would have become independent would have obvious negative repercussions on the EU, but no positive ones. It would see one of its members becoming weaker, its own balkanisation would be encouraged, it would become more difficult to govern and it would be less able to make important decisions quickly. On the flip side of the coin, it is quite difficult to imagine which advantages this would bring to the EU. The EU would therefore have no interest in encouraging or admitting the partition of one of its Member States, on the contrary.

## V Difficult Bilateral Issues of Succession Would Have to Be Solved before the Procedure of Accession to the EU Could Begin

The bilateral problems which need to be solved in partitioning a State, between the successor State and the newborn State, as in the two cases examined here, would be numerous and difficult. Most of these problems would be of such importance that they would have to be solved through an amicable agreement between the predecessor and the new State as a prerequisite to starting any eventual process of accession to the EU.

Let us consider the example of Scotland, were it to have voted to become an independent State in the 18 September 2014 referendum.[22]

[20] See the list in Appendix 8, Jean-Claude Piris, *The Lisbon Treaty* (Cambridge: CUP, 2010), pp. 386–397 (for a new edition of this book in Italian, up to date in 2013: *Il Trattato di Lisbona* (Milan: Giuffré, 2013), Appendix 8 is at pages 461–474).

[21] Television screens are already necessary to allow all the participants to see the person speaking during meetings.

[22] See Centre for European Reform, 'The EU and an independent Scotland' (23rd July 2014) <http://centreforeuropeanreform.blogspot.be/2014/07/the-eu-and-independent-scotland.html>, accessed 25 July 2016: 'the EU will adamantly refuse to mediate between London and Edinburgh [. . .] So full prior London/Edinburgh agreement on, for example,

Bilateral issues to be addressed between the British authorities and the future Scottish authorities had, apparently, not been a subject of any prior negotiation before the referendum, even informally. The resolution of the key issues analysed below would therefore have had to have been negotiated after the referendum, but before the negotiations of accession to the EU with its twenty-eight members:[23]

### A. *The Issue of the Future Currency of an Independent Scotland Would Have Been of Direct Concern for the EU*

If the predecessor Member State had used the euro as its currency, the question whether the new non-successor State could also retain the euro as its currency or if it would have to create its own currency would have arisen. The latter hypothesis would, in the absence of an international treaty having entered into force in due time, be the only legally correct answer, albeit itself raising complex political and economic issues.[24] In any case, even if the successor State did not have the euro as its currency, the newborn State, as a candidate for membership, would be obliged to establish its own central bank and to respect all the relevant provisions of the EU Treaties.[25] The issue of the future currency of an independent Scotland would have been both a bilateral issue between the UK and Scotland and an issue for the EU as such.

Before the 2014 referendum, the Scottish Government had declared that, if Scotland became independent, it would like to continue to use the Pound Sterling and to remain in a monetary union with the remainder of the UK. The British authorities had firmly and immediately rejected this prospect. Taking the crisis of the Eurozone as an example not to be followed, they pointed out that a monetary union without a corresponding economic and fiscal (budgetary) union would entail

the division of UK assets and liabilities, and future currency and regulatory arrangements, would be a certain Brussels pre-condition for membership'.

23 See S. Tierney, previously cited, at p. 9: 'as the Electoral Commission has suggested, there would still be a range of issues to be resolved between Scotland and the UK concerning the terms of independence, which could mean that these negotiations will by no means be straightforward'.

24 Two States which are not members of the EU are currently using the euro as their currency, without having been authorised to do so by the EU: Kosovo and Montenegro. Very small States, such as Monaco or the Holy See, have been authorised through an agreement concluded with the EU, to use the euro as their currency.

25 See, in particular, Article 131 TFEU, as well as Article 140 and the following Articles of the same Treaty.

serious risks. Bilateral negotiations would therefore have been necessary, and an outcome difficult to envisage, given that remaining in a budgetary and economic union with the remainder of the UK had been expressed as unacceptable by the Scottish Government. The independentists made declarations implying that were the UK to insist, Scotland might consider refusing to share a part of the public debt.[26] It is impossible to know how the bilateral negotiation would have finished.

On the EU side, any new Member State, when accepting to be bound by the EU Treaties, undertakes to adopt the euro as its currency on the day it fulfils the necessary conditions required by the Treaties. Would Scotland have requested a waiver from that Treaty obligation? Would such a request have been accepted by the twenty-eight Member States? Would a statement by Scotland on its willingness to adopt the euro in an uncertain future have been enough?[27] What about the requirement for all EU Member States to have an independent Central Bank, if Scotland were to go on using the Pound with the UK's agreement? Would it have its own independent Central Bank, different from the UK's? These questions are difficult to answer and could be used as legal objections by any EU Member State not be keen (for domestic reasons) to accept the admission of a new State born from a secession.

### B. *The Question of Boundaries between an Independent Scotland and the Remainder of the United Kingdom Would Also Have Been of Direct Concern for the EU*

According to Article 7 of Protocol No. 19 attached to the EU Treaties (already quoted), any candidate State must undertake to be part of the Schengen area when it will have fulfilled the necessary conditions required by the Treaties.[28] Thus, in principle, once it would have fulfilled these conditions, Scotland would have had to establish border controls

[26] See C. Kaeb and D. Scheffer, 'Scottish Independence Insta-Symposium: The Legal Terrain Following a Yes Vote for Scottish Independence' (2016) *Opinio Juris*, <http://opiniojuris.org/2014/09/15/scottish-independence-insta-symposium-legal-terrain-following-yes-vote-scottish-independence/>, accessed 25 July 2016: 'if Westminster insists that UK will be the continuator State of the United Kingdom and refuse a currency deal, Scotland can beg off sharing the UK debt and let Westminster shoulder the entire estimated burden of £ 1.6 trillion bt 2016–2017'.

[27] See Centre for European Reform (note 22).

[28] Currently, six Member States are not part of the Schengen area: four because they do not yet fulfil the necessary conditions (Bulgaria, Croatia, Cyprus and Romania), and two, the Republic of Ireland and the United Kingdom, because they obtained an opt-out (Protocol No. 20). The three EEA EFTA States (Iceland, Liechtenstein and Norway) participate in the Schengen area on the basis of specific agreements concluded with the EU. A few very small States, such as the Principality of Monaco, also participate in the Schengen area.

with the remainder of the United Kingdom, including on the land border with England, given the fact that the UK is not part of the Schengen area. Would Scotland have requested an exemption from that obligation? This would probably have been the case. With good political will, a compromise could have been found, for example with the promise to join the Schengen area 'if and when' Ireland and the United Kingdom would.[29]

However, nobody knows if all EU Member States would demonstrate good political will in such a case. What about if their political authorities felt, rightly or wrongly, that the very existence of their State could be affected in the future by what they would consider as a political encouragement – or at least open a door – to secessionism? It is a fact that, legally, such a compromise would require a formal derogation from the EU Treaties, to be included in an Accession Treaty, and that it would therefore have to be ratified by each of the Twenty-Eight. Such ratification would certainly raise delicate political questions in some EU Member States, at least in Cyprus, Greece and Spain.

### *C. The Military and Defence Issue and the Fate of the British Military Bases in Scotland Would Have Been a Difficult and Sensitive Problem*

The supporters of Scottish independence declared that they wanted to close the British military submarine bases based in Scotland, if it became an independent State. This would have forced the departure of the British nuclear submarines, which constitute an essential element of the British policy of military deterrence. This would have been a strategic problem for the UK and NATO. Would an independent Scotland have applied to become a Member of NATO? In any case, this would have weakened the security of Europe, in a period when it is more important to strengthen it.

### *D. Finally, the Difficult Issue of Sharing the Public Debt, State Property and Public Archives of the UK Predecessor State between the Rump UK, as the Successor State, and Scotland, as the Newborn State, Would Also Have to Be Solved*

History has shown that these questions may be difficult to solve. As indicated above, international law and historic precedents would not have been of any help. These are problems which need to be solved on a case-by-case basis through bilateral negotiations.[30] Preliminary

[29] See Centre for European Reform (note 22).

[30] See R. Hazell, 'Press Release: Uncertainties in SNP White Paper strengthen argument for second referendum' (26 November 2013) <https://www.ucl.ac.uk/constitution-unit/constitution-unit-news/261113>, accessed 5 July 2015: 'The Czech-Slovak divorce [. . .]

declarations on the issue (for instance, Scotland's possible refusal to share the burden of the UK public debt) showed how difficult the problem of public debt could have been.

## VI What Would the Situation of the Newborn State's Economic Operators and Citizens Be, before the Entry into Force of Any New Arrangement or Accession Treaty with the EU?

The situation referred to above is one where a part of the territory of a Member State (e.g. Scotland) secedes on a date when neither an accession treaty, nor another international agreement with the EU, even *ad interim*, would have been concluded and entered into force. In that case, the newborn State would unavoidably become, at least temporarily, a third country vis-à-vis the EU. That would be an undesirable outcome which the Parties concerned should try to avoid, but it would probably happen, at least for a period.

What would the legal situation be if that happened? To tell the truth, there is no legal basis whatsoever to find the persistence of 'acquired rights of EU citizenship'. All persons having lost the citizenship of an EU Member State at the date of the independence of the newborn State, would have automatically lost their EU citizenship at the same time. As a result, they would not be able to keep the advantages of their lost EU citizenship.[31] This includes the right of movement from, and to, all EU Member States, the right to vote and to be a candidate in the European Parliament, etc.

Accordingly, the short answer to the question above is that economic operators and natural and legal persons of both Scotland and of all EU Member States would, as from the date of Scotland's independence, have to adapt themselves to a new legal situation. They would no longer benefit from the rights attached to the EU citizenship. Their situation would be governed by a new legal framework. That framework might still

required 31 Treaties and 12,000 legal agreements to effect the separation. Many of the agreements were still being negotiated years later'.

[31] For another legal opinion, see J. Herbst, 'Observations on the Right to Withdrawal from the EU: Who are the "Masters of the Treaties"?', *German Law Journal*, 6(2001), 1755. The author's reasoning is (wrongly in my view) based on a single sentence in the judgment in Case C-26/62, the famous *Van Gend and Loos*, which was in no way (obviously in a 1963 judgment) addressing this question, but stating that Community law was a new legal order of international law which concerned not only the States but also their nationals, and that this law was becoming part of their 'legal heritage' (I would add 'as long as they remain EU citizens, i.e. nationals of a Member State of the EU!').

partly be based on the national laws still in force, despite having been adopted in order to apply EU Directives, as long as those laws were not abrogated.

Those who had a right to permanent residence could keep it, as a right derived from the ECHR (see the case law of the ECHR, e.g. *Kuric*). They could continue to exercise their rights, based on their particular contracts and in conformity with the applicable national and local laws and regulations. Those with no right to permanent residence, and especially the unemployed, could in theory be forced to leave, according to national and local rules on immigration.

The right to work of non-national residents would be dependent upon the national law of the new State, like the rights they would have acquired while working in other EU States. In the same vein, Regulation 883/2004 on social security would no longer apply to citizens of the newborn State, as Article 2 of that Regulation limits its scope to nationals of a Member State, stateless persons and refugees. Pensions and social security benefits might therefore be limited by the newly applicable national law, if no agreement were concluded between the EU Member State concerned and the newborn State.[32]

Some EU laws would continue to apply to Scottish citizens, because their provisions grant nationals of third countries certain rights and benefits. This is the case for the right of residence or the right to work, because there are EU directives on family reunification, on long-term residents, and on students.

As this would likely lead to difficult human situations and to legal disputes, it is probable that solutions, at least *ad interim*, would be found.

Agreements to that effect would be based on classic international law and in particular on the principle of reciprocity. This means that all rights obtained in favour of Scottish citizens in EU countries (which will, on some subjects at least, not be able to negotiate individually with Scotland as they are all bound together by EU law) will have to be granted to nationals of all twenty-eight EU Member States. In the absence of such an immediate ad hoc agreement, even *ad interim*, the situation of some individuals could become difficult. If an agreement was not concluded between the EU and Scotland in the short to medium term, this difficulty would get worse.

As for the EU citizens residing in the newborn State, they would lose their right to free movement and residence in that State, as well as their

[32] See A. Schrauwen, 'Secession and the Loss of Rights for EU Citizens', (note 13).

right to vote and to stand as candidates in elections to the European Parliament and in municipal elections.[33]

## VII What Other Options, Other than EU Membership, Would Be Possible for the Establishment of a Structured Relationship between the EU and a New State Born from the Partition of an EU Member State?

To the extent that the new State would decide not to become a candidate to the EU, or that it failed in its bid for admission, it could become a candidate to join the European Economic Area (EEA). This would allow it to join the three European Economic Area (EEA), European Free Trade Association (EFTA) States (Iceland, Liechtenstein and Norway), which are both in EFTA and in the EEA. This would allow it to participate largely in the internal market. It would then be required to follow the EU legislation for the internal market, as well as the future evolution of that legislation, without being able to significantly influence its adoption and content.

The finalisation of such participation would take time, as it would require the negotiation of treaties of accession both to EFTA and to the EEA. These Treaties would then have to be ratified by the three aforementioned States, as well as by the twenty-eight Member States of the EU and by the EU itself.[34] The process would be facilitated because the newborn State would already be applying the current pertinent EU legislation. Signature could also be accompanied by a provisional application of some of the contents of the Agreement, before its entry into force.[35]

Any other legal alternative would be less advantageous for the newborn State. None of these alternatives would allow it to participate fully, or almost fully, in the internal market, which would be detrimental to its external trade. These other options would consist in trying to negotiate and conclude either:

- multiple sectorial agreements with the EU ('Swiss option');[36]

[33] See J.-T. Arrighi et al., 'Franchise and electoral participation of third-country citizens in the European Union and of European Union citizens residing in third countries', (*European Parliament Study*, 2013).

[34] The Treaty of accession to EFTA would also need to be negotiated with and ratified by Switzerland.

[35] For the EU, this is legally possible on the basis of Article 218(5) TFEU.

[36] The EU is now negotiating with Switzerland, on the basis of a mandate of negotiation provided by the Council to the Commission and to the European External Action Service

- an Association Agreement with the EU ('Ukrainian option'); or
- an Agreement with the EU on the establishment of a customs union and a free trade agreement ('Turkish option').[37]

## VIII Conclusion

To conclude, I will make four observations. First, neither international law, nor EU law, forbid the partition of an EU Member State. A new State born from such a partition could ask to become an EU Member State, alongside the predecessor State. In that case, the procedure followed for its birth, as well as its constitution, will have to respect the Rule of Law and, to begin with, the Constitution of the State of which it was previously an integral part.

Second, in both the cases examined in this chapter, Catalonia and Scotland, neither Spain nor the UK consulted or even informed their EU partners[38] and the EU institutions, before or after the September/November 2014 events. It would also appear that the European Council has never been informed of the issue.

Yet the EU and its other Member States were significantly concerned. The partition of one of its members would have had serious negative consequences for the EU itself. It would also have entailed risks of contagion for other Member States.

We must stress the fact that the EU is far from being a classic Intergovernmental International Organisation. The federal elements of its architecture and of its policies are developing rapidly, in particular with the solutions needed to end the Eurozone crisis. We must view the

(EEAS) in May 2014, a horizontal agreement which aims to impose on Switzerland much stricter rules than currently: delays to implementing the relevant new EU legislation, acceptance of an important role both for the European Commission and for the Court of Justice of the EU, suspension of one or all agreements if a decision of the Court is incorrectly applied.

37 Both Agreements with Turkey and Ukraine do not confer on these States a full access to the EU/EEA internal market.

38 However, it seems that this policy of discretion has now come to an end, at least concerning Spain. According to public media, the Spanish Government begun to inform its main partners. Following that, several leaders, including David Cameron, Prime Minister of the UK, François Hollande and Manuel Valls, respectively President and Prime Minister of France, Angela Merkel, Chancellor of Germany, and Barak Obama, President of the USA, have expressed themselves publicly. Their comments were warnings of the need to respect the Rule of Law and of their preference for a united and strong Spain.

regional secessionist trends in some EU Member States through a federal perspective, as demonstrated by Professor Josu De Miguel Barcera:[39] 'In international law it is often said that secession (in the context of the European Union) is an internal matter for the Member States. However, in our opinion the political and legal system of the Union can be characterized also federally, which prevents the national and regional authorities to carry out unilateral acts that go against the principle of Community federal loyalty and European citizenship'.[40] This is one additional reason why it would have been reasonable to discuss these issues in the European Council, as well as in the European Parliament and with the European Commission.

Third, in both cases, the information provided to the EU citizens was poor and politically biased. As a minimum, an official clarification of issues of EU law, by the EU itself, was needed. It would have helped the EU citizens directly concerned to make up their minds, by helping them get accurate information. It would have been opportune to make public information available on the consequences of the partition of an EU Member State, in terms of what relations the newborn State could envisage with the EU.

I strongly feel that in the future, official answers should be provided publicly to the questions raised by regional secessions which directly concern the EU.

All EU citizens should know the truth: 'rejoining' the EU, after a secession from an EU Member State, would be legally possible if pursued in accordance with the correct procedure and while respecting the Constitution of the State of origin. However, such a course should not be taken for granted, given the absence of automaticity and the huge legal and political difficulties that this would entail.

Fourth, traditional diplomatic rules of classical international law protocol[41] should no longer be applied automatically within the EU, in

[39] J. de Miguel Bárcena, 'La cuestión de la secesión en la Unión Europea: una visión constitucional', *Revista de Estudios Políticos*, 165 (2014), 1: 'Contrariamente a lo que se suele afirmar, la secesión de partes de un territorio no es una cuestión de carácter interno, sino que afecta al sistema político europeo en su conjunto, en la medida que es una forma de integración federal donde no caben actos unilaterales que quebranten el principio de lealtad federal de la Unión y la ciudadanía europea que ha ido conformándose en las últimas décadas'.

[40] Abstract in English.

[41] See, for instance, Article 2(7) Charter of the United Nations: 'Nothing contained in the present Charter shall authorize the United Nations to intervene in matters which are essentially within the domestic jurisdiction of any state [. . .]'.

the manner in which they are applied between other States or in other Intergovernmental Organisations, such as the United Nations. The political interdependence between EU Member States is now such that the taboo which prevented any exchange of views about problems which are mainly or partially 'internal' to a Member State is no longer justified. This would, in any case, be necessary when these problems, and their solutions, directly or indirectly affect other Member States, as well as the EU as such. Today, budgetary decisions and the economic policies of each member of the eurozone have a direct and significant impact on other members of the monetary zone. In the same way, a major national policy decision, as exceptional as the possible partition of a Member State, would significantly affect other Member States, as well as the EU.

Pretending that regional secessionism in a given State of the EU is a matter which is exclusively an internal affair is simply not true. Realism on this point should lead to the recognition that such an issue must be the subject of discussion for all parties affected, including in the framework of the EU institutions.[42]

The European Union cannot pretend to ignore an issue which might lead to a weakening of some of its members and of the EU itself, as well as having serious strategic and political effects on the future of Europe in the world.

[42] On this subject, see the interesting article by F. de Carreras Serra, 'Unión Europea y Secesión de Estados Miembros. ¿Deben intervenir las Instituciones Europeas?', *UNED, Teoría y Realidad Constitucional*, 33(2014), 271–282. See Abstract in English: 'The European Union has reached such a high degree of integration that a secession on any of its Member States would cause very negative consequences. In this case, should the European Institutions consider this problem as merely an internal problem of the Member State, in accordance with international law? Or should they take part and intervene, with appropriate mechanisms, in order to protect the European Union and its objectives? This is the dilemma that the author of this article faces'.

7

# The Reach and Resources of European Law in the Scottish Independence Referendum

KENNETH A. ARMSTRONG

## I Introduction

Referendums tend to be dominated by internal constitutional preoccupations. The domestic constitutional context can be both the object of a referendum and the source of norms for its substantive and procedural legality.[1] In the specific context of the 2014 referendum on Scottish independence, much was made of the idea that the referendum was to be 'made in Scotland'.[2] Indeed, this interior perspective could give rise to a certain hostility towards 'external' voices and perspectives. Yet the exterior normative world of European law reached into and provided significant resources which framed important aspects of the independence referendum.

The term 'resources' is used as a way of opening up the analysis of the impact of European law beyond a world of formal compliance with rules and norms. It refers to a range of legal sources – primarily EU sources but also including references to Council of Europe instruments – and includes not only first order procedural and substantive standards of legality but also legal concepts such as 'citizenship' and legal ideologies which seek to place European law at the analytical

[1] See generally, Stephen Tierney, *Constitutional Referendums: The Theory and Practice of Republican Deliberation*, (Oxford: OUP, 2012).

[2] For example, we find this in the Scottish Government's publication *Scotland's Future: from the Referendum to Independence and a Written Constitution*: 'Under the Edinburgh Agreement, the referendum will be made in Scotland', <www.gov.scot/Resource/0041/00413757.pdf>, accessed 25 August 2015. The UK Government also used similar language in its consultation document on the referendum where it states that: 'We want to assist people in Scotland, in all reasonable ways, to participate in a referendum "Made in Scotland", whose outcome is legal, fair and decisive': HM Government, *Scotland's Constitutional Future* <www.gov.uk/government/uploads/system/uploads/attachment_data/file/39248/Scotlands_Constitutional_Future.pdf>, accessed 25 August 2015.

forefront. It is how these resources are deployed in a process of constitutional contestation by political and social actors – the 'Yes' and 'No' sides of the campaign; academic lawyers, legal practitioners and courts; the media and the public – which is of interest. To put it more concretely, this chapter evaluates the reach and resources of European law in three specific examples of debates conducted in the course of the Scottish independence referendum campaign. The first example concerns debates about the legality of secession/independence. The second example unavoidably grapples with the exterior world of EU law in the form of the question of whether there could be continuity in the application of EU law to an independent Scotland whether through accession or treaty renegotiation. The third example is an expansion of the second example and highlights the role played by different EU law subjects – 'citizens' and 'Member States' – either in supporting or in resisting claims concerning the effects of independence upon the continuous enjoyment of EU law rights.

The aim of this chapter is to stand back and evaluate what we can say about and learn from the referendum experience in terms of the reach and deployment of the resources of European law within 'internal' constitutional politics. The approach taken in this analysis is broadly informed by scholarship on 'Europeanisation'.[3] Political science scholarship has identified three main potential objects of Europeanisation: policy, politics and polity, with a somewhat greater attention towards the Europeanisation of policy and politics rather than the national polity. From a legal perspective, Europeanisation analysis typically concerns itself with domestic compliance with EU law and has also largely focused on studies which evaluate the impact of substantive EU law on a particular area of national policy, or the familiar strand of scholarship which focuses on the domestic judicial reception of EU structural doctrines such as direct effect or supremacy. Here it is the polity which is brought to the fore, in an effort to look beyond issues of compliance, to understand how the resources of EU law are deployed within polities at a moment of constitutional contestation – a referendum campaign.

[3] See generally: Theofanis Exadaktylos and Claudio M. Radaelli, 'Research Design in European Studies: The Case of Europeanization', *Journal of Common Market,* Studies, 47(2009), 507; Kevin Featherstone and Claudio M. Radaelli (eds.), *The Politics of Europeanization* (Oxford: OUP, 2003); Paolo Graziano and Maarten Peter Vink (eds.), *Europeanization: new research agendas* (London: Palgrave Macmillan, 2007).

This chapter also adds to a rich and increasingly important body of research on referendums in the EU,[4] particularly research which explores the role and relevance of referendums in the constitutional politics of the EU. This chapter flips this round and explores the role and relevance of Europe in domestic constitutional politics during referendum campaigns. However, the contribution is modest. It does not aspire to develop a robust conceptual or analytical taxonomy and instead adopts a more narrative and discursive analysis focusing on a single study of the Scottish independence referendum. However, as an organising device it seeks to highlight three different potential uses of the resources of EU law in the constitutional politics of referendums. It suggests that these external resources may be harnessed to: (1) inform and direct; (2) contest and constrain; or (3) amplify and resonate, domestic political narratives, choices and claims.

The European resources which 'inform and direct' are those which are absorbed into the domestic system and shape how the constitutional system operates, even when managing a seemingly internal constitutional issue. This could include norms and rules about how referendums should be conducted. It connotes an idea that even national constitutional systems might become Europeanised in the sense of evolving and adapting by absorbing processes and standards which have their origins outside the national constitutional order. The use of European resources to 'contest and constrain' suggests that such exterior resources emerge as alternative or indeed rival claims to those being advanced in a domestic constitutional discourse. At its strongest, it is the idea of European law as a 'trump' which takes certain matters out of domestic contestation. European legal resources would therefore displace inconsistent national legal rules and otherwise place external legal limits on domestic political choices. By contrast, resources which 'amplify and resonate' highlight the coexistence of intra- and extra-constitutional values, norms and processes and explore the manner in which each can be viewed as expressive of the other, highlighting patterns of consistency and compatibility, but without a hierarchical relationship between the internal and external normative dimensions. So for example, it would be the consistency of a domestic constitutional claim with the norms, values or procedures encoded in European resources which would help amplify or indeed bootstrap the domestic claim.

[4] For example, Carlos Closa, 'Why convene referendums? Explaining choices in EU constitutional politics', *Journal of European Public Policy*, 14(2007), 1311; Fernando Mendez et al., *Referendums and the European Union: A Comparative Inquiry* (Cambridge: CUP, 2014).

Overall, the analysis suggests that attempts to use European legal resources to contest and constrain political choice have generally failed to have the sort of 'trumping' effect that those relying upon them might have wished. Instead, we find more examples of the use of these resources to amplify and resonate with domestic narratives, choices and claims.

## II The Legality of Independence

The Scottish independence referendum gave rise to legal questions and issues of legality.[5] In the discussion that follows, two obvious legal dimensions are explored. The first is the procedural dimension and highlights issues relating to the legality of the process of separating, including the legality and constitutionality of a referendum on independence. The analysis draws attention to the facilitative nature of the UK's political constitution and the absence of either strong domestic or external legal controls on how a referendum is conducted, and indeed what triggers a referendum.

The second dimension explores issues of substantive legality and the normative 'fit' between independence claims and the international and European legal systems. The core contention is that the EU legal order's claim to autonomy, and its extension of legal subjectivity beyond states to citizens, played powerfully in the Scottish independence debate as a rival account of the legality of secession/independence to that habitually offered by public international law. The views of experts from the fields of public international law and of European law were advanced by their authors and then borrowed and contested by academics, policymakers and politicians. Yet the narrative of a European legal order open to the accommodation of independence claims has itself been strongly resisted by European legal scholars, for whom there is a fundamental incompatibility between disruptive nationalism and the discipline of European constitutionalism.

### A. *The Legality of the Referendum Process*

It is worth briefly narrating the salient aspects of the Scottish independence referendum process. Not only is this necessary to illustrate the wider discussion, it usefully contrasts the Scottish situation with the rather more difficult legal obstacles which have been encountered by

[5] For an exploration of some of the more detailed legal aspects of the Scottish independence referendum, see especially, Stephen Tierney, 'Legal Issues Surrounding the Referendum on Independence for Scotland', *EuConst*, (2013), 9359.

separatist movements in Catalonia, where the legality of an independence referendum has been successfully constitutionally challenged.

## I General Constitutional Context

The United Kingdom lacks a single written constitutional text which could act as a normative benchmark against which to evaluate the legality of a referendum on Scottish independence. Instead, the UK has a very flexible and largely procedural constitution, which empowers the Executive to look to the UK Parliament to enact, repeal and revise laws across a range of issues, including those which might otherwise form the content of a written constitution. This allows the political landscape to be changed without strong internal legal controls.[6]

Although referendums are not quite the constitutional novelty they once were in the UK, there have only ever been three UK-wide referendums: to confirm the UK's EU membership in 1975; to consider (but reject) the use of an alternate vote system in general elections; and in June 2016, a referendum on whether the UK should remain a member of the European Union. Indeed, as Bogdanor has pointed out,[7] in a constitutional system premised on the sovereignty of Parliament, until the 1970s there was a view that referendums were not really constitutional. The difficulty of reconciling referendums with parliamentary sovereignty has been well illustrated in the aftermath of the 2016 EU membership referendum with legal actions being brought to demand that the UK Parliament be given a role before the Article 50 TFEU withdrawal mechanism is triggered by the UK Government.

It was with the move towards the devolution of powers to Scotland and Wales from 1997 onwards that changes to the constitutional landscape were accompanied by resort to referendums, whose legality was prescribed in law through legislation enacted by the Westminster Parliament.[8] However, it ought to be clear that significant constitutional

[6] It should be noted that certain statutes have been treated by UK courts as 'constitutional statutes' in the sense that their provisions can only be repealed expressly and not merely impliedly by later laws. As Feldman highlights, the UK does not have a category of 'organic' laws similar to that found in Continental European jurisdictions which have an enhanced constitutional status and which are the product of special legislative processes: D. Feldman, 'The Nature and Significance of "Constitutional" Legislation', *Law Quarterly Review*, 129 (2013), 343.

[7] Vernon Bogdanor, 'The Referendum on Europe, 1975', *The Gresham Lectures*, www.gresham.ac.uk/lectures-and-events/the-referendum-on-europe-1975, accessed 5 February 2016.

[8] Referendums (Scotland and Wales) Act 1997. The situation in Northern Ireland was different. The referendum which preceded the establishment of the devolved institutions

change can occur in the UK in the absence of referendums. The legality of constitutional change, including territorial separation, is somewhat distinct from the legality of the process that produces such change.

There is no general legislative framework or judgment of the Supreme Court which mandates the circumstances in which a referendum will be triggered. The one exception is the European Union Act 2011. It specifies the circumstances in which any future transfer of powers from the UK to the EU will – or will not – require a referendum to be held. Of course, this does not implement any requirement of EU law since the treaties leave it to the national constitutional systems to decide the circumstances in which EU-related referendums are held. However, it highlights the significance of the European context as a source of influence upon domestic constitutional politics. Importantly, the Act seeks to take the otherwise discretionary political decision of the Executive to hold a referendum out of its hands and instead legally mandates referendums in specific circumstances as a choice of the Legislature. Yet this framework is neither relevant for a referendum on UK membership of the EU itself – which followed the normal path of specific legislative enactment[9] – nor is it relevant for an independence referendum other than to highlight the increasing normalisation of referendums within the UK constitutional landscape.

The UK Parliament's other relevant intervention is in the form of the Political Parties, Elections and Referendum Act 2000. Although the primary purpose of the Act is to regulate donations to, and campaign expenditure by, political parties, it also established an Electoral Commission and lays down a limited number of generic requirements as to the conduct of referendums, including giving the Electoral Commission a role in the setting of referendum questions. While this Act did not directly govern the Scottish independence referendum, as discussed further, its principles and the institutions it created were not irrelevant to the specific legal framework adopted for the conduct of the referendum.

What this brief discussion highlights is that the legal frameworks governing referendums in the UK tend to evidence a relatively bespoke approach to the management of constitutional issues rather than the operation of generic legal frameworks. In part this is due to the absence of a longer-run tradition of referendums and in part due to the highly instrumental, and facilitative nature, of the UK constitution. However,

was a product of an international agreement negotiated between the British and Irish Governments: the Belfast ('Good Friday') Agreement.

[9] The European Union Referendum Act 2015.

it also means that from a procedural perspective the legality of a referendum is not wholly distinct nor abstracted from the immediacy of the constitutional circumstances giving rise to the referendum. As we will now see, the consensual approach adopted between the Scottish and Westminster governments ensured that the Scottish independence referendum had a secure legal foundation. In other circumstances, it might prove less easy to provide that foundation.

## II The Legal Framework for the Independence Referendum

Turning from the general constitutional context to the more specific legal framework applicable to the Scottish independence referendum, the Scotland Act 1998 importantly reserves matters relating to 'the Constitution' to the Westminster Parliament. More particularly, Schedule 5 to the Act reserves matter relating to the Union between Scotland and England to the UK Parliament. That would seem to be a clear impediment to the competence of the Scottish Parliament to legislate for a binding referendum on independence. However, instead of this legal default resulting in constitutional contestation and litigation, it triggered a process by which the governments in Scotland and the UK would ultimately adopt a political agreement – the Edinburgh Agreement – which would pave the way for a legal referendum whose result would be accepted by both governments. The result of the Edinburgh Agreement was that an Order in Council was made under Section 30 of the Scotland Act 1998 to amend Schedule 5 to allow the Scottish Parliament to legislate for a referendum under certain conditions, not least of which was that there must only be one ballot paper giving voters a choice between only two responses. This ensured that the referendum would be a straight up and down vote on independence. The Scottish Parliament subsequently enacted the Scottish Independence Referendum Act 2013 and the Scottish Independence Referendum (Franchise) Act 2013.

The Edinburgh Agreement specifically acknowledged the relevance of the Political Parties, Elections and Referendum Act, and both governments agreed that the referendum rules should be based on the Act, but modified to the particular circumstances of the Scottish referendum. Specifically, in terms of the referendum question, the then Deputy First Minister of Scotland, Nicola Sturgeon requested the advice of the Electoral Commission on the referendum question.[10]

[10] Electoral Commission, *Referendum on Independence for Scotland: Advice of the Electoral Commission on the Referendum Question* <www.electoralcommission.org.uk/__data/

The point of rehearsing what is a relatively familiar account, both of UK constitutional law and of the more particular context of the referendum on Scottish independence, is to highlight that the legality of the referendum was ultimately not at issue from a domestic constitutional perspective. The flexible and procedural nature of the UK constitution allows legislation to be an instrument of executive power, largely free of internal constitutional restraint. What then of external legal resources and their conditioning of the legality of the referendum?

## III External Legal Resources

In exercising its functions, the Electoral Commission has had regard to the Code of Good Practice on Referendums prepared by the Council of Europe's 'Venice Commission'.[11] In giving its advice on the Scottish Independence Referendum, the Electoral Commission noted the recommendations of the Venice Commission to avoid referendum questions which suggested an answer, and to ensure the availability of objective information in advance of voting.[12] In terms of setting the referendum question, the Electoral Commission tested the original version of the referendum question: 'Do you agree that Scotland should be an independent country? Yes/No'. It concluded that the inclusion of 'Do you agree' might result in a leading question and it proposed instead that the question be simplified to: 'Should Scotland be an independent country? Yes/No'. This formulation was adopted by the Scottish Government. In the context of the UK referendum on EU membership, the Electoral Commission went a step further in recommending a move away from a question which elicits Yes/No answers precisely because of risks that framing a question in such a way might be thought to push voters one way rather than another. The point is not, therefore, that European resources are being deployed to contest or constrain constitutional choices, but rather that at least the ethos of the Venice Commission recommendations has been absorbed into the work of the Electoral

assets/pdf_file/0007/153691/Referendum-on-independence-for-Scotland-our-advice-on-referendum-question.pdf>, accessed 5 February 2016.

11 European Commission for Democracy through Law (Venice Commission), *Code of Good Practice on Referendums* CDL-AD (2007) 008, www.venice.coe.int/webforms/documents/default.aspx?pdffile=CDL-AD(2007)008-e, accessed 5 February 2016.

12 Electoral Commission, *Referendum on Independence for Scotland: advice of the Electoral Commission on the proposed referendum question* (2013), www.electoralcommission.org.uk/__data/assets/pdf_file/0007/153691/Referendum-on-independence-for-Scotland-our-advice-on-referendum-question.pdf, accessed 5 February 2016.

Commission as a form of good practice when it carries out its function of advising on referendum questions.

Where we did see an attempt to deploy European resources to contest and constrain constitutional choice was in respect of potential and actual legal challenges to the referendum franchise. There was an attempt to mount a legal challenge to the exclusion from the referendum franchise of Scots resident in the UK (but outside of Scotland) but this failed to make it to court due to lack of financial resources. Legally-aided prisoners did, however, bring a legal challenge to their exclusion from the franchise, with the case ending up on appeal to the UK Supreme Court.[13] In the course of giving judgment, the judges of the Supreme Court considered arguments about the respective relationships between UK law and the law of the European Convention on Human Rights, EU law and international law more broadly. While these arguments focused specifically on the issue of the franchise, they also entailed discussion of the legality (and indeed, necessity) of a referendum as a constitutional process.

As regards the compatibility of the referendum franchise with European and international legal resources, the relevant question before the UK Supreme Court was *inter alia* whether the blanket exclusion of prisoners from the franchise was (a) a breach of the right to vote in free elections as conferred by Article 3, Protocol 1 to the European Convention on Human Rights (ECHR; (b) a breach of the right to vote in periodic elections found in Article 25 of the International Covenant on Civil and Political Rights (ICCPR); or (c) a breach of EU law. The EU law point – whether the exclusion from the franchise of Scottish prisoners was legal given that a vote for independence could result in a change in both national and EU citizenship status – was given very little close examination. The Court concluded that the issue of citizenship would form part of the post-referendum negotiations rather than being determined by the referendum itself. The more interesting aspects of the Supreme Court's judgment lie in the treatment of the ECHR and ICCPR.

For the majority, the case law of the Strasbourg Court on the scope of application of Article 3, Protocol 1 ECHR suggested that it only applied to elections to legislatures but and not to referendums. However, certain members of the Court were less willing to see this case law as quite so clear cut, noting both a capacity for development in the Strasbourg case law itself and indeed within national courts' application of Convention

[13] *Moohan and Another* v. *Lord Advocate* [2014] UKSC 67.

rights. And while the leading judgment emphasised the different legal effects of an ECHR incorporated into UK law through the Human Rights Act 1998 and an ICCPR which was not so incorporated – the traditional dualist perspective – Lord Kerr was more inclined towards a coherent interpretation of the two instruments in ways which might suggest a more dynamic interpretation of the existing Strasbourg case law than other members of the Court were apparently willing to entertain. Accordingly, although the legal challenge foundered, it is clear that external legal resources were deployed in reviewing the legality of the referendum franchise.

Two members of the Court also commented on the role and function of the independence referendum itself. Viewed from the perspective of the UK constitution, for Lord Hodge, the issue of whether Article 3, Protocol 1 ECHR, required the independence referendum franchise to be extended to prisoners had to be placed in the context of a constitutional order in which, as intimated earlier, a referendum is not itself demanded or required in order for independence to come about (a sovereign UK Parliament could simply enact legislation). Considering this from the exterior perspective of the ECHR, Lady Hale concluded that nothing in Article 3, Protocol 1 ECHR demanded a referendum prior to independence. In this way, in the absence of legal norms at either domestic or international levels mandating a referendum, the conduct of that referendum would be subject to relatively limited legal scrutiny.

In sum, the Scottish independence referendum process was in many ways a very British affair and a good illustration of the procedural, political constitution at work. But it was not a process entirely free from European influences. Although attempts to deploy European law to contest and constrain political choices about the scope of the referendum franchise failed, the resources were nonetheless invoked in the context of the litigation over the referendum franchise. Moreover, the failure of these external norms to be more demanding as to the conduct of referendums resonated with the domestic constitutional position in which referendums are discretionary and a matter of political choice. Therefore, aside from the relatively general way in which the Venice Commission's principles might be said to inform the domestic approach to the conduct of referendums in the UK – at least in terms of setting the referendum question – the resources of European law tended simply to highlight the absence of strong legal controls over the conduct of referendums and resonated with the UK's essentially political constitution.

### B. *From Process to Substance*

The analysis now turns from the legality of the referendum process to the legal issues surrounding what that process might have produced: an independent Scotland. The international status of such an independent state, its international rights and responsibilities and its membership of key international organisations, all became part of internal political contestation during the referendum campaign. However, what is particularly noteworthy is the manner in which different, and indeed rival, external normative resources were exploited to support or contest competing claims about the consequences of independence. We begin with the reach of the resources of international law into the domestic debate before turning more directly to the issue of the normative fit between secession/independence and European integration.

#### I The Resources of International Law

While international law does not create a right of unilateral secession, that does not mean that international law denies itself, or lacks, conceptual resources through which to seek to determine the consequences of territorial reconfiguration, including in circumstances where self-determination is being claimed.[14] Indeed, contemporary international law scholarship has searched for a more comprehensive approach which seeks better to relate the reasons, circumstances and context of independence claims to how the international legal order should respond (and respond over time).[15] That an independent state emerges from an internal constitutional process and through democratic means ought not to

[14] For example, James Crawford, 'State practice and international law in relation to secession', *British Yearbook of International Law*, 69(1999), 85; James R Crawford, *The Creation of States in International Law* (Oxford: OUP, 2006). Beyond academic writings, there is the important judgment of the Canadian Supreme Court in respect of the claimed right of Quebec to secede: a judgment which dealt not only with the interior constitutional law of Canada but also whether a right to secede was to be found in international law: *Reference Re Secession of Quebec* [1998] 2 SCR 217. For academic discussion of the Quebec secession case, see, for example, Sujit Choudhry and Robert Howse, 'Constitutional Theory and The Quebec Secession Reference', *Canadian Journal of Law and Jurisprudence*, 13(2000), 143; Mark D Walters, 'Nationalism and the Pathology of Legal Systems: Considering the Quebec Secession Reference and its Lessons for the United Kingdom', *Modern Law Review*, 62(1999), 371.

[15] Robert Howse and Ruti Teitel, 'Humanity Bounded and Unbounded: The Regulation of External Self-Determination under International Law,' *The Law & Ethics of Human Rights*, 7(2013), 155; Susanna Mancini, 'Secession and Self-Determination', in Michel Rosenfeld and András Sajó (eds.), *The Oxford Handbook of Comparative Constitutional Law* (Oxford: OUP, 2012).

be irrelevant from the perspective of international law. Certainly, this would be at the core of any claim by an independent Scotland to external recognition by the international community. After all, this was not to be an act of unilateral secession but a rather more consensual and negotiated process, as expressed in the Edinburgh Agreement, the legislative interventions of both the UK and Scottish Parliaments, and the referendum itself.

However, rather than the Scottish secession/independence claim being challenged from the perspective of international law, the debate focused more narrowly on how international law ought to conceptualise and treat a newly independent Scotland, particularly with a view to settling arguments about post-independence international rights and responsibilities and membership of international organisations. In an Opinion authored by eminent international lawyers James Crawford and Alan Boyle for the UK Government,[16] it was suggested that post-independence, the UK would act as a 'continuator' state with an independent Scotland as a 'successor' state. This conclusion had certain consequences.

On the one hand, this approach resonated with and amplified the domestic legality and legitimacy of the independence referendum. If the effect of independence had been instead to dissolve the United Kingdom as a legal entity – in effect, producing two new states – the legitimacy of a referendum which only enfranchised a minority of the persons affected could not plausibly be defended and it is wholly inconceivable that the Westminster Parliament would have given its consent to the referendum being held in the first place. On the other hand, the conclusion that the UK would be a continuator state was not entirely convenient for claims being made by the Scottish Government about the continuity which an independent Scotland would expect to enjoy in its international relations, and insofar as the advice supported the position being taken by the UK Government as to the continuator state status of the UK, it was described by the then Deputy First Minister, Nicola Sturgeon, as 'arrogant' and betraying a 'near-colonial attitude'.[17] The idea that the UK would simply carry on meant that it would be harder for proponents of independence to counter the logical argument that if Scotland was no longer part of the UK, it

[16] James Crawford and Alan Boyle, 'Opinion: Referendum on the Independence of Scotland – International Law Aspects' in HM Government, *Scotland Analysis: Devolution and the Implications of Independence (Annex A)*, (2013).

[17] Quoted in *The Guardian* newspaper, 'David Cameron tries to put the brakes on Alex Salmond', 11 February 2013.

would no longer be part of a Member State of the EU, and so would need to seek EU accession from the outside: something which the Scottish Government had made clear it did not believe to be correct. Moreover, institutions like the Bank of England would clearly be retained by the UK and along with it, control over the currency and monetary policy; a very difficult issue for those who might claim that the pound belonged to Scotland as much as to the rest of the UK. As for the division of assets and liabilities, while there was specific contestation around particular assets, more generally the thrust of the debate related on the assets side to the start-up costs of a newly independent state – what assets would carry over and what would have be to put in place (e.g. buildings and infrastructure); and on the liabilities side to the apportionment of deficit and debt, not least in the wake of the effects of the global economic crisis on national balance sheets.

And yet these specific issues, and the resources of international law, were increasingly sidelined by a more specific focus on the issue of an independent Scotland's EU membership and the idea that the resources of European law were more open to the possibility of continuity in an independent Scotland's international relations. As will be discussed later, the appropriate legal mechanism through which to effect EU membership was itself the subject of specific contestation. For the moment, it is important to keep the issue of the mechanism of EU membership distinct from the question of whether European law offered an alternative or rival resource to international law in its capacity to recognise and accommodate Scottish independence.

## II Secession/Independence and European Integration

A turn to European legal resources might simply be an entirely instrumentalist strategy of seeking out resources to contest, or support, claims about the legality and legal consequences of independence, but without any strong commitment to one set of resources over another. Indeed, it would hardly be a surprise to find that politicians in particular would be inclined to instrumentalise legal texts and legal opinions in order to contest and constrain the claims and narratives of their opponents while also using these resources to amplify, and resonate, their own claims and narratives. The analysis in the preceding section is indicative of such an instrumentalist deployment of European legal resources. Yet for actors within the legal community – academics as well as practitioners – there may be rather more at stake, with the availability and use of legal resources signifying stronger value commitments and expressive of (competing) ideas about the relationship between law and the experience of European integration. One dimension refers to the relative appropriateness of framing legal issues from the perspectives of either international or European law, while a second dimension considers the fit between European law/European integration and independence movements.

**A. The Normative Pull of *Vangendeology*: EU and International Law as Normative Rivals** The Crawford and Boyle analysis of the consequences of independence relied upon the concepts and categories of public international law. In so doing, their evaluation was clear that (a) membership of international institutions was a distinct and different question from issues surrounding the legal status, or statuses, to be ascribed in international law to newly formed territories, and (b) as regards the European Union, there might well be more specific considerations at play. In that respect, the analysis was parsimonious, modest and entirely open to the idea that international law could accommodate a more specific European legal answer to the particular issue of the status of an independent Scotland within the EU. By contrast, European legal actors have often tended to seek to distance EU law from public international law, with the judgment of the Court of Justice in *Van Gend en Loos* as the talisman for a legal ideology of the autonomy and distinctiveness of the EU legal order: *Vangendeology*.

*Vangendeology* manifests itself in a number of different ways and is practised by EU law practitioners and academics alike.[18] Later, the discussion will highlight its emphasis on the legal subjectivity of citizens and how that played into the referendum campaign. For the moment, attention is simply drawn to the effects of *Vangendeology* in making EU law the primary, if not sole frame of reference, for thinking about secession/ independence even if – as the Crawford and Boyle analysis itself suggested – this was something that international law was itself open to.

The apparent rivalry between international law and EU law was repeatedly played out in the specific context of whether an independent Scotland could enjoy continuity in the application of EU law through membership following independence. But in the course of that

[18] For a good example of an academic commentary on the Scottish independence referendum from the interior world of EU law, refracted through the prism of *Vangendeology*, see S. Douglas-Scott, 'Why the EU should welcome an independent Scotland', (8 September 2014) <www.verfassungsblog.de/en/eu-welcome-independent-scotland-2/>, accessed 5 February 2016.

contestation, the resources of EU law – in particular the values articulated in the EU treaties – were often referred to in ways which might, wittingly or unwittingly, support the legality and legitimacy of the independence claim itself. Indeed, it is particularly striking that the Scottish Government repeatedly emphasised the compatibility between the independence process and the values of the EU treaties. In the document it produced during the referendum campaign on 'Scotland in the European Union',[19] the Scottish Government stated that the general context within which an independent Scotland would negotiate its future relationship within the EU was to be found in the values of the EU found in Article 2 TEU. But it went further in suggesting that 'the process by which Scotland will achieve independent statehood is wholly consistent with these principles'.

For eminent European legal practitioners like Sir David Edward, the new legal order announced in *Van Gend en Loos* was the appropriate starting point for any consideration of the relationship between the EU and an independent Scotland.[20] Sir David drew on Article 2 TEU in his evidence to the Scottish Parliament,[21] emphasising in particular the principles of 'democracy', 'non-discrimination' and 'solidarity' as well as protection of the 'rights of persons belonging to minorities'. If the independence process could be portrayed as possessing a normative fit with Article 2 TEU, then for Sir David Edward the obligation of sincere cooperation and mutual respect between the EU and its Member States – also found in Article 4 TEU – suggested a negotiated path towards not just independence but also EU membership. The Scottish Government relied on this evidence to support its argument that an independent Scotland would then negotiate its EU membership from 'inside'.

In this way, as between the rival resources of public international law and EU law, the former did not appear to directly contest the legality of Scottish secession/independence while suggesting certain possibilities as to the distribution of post-independence rights and responsibilities,

19 Scottish Government, *Scotland in the European Union*, (2013) <www.gov.scot/Resource/0043/00439166.pdf>, accessed 5 February 2016.

20 David Edward, 'EU Law and the Separation of Member States', *Fordham International Law Journal*, 36(5) (2013), 1. In a similar vein which adopts and extends *Vangendeology* in preference to international law, see Daniel Kenealy and Stuart MacLennan, 'Sincere Cooperation, Respect for Democracy and EU Citizenship: Sufficient to Guarantee Scotland's Future in the European Union?', *European Law Journal*, 20 (2014), 591.

21 Scottish Parliament, European and External Relations Committee (23 January 2014) <www.scottish.parliament.uk/S4_EuropeanandExternalRelationsCommittee/Meeting%20Papers/Public_papers_23_Jan_2014.pdf>, accessed 5 February 2016.

whereas the latter appeared to amplify and resonate the domestic constitutional path to independence, while offering an alternative account at least of how an independent Scotland might secure continuity in the territorial reach of EU law.

**B. Normative Resistance: European Integration and Nationalism** Any idea of a degree of fit and affinity between the values and principles of the EU and independence movements has been challenged by Joseph Weiler. His argument, as developed in his essay in Chapter 2 of this volume, and elsewhere,[22] is essentially that there is a fundamental incompatibility between the motivations and impulses that gives rise to independence movements and the ethos of the European Union as a mechanism for disciplining nationalism. Indeed, insofar as EU membership is a vehicle through which European states have stabilised and democratised in line with the values contained in Article 2 TEU, then the less desirable it may be to accommodate secessionist movements which destabilise those states. If the EU can be said to have rescued the European nation state by turning those states into 'Member States',[23] then anything which threatens the identity and vitality of those Member States could be argued to be inauthentically European.

The difficulty with Weiler's position is that while it might leave the door open to the accession of new states born of the failure or the oppression of other states, it closes the door on a democratic and constitutional process of self-determination; or as Neil Walker suggests, 'it does not take a people's own view of their preferred collective future seriously enough'.[24] As the Scottish Government contended, '[T]hroughout its history the guiding principle of the EU has been enlargement of its membership, not contraction'. Of course, to deny Scotland EU membership would not result in a contraction of membership given that it is the UK, and not Scotland, that holds membership. Nonetheless, the claim that the EU is a product of enlargement – itself the result of a post-war territorial reconfiguration – is well made. There is no obvious reason why, on normative grounds, the EU

[22] Joseph Weiler, 'Catalonian Independence and the European Union', *European Journal of International Law*, 23(2012), 909.

[23] See Chris J. Bickerton, *European Integration: From Nation-States to Member States* (Oxford: OUP, 2012).

[24] Neil Walker, 'Scotland and the EU: Comment by Neil Walker' (9 November 2014), <www.verfassungsblog.de/scotland-eu-comment-neil-walker/>, accessed 5 February 2016. See N. Walker 'Internal Enlargement in the European Union: Beyond Legalism and Political Expediency', Chapter 3, in this volume.

should set its face against accession for newly formed European states, without some examination of the constitutional and legal qualities of the process by which independence has come about and the capacity of the new state to meet EU normative standards and substantive obligations. After all, that is the essential function of the Article 49 TEU accession process.

While these opposing perspectives can be found within academic and elite political discourses, in many ways there was very little popular political contestation around the central proposition of 'independence within Europe'. One explanation for this might well be that the issue of EU membership had itself been taken out of the hands of voters. Notwithstanding the impact of EU membership upon the exercise of sovereign authority, it was never suggested that there ought to be a referendum on whether an independent Scotland ought to be part of the EU or whether, like Norway, it might choose to exist outside the EU. Scottish membership of the EU was treated as an uncontestable political and legal fact. Rather, the point at which the issue gained more traction within the popular political discourse was the suggestion that if Scotland remained part of the UK, a future UK-wide referendum on EU membership might see the UK and Scotland outside of the EU even if a majority in Scotland were to vote to remain in the EU. The result of the EU referendum held in June 2016 was precisely that with a small UK majority in favour of leaving the EU, while voters in Scotland voted more decisively for the UK to remain a Member State.

Whether one took the view that EU law offered a fertile or hostile legal context through which to reflect on the legality of independence and its consequences, it is perhaps an indication of the normative pulling power of *Vangendeology* that the resources of European law were foregrounded while international law was relegated to a more peripheral position. This might have been the inevitable consequence of international law's own struggles with independence claims and the limits of its own resources. Yet it is not clear that EU law provided more definitive answers, and as the discussion in the section which follows illustrates, not only were the normative arguments about EU membership unresolved, so too were the technical and procedural issues.

## III EU Membership and the Constitutional Politics of Scottish Independence

During the independence referendum campaign, opposing sides in the debate contested the legal basis for the continuing application of EU law in a post-independence Scotland. In the post-2014 period, the issue of EU membership continues to inform and direct the political debate over Scottish independence. Indeed, the result of the 2016 EU membership referendum has further fuelled discussion about the position of Scotland in a post-'Brexit' UK and EU. Thus, while we have noted that the UK generally lacks specific legal triggers for referendums, the changing constitutional politics of the UK, pre- and post-2014, mean that the EU context exerts significant domestic constitutional purchase.

### A. *Continuity of Governance? Transitioning to EU Membership*

Scotland is not, and never has been, a Member State of the EU. Article 52 TEU explicitly lists the Member States of the Union to which the treaties shall apply and Scotland is not listed as a Member State. Rather it is the United Kingdom of Great Britain and Northern Ireland which is listed and the application of EU law in Scotland derives from its status as a constituent territory of the United Kingdom. There was, therefore, a not implausible argument that if Scotland ceased to be a UK territory, then the scope of application of EU law could not apply to a territory which was not itself either a Member State or a constituent territory of a Member State. But for the Scottish Government, it was equally unconscionable that the effect of independence could be the involuntary disapplication of EU law to Scotland. It is this contestation around EU membership which is analysed here.

The obvious legal basis for an independent Scotland's EU membership would be an Article 49 TEU accession process under the conditions and procedures laid down in that provision. Yet that route presupposed that an application for membership would follow from the internal process of separation from the UK. Given that Article 49 TEU refers to the application being made by a 'European state', it would seem to be a necessary element of the capacity to invoke Article 49 TEU that Scotland had, in fact and law, become an independent state. In an important way, the initiation of an Article 49 TEU process would be a significant and early exercise of an independent Scotland's external sovereignty, highlighting not only its political and legal capacity as an international actor, but also bringing with it the recognition of its status by the EU and its Member States through the accession process. Notwithstanding the potential attractiveness of a formal accession process, there was, however, an obvious problem in terms of a hiatus between the moment of independence and the acquisition of EU membership.

The exact length of such a hiatus was open to debate. On one view, it could be suggested that no negotiations on membership could start until there was an independent state, with its own government, possessing the political and legal authority to enter into a negotiation process, leading to a binding result. After all, if one of the functions of the accession process is to determine the capacity of a state to fulfil its obligations under the treaties, it might be difficult definitively to make such a judgment until the institutions and processes for self-government were fully in place. If this approach was followed then the delay in membership would be considerable given that the negotiations for accession would need to be concluded, an agreement adopted and then ratification completed, in all the Member States. This would make the Scottish Government's claim that EU membership could be secured in eighteen months seem rather optimistic. Another view was that in practice the substantive negotiations – or the bulk of them – could be undertaken in advance of formal separation with an accession agreement ready for signature as soon as possible following independence – perhaps with some interim arrangements being adopted to ensure continuing access to the Single Market, pending the formal ratification and entry into force of the agreement.

The Scottish Government instead sought to find a legal mechanism which would support its preference for a seamless, or at least, continuous application of EU law rights within an independent Scotland. Hence its proposal that an independent Scotland would acquire EU membership through a renegotiation of the treaties via Article 48 TEU. The idea being advanced was that Scotland – as a constituent entity of an existing Member State – was not in the same position as other potential accession states and could for that reason seek membership from 'within'.

Relying on a negotiated membership had certain tactical advantages for the Scottish Government. As intimated previously, by focusing on 'negotiation', it is much easier to avoid answering specific questions about likely outcomes, such as the choice of currency, the division of assets and liabilities, or EU membership. These issues become displaced to a later date, with the emphasis turning instead to the referendum as providing a mandate to negotiate. More specifically with regards to EU membership, any potential difficulties in the conduct of post-referendum negotiations could be laid at the door of the UK Government who would be expected to pilot such negotiations on behalf of the Scottish Government. Accordingly, if negotiations with EU institutions and

Member States ran into difficulties, then culpability could be attached to Westminster rather than Holyrood. In this way, the Article 48 TEU route created a multilevel political structure for negotiations with attendant possibilities for a familiar pattern of blame-shifting between sub-national and national levels.

In early 2014, there was a significant debate among legal academics and practitioners about the relative uses of Articles 48 and 49 TEU. Indeed, in light of the earlier discussion, while the domestic constitutional context offered little by way of points of legal conflict, it was this exterior legal context that created legal contestation. Yet instead of one view or another clearly prevailing, legal irresolution risked a descent into political irrelevance, with neither side in the debate capable of instrumentalising European legal resources towards domestic political ends.

However, the absence of a determinative resolution to the Article 48/49 TEU debate, and the failure of opponents of independence to take the issue out of political contestation, left open the possibility of some kind of negotiated continuity of effect in the application of EU law to an independent Scotland. Indeed, for proponents of independence, the idea that independence entailed continuity externally, amplified and resonated with certain narratives about internal continuities in governance. Although the arguments for Scottish independence necessarily highlighted what would be new and different, and allegedly better about Scottish self-government, at the same time, a number of key aspects of governance would apparently remain the same. This was not to be a republican moment with an independent Scotland severing links with the UK monarchy. An independent Scotland would also remain part of a common travel area (including the UK and the Republic of Ireland) outside of the Schengen area, thereby ensuring that no new border controls would be created between Scotland and what remained of the United Kingdom. Highly significantly, there was to be no new Scottish currency, nor the adoption of the Euro, but rather maintenance of sterling as a common currency, albeit that the precise details of how this would operate were never resolved prior to the referendum. The claim that a vote for independence would not result in Scotland losing its ties to the European Union resonated with, and amplified, this important continuity of governance narrative. As the Scottish Government's White Paper put it, '[. . .] Scotland's transition to independent membership will be based on the EU Treaty obligations and provisions that currently apply to Scotland under our present status as part of the UK. It will avoid disruption to Scotland's current fully integrated standing within the legal, economic, institutional, political and social framework of the EU'. It is these continuities in governance – internal and external – which facilitated a depiction of Scotland's independent future as more than 'Devo Max' but less than a complete rupture from its past.

### *B. Post-2014 – The Continuing Resonance of EU Membership*

The capacity for EU membership to resonate within UK political discourse lost little of its energy following the referendum result. The issue of the UK's EU membership had been contained under the Conservative–Liberal Democrat Coalition Government between 2010 and 2015, with the Balance of Competence Review serving to bridge Conservative hostility and Liberal Democratic enthusiasm towards European integration. However, the Conservative Party made clear that if it formed a government in 2015 there would be an in/out referendum on EU membership prefaced by an attempted renegotiation of the UK's terms of membership. Following the Conservative's election victory in May 2015, legislation was enacted providing for a UK-wide referendum in 2016. However, the electoral victory of the Conservative Party in the UK has been matched by the success of the Scottish National Party in winning fifty-six out of fifty-nine UK parliamentary seats in Scotland in the 2015 General Election. It is this electoral success – in both UK and Scottish elections – which keep nationalist ambitions for future independence alive. Moreover, the prospect of a Conservative government overseeing a referendum resulting in UK withdrawal from the EU – and with it a cessation of the application of EU law in Scotland–led the Scottish First Minister to make two constitutionally significant pronouncements.

Echoing statements made during the referendum campaign about the risks of Scotland involuntarily being taken outside the EU, the First Minister suggested the possibility of a double-majority referendum vote that would only see the UK withdrawing from the EU in the event of a majority of electors both in the UK as a whole and within each constituent nation voting for withdrawal. An amendment to the EU Referendum Bill to this effect was proposed by a number of SNP MPs.[25] In effect, this would give a constitutional veto to a minority

[25] The following amendment was proposed:
'Declaration of intent for withdrawal from the EU

section of the population and the amendment was not adopted. But it signified something of a more federated constitutional politics in the wake of the independence referendum, with membership of the EU acting as a significant context for its expression.

The second pronouncement was of a 'triple-lock' against a further referendum on independence. In an early attempt to signal that a second referendum was not being immediately contemplated, the First Minister noted that another referendum would not be held unless, (1) there was a material change in circumstances justifying another plebiscite; (2) the referendum proposal was included in an SNP manifesto for Scottish parliamentary elections; (3) a majority of the electorate voted in favour of independence. While leaving open what might constitute a 'material' change, the example of a UK withdrawal from the EU was identified as one such possibility. With the 2016 EU referendum result in favour of the UK leaving the EU, the question of Scotland's constitutional position within the UK has remained inextricably tied to the UK's relationship with the EU. A second independence referendum has been suggested.

## IV Legal Subjects: Citizens and Member States

Those acquainted with the doctrinal content of EU constitutional law will be all too familiar with the following passage from the CJEU's judgment in *Van Gend en Loos*:

> [T]he Community constitutes a new legal order of international law for the benefit of which the states have limited their sovereign rights, albeit within limited fields, and the subjects of which comprise not only Member States but also their nationals.

The emphasis in this passage – and in EU law subsequently – has been away from Member States as subjects of EU law towards the legal subjectivity of the nationals of Member States. This trajectory in the legal discourse and thinking was given added impetus by the conferral on nationals of the Member States of the status of 'citizen of the EU' (Article 20 TFEU). It is the recognition of the legal subjectivity of EU citizens and

The Secretary of State will present to Parliament a declaration of intent for withdrawal from the European Union if –

(a) a majority of total votes cast in the referendum in the United Kingdom are against the United Kingdom remaining a member of the European Union, and

(b) a majority of the votes cast in the referendum in each of England, Scotland, Wales and Northern Ireland are against the United Kingdom remaining a member of the European Union'.

its influence upon the Scottish independence referendum debate that is of particular interest here.

The legal status of citizenship has afforded new legal resources for EU nationals in a variety of ways.[26] Yet for the most part, it is a status whose exercise and normative purchase lies primarily in a Member State other than that of which the citizen is a national. Except in well-circumscribed circumstances,[27] it would seem to be a status of limited relevance to claims by nationals of a Member State against that Member State. However, it is in the context of the *Rottmann* case that the seeds of an argument of potential use in the independence referendum can be found.[28]

In essence, what was at issue in *Rottmann* was the scope of the autonomy enjoyed by a Member State in its decisions regarding withdrawal of the status of nationality of that Member State. The status of nationality depends on the specific and different laws of each of the Member States. Member States adopt varied policies as to who may become their nationals, but once so recognised, those nationals derive rights as EU citizens under the conditions and limits laid down in EU law. However, it is obvious that withdrawal of a right of nationality may then have the consequence that the individual concerned loses his or her rights as an EU citizen. This was the situation in *Rottmann* where an individual had dishonestly acquired German nationality, and as a matter of Austrian law, lost his Austrian nationality. Once the deception was discovered, he subsequently lost his German nationality, but without automatically reacquiring Austrian nationality. While questions of nationality fall within the competence of the Member States, in a manner familiar to EU lawyers, the CJEU nonetheless adopted the position that the exercise of that competence had to have due regard for EU law. More specifically, the loss of nationality has to be amenable to judicial review, in which it is for the national court to determine whether the legitimacy of a loss of nationality on grounds of deception is proportionate, having regard to the consequences of the loss of rights for the individual (and, where appropriate, other family members), while also having regard to the gravity of the deception permitting a Member State to withdraw nationality.

[26] See Shaw's contribution to this volume, in Chapter 9, and more generally, J. Shaw, 'The Interpretation of European Union Citizenship', *Modern Law Review*, 61(3) (1998), 293.

[27] See Case C-34/09 *Ruiz Zambrano*, EU:C:2011:124, and subsequent case law.

[28] Case C-135/08 *Janko Rottmann*, EU:C:2010:104.

The *Rottmann* ruling is therefore a typical example of proportionality-based interest-balancing where the specific outcome for the individual is left to the national court to determine. Its entire focus is on the capacity of judicial review – and courts as non-majoritarian institutions – to afford due process to an individual who risks a loss of legal status. Yet in the context of the Scottish independence referendum, the implications of the status of citizenship of the EU, in general, and the legal consequences to be derived from the *Rottmann* judgment, in particular, were given a far wider and dramatic meaning and scope of application.

In short, it was argued that if an independent Scotland was forced to apply for EU membership 'from the outside', the loss of the enjoyment of EU citizenship rights pending formal accession to the EU would be tantamount to a failure to have due regard for the rights which EU law conferred on current EU nationals, as subjects of European law, in terms that would appear contrary to the judgment in *Rottmann*. For the Scottish Government, it was not merely politically undesirable to contemplate a formal accession process under Article 49 TEU, it would in its view, be contrary to the legal entitlements of EU citizens for there to be a loss or suspension of the rights they enjoyed pending accession, rather than finding a means of ensuring a seamless, or at least continuous, application of EU law in Scotland.

The identification of EU nationals as legal subjects within EU law was an innovative means of contesting the claim that a legal route to EU membership had to be pursued via Article 49 TEU. It also gave a more substantive and human dimension to the idea that an independent Scotland ought to be inside the EU. Again, this amplified a narrative of a tamed nationalism in which a vote for independence would not be wholly disruptive but indeed would secure continuities in the life, work and experiences of ordinary citizens.

Yet it could equally be suggested that as the consequences of the referendum vote were clear – particularly that separation from an EU Member State would entail a consequential cessation of the application of EU law to the separating territory – then the loss of citizenship status would not be unknown or involuntary but rather a necessary consequence of the decision to separate. Moreover, it is important to be clear about which group of citizens we have in mind. There are two key groups to consider:

- EU nationals residing in Scotland
- Scottish nationals residing in other EU Member States.

In the event that Scotland separated from the UK and, for that reason, was outside the EU pending accession, then there would be a potential loss of rights for those EU nationals resident in Scotland. The substance of those rights could, however, be protected as a matter of domestic law if the Scottish Parliament legislated to extend to those nationals the rights they would have enjoyed had Scotland remained a constituent nation of an EU Member State (particularly in view of its stated ambition of early EU membership). Of course, this would be a discretionary exercise of national political authority, rather than a legal entitlement derived independently from the EU legal order. Nonetheless, a protective mechanism was available. It is also worth recalling that migrant EU nationals resident in Scotland were not excluded from the referendum franchise and to that extent, had a 'voice' in the process.

UK nationals resident in another Member State possess EU citizenship rights and this would include Scottish-born UK citizens insofar as they retained UK nationality. It would naturally be a matter for the UK Government to determine its policy on retention and acquisition of UK nationality post-independence. That policy could entail retention of UK citizenship unless, or until, another nationality was acquired or even a transitional retention of UK citizenship, precisely to protect existing EU citizenship rights pending formal EU accession by a newly independent Scotland (which might also be seen as a practical application of the *Rottmann* principle). On the other hand, a decision by a Scottish-born UK citizen to adopt post-independence Scottish nationality and to renounce UK nationality would be an act made in the knowledge that, in the absence of accession, Scotland would not be an EU Member State and the decision would entail a voluntary loss of EU citizenship rights. Children born in an independent Scotland who acquired Scottish nationality would not experience a withdrawal of EU citizenship rights as they would never have possessed them.

So, the force of the argument premised upon an urgent need to protect EU citizenship rights is not compelling,[29] while the stretching of the *Rottmann* ruling – a case emphasising the importance of judicial review and due process to protect rights of individuals – to a wholly different context of the collective exercise of democratic choice is a step too far. Which is not to argue for blindness towards the legal

[29] Kenealy and Maclennan similarly conclude that the citizenship argument is not compelling in terms of being generative of EU membership for an independent Scotland: above (note 20).

subjectivity of citizens, but rather to suggest that mere recognition of that subjectivity could not constitute a legal trump, or bootstrap, for claims that a vote for independence necessarily demanded the continued application of EU law to Scotland, outside of a formal accession process under Article 49 TEU.

It is also important to recognise that this focus on the legal subjectivity of individuals – the legacy of *Vangendeology* – came at the expense of a deeper consideration of 'Member States' as subjects of EU law. While the EU treaties may be more than an agreement between Member States and while the subjects of EU law are more than its constituent Member States, this hardly means that Member States are an irrelevant legal category. For example, the obvious counter-argument to the idea that Article 48 TEU could constitute a legal basis for an independent Scotland's EU membership, would be to note that it is a means of amending the treaties as they apply to the Member States. It changes the rules for the Member States; it does not change the legal identity of the Member States (German unification changed its territorial scope not its legal identity as a Member State). By contrast, Article 49 TEU is the legal means by which an entity becomes a 'Member State' of the EU. To acquire that identity, there is a process for verifying that an entity is capable of taking on the responsibilities of a Member State, and a constitutional process by which the existing Member States accept the new member to their club. One does not need to be a crude realist or ideological intergovernmentalist to suggest that what is at least as relevant to a legal understanding of the roles of Articles 48 and 49 TEU is an understanding of the legal subjectivity of Member States. To put it more directly within the themes and claims explored in this essay, the resources of EU law are plural rather than singular and whatever may be the relevance of recognising citizens as EU legal subjects, this cannot be at the expense, or to the exclusion, of Member States as subjects of EU law whose identity and agency still matters.

## V Conclusions

The electorate in Scotland voted against independence and by a margin that was perhaps greater than some expected. But the first important conclusion to draw from the referendum on Scottish independence is that referendums often do not bring finality to political contestation despite the binary – and even the binding – nature of referendum ballots. Post-referendum electoral success for the Scottish National Party has emboldened those who still believe that Scotland's future is as an independent state. The issue of Europe – more particularly the referendum on the UK's membership of the EU – has, once again, ignited the debate about Scottish independence and the potential for a second independence referendum.

The political contestation which surrounds referendums and the difficulty in forecasting the potential economic, political and social consequences of a straight yes/no decision may create a yearning for certainty. It is to law that one might turn to provide clarity. However, the second conclusion we can draw is that while legal issues frame both the referendum process and the substantive issues at stake, certainty can prove illusory. The aim of this essay has been to highlight that the legal sources and resources are not solely domestic and interior to the particular polity engaged in a referendum but include exterior resources. Political, economic and social actors deploy these resources in the course of their political contestation, but they often do so instrumentally, to try and defeat an opponents' arguments by taking an issue outside the debate and outside politics. Law is appealed to as a 'trump' card to contest and constrain political choices and claims, yet the experience of the Scottish referendum illustrates how little capacity legal norms have to work in this way. Rather, law acts as a resource through which to direct and inform domestic political narratives, claims and choices or to resonate with, and amplify, those narratives, claims and choices. Law is part of political contestation; it neither stands outside politics nor defeats it.

European legal resources proved prominent in the Scottish referendum debate. This is hardly surprising given the importance that the Scottish Government attached to the continuity of application of EU law to Scotland through EU membership. The irresolution over the correct legal basis or route to EU membership might be viewed as suggesting that law is not only not a trump card, it has relatively limited utility as a resource. Yet the technical debate was a way into a wider discussion about what EU membership means and for which legal subjects. *Vangendeology* offers up a vision of the EU as expansionary, value-oriented and engaged with citizens as legal subjects. Weiler's alternative narrative sees the EU as a disciplinary device which works through the voluntary agency of Member States while placing demands on those states in terms of the conditions of membership and value-commitments, including the taming of nationalism. As ideal-types, they are useful legal paradigms and prisms through which to reflect upon the issues facing the EU including substate secessionist movements.

Yet it is the UK referendum on EU membership that has proved to be the bigger test for these paradigmatic ways of viewing the EU. Voters in England and Wales have clearly rejected the demands of EU membership and found little in the resources of subjective legal rights to compensate. Voters in Scotland and Northern Ireland have taken a different view. The irony of the result of the 2014 independence referendum may well be that while Scotland voted to remain part of the Union with the rest of the UK, in the 2016 EU referendum, much of the rest of the UK voted not only to leave the EU but also to unsettle the Union of the constituent nations of the UK itself.

8

# The Political Rights of EU Citizens and the Right of Secession

MANUEL MEDINA ORTEGA

## I Introduction: The Right to Secede as a Political Right of EU Citizens

When Alex Salmond, First Minister of Scotland, announced his intention to call for a referendum on the independence of his region, he rejected objections alleging that separation from the UK would entail exclusion from the EU, and he claimed that the citizens of Scotland, as European citizens, had a democratic right to stay in the Union even if they chose to establish an independent State. This political statement was further elaborated from a legal perspective by Aidan O'Neill, Q.C., on the basis of the case law of the EU Court of Justice on the fundamental status of European citizenship,[1] and later developed by the proponents for the independence of Catalonia and other regions in the EU Parliament.[2] In accordance with this line of reasoning, a part of a Member State would have an unconditional right to secede and the EU institutions could do nothing but recognise the will of the people of the seceding region by accepting it as a Member State through a process of 'internal enlargement', without having to go through the admission requirements established in the Treaties. This chapter discusses this line of reasoning and its validity as a way to avoid the stringent requirements established in the EU Treaties for the admission of new

[1] See Jo Shaw, 'EU Citizenship and the Edges of Europe', in *The Europeanization of Citizenship in the Successor States of the Former Yugoslavia*, (2012) CTSE Working Paper Series, Working Paper 2012/19, p. 8. See also J. Shaw 'Unions and Citizens: Membership Status and Political Rights in Scotland, the UK and the EU', Chapter 9 in this volume

[2] Amendment 37 by MEPs, R. Tremosa i Balcells, I. Bilbao, A. Miranda, F. Brepoels and R. Romeva to the Foreign Affairs Committee Draft Report of M. E. Koppas on enlargement (2012/2025(INI)), 3 April 2012.

Members. Section II deals with the legal and political problems raised in Catalonia in this respect.

Section III considers the nature of the fundamental rights of EU citizens and discusses the possibility that the inhabitants of a region may decide on their separation from a Member State and the consequences thereof. The political rights of EU citizens derive from the recognition of shared democratic values by the Union and its Member States. The Member States are obliged by the Treaties to recognise and enforce these democratic values. It is doubtful, however, whether this obligation includes a duty to recognise a unilateral declaration of independence by a region of one of the Member States, as this might run counter to the respect of the fundamental functions of the Member States and their right to maintain their territorial integrity. Section IV looks at the contradiction between the duty to recognise the political rights of EU citizens and the principle of respect for the territorial integrity of the Member States. As the EU is a 'Union of States', the principle of the territorial integrity of the Member States prevails over a hypothetical right of the regions to be recognised as independent States, even if that might seem to run counter to democratic values.

Section V discusses the difference in nature between EU citizenship and national citizenship. EU citizenship derives from national citizenship: the severing the link of citizenship of the inhabitants of a seceding region from their Member State entails the loss of EU citizenship. If secession occurs, the EU might be obliged to adopt transitional arrangements to safeguard the rights acquired under EU law by the inhabitants of the seceding territory, pending the admission of that region into the EU as a new Member State. The recognition of these rights by the EU institutions could not go so far, however, as to deprive the secession of any legal effect. The new independent region would find itself, in principle, out of the realm of EU law and their citizens may only avail themselves of EU citizenship if they remain recognised as citizens of their original Member State, or if they acquire the citizenship of another Member State, which could be from the seceding region itself if it is accepted as a new Member (Section VI). Section VII concludes that the political rights of EU citizens do not include the right of the citizens of the seceding region to have their new independent entity recognised as a Member State of the EU without having to go through the formal admission procedure established by the Treaties.

## II The Case of Catalonia

The EU is an international organisation made up of independent States. Article 1(1) TEU provides that 'the High Contracting Parties establish among themselves a European Union [. . .] on which the Member States confer competences to attain objectives they have in common'. As an international organisation, the EU is based on the principle of conferral: 'the Union shall act only within the limits of the competences conferred upon it by the Member States in the Treaties to attain the objectives set out therein' (Art. 5(2) TEU). Under this principle, 'competences not conferred upon the Union in the Treaties remain with the Member States' (Arts. 4(1) and 5(2), last sentence TEU).

The Union is bound to 'respect the equality of Member States before the Treaties, as well as their national identities, inherent in their fundamental structures, political and constitutional, including ensuring the territorial integrity, maintaining law and order and safeguarding national security' (Art. 4(2) TEU).

The secession of a part of the territory of a Member State is not foreseen by EU law. A pronouncement by an EU institution on such a process would be *ultra vires*. The rules of general international law would apply since, as the European Court of Justice ruled in *Hungary* v. *Slovak Republic*, 'international law is part of the European Union legal order and is binding on the institutions'.[3] The right to secession is recognised as a general principle in international law only in the context of decolonisation. For the rest, general international law considers separation of a part of a State to be a matter of fact, not of law. Recognition by other States or international organisations, of the independence of a part of a State, is not binding on the State to which that region belongs or on any other State. In the *Kosovo* case, the International Court of Justice left open the question of the duty of the international community to recognise the secession of a part of the territory of a Member of the UN. In the *Kosovo* Advisory Opinion the Court stated that 'the adoption of the unilateral declaration of independence of 17 February 2008 did not violate international law, Security Council Resolution 1244(1999) or the Constitutional Framework, but it failed to state that international law imposed a duty to recognise that declaration.[4]

[3] Case C-364/10 *Hungary* v. *Slovak Republic*, ECLI:EU:C:2012:630, para. 44.

[4] '*Accordance with International Law of the Unilateral Declaration of Independence in Respect of Kosovo*', Advisory Opinion of 22 July 2010 [2010] *International Court of Justice, Reports of Judgments, Advisory Opinions and Order*, p. 452, para. 122.

The legality of the secession of a part of a State is determined by the constitutional law of the State to which it belongs. If the national constitution is 'flexible', the procedure for a part of a State to become independent may be relatively simple.[5] This was the case of the failed attempt to separate Scotland from the UK. The House of Commons was the only institution which could decide on calling a referendum for secession and on the consequences attached thereto. If the national constitution is 'rigid', the accession to independence of a part of a country may be subject to special conditions or may not be admissible at all. The 1978 Spanish Constitution does not recognise a right to secession of its component units. Article 2 states that the Constitution 'is based on the indissoluble unity of the Spanish Nation, which is the common and indivisible Fatherland of all Spaniards'.[6]

The relevance of a national constitution for the secession of a part of its territory becomes clear when we compare developments in the attempts to separate Catalonia and Scotland from their respective States.[7] On 25 January 2012, Alex Salmond, First Minister of Scotland, announced his intention to call a referendum on independence in the autumn of 2014. The British Prime Minister, David Cameron, stated at first his direct opposition to this proposal. Ten months later, on 15 October, he reached agreement with the First Minister on the conditions for such a referendum. The polls on 18 September 2014 showed that a majority of the Scottish people was against secession. The whole process developed smoothly, without any significant hitch.

The attempt to obtain the independence of Catalonia has followed a more complex and disruptive path. Catalonia had been part of the Kingdom of Aragon since the Twelfth Century. In the Fifteenth Century King Ferdinand II of Aragon married Queen Isabella of Castile and the two crowns merged to form a 'personal union' which eventually gave birth to the Kingdom of Spain. During the Spanish War of Succession of 1700–1714, the French Bourbon candidate found support in the former territories of Castile, while Aragon sided with the Habsburgs. Barcelona

[5] See Carlos Closa, 'Constitutional Rigidity and Procedures for Ratifying Constitutional Reforms in EU Member States', in Arthur Benz and Félix Knüpling (eds.), *Changing Federal Constitutions: Lessons from International Comparison* (Toronto: Opladen, 2012).

[6] See César Colino and José Antonio Olmeda Gómez, 'The Limits of Flexibility for Constitutional Change and the Uses of Subnational Constitutional Space: The Case of Spain', in Benz and Knüpling (note 5), pp. 191–210.

[7] Cf. Kenneth A. Armstrong 'The reach and resources of European law in the Scottish independence referendum', Chapter 7 in this volume.

endured a long siege by the combined Castilian and French forces. The new Bourbon king took revenge for the support given by Aragon to his rival and abolished the traditional privileges of this region, including Catalonia. These historical events have been alleged by Catalan nationalists to demand a special status for Catalonia within Spain, including the right to use the local language.

The Spanish Second Republic, between 1931 and 1936, recognised the right of some regions to have their own self-government. Catalonia was the only part of Spain which established its own regional government before the outbreak of the 1936–1939 Civil War. Self-government was also granted to the Basque Country after the outbreak of the Civil War. A regional charter for Galicia was voted in a referendum in 1936, shortly before the military uprising, but it was not approved by the national parliament as the entire region fell almost immediately under the control of the military rebels. In 1934, the Catalan Government, under Lluis Companys of *Esquerra Republicana de Catalunyna* (ERC), declared independence from Spain and the Central Government resorted to military force to quell the rebellion. The leaders of the revolt, including Companys, were given prison terms. The left-wing coalition known as the 'Popular Front' which won the 1936 elections, restored the Government of Catalonia. Once the war ended, General Franco put an end to the self-government of Catalonia and to the pro-independence movement. Catalan nationalists went into exile, were sent to prison or were executed, as was the case of President Companys.

After the death of General Franco in 1975, the transitional government of Adolfo Suárez ('*Unión de Centro Democrático*', [UCD]), installed a provisional government in Catalonia under the leadership of the nationalist leader in exile Josep Tarradellas. The 1978 Constitution established the legal framework for a semi-federal State where the regions could acquire self-government. Catalonia was once more the first region to approve its own Charter in 1979. Two main nationalist organisations developed at the time, '*Convergéncia I Unió*' (CiU), led by Jordi Pujol, and '*Esquerra Republicana de Catalunya*' (ERC), which has experienced repeated changes of leadership. While ERC maintained a pro-independence position, CiU followed a more opportunistic line, acting as a moderating force in the Spanish political arena. It has continuously sought alliances in Madrid, left and right, aiming to increase the powers of the Catalan Government.

The status of Catalonia was buttressed in 2006 by a new Charter sponsored by the Socialist Government of Rodríguez Zapatero.

The People's Party, then in opposition, challenged the new Charter before the Constitutional Court, which voided its most important provisions in June 2010, including the articles which declared that Catalonia was 'a nation' and which gave official priority in Catalonia to the Catalan language over the 'Castilian' or 'Spanish' language which, under the national Constitution, is an official language across Spain.[8] This decision of the Constitutional Court caused discontent in Catalonia and led to more radical demands. A broad section of the Catalan public opinion switched from the previous demands for a greater degree of self-government to a tougher line of outright independence. In the wake of this wave of discontent, the November 2010 regional elections gave a majority of seats in the Catalan Parliament to the nationalist parties. The coalition led by the Socialists, which had held the Government of Catalonia until then, was replaced by a new coalition led by the two moderate nationalist parties '*Convergéncia Democrática de Catalunya*' (CDC) and '*Unió Democrática de Catalunya*' (UDC), which had stood together in all the elections since 1977 under the common cartel name '*Convergéncia i Unió*' (CiU).

On 23 January 2013, the Catalan Parliament adopted a 'Declaration on Sovereignty' which proclaimed its right to self-determination and announced that a referendum on independence be held in 2014.[9] On October 29, the Spanish Parliament rejected the right of the Catalan Parliament to make such a declaration. The Spanish Parliament based its denial of the right to self-determination on two provisions of the Spanish Constitution: Article 2, which proclaims 'the indissoluble unity of the Spanish nation', and Article 1(2), which declares that 'national sovereignty resides with the Spanish people'. A 'part of the people' could not decide by itself on this issue without taking into account the will of the rest of Spain.[10]

[8] Judgment 31/2010, 28 June 2010. Cf. special issue on this judgment in the *Revista catalana de dret public*, No. 43, December 2011.

[9] Resolution 5/X approving the Declaration on sovereignty and the right to decide of the people of Catalonia, 250-00059/10 and 250-00060/10, DSPC-P 4, *Butlletí Oficial del Parlament de Catalunya* 7, *Diari de Sessions del Parlament de Catalunya*, P.4, 23 de enero de 2013, pp. 60–61. See Christopher K. Connolly, 'Independence in Europe: Secession, Sovereignty, and the European Union', *Duke Journal of Comparative and International Law*, 24(2013), 51–195, at 55–59.

[10] *Diario de sesiones del Congreso de los Diputados. Pleno y Diputación permanente*, N° 151, 29 October 2013, pp. 47–57 (debate) and 75 (vote). Text of the draft resolution, *Boletín Oficial de las Cortes Generales. Congreso de los Diputados. X Legislatura. Serie D: General*, N° 347, p. 7, doc. 173/000113, and p. 9, doc. 173/000114. Resolution, ibid., N° D-354, 7 November 2013, pp. 26 and 28.

The Constitutional Court has since consistently rejected the validity of the pronouncements of the Catalan Parliament, of the Catalan Government on their right to assert independence and on the right of the people of Catalonia to decide on this issue through a plebiscite. The Constitutional Court had maintained in its 2010 resolution the validity of Article 22 of the 2006 Charter, which reserved to the Central Government the right to call a referendum on secession. That Article complied with the Constitution because it denied the regional Government the right to organise such a referendum. The Central Government ought to have the last word on the approval a referendum on this issue as it retained the exclusive competence to decide on this matter. Previously, in 2008 the Constitutional Court had annulled a Decree of the Basque Government on a similar referendum in that region.[11] The Constitutional Court stated on that occasion that only the Central Government was competent to decide on this issue. It also said that neither a region nor the State as a whole could call for a referendum on the self-determination of a part of the State without the adoption, beforehand, of a constitutional amendment. A referendum on this issue could not be disguised as a 'non-binding consultation' as the Basque Government had attempted to do at the time. On 11 July 2013, the Constitutional Court suspended resolution 5/X of the Catalan Parliament on 'the sovereignty and the right of the Catalan people to decide', and it voided this resolution on 25 March 2014.[12] The Constitutional Court stated at the time that the national legal order was based on the 'exclusive and indivisible sovereignty of the Spanish people' and that a regional government could not call on its own a referendum on self-determination.[13]

The Catalan Parliament adopted Act 10/2014 on 26 September 2014, which authorised the Catalan Government to organise 'popular consultations'. This Act was also challenged by the Central Government and the Constitutional Court declared it null and void.[14] In an attempt to

[11] Judgment 103/2008, 11 September 2008, *Boletín Oficial del Estado*, N° 245, 10 October 2008, Supplement, p.3.

[12] Judgment 42/2014, 25 March 2014, *Boletín Oficial del Estado*, N° 87, 10 April 2014, Section TC, p. 77. Cf. Víctor Ferreres Comella, 'The Spanish Constitutional Court Confronts Catalonia's "Right to Decide" (Comment on Judgment 42/2014)', *European Constitutional Law Review*, 10 (2014), 571–590.

[13] Pablo José Castillo Ortiz, 'Framing the Court: Political Reactions on the Declaration of Sovereignty of the Catalan Parliament', *Hague Journal of the Rule of Law*, 7 (2015), 27–47 (published online 1 September 2015).

[14] Judgment 32/2015l, 23 February 2015, *Boletín Oficial del Estado*, N° 64, 16 March 2015, Section TC, p. 213.

circumvent the prohibition by the Constitutional Court of a formal referendum or 'popular consultation', the Catalan Government chose a less formal procedure which consisted in providing assistance to an informal 'citizens' participation process' organised by social movements. The Central Government challenged anew this form of indirect support by the Government of Catalonia for the independence process. The Spanish Attorney General at the time requested criminal charges be brought before the ordinary courts of justice against some members of the Catalan Government, including its President, who had been active in the support for this alternative 'citizens' participation process', and accused them of disobeying the Constitutional Court. The informal consultation was declared unconstitutional.[15] The Criminal Section of the Supreme Court of Catalonia is now conducting criminal proceedings against the President and other members of the former Catalan Government for having given support to this informal consultation process. At the same time, and without a direct relationship with the proposals for independence, the ordinary courts of justice are conducting criminal proceedings on charges of corruption against some leading members of the ruling '*Convergência Democrática de Catalunya*' (CDC), including its founder and former leader Jordi Pujol, and against all the members of his family. The leaders of CDC have accused the central PP Government of pushing for judicial action against the Catalan Government and the CDC as a form of political blackmail. On 16 October 2015, the People's Party rushed several amendments to the Statute of the Constitutional Court through the *Cortes Generales*, empowering this body to restrain active support for secession by the regional authorities and ultimately to allow the Central Government to take over some of the powers entrusted to the regional governments if they fail to comply with the resolutions of the Constitutional Court.[16]

The Catalan president dissolved the Catalan Parliament and called for new elections to be held on 27 September 2015. He called them a 'plebiscite' and announced that in case the pro-independence parties obtained a majority in the Regional Parliament the new government would proclaim independence within eighteen months without further

[15] Judgment of 11 June 2015, No. 138/2015, *Boletín Oficial del Estado*, N° 138, 6 July 2015, p. 56313.

[16] Organic Law 15/2015 of 16 October, amending Organic Law 2/1979 of 3 October of the Constitutional Court, for the purpose of enforcing the resolutions of the Constitutional Court as a guarantee of the rule of law, *Boletín Oficial del Estado*, No. 249, Saturday 17 October 2015, Section I, pp. 95657–96659, No. 11160.

negotiations with the Central Government. The parties and social movements opposing independence rejected the idea that the new regional elections could constitute a plebiscite, as the elections to the regional parliament could not have an effect not envisaged by the Constitution. The call to regional elections for the purpose of declaring unilateral independence led to a split in the traditional allies of '*Convergéncia Democrática de Catalunya*' (CDC) and the more moderate nationalists of '*Unió Democrática de Catalunya*' (UDC), who announced the end of their electoral alliance with CDC, which had existed since the restoration of democracy in 1977, and chose to stand alone in the 2015 elections. The two main parties now supporting independence, CDC and '*Esquerra Republicana de Catalunya*' (ERC), formed a new electoral coalition called '*Junts pel Sí*' (JxS, 'Together for the Yes Vote'). The new coalition was headed by Raúl Romeva, who had been elected to the European Parliament on a 'United Left-Green' list, and included several candidates representing pro-independence social movements. The leaders of the CDC and ERC, Artur Mas and Oriol Junqueras, took the modest fourth and fifth positions in that list. The leftist '*Coalició de Unitat Popular*' (CUP), which also favoured independence, submitted a separate list of candidates. During the electoral campaign the CUP stressed its ideological differences with the JxS list and committed itself not to support Artur Mas as the new president of Catalonia due to his association with the corruption scandals which had tainted his party and his government.

The electoral results were mixed. JxS was the most voted list, with 39.54 per cent of the popular vote and sixty-two seats, but short of the absolute majority of sixty-eight seats needed to form a government on its own, while CUP got 8.20 per cent of the electorate and ten seats. The two pro-independence lists obtained together an absolute majority in the Catalan Parliament, with seventy-two seats out of a total of 135, but not a majority of the popular vote, with only 47.7 per cent of the electorate. The lists not supporting independence, with sixty-three seats, had obtained a majority of the electorate, with 52.26 per cent of the popular vote. The anti-independence lists did not share, however, a common position on the core issue of separation from Spain. While the '*Partido Socialista de Catalunya*'(PSC), the '*Partido Popular*' (PP) and '*Ciudadanos-Citadáns*' (C´s) opposed independence, the coalition '*Sí que es pot*' ('Yes, we can') formed by '*United-Left-Greens*' and '*Podemos*' ('We Can') supported the right of the Catalan people to decide on the issue of independence without committing themselves expressly in favour of independence. The results may be considered a tie, with roughly half of the voters favouring independence and the other half opposing it. The parties opposing independence claimed that the absolute majority of seats obtained by the two lists supporting independence was not sufficient to grant legitimacy to a unilateral declaration of independence, as they had not obtained the majority of the popular vote. The members of the two pro-independence lists, along with five members of the '*Sí que es pot*' electoral list, voted a non-partisan representative of the pro-independence movement, Carme Forcadell, as chairwoman of the Parliament, who ended her inaugural speech with a *vivat* to the Catalan Republic. As soon as the new Parliament was installed, the two pro-independence lists submitted a draft resolution affirming the right of Catalonia to declare independence and to disobey Spanish law.[17] The draft resolution was adopted on 9 November with the seventy-two votes of the pro-independence parties against the sixty-three votes of the other parties. It announced the purpose of the new majority 'to disconnect from Spain' and made a 'solemn proclamation' on beginning the construction of a Catalan republic.[18] It did not take long for the Constitutional Court to void this Declaration.[19]

The draft resolution on the unilateral declaration of independence had a strong impact on the rest of Spain. During the 2011–2015 Parliament in the *Cortes Generales* in Madrid, the main national parties, PP, PSOE, UPYD and *Ciudadanos*, had formed a common front against the attempts of the Catalan nationalist parties to seek independence through unilateral declarations. The Spanish parliamentary elections of 20 December 2015 maintained a majority of seats in the *Cortes* in Madrid for the anti-secessionist parties, but gave a substantial minority of seats to a coalition of left-wing parties supporting the right to self-determination of the regions, centred around the new left-wing party *Podemos*. Negotiations to establish a left-wing coalition government at the beginning of the new legislature in 2016 are been influenced by their substantial differences with the Socialist Party on this issue. After protracted negotiations between CUP and JxS, an agreement was reached to install the mayor of Gerona, Carles Puigdemont, a member of CDC, as President of Catalonia, thus

[17] Draft resolution 25/2, 27 October 2015.

[18] Resolution 1/XI of the Parliament of Catalonia, 250-00001/11, *Butlletí official del Parlament de Catalunya.*

[19] No. 6330-2015, under Title V *LOTC.*

dropping former President Mas.[20] The two pro-independence parliamentary groups committed themselves on this occasion to pursue the independence project. In the meantime, *CDC* formed a new coalition to incorporate social movements and new small parties favouring independence, named '*Democrácia i Llibertat*' ('Democracy and Freedom', DiL).

Public opinion polls show that although independence has the support of almost fifty per cent of Catalans, when the question is raised that independence could lead to the departure of Catalonia from the EU, support for independence considerably weakens.[21]

## III Secession as a Fundamental Right of EU Citizens

Supporters of the right of regions to obtain independence claim that EU citizens have a right to decide on how they organise their political communities. A very articulate line of reasoning in support of this position has been put forward by Joan Ridao, a professor of Constitutional Law at the University of Barcelona and a former spokesman for '*Esquerra Republicana de Catalunya*' in the Spanish Congress of Deputies, and Alfóns González Bondía, a professor of Constitutional Law at the Rovira i Virgili University in Tarragona. They consider that the EU is a '*sui generis*' political entity in blending the traits of an international organisation with those of a federal State or a confederation of States. The hybrid character of the EU has led its institutions to solve practical problems, in some cases in accordance with the rules on the functioning of international organisations, and in other cases with those of federal or confederate systems of government. The choice of either model depends, in each case, on their adequacy to achieve the aims, goals and principles of the EU.[22] Ridao and González Bondía believe that the European integration model

[20] Puigdemont was elected on 10 January 2016 by the sixty-two deputies of *JxS* and eight members of the *CUP* against the sixty-three members of the other groups, with the abstention of two of the *CUP* members

[21] See the results of a public opinion poll conducted by Metroscopia, '*El País*', 30 October 2015. Cf. Javier Tajadura Tejada, 'Más allá de un asunto interno: secesionismo e integración europea' (2014) Real Instituto Elcano, ARI 64/2014, 22 December 2014.

[22] Joan Ridao Martín and Alfonso González Bondía, 'La Unión Europea ante la eventual creación de nuevos Estados surgidos de la secesión de Estados miembros' ('The European Union and the Eventual Establishment of New States Emerging from the Secession of Member States'), *Revista de Derecho de la Unión Europea*, 27(July–December 2014), 363–389; and the reply by Enrique Linde Paniagua, 'Contestación al trabajo de Ridao y González Bondía: La secesión de territorios de Estados miembros de la Unión Europea, que se fundan en ideologías nacionalistas, es contraria a los principios democráticos que rigen en los Estados occidentales y en la Unión Europea', ibid., 391–411.

is now closer to a federation than to an international organisation. The institutional structure of the EU is well adapted to the federalist structure, as it is based on multiple centers of powers and it attempts to strike a balance between the various levels of government. The EU is based on a power-sharing mechanism between the common institutions and the Member States and this arrangement resembles the federal model.[23]

The recognition of fundamental rights by Article 6 TEU, and by the European Charter on Fundamental Rights, brings the EU closer to the federal model. The protection of human rights by the common institutions is intended to reinforce European identity through the incorporation of common fundamental values and principles in the European integration process. Democracy is one of those fundamental values and is an essential element of the national constitutions of the Member States. Article 10(3) TEU recognises, for every EU citizen, 'the right to participate in the democratic life of the Union'. It further states that 'decisions shall be taken as openly and as closely as possible to the citizen'. The prevalence of the Rule of Law is also an essential element of the EU. The recognition of European citizenship constitutes an example of federalism, as it establishes a direct link between the institutions and the peoples of the EU. The incorporation of the common values and principles in the Treaties should prevent the downgrading of the EU into an organisation where decisions can be adopted without due regard for the will of the citizens, or where fundamental human rights are ignored by the institutions or by the Member States.[24]

On the issue of the right to secession of a part of a Member State, Ridao and González Bondía underline the contradiction between the recognition by the EU Treaties of the democratic values in Article 2 TEU and the duty to respect the 'fundamental structures, political and constitutional' of the Member States, 'including ensuring the territorial integrity of the State' under Article 4(2) of the same Treaty. 'Faced with this apparent antinomy a reasonable doubt arises on what the EU should do in a situation in which it would have to abide by the obligations arising from both provisions and where that would not be possible'.[25] They conclude that the Commission could bring proceedings against a Member State before the European Court of Justice for breach of the Treaties under Article 258 TFEU if that State ignores the fundamental rights of the EU citizens.[26]

[23] Ibid., 365. [24] Ibid., 367–369. [25] Ibid., 374. [26] Ibid., 377.

## IV Fundamental Human Rights versus the Integrity of the Member States

The weakness of this line of reasoning lies in the fact that EU law, as interpreted and applied by the Court of Justice, does not recognise a right to bring a claim before it for violations of the political rights of EU citizens outside the situations expressly contemplated by the Treaties, or by specific rules adopted by the common institutions. Article 51(1) of the Charter of Fundamental Rights states that its provisions 'are addressed to the institutions, bodies, offices and agencies of the Union with due regard for the principle of subsidiarity and to the Member States only when they are implementing Union law'. Article 51(2) declares that 'the Charter does not extend the field of application of Union law beyond the powers of the Union or establish any new power or task for the Union, or modify powers and tasks as defined in the Treaties'. We have already seen the strong language of Article 4(2) TEU on the preservation of the territorial integrity of the Member States. It could not be otherwise, as the Treaties are the creation of the Member States. As long as the Member States do not give up their sovereign rights, they are the sole masters of the Treaties. The Opinion of the Court of Justice on the Draft Treaty for Accession of the EU to the European Convention on Human Rights has reaffirmed these fundamental principles of EU law.[27] Advocate General Julianne Kokott stated[28] that the principle of conferral deprives the Union of a general competence in the field of human rights and fundamental freedoms (point 34).

The EU is based on the overriding position of the Member States. The EU lacks a comprehensive administration of its own. It can only work with the cooperation of the national administrations. The citizens' political rights contained in Title V of the Charter of Fundamental Rights are basically limited to the right to vote and the right to stand for elections to the European Parliament and at municipal elections. The principle of conferral of Article 5(2) TEU requires a formal amendment to enlarge the scope of these rights. Article 51 of the Charter acts as a straightjacket against the recognition of new political rights without the unanimous consent of all the Member States. This Article also provides that due regard must be paid to the principle of subsidiarity and to the allocation of powers established by the Treaties. Above all, 'the Charter does not extend the field of application of Union law beyond the powers of the

[27] Opinion 2/13 of 18 December 2014, ECLI:EU:C:2014:2454.
[28] Of 13 June 2014, ECLI:EU:C:2014:2014:2475.

Union or establish any new power or task for the Union, or modify powers and tasks as defined in the Treaties' (Article 51[2]). The protection of fundamental rights is guaranteed by different legal instruments: the national laws of the Member States, EU law, and the Convention on Fundamental Rights of the Council of Europe.[29] The primacy of EU law prevents the enforcement of a compulsory rule of EU law from being made conditional on respect for particular fundamental rights recognised by national constitutions.[30] Advocate General Cruz Villalón has said that it is 'an all but impossible task to preserve *this* Union, as we know it today, if it is to be made subject to an absolute reservation, ill-defined and virtually at the discretion of each of the Member States, which takes the form of a category described as ′constitutional identity'.[31]

## V EU Citizenship versus National Citizenship

The theory of the 'internal enlargement', as expounded by Scottish, Catalan and other pro-independence movements within the EU and as explained above, claims that the citizens of a seceding territory have the right to retain their EU citizenship after secession and that the EU would have no option but to recognise the democratic will expressed by those citizens if they choose to create a new political entity within the EU. The new State would become a Member of the EU without formal admission, as the seceding territory is already a part of the EU. Against this point of view it must be recalled that EU citizenship is vicarious to national citizenship. Article 20(1) TFEU states: 'Every person holding the nationality of a Member State shall be a citizen of the Union. Citizenship of the Union shall be additional and not replace national citizenship'. If a part of a Member State secedes, their citizens would lose their EU citizenship. They could not claim rights as EU citizens under EU law after secession, including any right to have their political community recognised as a Member State, without formal admission to the EU.

29 Cf. Astrid Epiney, 'Le champ d′application de la Charte des droits fondamentaux : l′arrêt *Fransson* et ses implications', *Cahiers de droit européen*, 15(2014), 283–303.

30 Case C-399/11 *Melloni* v. *Ministerio fiscal*, ECLI:EU:C:2013:107, para. 58. Cf. Edouard Dubout, 'Le niveau de protection des droits fondamentaux dans l′Union Européenne : unitarisme constitutif *versus* pluralisme constitutionnel. Réflexion autour de l′arrêt *Melloni*', *Cahiers de droit européen*, 49(2013), 293–317.

31 Opinion of 14 January 2015, in Case C-62/14 *Gauweiler and Others* v. *Deutscher Bundestag*, ECLI:EU:C:2015:7, para. 59.

The supporters of the 'internal enlargement' theory emphasise the importance that Article 2 TEU lends to democracy as a fundamental value of the Union.[32] The will of the citizens of a part of a Member State to establish an independent State should be recognised accordingly. Kenneth A. Armstrong has pointed out, however, that 'the spirit of *Van Gend en Loos* and its progeny within the EU jurisprudence is that the Union is founded on the rule of law as well as the principle of democracy' and that 'the identity of the EU as a distinct legal order is inextricably bound up with the idea that it is a rules-based organisation in which exercises of political discretion are subject to legal control'.[33] The recognition of the democratic values in the primary law of the EU cannot give rise to a right of the citizens of the territory of one of the Member States to set up an independent State, because secession entails the loss both of that State's citizenship and of EU citizenship. Non-EU citizens cannot claim the rights recognised by the EU Treaties for EU citizens, including the political right to set up a democratic form of government. The political rights of non-EU citizens are outside the ambit of EU law. Once a part of a State ceases to be a part of the EU, the rights of its citizens may only be acknowledged under the rules of general international law, not under EU law. There is no continuity between the political status of the citizens of a Member State, who are as such citizens of the Union, and that of the citizens of a part of a seceding territory, who lose their EU citizenship as a result of secession.

The establishment of a European citizenship is one of the aims of the EU (Preamble to the TEU and Recital 10 and Article 20(1) of the TFEU). The EU Court of Justice has stated that 'Union citizenship is destined to be the fundamental status of nationals of the Member States'[34].

[32] Sir David Edward, 'EU and the Separation of Member States' (2013) 36 Fordham Inter'l LJ, 1151 ff.

[33] Kenneth A. Armstrong 'An Independent Scotland in the European Union: Pathways, Pitfalls, and Legal Perspectives' *Cambridge Journal of International and Comparative Law*, (2014), vol. 3 n. 1 181–195, at 185. See also K. Armstrong 'The Reach and Resources of European Law in the Scottish Independence Referendum', Chapter 7 in this volume

[34] See, among others, the following decisions of the European Court of Justice: Case C-184/99 *Grzelczyk* ECR I-6193, ECLI:EU:C:2001:458, para. 31; Case C-224/98 *d'Hoop* [2002] ECR I-1619, ECLI:EU:C:2002:432, para. 28; Case C-413/99 *Baumbast* [2002] ECR I-7091, ECLI:EU:C:2002:493, para. 82; Case C-184/02 *García Avelló* [2002] ECR I-11613, ECLI:EU:C:2003:539, para. 21; Case C-403/03 *Schempp* [2005] ECR I-6421, ECLI:EU:C:2005:446, para. 15; Case C-209/03 *Bidar* [2005] ECR 2119, ECLI:EU:C:2005:169, para. 31; Case C-103/08 *Gottwald* [2009] ECR I-9117, ECLI:EU:C:2009:597, para. 23; Case C-75/11 *Commission* v. *Austria*, ECLI:EU:C:2012:605, para. 38. On the development of the status of EU citizenship: Koen Lenaerts and José Antonio Gutiérrez-Fons, 'Ruiz-

The Treaties and the Charter of Fundamental Rights refer mainly to the rights of EU citizens in the context of economic integration, in order to facilitate the development of the single market, mostly as the right to move and reside freely within the borders of the EU. Some of the rights of EU citizens relate, however, to the organisation of their political communities. This is the case of the freedom of association and the right to belong to political parties at the EU level (Art. 12 TFEU), the right to vote and to stand as a candidate for municipal elections and for elections to the European Parliament (Arts.40 and 39), and the right to address petitions to the EU institutions (Art. 44). These rights may be referred to as the 'political rights of EU citizens', as opposed to the individual rights protected by the core body of EU citizenship. The European case law does not support a wholly independent status for EU citizenship, but links it to national legislation. In *Eman-Sevinger* the Court stated that 'while in the current state of Community law there is nothing concerning the right to vote to the European Parliament by reference to the criterion of residence in the territory in which the elections are held, the principle of equal treatment prevents, however, the criteria chosen from resulting in different treatment of nationals who are in comparable situations, unless that difference in treatment is objectively justified'.[35] In *Gibraltar* the Court extended the electoral rights to the residents of a part of a Member State who could not be considered citizens of the EU.[36]

Zambrano (C-34/09) o de la emancipación de la ciudadanía de la Unión a los límites inherentes a la libre circulación' (October–December 2011) 40 *Revista española de Derecho europeo*, 493–521; Susanne K. Schmidt, 'Who Cares about Nationality? The Path-Dependent Case of the ECJ from Goods to Citizens', *Journal of European Public Policy*, 19(2012), 8–24; Hannette van Eijken and S. A. de Vries, 'A New Route into the Promised Land? Being an European Citizen after Ruiz-Zambrano', *ELR*, 36 (2011), 704–721; Carlos Closa, 'La ciudadanía europea: el estatuto de un sujeto político inacabado', in Iván Llamazares and Fernando Reinares Nestares (eds.), *Aspectos políticos y sociales de la integración europea* (Valencia: Tirant lo Blanch, 1999), pp. 69–92, and 'Constitutional Prospects of European Citizenship and New Forms of Democracy', in Giuliano Amato, H. Bribosia and Bruno De Witte (eds.), Genése et destinées de la Constitution européenne (Genesis and Destiny of the European Constitution) (Brussels: Bruylant, 2007), pp. 1037–1063; Gregorio Garzón Clariana, 'Les droits politiques des citoyens de l'Europe: les vingt premières annèes' (2013) 13 ERA Forum, pp. 545–567; Manuel Medina Ortega, 'El estatuto politico del ciudadano europeo' (2012) 12 Anuario español de Derecho internacional privado, 519–536

35 Case C-300/04 *Eman-Sevinger* [2006] ECR I-8055, ECLI:EU:C:2006:545, para. 2.

36 Case C-145/04 *Spain* v. *UK* [2006] ECR I-7917, ECLI:EU:C:2006:543. See also the judgment of the European Court of Human Rights of 18 February 1999, *Matthews* v. *UK* [GC] App. No. 24833, ECHR 1999-I, which established the basis for the EU Court of Justice decision.

The 1986 Single Act signalled the transition from an integration process addressed primarily to achieve economic goals to another aimed at attaining political union. Recital 3 of its Preamble declared the will of the governments 'to work together to promote democracy on the basis of the fundamental rights recognised in the constitutions and laws of the Member States, in the Convention for the Protection of Human Rights and Fundamental Freedoms and the European Social Charter, notably freedom, equality and social justice'. Its Recital 4 referred to 'the wishes of the democratic peoples of Europe, for whom the European Parliament, elected by universal suffrage, is an indispensable means of expression'. The 1992 Maastricht Treaty purported to establish a European citizenship and 'to enhance the democratic and efficient functioning of the institutions' (Preamble, Recital 5).

The German Constitutional Court (*Bundesverfassungsgericht*) sees a substantial difference of 'density' (*Dichte*) between EU citizenship and the citizenship of the Member States.[37] The fact that European citizenship is derived from the citizenship of the Member States makes it a 'light' citizenship by comparison with the strong link between European citizens and their national States.[38] Jo Shaw has explained that when the Court of Justice says that 'the Union citizenship is destined to be the fundamental status of nationals of the Member States' it is outlining an aspiration and not claiming that it is presently the case.[39]

## VI Transitional Rights of the Citizens of Seceding Territories

Secession of a part of a Member State will normally entail the loss of EU citizenship rights by its population. Admission of a new independent State created by secession is only possible following the procedure for accession foreseen by the EU Treaty. Any attempt to short-circuit that procedure through an amendment to the Treaties would not be helpful. The amendment procedure normally takes longer than the admission procedure and requires, in any case, the consent of all the Member States.

[37] *Bundesverfassungsgericht*, Second Senate, Judgment of 12 October 1993, *BVerfGE* 89, 155, para. 97.

[38] William Maas, 'Unrespected, Unequal, Hollow? Contingent Citizenship and Reversible Rights in the European Union', *Columbia Journal of European Law*, 15 (2009), 265–280.

[39] *Citizenship: Contrasting Dynamics at the Interface of Integration and Constitutionalism* (2010) European University Institute, Robert Schuman Center for Advanced Studies, European Democracy Observatory on Citizenship, *EUI Working Paper*, RSCAS 2010/60, p. 1. See also J. Shaw 'Unions and Citizens: Membership Status and Political Rights in Scotland, the UK and the EU′, Chapter 9 in this volume.

If it can reasonably be expected that the newly independent entity will be accepted as a Member State, the recognition of a transitional status for residents of the seceding territory could be considered. This could have been the case for the citizens of Scotland, as the referendum for secession was negotiated in a friendly manner between the governments of Scotland and the UK. In the spirit of friendly relations between a rump UK State and a seceding Scotland, the UK could have been expected to facilitate the entry of an independent Scotland in the EU. If the citizens of Scotland had been left outside the EU for a short period pending the formal admission of Scotland as a new Member, it would have made sense to establish transitional arrangements to maintain their rights as EU citizens in the interim. As the referendum went against secession, no such precedent in this respect was established, however.

The Spanish Government, on the contrary, has consistently rejected any claims that might lead to the recognition of the right of the people of Catalonia to establish an independent State, due to the limitations imposed by the Constitution. It has been supported in this respect by the Constitutional Court and a substantial majority of the national Parliament. Under the present circumstances, if Catalonia secedes it could take a long time for an independent Catalan State to be accepted into the EU. Transitional status could be considered for the residents of Catalonia only if all the Member States, including Spain, were ready to accept it as a new Member State.

A transitional EU status of citizenship could be recognised for the residents of a seceding part of the territory of a Member State. Both the *Matthews* decision of the European Court of Human Rights and the *Gibraltar* judgment of the European Court of Justice supported the recognition of political rights derived from EU citizenship for persons who were not citizens of a Member State. Future negotiations for eventual secession of a part of the territory of a Member State could thus, and possibly should, include a definition of the political rights of the residents of that territory during the transitional period, pending its admission to the EU as a new Member State, if that is feasible.

## VII Conclusions

The political rights of EU citizens do not include a right to secession for parts of the territory of a Member State. Under international law, the right to secession is subject to the provisions of the national constitutions. Where, as in the case of the UK, the Constitution is flexible, an act of Parliament may provide an adequate legal basis for the secession of a part of its territory. The Spanish Constitution, on the other hand, does not recognise such a right. EU institutions must abide in any case by the provisions of Article 4(2) TEU which impose the duty to 'respect the equality of Member States before the Treaties as well as their national identities, inherent in their fundamental structures, political and constitutional, inclusive of regional and local self-government', as well as the 'essential State functions, including ensuring the territorial integrity of the State'.

Taking into account that under Article 20(1) TFEU, EU citizenship derives from the citizenship of the Member States, secession of a part of the territory of a Member State entails the loss of EU citizenship for the residents of the seceding region. The political rights derived from EU citizenship will be lost with independence from a Member State of the EU. There is no right of the citizens of the seceding territory to have it recognised as a Member State of the EU without following the procedure established in the Treaties for admission of States. 'Internal political enlargement' through mere recognition of the independence of a part of the territory of a Member State is not possible. The seceding territory may only return to the EU after complying with the requirements for admission established in Article 49 TEU.

If it can be expected that the seceding territory will be admitted to the EU as a new independent State within a reasonable period, an interim status could be considered for the residents of the seceding territory. Such an interim status would have to be approved, however, by the State from which the territory seceded. Otherwise, the residents of the seceding territories will lose their rights as EU citizens.

9

# Unions and Citizens: Membership Status and Political Rights in Scotland, the UK and the EU

JO SHAW*

## I Introduction

The primary objective of this volume is to analyse aspects of the putative withdrawal of a Member State from the European Union and/or the secession of a 'region' from a (Member) state. This raises important legal, political and normative questions, with few precedents to help us. This chapter uses the lenses of citizenship to explore the interaction between the two dimensions of 'troubled membership', applying a law-and-politics approach which locates legal change in its broader political context and focuses on the contestation of the boundaries of polity membership.[1] After setting the scene (Section II), the chapter explores the content of a possible future Scottish citizenship regime (Section III) and then examines the intertwining of formal legal membership and political citizenship in respect of both the Scottish referendum and the UK's 2016 EU referendum (Section IV). The threads are drawn together

* This paper draws on J. Shaw, 'Citizenship in an independent Scotland: legal status and political implications' CITSEE Working Paper 2013/34 and J. Shaw 'Citizenship in an independent Scotland', Evidence submitted to the European and External Relations Committee of the Scottish Parliament, 15 May 2014. I am grateful to the editor for very helpful guidance on reshaping a first draft of this paper. I alone remain responsible for errors.

1 Space precludes a detailed discussion of how the two referendums discussed in this chapter have come about or an analysis of the referendum debates themselves. Suffice it to say that the holding of referendums – constitutional or otherwise – represents the outcome of a political process (Stephen Tierney describes it as an 'inauspicious history' in the UK context: S. Tierney, 'Reclaiming Politics: Popular Democracy in Britain after the Scottish Referendum', *The Political Quarterly*, 86 [2015], 226–233), and is apt to show that one side or indeed both see a political advantage in invoking the notion of a plebiscite.

in the conclusion (Section V) through a discussion of how the EU referendum outcome is directly impacting upon the issue at the heart of the Scottish referendum debate, namely the ongoing viability of the UK as a union state.

## II Setting the Scene: Citizenship and Constitutional Change in Scotland, the United Kingdom and the European Union

As an example of troubled membership, the situation in the UK is unique. Two unions are simultaneously contested. The 300-plus-year Union between England and Scotland, which formed the basis of what we now know as the United Kingdom of Great Britain and Northern Ireland, was directly challenged in a September 2014 referendum on Scottish independence. This referendum was framed by a political agreement between the Scottish and UK Governments (the so-called Edinburgh Agreement),[2] implemented by legislation in the Westminster and Scottish Parliaments.[3] In the event, Scotland voted by a margin of 55 per cent to 45 per cent to remain in the UK.

The forty-year 'union' brought about by UK accession to the European Communities on 1 January 1973 has also been contested. On 23 June 2016, the UK voted in a referendum on EU membership. Since the Treaty of Lisbon, such a national referendum has been validated as a legitimate political trigger for constitutional change, with Article 50 TEU now regulating the terms of consensual withdrawal from the Union generated by the initiative of a Member State.[4] By a margin of 52 per cent

[2] *Agreement between the United Kingdom Government and the Scottish Government on a referendum on independence for Scotland*, Edinburgh, 15 October 2012, <www.gov.scot/About/Government/concordats/Referendum-on-independence>, accessed 19 July 2016.

[3] The UK/Westminster Parliament and the Scottish Parliament both adopted an Order in Council under Section 30 of the Scotland Act 1998, to allow a single question referendum to take place on the question of Scottish independence, with details, including the date, the franchise and the question to be determined by legislation adopted by the Scottish Parliament. This alters the schedule of powers reserved to the UK Parliament under the current devolution settlement. The Scottish Independence Referendum Act 2013 and the Scottish Independence Referendum (Franchise) Act 2013 set out the details of the referendum.

[4] See C. Closa 'Interpreting Article 50: Exit, Voice and. . .What About Loyalty?', Chapter 1 in this volume; C. Hillion 'This Way, Please! A Legal Appraisal of the EU Withdrawal Clause', Chapter 11 in this volume and A. Łazowski 'Be Careful What You Wish for: Procedural Parameters of EU Withdrawal', Chapter 12 in this volume.

to 48 per cent on a turnout of more than 72 per cent (higher than the 66 per cent turnout in the 2015 UK General Election), the voters of the UK answered 'Leave' to the question 'Should the United Kingdom remain a member of the European Union or leave the European Union?'.

In both cases, a 'yes' or 'leave' vote was always going to bring about a new constitutional situation with uncertain consequences. It would provide an important (and legally challenging) case study of how polities emerge, evolve, decay and sometimes disappear over time. This would have significant effects on citizenship regimes, as polity change brings about constitutional change and new sites of contestation over belonging and membership. The outcome is all the more complex because in recent years, we have seen the decline of the so-called Westphalian states system as the exclusive underpinning element of citizenship, and the rise of a variety of semi-sovereign polities at the regional, national, supranational and international level, often conferring a range of citizenship-like rights upon individuals on a territorial or a jurisdictional basis. In the context provided by the EU treaties and other international and transnational legal instruments, polities emerge and evolve not just under the shadow of the law, but through the law itself, under the shadow of politics, political practice and constitutional principles, such as the principles of democracy and human rights. In like manner, as political space is restructured, the different legal frameworks governing membership statuses and rights emerge, evolve, decay and sometimes disappear, sometimes under conditions of considerable legal uncertainty as regards the implications of, and for, domestic law, EU law and international law.

But the need to connect the individual and the polity or polities occupying the territorial or legal space or spaces within which the individual resides, works or travels, or to which he or she otherwise enjoys a connection, is an enduring one. It is one that sets many of the boundaries of the most significant life opportunities, both in principle and in practice. Being born with, or subsequently acquiring, the citizenship status of certain states[5] currently conveys significant life

[5] The point is well illustrated by reference to the increase in the share of non-EU born EU citizens as part of the overall population of EU citizens resident in the UK between 2004 and 2015: see Commentary, *Recent Trends in EU nationals born inside and outside the EU* (16 July 2015). <www.migrationobservatory.ox.ac.uk/sites/files/migobs/commentary-recent%20trends%20eu%20nationals_0.pdf>, accessed 19 July 2016. To put it another

opportunities not available to others.[6] This was one reason why many saw the prospect of continued or renewed EU membership for Scotland after independence as a central element of the argument that a small Scotland could be a viable and prosperous state. EU citizenship, although not a new 'nationality' as such but rather a bundle of rights associated with a legal status which derives its scope not just from the EU treaties but also (primarily) from national citizenship laws, was seen as a vital element of the EU membership package, both for putative Scottish citizens and for those coming to, or resident in Scotland, who would enjoy free movement rights if Scotland remained a Member State. Equally, EU citizenship has been a factor in the UK EU referendum debate, especially as free movement rights have become a highly contested element of UK politics.[7] In sum, while the death of national citizenship is frequently announced, it in fact retains an enduring importance which becomes particularly acute at the moments which polities emerge, evolve, decay or disappear; and in the EU context it is supplemented in important ways by EU citizenship. This premise lies at the heart of this chapter.

The possible creation of an independent Scotland (iScotland), with an uncertain status in relation to the EU as well as to the rest of the UK (rUK), has significant citizenship implications. The primary question concerns the identification of who the Scottish citizens that might benefit from EU citizenship are. To avoid uncertainty in the event of secession, it is reasonable to expect that prior to any independence referendum, especially one conducted under democratic conditions and framed by law, it should already be more or less clear who the *ab initio* citizens of the new state would actually be. And one of the first acts of any new state must always be to define by law the new citizenry not only for the moment of independence but also *for the future*, by determining the rules on the future acquisition and/or transmission of citizenship at birth and thereafter. The next section explores these issues.

way, the prior acquisition of the citizenship of an EU Member State seems to have become a significant factor in migration to the UK.

6 A. Shachar, *The Birthright Lottery. Citizenship and Global Inequality* (Cambridge MA: Harvard University Press, 2009); B. Milanovic, 'Global Inequality in Numbers: In History and Now', *Global Policy*, 4 (2013), 198–208 refers to a 'citizenship premium' enjoyed by citizens of rich states.

7 J. Shaw, 'Between Law and Political Truth? Member State Preferences, EU Free Movement Rules and National Immigration Law', *Cambridge Yearbook of European Legal Studies*, 17(2015), 247–286.

But the territorial boundaries of membership regimes rarely coincide precisely with formal legal membership, and many benefits are conferred by states upon lawfully resident non-citizens, sometimes as a result of international obligations which states choose to take on as well as those which are associated with membership of certain organisations, such as the Council of Europe or the European Union. In particular, EU Member States are obliged by EU law to ensure equal treatment for non-national EU citizens in certain areas, pursuant to the EU treaties and secondary legislation. Indeed, sometimes they choose to provide for such equality without any supervening obligations. That the UK has permitted EU citizens to vote in Scottish Parliament and other devolved elections, as well as in the referendum on Scottish independence, is an example of this type of asymmetry between legal membership and political rights. The provision made under UK law goes well beyond the EU rules on local electoral rights for resident EU citizens under Articles 20 and 22 TFEU. That said, EU citizens were not able to vote in the referendum on EU membership, as we shall see in Section IV.

In addition, external non-resident citizens also often benefit under national law from a range of rights extending beyond the right to return, often including the right to vote in some or all elections.[8] Again, EU law has some effects in this domain. EU citizens returning to their home state after exercising their free movement rights are protected, in respect of certain non-discrimination and family reunification rights, by EU law.[9] But EU law *does not* guarantee free movers external electoral rights *outside* the territory of the home state, although some commentators and NGOs have argued that it should do. As we shall see, no external citizens voted in the Scottish referendum, but those absent from the UK for fifteen years or fewer were able to vote in the EU referendum.

There are, therefore, significant tensions between being a (national and EU) citizen and exercising political citizenship, especially where there are potentially shifting polity boundaries in a multi-level constitutional framework such as Scotland/UK/EU. In order to explore these tensions, this chapter uses the analytical framework of the citizenship regime. This combines the status of legal membership with the body of 'citizenship rights'. Studying citizenship regimes can reveal the 'lived

[8] R. Bauböck, 'Morphing the Demos into the Right Shape. Normative Principles for Enfranchising Resident Aliens and Expatriate Citizens', *Democratization*, 22 (2015), 820–839.

[9] Case C-370/90 *Surinder Singh* ECLI:EU:C:1992:296.

details'[10] of a polity and illuminates both the constitutional and the practice dimensions of the 'we'. There has been, as Sandra Seubert has noted, a discernible 'turn to practice' in the context of citizenship studies over the years, bringing in both the formal and informal dimensions of citizenship laws and practices.[11] The contestation of the boundaries of citizenship regimes (membership status and rights) helps us to understand the broader nature of the polity and the shifting constitutional landscape. Moreover, the effects of referendums are not simple top down read-offs from ballot box results. They can, and do, also have complex indirect effects upon the citizenship regimes of the polities affected, before, during and after referendum campaigns.

Such a citizenship-focused analysis can provide useful insights wherever there are active and politically well-supported secessionist and/or withdrawal movements, raising claims in the context of mainstream politics, and not just in the Scotland/UK context. However, this paper will concentrate solely upon the case of UK/Scotland, where the September 2014 referendum on independence resulted in a vote of 55 per cent in favour of remaining in the UK. This demonstrated that there is a substantial groundswell of opinion in favour of independence in Scotland, although not a majority at the time of the referendum.[12]

The outcome of the EU referendum for the UK was closer than that in Scotland in 2014 (52/48 as against 55/45) and demonstrated significant territorial disparities in terms of support for leave/remain across the UK.[13] Sixty-two per cent of people in Scotland voted in favour of the UK remaining in the EU. Meanwhile, England voted 53.5/46.5 for leave (although most of London voted heavily to remain), Wales voted 52.5/47.5 to leave, and Northern Ireland voted 56/44 to remain, with a distinct divergence across the two communities in the province. There are important respects in which the continuing debate about Scottish independence, which the 2014 referendum did not entirely foreclose, are likely to influence the impact and eventual consequences of the EU

[10] K. L. Scheppele, 'Constitutional Ethnography: An Introduction', *Law and Society Review*, 38 (2004), 389–406.

[11] S. Seubert, 'Dynamics of Modern Citizenship Democracy and Peopleness in a Global Era', *Constellations*, 21 (2014), 547–559.

[12] For an overview see T. Mullen, 'The Scottish Independence Referendum 2014', *Journal of Law and Society*, 41 (2014), 627–640.

[13] For details of the EU referendum results, see <www.electoralcommission.org.uk/find-information-by-subject/elections-and-referendums/upcoming-elections-and-referendums/eu-referendum/electorate-and-count-information>, accessed 19 July 2016.

referendum and may have influenced the clear difference in orientation discernible between the Scotland, on the one hand, and England and Wales on the other.

In any altered constitutional situation, whether that results from a secession or a withdrawal referendum, there will be changes to the conditions of political membership in all of the polities affected, demanding political intervention to facilitate the 'right-sizing' of the demos in terms of both membership status and political rights. Even just the threat or suggestion of change can have implications for the notion of 'who we are'. Do we define ourselves, for example, by reference to a territory and residence or a distinct ethnicity? Who should have a say? Defining citizenship in new (and renewed) states under democratic conditions of secession or withdrawal means grappling with the central question of democratic participation and the right to vote as a paradigmatic expression of how the 'we' in any new polity is defined. It raises important and complex citizenship questions for which there is little obvious precedent, especially where the UK has voted to withdraw from the EU and this is likely to have a knock-on effect on the Scottish independence movement and the UK's territorial integrity.

## III Citizenship in a New State: How It Might Work in Scotland

### A. *The Purposes of Citizenship Laws*

Citizenship laws have a number of complementary societal purposes.[14] Perhaps the most important is the assurance of a stable population, especially through the transmission of 'membership' across generations, where most people acquire citizenship involuntarily at birth. But citizenship laws also determine the degree of territorial inclusivity by setting out the terms under which long term resident immigrants can become citizens. In addition, they will determine whether citizenship must be an exclusive relationship, or whether a person may hold dual or multiple citizenships. Citizenship laws also regulate issues such as special ties to the state, or other forms of genuine link for those who have left the territory or are attached to it only by descent from a citizen born in the territory, by providing for preferential naturalisation and/or citizenship by descent. Citizenship laws not only regulate who can *acquire*

[14] M. Vink and R. Bauböck, 'Citizenship Configurations: Analysing the Multiple Purposes of Citizenship Regimes in Europe', *Comparative European Politics*, 11(1) (2013), 621–648.

citizenship, but also who *loses* it, whether through absence from the territory, through voluntary acts of renunciation or as a result of an act of deprivation, for example decisions taken by state authorities on public interest or national security grounds. Finally, and perhaps most significantly for our purposes in this chapter, citizenship laws generally set the *prima facie* boundaries of political *demos*, in the sense of providing – in most cases – the preliminary determination of who can vote and who can stand for election, especially in national elections.

In new states, all of these issues and more come to the fore, as the new state will have to define its own citizenry *ab initio*. Law and politics will influence the outcome. In iScotland, a distinctive politics of identity would certainly be important, as would Scottish demography. The design of citizenship laws would offer one of the routes by which iScotland could simultaneously both distinguish itself from rUK (e.g. in respect of the conditions it might place on naturalisation, in its approach to the transmission of citizenship outside the territory, or in its approach to rights attaching to citizenship), whilst at the same time reassuring new Scots about the validity and durability of their continuing social and economic ties across these islands. This latter is part of a tactic of postulating secession as a relatively 'soft' process in which some key aspects of life would not change, or would change little, and in which changes would come about consensually and through democratic processes.

### B. *The Scottish Context – an Emerging Distinctive Identity against a History of Emigration*

Even though Scotland has not been an independent state for more than 300 years, claims about the nature of Scotland as a 'nation' within the UK have always been closely intertwined with the ebbs and flows of a distinctive Scottish identity *within* the ebbs and flows of the British state.[15] This can be seen most clearly after the Second World War, when stronger movements for greater self-government and independence emerged in Scotland.

Between the 1970s (when it had its first major electoral breakthroughs) and 2007, when it first formed a minority government under the devolved powers of the Scotland Act 1998, the Scottish National Party

[15] M. Pittock, 'Scottish Sovereignty and the Union of 1707: Then and Now', *National Identities*, 14 (2012), 11–21.

(SNP) has transformed into 'civic nationalist' party.[16] Territory and residence, not descent or ethnicity, have become the central elements of attachment to Scotland in elite discourse and, to a degree, in the public imagination.

In addition, as Jonathan White has highlighted, the prevailing identity-based approach to politics in Scotland has latterly partly shifted towards a partisan approach based on opposing austerity as an economic policy.[17] By adopting the trope of opposition to austerity as a badge of identity, the SNP has gone beyond regionalism and the politics of territory, and posed itself as lying at the heart of a larger alternative narrative for British politics as well as just Scottish politics.

This basis for a national sense of self has grafted itself comfortably onto the sense of Scottishness which emerged after 1979. The election of Margaret Thatcher's first conservative government, which saw cold winds of deindustrialisation sweeping through much of Scotland, followed hard on the heels of the March 1979 devolution referendum, in which the SNP called for a vote to reject what it saw as an inadequate settlement proposed by Westminster. The proposal to institute devolved institutions failed, even though it was supported by a majority at the ballot box, because the required threshold of 40 per cent of the registered electorate supporting the initiative was not met. Throughout the eighteen years of Conservative Party government, a strong sense of grievance at the imposition of policies by outsiders and a lack of control of the instruments of government developed. Conservative Party support (and parliamentary representation) collapsed completely in Scotland, from a high point of more than 50 per cent in 1955 to a low point of less than 15 per cent in 2015. Initially, the decline of the Conservative vote resulted in Labour Party dominance. Labour had led the very popular pro-devolution movement before and after 1997. More recently, as Labour became increasingly compromised by its thirteen years in (Westminster) power, including the years of the global financial crisis, and its adherence to a neo-liberal anti-austerity rhetoric, the SNP has emerged as the utterly dominant actor in Scottish politics in the mid-2010s.

16 M. Leith, 'Scottish National Party Representations of Scottishness and Scotland', *Politics*, 28 (2008), 83–92; Andrew Mycock, 'SNP, identity and citizenship: Re-imagining state and nation', *National Identities*, 14 (2012), 53–69.

17 J. White, 'When Parties Make Peoples', *Global Policy*, 6(1) (2015), 106–114.

It secured a landslide fifty-six of the fifty-nine Scottish seats in the 2015 UK General Election, as well as a more substantial Yes vote in the 2014 referendum than was predicted by the polls and expert observers when the campaign started. 2016 saw it re-elected, albeit no longer with an outright majority, as the dominant force in the Scottish Parliament and able to form a minority government.

This sense of Scottish identity is also sustained by a perception that Scots are somehow more egalitarian and more interested in strong welfare state institutions than are the English, and that they are less animated by the hostility to immigration (and indeed free movement), which is an important factor in negative attitudes towards the EU in England.[18] Although this perception of greater attachment to egalitarianism barely finds support in public opinion or social attitudes-based research, it is strongly articulated electorally in terms of different voting patterns in Scotland to England, largely because of how Scots have built certain myths into their identity and their belief systems.[19] It has influenced perceptions of what a future Scotland ought to look like, and how it should regulate both citizenship and citizenship rights. Alongside these changes, the SNP has transformed itself from an anti-European[20] to a pro-European party, brandishing the slogan of 'Scotland in Europe', to sustain the idea that small states are those that do best from EU integration.[21]

Scotland's distinctive landscape of electoral support for parties and political elite preferences has also long played out in stronger popular support for the UK to remain in the EU, with 64 per cent of voters indicating in the British Election survey that they would vote to

[18] J. Portes, 'Free movement: here to stay?' (10 January 2016) *NIESR* Blog, <www.niesr.ac.uk/blog/free-movementhere-stay#.VpOgP_HezTE>, accessed 19 July 2016.

[19] A. Henderson, 'The myth of meritocratic Scotland: political cultures in the UK', in P. Cowley and R. Ford (eds.), *Sex, Lies and the Ballot Box* (London: Biteback Publishing, 2014); and A. Henderson, C. Jeffrey and R. Lineira, 'National Identity or National Interest? Scottish, English and Welsh Attitudes to the Constitutional Debate', *The Political Quarterly*, 86 (2015), 265–274.

[20] In the 1975 referendum, the SNP campaigned for the UK to leave 'the common market', because initially it believed that this was the direction in which public opinion was heading. See J. Mitchell, 'The EU Referendum: Unpredictable in Scotland and the UK' (1 December 2015) *European Futures* Blog, <www.europeanfutures.ed.ac.uk/article-2246>, accessed 19 July 2016. In the event, every part of Scotland voted to remain in the EEC, apart from Orkney and Shetland.

[21] J. Shaw, 'Scotland: 40 Years of EU Membership', *Journal of Contemporary European Research*, 8 (2012), 547–554.

remain in the EU, and 24 per cent indicating they would vote to leave.[22] This support was present across voters for all of the main parties in Scotland, including the Conservatives. In the event, Scotland split 62/38 with no single Council area voting 'Leave'. From early on in the campaign a crucial and potentially painful difference between Scotland and the rest of the UK was visible.[23] In the event there was a fourteen-point difference between the outcomes in Scotland and the UK as a whole.

Finally, it is worth noting the demography of modern Scotland. For many centuries, Scotland has been a country of emigration. However, the picture has become more complex in recent years. The historical patterns of emigration continue – with perhaps a million persons born in Scotland not resident there at present (against a current population of around 5.4 m).[24] But Scotland has also become a migration destination and there are increasing numbers of non-UK citizens and non-UK born UK citizens resident in Scotland (as well as continuing high levels of mobility between Scotland and the rest of the UK). Scotland mirrors patterns of immigration visible elsewhere in the UK, although with smaller numbers of migrants.[25] Citizenship laws would thus grant Scotland one means to respond to its distinctive demographic challenges in terms of a relatively stagnant population and – in common with other advanced post-industrial states – an ageing population,[26] as well as to express the distinctive identity politics sketched above.

22 J. Curtice, *Britain Divided? Who supports and opposes EU Membership, What UK Thinks* (October 2015) Analysis Paper 1, <http://whatukthinks.org/eu/wp-content/uploads/2015/10/Analysis-paper-1-Britain-divided.pdf>, accessed 19 July 2016.

23 'Scots want to stay in EU, as the rest of Britain wants to say goodbye, says new poll' (2 November 2015) *The Herald*, <www.heraldscotland.com/news/13187523.Scots_want_to_stay_in_EU__as_the_rest_of_Britain_wants_to_say_goodbye__says_new_poll/>, accessed 19 July 2016. Nigel Farage famously described the 'Brexit' campaign in Scotland in February 2016 as 'a bit embryonic', see G. Campbell, 'Brexit campaign "embryonic" in Scotland' (1 February 2016) *BBC News* <www.bbc.co.uk/news/uk-scotland-scotland-politics-35458658>, accessed 19 July 2016.

24 See 'Scotland Analysis: Devolution and the implications of Scottish Independence' (2013) Cm 8544, at 20; and J. Carr and L. Cavanagh, 'Scotland's Diaspora and Overseas-Born Population' (2009) Scottish Government Social Research.

25 For an overview, see Migration Observatory Commentary, 'Bordering on confusion: International Migration and Implications for Scottish Independence' (16 September 2013), <www.migrationobservatory.ox.ac.uk/commentary/bordering-confusion-international-migration-and-implications-scottish-independence>, accessed 19 July 2016.

26 Scottish Parliament Finance Committee Report, 'Demographic Change and an Ageing Population' (11 February 2013) 2nd Report, 2013 (Session 4), <www.scottish.parliament.uk/S4_FinanceCommittee/Reports/fiR13-02_rev.pdf>, accessed 19 July 2016.

### C. *Theory into Practice and Identity Politics into Law: What Would Scottish Citizenship Look Like?*

There is guidance from both state practice and international law instruments to assist lawmakers in the creation of new norms of citizenship in seceding states. Scotland has no modern history of statehood – and no historical citizenry – on which to draw, and thus the 'restored state' model of new citizenship used in some states[27] cannot be invoked. Moreover, the 'federal' model of new citizenship building is not applicable, given the limited character of the UK's asymmetric devolution arrangements. Unlike the former federations Yugoslavia or Czechoslovakia, there is no former 'republican' or regional level citizenship, in a formal sense, on which to draw.[28] Consequently, iScotland would probably use the third model of *ab initio* citizenship building for new states, namely the residence-based or territorial model. This approach would be tempered by continuing close relationships across these islands, not only between iScotland and the rUK but also with Ireland, which itself became independent from what we now call the United Kingdom by a complex (and often violent) process between 1919 and 1922. Ireland's own citizenship regime, built up over many years, remains partially entwined with that of the UK in ways which relate to the earlier independence process, to ongoing patterns of migration and – more recently – to the Northern Ireland peace process.[29] Many of these key points were noted in UK Government commentary on proposals for Scottish citizenship.[30]

In international law, the most important principle concerns protection against statelessness occurring as a result of the creation of a new

[27] See O. Shevel, 'The Politics of Citizenship Policy in New States', *Comparative Politics*, 41 (2009), 273–291.

[28] J. Shaw and I. Štiks (eds.), *Citizenship after Yugoslavia* (London: Taylor and Francis, 2012).

[29] B. Ryan, Written Evidence to the Scottish Affairs Select Committee (August 2012) <www.publications.parliament.uk/pa/cm201213/cmselect/cmscotaf/139/139we02.htm>, accessed 19 July 2016.

[30] Scotland Analysis, 'Borders and Citizenship' (January 2014) Cm 8726, <www.gov.uk/government/publications/scotland-analysis-borders-and-citizenship>, accessed 19 July 2016; J. Crawford and A. Boyle, 'Opinion: Referendum on the Independence of Scotland – International Law Aspects', published as Annex A to Scotland Analysis, 'Devolution and the implications of Scottish independence' (February 2013) Cm 8554, <www.gov.uk/government/uploads/system/uploads/attachment_data/file/79408/Annex_A.pdf>, accessed 19 July 2016.

state.[31] We should also bear in mind that the European Convention on Nationality (which the UK has not ratified) offers benchmarks in relation to key principles such as non-discrimination. As for EU law, its impact is far more attenuated. There has been little impact, on the part of EU law, as regards the cases of new citizenship regimes in Europe since 1989, although there is some evidence of pre-accession influence.[32] As for the existing Member States, some have argued that there is potential for EU law influence to grow, subsequent to the judgment of the Court of Justice in the *Rottmann* case.[33] This concluded that in certain respects national rules on loss of citizenship fell within the scope of EU law and could be affected by the imperative of protecting the essence of EU citizenship.[34]

Before the referendum campaign began, there were few hints as to what future Scottish citizenship might look like. The points about territory and a sense of an inclusive and egalitarian identity discussed above can be found in the Scottish Government 2009 White Paper *Your Scotland. Your Voice*:[35]

> Citizenship in an independent Scotland will be based upon an inclusive model. Many people in Scotland have ties to the rest of the United Kingdom, including familial, social and economic connections. An independent Scotland could recognise the complex shared history of Scotland and the United Kingdom by offering shared or dual citizenship.

A related 2009 document on *Europe and Foreign Affairs* also mentioned the importance of people identifying 'with the community in which they live and [feeling] valued and part of Scottish society'.[36] The inclusive

[31] On this, see the Draft Articles of the International Law Commission on Nationality of Natural Persons in relation to the Succession of States, 1999, <www.unhcr.org/5465e1ca9.pdf>, accessed 19 July 2016.

[32] J. Shaw, 'The constitutional mosaic across the boundaries of the European Union: citizenship regimes in the new states of South Eastern Europe', in N. Walker, S. Tierney and J. Shaw (eds.), *Europe's Constitutional Mosaic* (Oxford: Hart, 2011), pp. 137–170.

[33] Case C-135/08 *Rottmann* v. *Freistaat Bayern*, ECLI:EU:C:2010:104

[34] See the extended commentary in J. Shaw (ed.), 'Has the European Court of Justice challenged Member State sovereignty in nationality law?', EUI Working Paper, RSCAS 2011/62.

[35] Scottish Government, 'Your Scotland. Your Voice. A National Conversation' (November 2009), <www.scotland.gov.uk/Publications/2009/11/26155932/0>, accessed 19 July 2016, at 135 (para. 8.22).

[36] Scottish Government, 'Europe and Foreign Affairs. Taking Forward our National Conversation' (Edinburgh, 2009), <www.scotland.gov.uk/Resource/Doc/283886/0086022.pdf>, accessed 19 July 2016, at 24–25 (para. 5.13).

model is 'designed to support economic growth, integration and promotion of diversity.'

The 2013 White Paper *Scotland's Future*, setting out the prospectus for independence, continues this line of thinking:

> At the point of independence, this Government proposes an inclusive model of citizenship for people whether or not they define themselves as primarily or exclusively Scottish or wish to become a Scottish passport holder. People in Scotland are accustomed to multiple identities, be they national, regional, ethnic, linguistic or religious, and a commitment to a multi-cultural Scotland will be a cornerstone of the nation on independence.[37]

*Scotland's Future* outlined a number of pathways to citizenship, both on and after independence. These are relatively standard when viewed in international comparison (see Table 9.1 below).[38]

Table 9.1 *Scottish Government comparison between status quo and hypothetical Scottish citizenship*

| Current status | Scottish Citizenship? |
|---|---|
| **At the date of independence** | |
| British citizen habitually resident in Scotland on day one of independence | **Yes, automatically** a Scottish citizen |
| British citizens born in Scotland but living outside of Scotland on day one of independence | **Yes, automatically** a Scottish citizen |
| **After the date of independence** | |
| Child born in Scotland to at least one parent who has Scottish citizenship or indefinite leave to remain at the time of their birth | **Yes, automatically** a Scottish citizen |
| Child born outside Scotland to at least one parent who has Scottish citizenship | **Yes, automatically** a Scottish citizen (the birth must be registered in Scotland to take effect) |
| British national living outside Scotland with at least one parent who qualifies for Scottish citizenship | Can **register** as a Scottish citizen (will need to provide evidence to substantiate) |

[37] Scottish Government, 'Scotland's Future' (November 2013) White Paper, <www.gov.scot/Publications/2013/11/9348>, accessed 19 July 2016, at 271.

[38] 'Scotland's Future', 273; also available at <www.gov.scot/Publications/2013/11/9348/11>, accessed 19 May 2017.

Table 9.1 *(cont.)*

| Current status | Scottish Citizenship? |
|---|---|
| Citizens of any country, who have a parent or grandparent who qualifies for Scottish citizenship | Can **register** as a Scottish citizen (will need to provide evidence to substantiate) |
| Migrants in Scotland legally | **May apply** for naturalisation as a Scottish citizen (subject to meeting good character, residency and any other requirements set out under Scottish immigration law) |
| Citizens of any country who have spent at least ten years living in Scotland at any time and have an ongoing connection with Scotland | **May apply** for naturalisation as a Scottish citizen (subject to meeting good character and any other requirements set out under Scottish immigration law) |

*Source: Scotland's Future,* November 2013

Specifically, the government proposed an approach to citizenship *ab initio* which combined residence with descent. Citizenship would be automatically attributed to those UK citizens habitually resident in Scotland on the date of independence and to those UK citizens who were born in Scotland and but were resident outside Scotland. No explicit reference is made to a right to choose on the part of those putative citizens who may have other citizenships, but the approach suggests that iScotland would have (at least potentially) a substantial number of external citizens, resident either in rUK or elsewhere. After independence, the routes to citizenship would either be automatic (at birth), by registration (for those with close ties) or on application for naturalisation as a citizen, subject to conditions.

If implemented, the overall scheme would probably have been somewhat broader than UK citizenship is at present, allowing also for registration by citizens of other states who have a grandparent who qualifies for Scottish citizenship. This suggested quite a strong focus on ethnically defined citizenship transmission across generations, notwithstanding the rhetoric of territorial and residence-based inclusion given such attention in the political documentation.

However, one proposed route to naturalisation was rather curious and raised some questions about the balance between territory, ethnicity and other forms of affiliation. This was the case of 'citizenship by connection'.

A person – regardless of nationality – could apply for naturalisation as a Scottish citizen on the basis of ten years of prior residency, whenever that might have been, and regardless of whether that residency was still subsisting. This possibility was intended to operate in addition to ordinary naturalisation for non-citizen residents. This is more liberal than ordinary naturalisation because it does not require residence at the time of application, although ten years of (past) residence is longer than the UK currently requires for naturalisation. This is an unusual mode of acquisition, without direct equivalent in other states, perhaps closest in character to the socialisation-based modes of acquisition found in some states, although these generally require residence as a condition.[39] It shades towards an arbitrary and overbroad preference for a group based on a dubious and undefined criterion of 'connection'. It is a category of citizenship acquisition which could easily be subject to 'deflection effects'. This is what occurs when a person of a first state exploits some condition (e.g. descent from former citizens or, in this case, earlier residence) in order to obtain the passport of a second state which they intend to use not in order to reside in that state (or at least not for more than a minimum of time) but in order to reside and work in a third state (in this case, by virtue of EU free movement laws or domestic arrangements made to accommodate Scottish citizens in rUK). The possibility that such deflection effects might operate to the rUK's detriment was highlighted in UK Government commentary on citizenship.[40]

In sum, iScotland's citizenship law seemed likely to be rather inclusive, not only on a territorial basis, but also on the basis of other connections to Scotland, including ethnicity and descent, as well as *past* residence. Such a broad citizenship law, perhaps overinclusive across some dimensions, presented an interesting contrast with the discussion – developed in the next section – of the *residence-based* franchise which was applied to the independence referendum, notwithstanding the loud objections of persons born in Scotland and now resident elsewhere, especially in England. For some, this franchise was *underinclusive*.

39 For more details, see the EUDO Citizenship Observatory's modes of acquisition databases, in particular mode A07: <http://eudo-citizenship.eu/databases/modes-of-acquisition?p=&application=modesAcquisition&search=1&modeby=idmode&idmode=A07>, accessed 19 July 2016.

40 See 'Borders and Citizenship' (note 30), at para. 4.48.

But any future Scottish citizenship law (which is bound to be contested, not only initially but for a longer period after independence by those who felt it was too restrictive, as much as by those who felt it was too inclusive) would not sit in isolation. Geographically and geopolitically, a new citizenship regime can never be an island, with its legal boundaries creating a hermetically sealed space. Scotland would be no different. *Scotland's Future* acknowledged this, but seemed to predict that a framework of softer citizenship boundaries might emerge. This tone was struck probably in order to provide assurance to Scottish voters that little would change in the citizenship sphere despite secession.

The proposals envisaged the possibility of a very substantial overlap between Scottish citizenship and rUK citizenship, involving mutual tolerance of dual citizenship. It is implicit in *Scotland's Future* that the Scottish Government envisaged that new Scottish citizens would have the right to opt (i.e. presumably to choose to be 'British' and/or 'Scottish'). It had perhaps looked, amongst other sources of inspiration, at the right of option in Northern Ireland as the guide for this.[41]

But this may be a situation that the rUK would choose to prevent, although we cannot at this moment predict how the rUK might react to such features of a Scottish citizenship regime. The rUK might, for example, consider the withdrawal – in accordance with international law and common state practice[42] – of UK citizenship from those resident in Scotland and enjoying the benefit of Scottish citizenship, who lacked a connection with the rest of the UK (e.g. those born in Scotland who had never been resident in the rest of the UK). Such a separation of citizenship regimes is what occurred, for example, when many former UK colonies and dominions became independent, and some have argued it would be the appropriate response in the Scottish case.[43] Furthermore, the rUK could adopt a hostile

[41] Northern Ireland Peace Agreement (Good Friday Agreement), April 1998, read in conjunction with Irish nationality law (see Ryan (note 29)).

[42] B. Ryan, 'At the Borders of Sovereignty: Nationality and Immigration Policy in an Independent Scotland', *Journal of Immigration Asylum and Nationality Law*, 28 (2014), 146–164.

[43] C. Yeo, 'Dual Citizenship and Scottish Independence', (15 September 2013) *Free Movement* Blog, <www.freemovement.org.uk/dual-citizenship-and-scottish-independence/>, accessed 19 July 2016, criticising *inter alia* Nick Barber, 'After the vote: the citizenship question', (4 August 2014) *UK Constitutional Law Association* Blog, <http://ukconstitutionallaw.org/2014/08/04/nick-barber-after-the-vote-the-citizenship-question/>, accessed 19 July 2016.

stance towards dual citizenship, thus making it hard even for those with a connection to both states to hold the two citizenships simultaneously.

But even if there were a large measure of separation between the two citizenship regimes, akin to that which occurred when the colonies and dominions became independent, there may not be a high degree of social acceptance of such a separation, if it ended up dividing families in ways which created anomalies or boundaries which were hard to understand. There would be pressure on those boundaries from those who found themselves just one side or the other, and long-term contestation of both the Scottish and the rUK citizenship regimes. Moreover, the numbers of (theoretical if not actual) dual citizens might still be quite large, given the degree of cross-border mobility across the UK.

Furthermore, experience with the creation of new states highlights that whether people choose to 'adopt' new citizenships that they are given after birth as a result of the establishment of new states often tends to be the result of pragmatic considerations. The decision to opt for more than one citizenship is frequently influenced by considerations such as access to travel documents, political rights, socioeconomic rights such as the right to live and work in more than one state, and access to welfare rights, perhaps with a dash of 'identity' thrown into the mix. For those who voted against independence, would taking a Scottish passport be seen as approving separation after the event?

The nestedness of citizenship regimes thus has both geopolitical and individual characteristics and consequences. There are complex interdependencies within citizenship regimes and between different regimes, often as a result of the piecemeal historical evolution of status, rights and identity. This is certainly true within the UK's current regime, where any attempts to change certain aspects of the regime (e.g. the UK's system of voting rights for Irish and certain Commonwealth citizens who are not subject to immigration control) in order to make the regime cohere around a specific model of attachment and polity membership, are likely to run aground on other aspects of the regime, such as the historically close links across these islands and the UK's imperial history.[44] The point about complex and hard-to-fathom membership models becomes ever clearer when we explore in more detail the

[44] J. Shaw, 'Citizenship and Electoral Rights in the Multi-Level "Euro-Polity": The Case of the United Kingdom', in H. Lindahl (ed.), *A Right to Inclusion and Exclusion? Normative Fault Lines of the EU's Area of Freedom, Security and Justice* (Oxford: Hart Publishing, 2009), pp. 241–253.

interactions between the legal status of citizenship and other dimensions of the concept of citizenship, in particular political rights, as voting is a paradigmatic expression of the democratic 'we'. This is the task of the next and final substantive section of this chapter.

## IV Citizenship and the Evolving Polity: 'Rightsizing' the Demos

A new citizenship regime is the product of a political act of self-determination. In the Scottish case, that act of self-determination, taking the form of a referendum, is rightly characterised by Rainer Bauböck as consensual and democratic in character, rather than remedial.[45] A similar point can be made about a vote on state membership of the European Union, since the EU treaties now include a provision explicitly providing for the possibility of withdrawal, based on a negotiation between the withdrawing state and the other Member States (Article 50 TEU). But how should the self-determining 'we' be defined in these cases? Three groups of issues can be separated out:

- Who should vote in any independence referendum? Citizens? Residents? Some combination of the two? In the case of a referendum on EU membership (characterised by Eurosceptic forces precisely as an 'independence' referendum), are the questions (and the balance of interests) just the same as they are for a secession referendum *within* a state?
- In the event of a 'yes' vote creating a new state such as iScotland, who should be able to vote in the first general election in that newly constituted state? Has the vote to leave the EU, thus arguably reconstituting the sovereignty the UK, changed the constellation of interests which determine the scope of the general election franchise in the UK?
- And, finally, who might participate – and how – in any constitutional convention to prepare a long-term written constitution for the newly reconstituted state? This is presently only an issue for iScotland,[46] as despite the uncertainties to which it has given rise, there is no

[45] R. Bauböck, 'Regional Citizenship and Self-Determination', in R. Ziegler, J. Shaw and R. Bauböck (eds.), *Independence Referendums: Who should vote and who should be offered citizenship?* (2014) EUI Working Paper RSCAS 2014/90.

[46] As Aileen McHarg has noted in A. McHarg, 'The Constitutional Case for Independence', in A. McHarg, T. Mullen, A. Page and N. Walker (eds.), *The Scottish Independence Referendum: Constitutional and Political Implications* (Oxford: OUP, 2016). Available at DOI 10.1093/acprof:oso/9780198755517.003.0005. Constitutional questions may not have been to the fore in the referendum debate, but constitutional questions were

immediate suggestion that the leave vote in the EU referendum could lead to a constitutional reformation of the UK. However, as we shall discuss below, the UK is unlikely to be left constitutionally unchanged by the vote to leave the EU.

This section concentrates on the questions within the first bullet point from an empirical and a normative perspective, as the second and third sets of questions are speculative at present; however, the normative considerations discussed below could be applicable in those cases as well. With respect to elections to what would then be a *national* parliament, it would have been interesting to see whether iScotland would innovate and allow EU citizens to vote on the basis of the precedent set in respect of the devolved institutions (and in line with arguments led by a number of NGOs in the context of a European Citizens' Initiative).[47] This would reflect and build upon the present reciprocal arrangements between Ireland and the UK.[48] Furthermore, with respect to participation in a longer-term constitution-building process, leading to a likely written constitution for Scotland (in contradistinction to the current position in the UK),[49] a number of options for incorporating the interests of non-citizen residents might well have been on the table, for example via civil society participation.[50]

### A. *Legal and Constitutional Considerations: The Scottish Referendum*

The franchise for the 2014 referendum was settled by legislation, based on the Edinburgh Agreement. This handed the determination of the franchise over to the Scottish Parliament, where normally it was a matter reserved for the Westminster Parliament.

undoubtedly central to a deeper understanding of how the case for 'Yes' needed to be understood.

47 Let Me Vote was an unsuccessful European Citizens' Initiative (www.letmevote.eu/en/). The issues are discussed in depth in P. Cayala, C. Seth and R. Bauböck (eds.), *Should EU Citizens Living in Other Member States Vote There in National Elections?*, (2012) EUI Working Paper RSCAS 2012/32, available at <http://cadmus.eui.eu/bitstream/handle/1814/22754/RSCAS_2012_32.pdf?sequence=1>, accessed 19 July 2016.

48 J. Shaw, *The Transformation of Citizenship in Europe*, (Cambridge: CUP, 2007), pp. 251–263.

49 See further McHarg above (note 46).

50 A. Renwick, *After the Referendum: Options for a Constitutional Convention*, (London: The Constitution Society, 2014).

Under the Scottish Independence Referendum (Franchise) Act 2013, the referendum franchise was based on the local government and Scottish Parliament electoral register, with the addition of sixteen- and seventeen-year-olds. It was entirely residence-based and rejected the voting claims of non-resident 'Scots', whether they resided in the rest of the UK or elsewhere in the world, however recently they departed and however they claimed to be 'Scottish' (by descent, prior residence or birth). It therefore included resident EU, Irish and qualifying Commonwealth citizens (pursuant to a mix of UK law and EU law peculiar to the UK), but did not include any other non-citizens, including those who have indefinite leave to remain in the UK. It also excluded prisoners, in like manner to electoral franchises at all levels right across the UK.[51]

The exclusion of UK citizens with a connection to Scotland but no longer resident there encountered some public opposition, notably from London-based Scots. Some suggested that this exclusion was contrary to EU law,[52] although the issue was not tested in the courts. The inclusion of EU citizens resident in Scotland along with the other categories of residents (i.e. Irish and qualifying Commonwealth citizens), who are generally enfranchised under UK law, received relatively little comment in the media. While some elements within the resident EU-citizen community publicly embraced the opportunity to cast a ballot,[53] research suggests that for some, having the vote was seen as a burdensome privilege rather than an important opportunity for political self-determination.[54]

It is interesting to note that the nationals of the other Member States were not part of the electorate for the 1979 devolution referendum, which was conducted on the basis of the Westminster (i.e. national) franchise. This preceded the establishment of EU voting rights. But

[51] This was confirmed by the judgment of the Supreme Court in *Moohan and Another* v. *Lord Advocate* [2014] UKSC 67. A. Tickell, 'Litigating with a Blunderbuss: Prisoner Votes, Moohan v Lord Advocate and the Independence Referendum Franchise', *Edinburgh Law Review*, 19 (2015), 409–414.

[52] 'Legal Challenge to Scottish Expats Being Denied Vote in Independence Referendum' (14 March 2014) *Votes for Expats* Blog, <http://votes-for-expat-brits-blog.com/2014/03/14/legal-challenge-to-scottish-expats-denial-of-vote-in-independence-referendum/>, accessed 19 July 2016.

[53] See, for example, <www.facebook.com/EuCitizensForAnIndependentScotland>.

[54] E. Pietka-Nykaza and D. McGhee, 'Stakeholder citizenship: the complexities of Polish migrants' citizenship attachments in the context of the Scottish independence referendum', *Citizenship Studies*, 20:1, (2016), 115–129.

using the Westminster franchise would still have included in the franchise Irish and qualifying Commonwealth citizens who have *always* voted in *all* UK elections – a principle which was recognised by the Court of Justice in the *Gibraltar* case as being constitutional in character for the UK.[55]

Furthermore, since the 1979 referendum, certain external voters have been included in the UK Westminster elections franchise, albeit with a maximum time limit at present of fifteen years after departure from the UK.[56] The challenge of setting parameters for the inclusion of 'external' voters for the referendum would have been very tough. If 'external' voters had been included, presumably no distinction would have been drawn between those living in Paris and those living in London. Including external 'Scots' would have required significant innovation in comparison to existing electoral registration practices, and would have imposed additional costs (including allowing persons resident in one part of the UK to vote in another part of the UK), without an obvious improvement in the legitimacy of the process.

Finally, in 1997, a precedent was set that the devolution referendum was run using the local elections franchise (i.e. including EU citizens and limiting the franchise by reference to residence), and this then became the basis for the Scottish Parliament elections franchise from 1999 onwards. In sum, the outcome may seem peculiar (and it is unique in the EU context), but its probable rationale in the UK system has been to emphasise the *local* as opposed to *sovereign* character of Scottish Parliament elections.[57]

It was suggested, notably by Aidan O'Neill,[58] that the exclusion of non-resident Scottish-born UK citizens from the right to vote in the independence referendum was not compatible with EU law, because Member States – although they have the competence to determine a matter of national law such as the franchises in national elections or in a secession referendum – should act in compliance with EU law, including the principle of free movement, when exercising

[55] Case C-145/04 *Spain* v. *United Kingdom (Gibraltar)*, ECLI:EU:C:2006:231, discussed in Shaw, *Transformation of Citizenship* (note 48), pp. 180–187.

[56] See s. 141 Political Parties, Elections and Referendums Act 2000.

[57] See *AXA General Insurance Company Ltd v Lord Advocate* [2012] UKSC 122, in which the Supreme Court gave its view on the non-sovereign nature of the Scottish Parliament.

[58] A. O'Neill, '(Dis)enfranchisement and free movement', draft chapter, December 2015, on file with the author.

such a competence. The determination of the franchise is capable of affecting the extent to which individuals may exercise their free movement rights, because of the risk that the independence referendum would result in a vote for secession and that the new Scottish citizens (including those resident outside Scotland) may lose their EU citizenship and associated rights either for the shorter or the longer term. Member States must accordingly implement such a national competence in a manner not likely to impede free movement. Although this is a stretched definition of obstacles to free movement, O'Neill contended that the duties of the Member States extended that far nonetheless. He noted the interest that the European Commission has taken in the question of disenfranchisement of Member State nationals who are resident outside their state of citizenship, directing a Recommendation in particular at those Member States (including the UK) which limit the *national* voting rights of non-resident citizens.[59] For UK citizens resident for more than fifteen years outside the UK, the consequence of free movement is indeed disenfranchisement from participation in UK elections, and thus the possible loss of any right to vote in a national election unless they have taken up citizenship in the host state. But this may not be possible (or desirable) if, for example, the fifteen-plus-years absence from the UK has been spent in a variety of different host states, and/or if the host state does not permit dual citizenship. The European Commission has recognised the difficulties that this raises, and highlighted that the vast majority of Member States do make external voting rights available without time limitation, but the Commission's measure is just that: a Recommendation without binding force.

Overall, any attempt to invoke EU law is likely to be unsuccessful. Certainly, it is true to say that the Scottish Parliament, in adopting the Scottish Independence Referendum (Franchise) Act 2013, did not have regard to the potential implications in relation to EU free movement, and it is also the case that such a vote does has the capacity to affect the EU citizenship status of the putative citizens of a new state, because of the uncertainties of the (re)accession process. Moreover, since the referendum, the connections between EU citizenship and

[59] European Commission, Commission Communication addressing the consequences of disenfranchisement of Union citizens exercising their right to free movement, COM (2014) 33 final; European Commission, Commission Recommendation addressing the consequences of disenfranchisement of Union citizens exercising their right to free movement, COM (2014) 391 final.

national rules on the franchise seem to have been strengthened by the *Delvigne* case.[60] In this case, the Court of Justice held that French rules on the disenfranchisement of those who had committed a criminal offence (so far as they applied to European Parliament elections) fell within the scope of EU law and thus had to be justified as restrictions to the principle of universal suffrage enshrined *inter alia* in Article 39(2) of the Charter of Fundamental Rights as regards European Parliament elections (as well as in Article 14(3) TEU and Article 223 TFEU).

While this case opens up the possibility of a new level of scrutiny on restrictions on the right to vote in European Parliament elections by reference to EU law, it creates a connection between EU law and national voting rights rules only in that respect, and without regard to the free movement issue. Successful challenges to restrictions contained in such rules might have a knock-on effect (in the same way that the extension of the right to vote in Scottish Parliament elections and in the Scottish independence referendum could be seen as knock on effects of the EU local electoral rights when understood in the particular constitutional context of the UK), but it does not in itself create a direct connection between EU law and EU citizenship and regional secession referendums. To that end, it is important to understand the limitations of the *Delvigne* case, reinforced by Judge Lenaerts, the newly (2015) elected President of the Court of Justice, writing extra-judicially.[61] He noted that it is significant that what he calls the 'seminal' case of *Delvigne* proceeds by recognising the constitutional autonomy of the principle of representative democracy, long embedded in the provisions on European Parliament elections and given greater salience after the Lisbon Treaty entered into force. *Delvigne* is not a judicial reading into the provisions on EU citizenship of an 'incorporation doctrine', possible in a federal state such as the United States of America, which opens the way for the highest court in the polity to scrutinise all legal provisions for their adherence to fundamental rights doctrines. Indeed, such a conclusion would require a more capacious construction of the

[60] Case C-650/13 *Delvigne* v. *Commune de Lesparre Médoc and Préfet de la Gironde*, ECLI: EU:C:2015:648. See J. Shaw, 'Prisoner Voting: Now a Matter of EU law' (15 October 2015) *EU Law Analysis* Blog, <http://eulawanalysis.blogspot.co.uk/2015/10/prisoner-voting-now-matter-of-eu-law.html>, accessed 19 July 2016.

[61] K. Lenaerts, 'Linking EU Citizenship to Democracy', *Croatian Yearbook of European Law and Policy*, 11(2015), Editorial Note vii–xviii.

constitutional significance of EU citizenship than has thus far been admitted by the Court of Justice, despite the rhetoric that it is 'destined to be the fundamental status of the nationals of the Member States'.[62] Any other conclusion, said Judge Lenaerts, would be contrary to the allocation of competences between the EU and the Member States enshrined in the treaties, and would also overstep the judicial function, by instituting a judge-led reformation of the content of EU citizenship rights.

### B. *Legal and Constitutional Considerations: The EU Referendum*

The franchise for the referendum on UK membership of the European Union was fixed at an early stage, as was the question.[63] The EU Referendum Act 2015[64] laid down that the franchise would be based on the general election franchise, with provision made also for members of the House of Lords to vote, along with electors in Gibraltar who vote in European Parliament elections pursuant to the *Matthews* case.[65] One of the most contentious issues concerned the extent to which non-resident UK citizens would be enfranchised.[66] The decision to continue with the fifteen-year external voting restriction in the case of the referendum franchise might be thought contestable, as the abolition of the rule was included in the 2015 general election manifesto of the Conservative Party and is the subject of a promised 'Votes for Life' Bill, likely to come under discussion before the next anticipated general election (2020).[67] Questions were also raised regarding the exclusion of resident EU citizens, given that they had voted in the Scottish independence

[62] Case C-184/99 *Grzelczyk*, ECLI:EU:C:2001:458, para. 31. See J. Shaw, 'Citizenship: contrasting dynamics at the interface of integration and constitutionalism', in P. Craig and G. de Búrca (eds.), *The Evolution of EU Law* (2nd Edition, Oxford: OUP, 2011), pp. 575–609.

[63] The referendum was held on the question: 'Should the United Kingdom remain a member of the European Union or leave the European Union?', under s1(4) EU Referendum Act 2015.

[64] <www.legislation.gov.uk/ukpga/2015/36/contents/enacted/data.htm>, accessed 19 May 2017.

[65] *Matthews* v. *the United Kingdom*, App No. 24833/94, ECHR 1999-I.

[66] For analysis, see C. Hanretty, 'Does the #Brexit referendum franchise matter?' (15 May 2015) Blog, <http://chrishanretty.co.uk/blog/index.php/2015/05/25/does-the-brexit-referendum-franchise-matter/>, accessed 19 July 2016; and S. Peers, 'Who should get the vote in a Brexit referendum?' (29 January 2015) *EU Law Analysis* Blog, <http://eulawanalysis.blogspot.co.uk/2015/01/who-should-get-vote-in-brexit-referendum.html>, accessed 19 July 2016.

[67] For details, see I White, 'Overseas Voters' (23 March 2017) House of Commons Library Briefing Paper No. 5923.

referendum. The third issue raised was that of enfranchising sixteen- and seventeen-year-olds, who not only voted in the Scottish referendum but who have also, from 2016, voted in Scottish Parliament elections. Of all the points of contention, it was the latter which attracted most support in the Westminster Parliament. The House of Lords inserted an amendment to give sixteen- and seventeen-year-olds the right to vote, but this was reversed by the House of Commons.[68]

In the end, all attempts to vary the Westminster franchise along these lines failed, despite the arguments that each group – resident EU citizens, UK 'expats' and young voters – all have particularly high stakes in the outcome of the referendum. There may be good political or justice-based arguments for including those who are taking advantage of EU free movement rights (in whichever direction) in the decision on whether the UK remains a member of the EU or not, not least because EU citizens are selectively franchised in the UK at present. Irish citizens and Maltese and Cypriot citizens (as Commonwealth citizens) benefit from the existing rules.[69] Moreover, as all of these groups are outnumbered by 'sedentary' citizens and voters, the case could perhaps be made for giving them a say. But one reason for not including either group of voters was the view – driven by opinion polling – that the overall outcome was likely to be close (as indeed it turned out to be), and the government, which largely drove the 'scene-setting' part of the process, did not want to be subject to the accusation of loading the dice in advance of the vote, however small or large the group included or excluded actually was. In that context, the Westminster franchise represented a safe haven.

Returning to the arguments about EU law made previously, is there a more plausible connection to EU law in respect of the determination of the franchise for a referendum on state membership of the EU, as opposed to regional secession? In line with the free-movement-based argument made in respect of the inclusion of non-resident Scottish-born UK citizens in the Scottish referendum franchise, O'Neill argued that a similar case could be made in respect of the exclusion of EU citizens exercising their free movement rights (in either direction).

[68] For details of the passage of the bill, see <http://services.parliament.uk/bills/2015–16/europeanunionreferendum.html>.

[69] R. Ziegler, 'The "Brexit" Referendum: We Need to Talk about the (General Election) Franchise' (7 October 2015) *UK Constitutional Law Association* Blog, <https://ukconstitutionallaw.org/2015/10/07/ruvi-ziegler-the-brexit-referendum-we-need-to-talk-about-the-general-election-franchise/>, accessed 19 July 2016.

The legislature should be under a duty, he argued, to set up a referendum franchise that has regard to their interests.[70]

As Counsel representing two claimant non-resident UK citizens, Shindler and Maclennan, in a 2016 case in the English courts challenging the UK's EU referendum franchise,[71] O'Neill had an opportunity to have his argument reviewed by the judiciary at several levels. Before the Divisional Court, the April 2016 judgment acknowledged that the rule in Section 2 of the EU Referendum Act 2015 settling the categories of persons entitled to vote in the referendum was quintessentially an exercise of national sovereignty or competence. Significantly, the judges also accepted that such a national competence still has to be exercised with due regard to EU law, and in particular the impact that the exercise of such a national competence would have on the exercise of rights under EU law, in particular the right of free movement. Notwithstanding that conclusion, the court followed the earlier ruling of the Court of Appeal in the *Preston* case in relation to the fifteen-year rule and UK parliamentary elections[72] to the effect that such an exclusionary rule could not be regarded as a 'restriction' on the rights of free movement of EU citizens for the purposes of the test currently applied by the Court of Justice. Specifically, it is not a measure 'liable to dissuade or deter EU citizens from exercising their rights of free movement'.[73] As in *Preston* the court acknowledged that the fifteen-year rule represents a 'disadvantage' that results from choosing to reside outside the UK, but not every 'disadvantage' can be characterised as a 'restriction'. It is hard to formulate a legal test that might adequately capture how the disadvantage of losing the vote after fifteen years could be understood as a 'restriction' liable to dissuade a person from exercising their free movement rights in the first place. To suggest otherwise, according to the Court of Appeal in *Preston*, would not 'square with ordinary human experience', or with the 'inevitable uncertainties' of 'crowded human lives'. There are simply too many unforeseeable circumstances between the decision to exercise free movement rights and the withdrawal of voting rights.[74]

[70] See O'Neill, '(Dis)enfranchisement', above (note 58).

[71] *Shindler and Maclennan* v. *Chancellor of the Duchy of Lancaster and Secretary of State for Foreign and Commonwealth Affairs* [2016] EWHC 957 (Admin). For a brief comment, see H. Green, 'Expats lose Supreme Court bid for right to vote in EU referendum' (2 June 2016), <https://aberdeenunilaw.wordpress.com/tag/r-shindler-and-anor-v-chancellor-of-the-duchy-of-lancaster-and-another/>, accessed 19 July 2016.

[72] R (Preston) v. Wandsworth London Borough Council [2013] QB 687.

[73] Case C-192/05 *Tas Hagen* ECLI:EU:C:2006:676.

[74] *Preston* above (note 72) at para. 80.

The *Shindler and Maclennan* case proceeded quickly to the Court of Appeal, which handed down its judgment on 20 May 2016. This time, the court took a firmer line on the hard kernel of sovereignty at the heart of national decisions on the franchise on a referendum such as the one to be held in June 2016. Lord Dyson, the Master of the Rolls, concentrated his analysis on Article 50 TEU, and drew – in the absence of case law of the Court of Justice upon the matter – upon what he regarded as an influential analysis of that provision by the German Federal Constitutional Court in its judgment on the Treaty of Lisbon.[75] He picked out one comment in particular:

> Whether these [national constitutional] requirements [referred to in Article 50 TEU] have been complied with in the individual case can, however, only be verified by the Member State itself, not by the European Union or the other Member States.[76]

Accordingly, said Lord Dyson,

> It is clear from this analysis that the German Court did not accept that the domestic constitutional requirements applicable to a decision to withdraw were themselves subject to validation under EU law and could be overturned on grounds of incompatibility with the EU Treaties.

The Court of Appeal therefore distinguished the prior case of *Preston*, on the grounds that the settling of the franchise for a national decision about whether to withdraw is an exercise of national sovereignty – recognised under Article 50 TEU – about whether to be bound by EU law at all. It would, concluded Lord Dyson

> be contrary to [Article 50] if articles of another EU Treaty [i.e. TFEU] relating to citizenship and free movement were to intervene so as to determine the constitutional requirements to be adopted by a Member State which is deciding whether to leave the EU.

On that view, the claimants' case fell at the first hurdle – although in any event, the judges indicated that they also agreed with the lower court's view of the issue of 'restriction' of free movement. The Supreme Court approved the conclusions of the Court of Appeal without holding a full hearing on the matter. What was most instructive about this case was that we saw the terrain of the argument moving away from the issue of free movement. By placing the emphasis on the issue of sovereignty, the

[75] Judgment No 2 BvE 2/08, 30 June 2009, <http://www.bundesverfassungsgericht.de/entscheidungen/es20090630_2bve000208en.html>, accessed 19 May 2017.

[76] Para. 330.

Court of Appeal decisively moved the issue onto terrain where it could align itself with the traditionally sovereignty-sensitive German constitutional court on matters such as *Kompetenz-Kompetenz*. In view of the vote to leave the EU on 23 June 2016, and the extensive discussion of Article 50 TEU thereafter, this is an interesting move on the part of the court.

### C. *Normative Considerations: A Brief Note*

It is widely accepted that the franchise, at least for the Scottish referendum, was established as a result of a process of legitimate constitutional decision-making within the existing United Kingdom. Furthermore, it is likely that any other answer to the question of who should vote in that referendum would have been so indeterminate as to be illegitimate.[77] However, 'right-sizing' participation in votes such as independence referendums or referendums on membership of supranational associations such as the EU raises normative considerations as well as legal and practical complexities.[78]

Ruvi Ziegler has argued[79] that it is normatively desirable that there should be as much congruence as possible between those who are expected to be the citizens of a new state and those who vote in any independence referendum, on the grounds that this group represent the primary 'stakeholders' (adopting Rainer Bauböck's terminology for the normative basis on which citizenship should be granted)[80] in the referendum. His argument depends on accepting the principle that there should be a link between citizenship status and voting, which is widely, but not universally, accepted by commentators.[81] Indeed, with respect to many elections worldwide (especially but not only local elections), the vote is in practice accorded to many residents who do not (yet) have

[77] B. Ryan, 'The Scottish Referendum Franchise: Residence or Citizenship?', in Ziegler et al., 'Independence Referendums' (note 45).

[78] This is discussed at length in Ziegler et al., 'Independence Referendums' (note 45). Space precludes further discussion in this chapter.

[79] R. Ziegler, 'Kick Off Contribution', in Ziegler et al., 'Independence Referendums' (note 45).

[80] See R. Bauböck, 'Stakeholder Citizenship and Transnational Political Participation: a normative evaluation of external voting', *Fordham Law Review*, 75 (2007), 2393–2447.

[81] For critiques, see H. Lardy, 'Citizenship and the Right to Vote', *Oxford Journal of Legal Studies*, 17 (1997), 75–100; and D. Owen, 'Transnational citizenship and the democratic state: modes of membership and voting rights', *Critical Review of International Social and Political Philosophy*, 14 (2011), 641–663.

citizenship, and the UK has never had full congruence between citizenship and the franchise, more for reasons of historical accident than political principle.

Ziegler has argued that underinclusiveness (i.e. the exclusion of putative citizens) 'would undermine the legitimacy of the referendum, not least for disenfranchised persons affected by a new legal reality'. Overinclusiveness – that is, the inclusion of groups who would not be expected to receive citizenship – mandates that the scope of the putative citizenry should be rethought. Perhaps those groups *should* be offered citizenship. In Ziegler's view the Scottish independence referendum franchise did not satisfy the test of congruence, although he acknowledged that it would be a hard test to satisfy in practice, not least because of the challenge of identifying the putative *external* citizens. It would have been difficult, if not impossible, to establish an electoral register that additionally distinguished between former Scottish residents on the basis of whether or not they had been born in Scotland (i.e. the putative citizenship criterion according to the White Paper). In like manner, Ziegler has argued that the EU referendum franchise demands that the UK should take a closer look at its general election franchise.[82] However, there is another way of looking at overinclusiveness, as Ben Saunders has argued: it is generally better to err on the side of over rather than underinclusiveness, not least because – as he suggested – not all those who are offered the vote need exercise it.[83]

Rainer Bauböck, in contrast, defended the approach of setting a residence-based franchise, on the grounds that giving normative force to the 'regional citizenship' that currently delimits the scope of the franchise for the Scottish Parliament elections correctly reflects the character of the referendum in such a case. As a case of consensual self-determination in which the national and the regional legislatures had agreed upon the terms of the vote, the decision concerns whether to *upgrade* the regional citizenship which currently exists into that of an independent state. This is the only 'real' *demos* which exists. The citizens of an independent state are only a putative *demos*, and according to Bauböck:

[82] See Ziegler, 'Brexit' (note 69).

[83] B. Saunders, 'Not all who are enfranchised need participate', in Ziegler et al., 'Independence Referendums' (note 45). For an extended articulation of Saunders' position, see B. Saunders, 'Scottish Independence and the All-Affected Interests Principle', *Politics*, 33(2013), 47–55.

> The putative *demos* of an independent Scotland should not replace the existing *demos* of Scotland as part of the UK in a decision about independence because only the latter but not the former can be considered as democratically legitimate.[84]

This conclusion accords with the actual practice adopted in Scotland in 2014, even if that practice itself could be said to be based on a rather muddled notion of the regional *demos*, stemming from the highly contingent approach on the part of the UK over the years to the intertwining of citizenship and voting.

## V Conclusions: On the Intertwining of Citizenship and Voting

The task undertaken in this chapter has been to bring together two dimensions of troubled membership, each complex in itself: the challenge of establishing or re-establishing a citizenship regime, in particular after a secession referendum, and the definition of political citizenship in the context of consensual acts of self-determination leading to secession/withdrawal. In both cases, the constitutional particularities of the UK (and the likely challenges facing an iScotland), as well as normative considerations attendant upon the definition of the boundaries of the *demos*, hang not too far in the background. Moreover, these contestations are ongoing and do not attach simply to separate and definable 'moments' of constitutional change. Each of the overlapping polities we are studying is constantly mutating and adapting to the new conditions.

The point is well illustrated if we reflect on the intersection between the continuing Scottish independence movement (bolstered by a relatively narrow defeat in 2014), and the Eurosceptic movement, which pushed successive UK governments gradually closer to holding an in/out referendum on UK membership of the EU and triumphed in the 2016 EU referendum. For some, this amounts to juxtaposing Scottish nationalism and English nationalism, given the territorial disparities of the referendum results, although this downplays the complexities of navigating membership and attachment in a multilevel constitutional framework. The interactions between these two self-determination claims are complex and the outcomes which will flow from the result of the EU referendum are still hard to predict. Although the majority of the UK political elite remains avowedly Unionist, the distinct character of the

[84] Bauböck, 'Regional Citizenship' (note 45).

result was one of the voting scenarios which was self-evidently likely to place intense pressures upon the viability of the British union state. In that sense, the holding of an EU referendum to placate Eurosceptic forces is now widely accepted as having been a foolish political risk to take for those who support the continuation of the British state within its current boundaries.

Since the UK as a whole – led by the numerically superior English voting population – voted to leave, but Scotland, Northern Ireland and Gibraltar voted to remain, a series of major challenges now face the UK. This scenario did receive some attention in the press and among commentators in advance of the referendum, but the risks that it posed do not appear to have swayed the wider voting public.[85] Predictably, the Scottish First Minister Nicola Sturgeon (a supporter of independence) has worked hard to highlight the Scottish 'difference', appointing a Standing Council on Europe to advise her on how the benefits of Scotland's EU membership can best be preserved.[86] While Sturgeon has not ruled out the possibility of a second referendum on Scottish independence, it is significant that the new UK Prime Minister Theresa May (herself described as a 'reluctant Remainer') made her first visit after appointment to Edinburgh to see FM Sturgeon and stated that she would not trigger the formal withdrawal talks under Article 50 TEU until she had secured 'a UK-wide approach and objectives'.[87] This seems to suggest a prolonged period of uncertainty and negotiations.

It is also worth highlighting one other troublesome scenario which did not transpire, described by James Mitchell as 'the West Lothian

[85] See, for example J. Nickerson, 'EU referendum: Could a Brexit vote lead to a second Scottish independence referendum?' (6 January 2016) City AM, <www.cityam.com/231838/could-a-brexit-vote-lead-to-a-second-scottish-independence-referendum>, accessed 19 July 2016; F. Perraudin, 'Sturgeon: new Scottish referendum "probably unstoppable" if UK votes to leave EU' (16 October 2015) *The Guardian*, <www.theguardian.com/politics/2015/oct/16/nicola-sturgeon-new-scottish-referendum-probably-unstoppable-if-uk-votes-to-leave-eu>, accessed 19 July 2016; K. Hughes, 'Rough waters ahead for Scotland if the UK votes "no" in EU referendum' (16 August 2015) *Open Democracy*, <www.opendemocracy.net/can-europe-make-it/kirsty-hughes/rough-waters-ahead-for-scotland-if-uk-votes-'no'-in-eu-referendum>, accessed 19 July 2016.

[86] Scottish Government, 'First Minister forms group to advise on Scotland's relationship with the EU', (28 June 2016) <http://news.scotland.gov.uk/News/Standing-Council-on-Europe-25c6.aspx>, accessed 19 July 2016.

[87] 'May says won't trigger EU divorce until UK-wide approach agreed'(15 July 2016) *Reuters*, <www.reuters.com/article/us-britain-eu-scotland-may-idUSKCN0ZV1I0>, accessed 19 July 2016.

Question writ large'.[88] What would have happened if England and Wales had voted narrowly in favour of leaving, but Scotland had voted overwhelmingly in favour of remaining, in sufficient numbers to tip the overall balance of the result?[89] This would have been a situation in which Scotland was seen to have affected the fate of the whole United Kingdom in relation to EU membership against the 'will' of England and Wales. Might this have led to the UK 'expelling' Scotland, rather than Scotland choosing to secede?

And finally, beyond the possibilities offered by territorial politics and the reconfiguration of state boundaries, what types of individual solutions might citizens find in order to improve their options and life chances, both in relation to political voice and also to migration/return migration potential? For example, anyone born in Northern Ireland is able to opt for Irish citizenship in addition to UK citizenship (as are those with Irish parents or grandparents), and it seems the Northern Irish are choosing to do so in increasing numbers to offset the risk of the UK leaving the EU.[90] Moreover, up to six million people in the UK are said to be eligible to seek Irish passports based on having an Irish parent or grandparent. EU citizens in the UK may seek to combine UK citizenship, along with their existing citizenship, and likewise UK citizens resident in other Member States may also seek citizenship more actively than at present.[91] If, as seems anecdotally to be

[88] See Mitchell, 'Unpredictable' (note 20). The West Lothian Question is usually described in terms of Scottish MPs voting on matters that only affect England (or at least not Scotland), and was recently addressed through the introduction of a limited version of 'English Votes for English Laws' (EVEL) by means of Standing Order changes in the Westminster Parliament.

[89] S. Carrell, 'EU referendum: English votes to leave could be offset by rest of UK' (2 December 2015) *The Guardian*, <www.theguardian.com/politics/2015/dec/02/eu-referendum-english-votes-offset-by-scotland-wales-northern-ireland-uk>, accessed 19 July 2016.

[90] This option was cited in the Scottish context by Jim Gallagher: see J. Gallagher, 'Citizenship, Borders and Migration in an Independent Scotland' (September 2013) *Policy Primer*, <www.migrationobservatory.ox.ac.uk/policy-primers/citizenship-borders-and-migration-independent-scotland>, accessed 19 July 2016. I. Honohan, 'Britons are applying for Irish citizenship to get an EU passport. Is this a problem?'<http://blogs.lse.ac.uk/politicsandpolicy/britons-are-applying-for-irish-citizenship-to-get-an-eu-passport-is-this-a-problem/>, accessed 21 April 2017.

[91] On EU citizens naturalizing in the UK, see Migration Observatory, 'Naturalisation as a British Citizen. Concepts and Trends' (March 2015) <www.migrationobservatory.ox.ac.uk/briefings/naturalisation-british-citizen-concepts-and-trends>, accessed 19 July 2016. Discerning the naturalisation rates for UK citizens in other EU Member States is a much more difficult task.

happening,[92] larger numbers of citizens choose these options it could lead to a substantial reconfiguration of the 'we' who inhabit these islands. These considerations are in addition to the complex citizenship changes we would expect in the event of a Scottish secession from the rest of the UK.

At the time of writing, the matters under discussion were fluid in character. But the complexities of the UK's case of troubled membership are already visible, if not always easy to comprehend, because so many different aspects of the UK's constitutional constellation are brought into question.

This chapter does not seek to assert that the Scottish case provides some sort of paradigm that others might follow. Each case of regional 'trouble' in the EU (e.g. Catalonia, Flanders) is different, characterised by different constellations of political forces and constitutional contexts, and the UK is unique in (currently) compounding its regional 'trouble' with an additional question of whether the state as a whole should remain a Member State of the European Union. What this chapter has sought to do is to show that citizenship – as a legal status and as the basis for political membership – operates as a useful prism through which to observe the interplay of individual status and rights, of competing and overlapping legal orders, and of political contestations of belonging and membership.

[92] 'Thousands of Brits rush for EU passports after Brexit vote' (18 July 2016) *CNN Money*, <http://money.cnn.com/2016/07/18/news/uk-british-european-passports-citizenship-brexit/>, accessed 19 July 2016.

# 10

# Interpreting Article 50: Exit, Voice and . . . What About Loyalty?

CARLOS CLOSA*

## I Introduction

The explicit right to withdrawal enshrined in Article 50, far from being redundant for stating the obvious, may have subtly transformed the structure of the Member States' commitment to the EU. JHH Weiler[1] depicted these commitments by applying the notions of exit and voice borrowed from Albert O. Hirschmann's seminal analysis.[2] In a nutshell, Weiler argued that the implicit exit option in the European Union treaties led to an increase of voice (i.e. the control of governments on decision-making). This picture probably remained valid until the early 2000s until the Treaty of Lisbon formalised an explicit right to withdrawal. This has affected the traditional equilibrium between these two mechanisms: the explicit regulation of withdrawal provides a resource for the erosion of *loyalty* and changes the demands from *increasing voice* to *ex post selective exit* (i.e. partial exemptions from the EU *acquis* which add to already existing partial derogations obtained during treaty negotiations). In order to substantiate this thesis, Section II of this chapter presents the notions of exit, voice and loyalty as constructed by Hirschman and applied to the EU by Weiler. It then, in Section III examines the model of exit contained in the Treaty of Lisbon, arguing that formalisation produces significant legal and political effects. Section IV lists and describes

* I wish to thank Giuseppe Martinico, Oliver Garner, Maraijke Kleine and the participants in the EUI workshop on troubled membership in the EU for their valuable comments.An initial version of this chpater was published as *Carlos Closa Interpreting Article 50 : exit and voice and † what about loyalty? EUI RSCAS; 2016/71 http://cadmus.eui.eu/handle/1814/44487*

[1] J. H. H. Weiler, 'The Transformation of Europe' *The Yale Law Journal*, 100 (8) (1992), 2403–2483.

[2] Albert O. Hirschman, *Exit, Voice, and Loyalty: Responses to Decline in Firms, Organizations, and States* (Harvard MA: Harvard University Press, 1970).

a typology of these effects. The chapter then, in Sections V and VI, revises the rationale for exit from organisations such as the EU, turning towards the current demands raised against the threat of exit and concludes by discussing how this erodes 'loyalty'. Section VII describes how the formalisation of exit changes the voice mechanism and Section VIII concludes re-stating the case that the explicit exit provision in Article 50 erodes loyalty from Member States to the Union.

## II Interpretation of Withdrawal: Exit and Voice

In 1970, Hirschman constructed the notions of exit and voice as instruments which individuals and groups use to respond to the decline in the performance of products, firms, organisations and public corporations.[3] 'Exit' is an economic mechanism and consists of simply abandoning the product, organisation, firm, etc. Whilst Hirschman did not precisely define what an 'economic mechanism' is, most likely he meant that utility calculus informs exit decisions. 'Voice', on the other hand, is a more diffuse mechanism and one which belongs to the sphere of politics. The use of voice results less evident: basically, individuals, groups, etc. increase their demands for improvement and/or take a more active role to control the product/organisation. Voice and exit relate closely to each other: in the face of declining performance, voice serves to air dissatisfaction and increase involvement through various mechanisms, thus improving the product, organisation, etc. But this happens on the condition that exit is virtually ruled out. Hirschman[4] argues that the presence of the exit option can sharply reduce the probability that the voice option will be taken up widely and effectively. Later, he expanded his previous thesis and in his *Exit, voice and the state,*[5] Hirschman focussed on the significance of exit in relation to the state but he did not construct a systematic analysis nor did he elaborate on the relationship between exit and voice *within* the state, let alone the connection between these two mechanisms and loyalty. The connection between these mechanisms precisely in the case of organisations remains underexplored. Hirchsman constructed his reasoning aggregating the behaviour of individuals and, hence, the translation of these logical mechanisms to explain choices of units such as ′states' or 'organizations' must be taken with caution.

[3] Hirschman (note 2) [4] Hirschman (note 2), p. 76.

[5] A. O. Hirschman, 'Exit, Voice, and the State', *World Politics*, 31(01) (October 1978), 90–107.

In the *Transformation of Europe*, Weiler applied these categories to show how the EU had successfully closed selective exit (i.e. the selective application of EU law) in the foundational period while keeping full exit (leaving the Union) as an implicit option. To compensate for the selective closure of exit, Member States increased their voice, i.e. the political mechanism. This meant an increased role for the Council and the intergovernmental procedures for decision-making within the Community method itself. Full exit did not play any specific role in Weiler's construction of the relationship between voice and selective exit in the EU, even though he conceded that in the face of many lawyers' scepticism, withdrawal remained possible in principle.[6] He further convincingly argued that insisting on the possibility of withdrawal might be counterproductive, especially in an organisation like the EU.

The original treaties' silence on the issue created a certain interpretative vacuum on the exit option which the application of the posterior Vienna Convention on the Law of Treaties (1969) could help clarify. Although appeal to the Convention has formed the backbone of much legal argument, Article 4 conclusively establishes that 'the Convention applies only to treaties which are concluded by States after the entry into force of the present Convention'. The Convention would thus apply, in purity, after the first 'new' treaty amending the original ones (i.e. the Single European Act) entered into force in 1987 (the Convention entered into force on 27 January 1980).[7]

In parallel, the Luxembourg compromise and the generalisation of unanimity along with the growing involvement of the Council in decision-making (together with the ongoing efforts of governments to enlist their nationals in Community institutions such as the EP and the Commission to serve their cause), guaranteed states a voice in the EU. Doctrinally, exit options remained contentions but the 1974 UK referendum on withdrawal from the Communities proved, pragmatically, the existence of the right to withdraw. No one contested the British

[6] See his 'Alternatives to Withdrawal from an International Organization: The Case of the European Economic Community', *Israel Law Review*, 20(1985), 282–298. However, authors such as Schermers argued that unilateral withdrawal was not compatible with international organisations. H. G. Schermers, *International Institutional Law* (The Hague: Sijthoff & Noordhoff International Publishers, 1980), p. 29.

[7] Alternatively, conceiving the 1972 Treaty concerning the accession of the Kingdom of Denmark, Ireland, the Kingdom of Norway and the United Kingdom of Great Britain and Northern Ireland to the European Economic Community and to the European Atomic Energy Community as a reform of the original treaties, the Convention would apply to the EU from the entry into force of the later treaty (i.e. 1 January 1973).

government's assumed right to withdraw if it had wished after holding the referendum,[8] although a significant number of authors argued that the EU's *sui generis* nature precluded withdrawal.[9] After this episode, no other state claimed this right again until the German Constitutional Court, in its ruling on the Maastricht Treaty, constructed the right of withdrawal as a guarantee of national sovereignty and, hence, inherent to membership.[10] The Czech Constitutional Court also asserted the same view in its ruling on the Treaty of Lisbon precisely in reference to Article 50.[11]

While full exit implicitly formed part of the nature of the EU, the Single European Act (SEA) opened a path to a different modality of *selective exit* that the Treaty of Maastricht consolidated and later treaties enlarged: the progressive inclusion of opt-out provisions which allow the selective derogation of specific policies measures for specific states. In relation to

[8] See A. F. Tatham, 'Don't Mention Divorce at the Wedding, Darling!: EU Accession and Withdrawal after Lisbon', in A. Biondi, P. Eeckhout and S. Ripley (eds.), *EU Law after Lisbon* (Oxford: OUP, 2012), p. 128, at 144. He follows T. C. Hartley, 'International Law and the Law of the European Union: A Reassessment', *British Yearbook of International Law*, 72 (2001), 1, 22.

[9] In the 1980s Greenland withdrawal triggered a debate on whether a state could withdraw from the then EEC. Harhoff argued that the unlimited duration established in Article 240 of the Treaty of Rome meant an irrevocable commitment of the signatories and deduced from this that unilateral denunciation was illegal and contrary to the aim of the treaties. F. Harhoff, 'Greenland's withdrawal from the European Communities', *CMLRev*, 20 (1983). Other authors subscribing to this thesis were Jean Victor Louis, *The Community Legal Order*, (2nd edition, Luxembourg: Office for Official Publications of the European Communities 1990), p. 74; and Michael Akehurst, 'Withdrawal from international organizations', *Current Legal Problems*, 32(1979), 152. Louis however specified that the Community was dissoluble only by virtue of being a step in a gradual process towards union. However, a significant number of other authors argued that withdrawal was possible: J. H. H. Weiler, 'Supranationalism revisited – a retrospective: the European Communities after 30 years', in W. Mainhoffer (ed.), *Noi si mura* (Florence: EUI, 1983); Roy Pryce, *The politics of the European Community* (London: Butterworths, 1975), p. 55; and Paul Taylor, 'The European Community and the State: Assumptions, Theories and Propositions', *Review of International Studies*, 17 (2) (1991), 109–125. P. D. Dagtoglou opined '[W]hether withdrawal was excluded or not depended not on the aim to integrate "in abstracto", but only on the stage of integration actually reached "in concreto"' in P. D. Dagtoglou (ed.), *Basic problems of the European Community* (Oxford: Basil Blackwell, 1975). The EP legal affairs committee concluded that it was not possible to conclude on whether a state could withdraw from the EC, PE Doc 1-264/83, p. 9

[10] Decision of the German Federal Constitutional Court of October 12, 1993 in Cases 2 BvR 2134/92, 2 BvR 2159/92 *Re Maastricht Treaty* [BVerfG 89,155]

[11] Czech Republic Constitutional Court Judgment Pl. ÚS 19/08: *Treaty of Lisbon* I 2008/11/26.

the situation described by Weiler, EU law applies equally to all *participating* Member States but not all states participate equally. As I will argue below, the withdrawal threat creates the conditions for new modalities of selective derogation of the *acquis*: ex post partial derogation, such as the exceptions negotiated for the UK in the 2016 February Council Decision.[12] Before developing this argument further, Section III reviews the characteristics of the formalised exit provision.

## III The Formalisation of Full Exit

Article 50 of the Treaty of Lisbon explicitly regulates withdrawal. Allegedly, formalisation of withdrawal explodes two basic assumptions about the EU: that European integration is irreversible and that Member States have waived their right to dissolve the Union.[13] It also confirms the interpretations of the German and Czech constitutional courts mentioned above.

While recourse to the general rules of international law was possible in the absence of explicit provisions,[14] formalisation of the right of withdrawal in Article 50 neutralises the application of general rules of international law because of the principle '*lex specialis derogate legi generali*'. Releasing the EU from the strictures of international law means on the one hand, enhancing EU autonomy *vis-à-vis* that order, but on the other hand, it also means releasing Member States from the stricter conditions for withdrawal in international law.[15] Explicit regulation hardly represents a novelty in international public law since a significant number of international organisations regulate the same option along similar lines.[16] But an important caveat applies to this trend: while denunciation

[12] See Conclusions European Council meeting (18 and 19 February 2016) Brussels, 19 February 2016 (OR. en) EUCO 1/16 CO EUR 1 CONCL 1 http://www.consilium.europa.eu/en/meetings/european-council/2016/02/18-19/, accessed 27 February 2017

[13] Jochen Herbst, 'Observations on the Right to Withdraw from the European Union: Who are the "Masters of the Treaties"?', *German Law Journal*, 6(2005), 1755, at 1759. He appealed to both assumptions in order to argue that the legality of the right of withdrawal could be challenged.

[14] H. Hofmeister, 'Should I stay or Should I Go? – A Critical Analysis of the Right to Withdraw from the EU', *ELJ*, 16 (2010), 589 at 591.

[15] C. Hillion, 'Accession and Withdrawal in the Law of the European Union', in A. Arnull and D. Chalmers (eds.), *The Oxford Handbook of European Union Law* (Oxford: OUP, 2015), p. 126; and 'This way, please! A legal appraisal of the EU withdrawal clause' in this volume.

[16] In comparative international regulation, withdrawal is also in almost all cases an unconditional option and withdrawing states do not need to provide any kind of justification for this decision. Only the Organization for the Prohibition of Chemical Weapons (OPCW)

and withdrawal are a regularised component of modern *treaty* practice, they are not that common for *international organisations*.[17] Accordingly, if withdrawal regulation is not exceptional but not widespread either, the question which stands is why or for what purpose did the EU Member States decide to introduce an explicit provision on withdrawal, given the significant agreement among legal scholars about its facticity. If withdrawal was possible in any case, why bother mentioning it explicitly? A trend towards institutional isomorphism with other international organisations would not appear to explain the provision (at least not in the sense that this convergence is interpreted as a mechanism for reasserting the EU's international law nature).

Since the provision originated in the works of the Convention on the Future of Europe (2002–2003), its preparatory works provide some clues. One specifically legal response would be that Article 50 serves to dispel any legal doubts about withdrawal. The Praesidium of the Convention thus argued that even though withdrawal was possible, even in the absence of an explicit specific provision to that effect, its insertion clarifies the situation and allows the introduction of a procedure for negotiating, and concluding, an agreement between the Union and the withdrawing state.[18] Agreeing on the procedure before a specific instance

and the Organization for Eastern Caribbean States (OECS) construe the right to withdraw as deriving from a state deciding that extraordinary events, related to the subject matter of the Conventions, jeopardised their superordinate national interest (Arts. 16 and 24 respectively).

17 Laurence Helfer, 'Laurence (2005) Exiting treaties', 91 *Virginia Law Review*, 91 (2005), 1579–1648, at 1602.

18 Draft Constitution, 'Volume I Revised text of Part One' (2003) Conv 724/1/03 Rev 1 Annex 2, <http://register.consilium.europa.eu/doc/srv?l=EN&f=CV%20724%202003%20REV%201>, accessed 5 July 2015, p. 131. Similarly, the House of Lords argued that the significance of Article 50 lay, therefore, not in establishing a right to withdraw, but rather in defining the procedure for doing so. House of Lords (2016). The process of withdrawing from the European Union European Union Committee 11th Report of Session 2015–16 HL Paper 138, <www.publications.parliament.uk/pa/ld201516/ldselect/ldeucom/138/138.pdf> accessed 27 February 2017. In contrast, the representative of the Austrian Government at the Convention, Hannes Farnleitner, argued that the provisions of the Vienna Convention on the Law of the Treaties provide a sufficient basis for termination of membership. Hannes Farnleitner, 'Suggestion for amendment of Article I-59' <http://european-convention.europa.eu/docs/Treaty/pdf/46/46_Art%20I%2059%20Farnleitner%20EN.pdf>, accessed 27 February 2017. The representatives of the Dutch Government argued that facilitating the possibility of withdrawal from the Union is contrary to the idea of European integration set out in the Preamble to the Treaty and captured in the expression of 'an ever closer union'. G. M. de Vries and T. J. A. M. de Bruijn, 'Suggestion for amendment of Article: 46 Suggestion for Part III' (2003), <http://european-convention.europa.eu/docs/Treaty/pdf/46/art46vriesEN.pdf>, accessed 27 February 2017.

of its application emerges is easier than achieving the same agreement against the background of an actual case of separation.[19] Notably, the provision does not clarify all of the necessary elements completely and some actors have rightly criticised it for this incompleteness, [20] although, from the opposite point of view, its openness offers significant margin for political discretion much needed in such a situation. The introduction of procedural clarification still begs the question why it is necessary to dispel doubts about something generally and implicitly agreed? Withdrawal was agreed in the context of a significant uplift in the EU's ambitions with the 2005 EU Constitution. The Praesidium argued that the provision was a political signal to anyone inclined to opine that the Union is a rigid entity which is impossible to leave. Thus, in line with theoretical interpretations of the right to exit, explicit formalisation of withdrawal functions as an 'insurance policy' against future uncertainty permitting a state to renounce to its commitments if the anticipated benefits of cooperation turn out to be overblown.[21] The existence of this 'insurance policy' enables states to negotiate more expansive or deepen substantive treaty commitments *ex ante*, although it raises troubling opportunities for strategic action *ex post*.[22] This was precisely the context of the EU Constitution: the right to withdraw was thus understood as a safety valve to reassure Member States that they would always be allowed to leave, should they be or become unwilling, to pursue the emboldened integration path embodied by the Constitutional Treaty.[23] This begs the question: why would a state wish to leave the EU? Section V discusses the logics for seeking exit but the next few paragraphs provide a fuller characterisation of article 50.

The peculiarities of withdrawal in the EU result from the interaction of its characteristics with the specific nature of the Union (as established by the Court in Van Gen den Loos)[24]. Article 50 recognises a *unilateral, unconditional* and *non-immediate* right to withdrawal.

- Unilateralism means that the right is totally independent of the will of the EU (EU institutions may not even opine on the departing Member

[19] Rostane Medhi, 'Brèves observations sur la consecration constitutionnelle d'un droit de retrait volontaire', in Paul Demaret, Inge Govaere and Dominik Hanf (eds.), *30 Years of European Legal Studies at the College of Europe/30 ans d'études juridiques européennes au Collège d'Europe: Liber Professorum 1973/74–2003/04* (Brussels: P.I.E.-Peter Lang, 2005).

[20] Hofmeister (note 14), 595. [21] Helfer (note 17), 1591. [22] Ibidem, 1591.

[23] Hillion (note 15) and Medhi (note 19).

[24] Case 26/62, NV Algemene Transport- en Expeditie Onderneming van Gend & Loos v. Netherlands Inland Revenue Administration, ECLI:EU:C:1963:1

State's communication) and the remaining Member States.[25] In relation to this, the Convention moved between two alternatives. On the one hand, some British representatives defended a strictly unilateral provision which would merely require a notification to the Council for withdrawal to become effective.[26] On the opposite side, most of the proposals and amendments submitted to the Convention on the issue sought either to eliminate explicit unilateralism or to introduce mechanisms to correct or limit it. For instance, the Badinter proposal subordinated the right to a compulsory agreement with the Union.[27] The final design reflects a compromise between these two and, because of this, the ultimate shape of the withdrawal right contains only a specific limitation to unilateralism: the obligation to follow the procedure established by Article 50, which renders alternative mechanisms (such as simply repealing the domestic legislation which gives EU law effect in a given Member State) illegal.[28] Beyond the notification and the requirement to seek an agreement, no other factors modify unilateral withdrawal. Some authors have tried to engineer a reasoning which brings the ECJ in as the final arbiter of this decision: since treaty provisions are justiciable, Article 50 places the ECJ in such a position and it could rule on disputes regarding the validity or not of withdrawing.[29] However, it seems

[25] Hofmeister (note 14), 592; Tatham (note 8), 152. Helfer (note 17) argues that withdrawal is fundamentally a unilateral act.

[26] Allan Dashwood Article 27 CONV 345/02. In reality, it was Peter Hain who submitted the Project entitled, *Traité constitutionnel de l'Union européenne* (Dashwood Project), CONV 345/02 Brussels, 15 October 2002.

[27] The Badinter proposal (*Une constitution européenne [Artículo 80]* CONV 317/02, 30 September 2002 http://european-convention.europa.eu/pdf/reg/en/02/cv00/cv00317.en02.pdf, accessed 27 February 2017) modified strict unilateralism by granting states the final right to withdrawal but it could only be exercised with the EU's agreement (Art. 80).

[28] HM Government, 'The process of withdrawing from the European Union', (2016) <www.publications.parliament.uk/pa/ld201516/ldselect/ldeucom/138/138.pdf>, accessed 5 June 2016, p. 13. Although the UK Government declared itself bound to follow the Article 50 procedure, surprisingly, it lays the main emphasis against illegal withdrawal on the practical effects of such behaviour on trade negotiations rather than on the illegality per se. (*Such a breach would create a hostile environment in which to negotiate either a new relationship with the remaining Member States, or new trade agreements with non-EU countries*). Equally, the House of Lords concluded that the process described in Article 50 is the only way of doing so consistent with EU and international law. House of Lords (note 18).

[29] R. J. Friel, 'Providing a constitutional framework for withdrawal from the EU: Article 59 of the draft European constitution', *ICLQ*, 53 (2004), 407–428, at 42; C. Hillion 'This Way, Please! A Legal Appraisal of the EU Withdrawal Clause', Chapter 11 in this volume.

doubtful that a withdrawing state proceeding according to its own domestic constitution would entrust the ECJ with the verification of this act although domestic courts may feel bound to refer an eventual question on the procedure to the ECJ. Unilateralism has been supported by arguing that the prevalence of the opposite principle (i.e. 'mutual agreement' between Member States and the EU) on this point would reduce the counter-centralisation force underlying the right of secession.[30]

- Unconditionality means that the exercise of the right to withdrawal is not subjected to any preliminary verification of conditions[31] nor is it even conditional on the conclusion of the agreement foreseen in the provision[32] (see below). Article 50 does not even mention the generic circumstances in which this right may be activated, and the proposals aired during the Convention, such as the existence of 'extraordinary circumstances' (such as revision of the Treaties) or conditioned on obtaining unanimous assent of Member States (which would be equivalent to requesting authorisation) were ruled out.[33] The Convention also ruled out the option of making withdrawal conditional upon completion of the withdrawal agreement: its *Praesidium* argued that if the right of withdrawal existed without explicit regulation, it could not then be made conditional upon the conclusion of such an agreement.[34] Nor could withdrawing in accordance to a country's *own constitutional requirements*, as explicitly required in the Article, be considered a condition.[35] The German

[30] Wolf Schäfer, 'Withdrawal legitimised? On the proposal by the Constitutional convention on the right of secession from the EU' (July/August 2003) *Intereconomics*, 182–185, at 185.

[31] Cf. Hillion Chapter 11 in this volume who argues that some conditions do apply; Herbst (note 13). According to Helfer, the overwhelming majority of the denunciation and withdrawal clauses do not require a state to provide any justification to quit a Treaty. Helfer (note 17).

[32] Hofmeister (note 14), 593.

[33] See for instance, Contribution by Mr Lamassoure, Member of the Convention 'The European Union: four possible models' (3 September 2002) CONV 235/02 Contribution 83 (05.09) <http://www.alainlamassoure.eu/liens/366.pdf>, <http://register.consilium.europa.eu/doc/srv?l=EN&f=CV%20235%202002%20INIT>, accessed 27 February 2017.

[34] Draft Constitution, 'Volume I Revised text of Part One' (2003) CONV 724/1/03 Rev 1 Annex 2, <http://register.consilium.europa.eu/doc/srv?l=EN&f=CV%20724%202003%20REV%201>, accessed 27 February 2017, p. 132. Also, Tatham (note 8). Surprisingly, the House of Lords (note 18) argues that withdrawal from the EU becomes final *only* once the withdrawal agreement enters into force.

[35] Cf. Clemens M. Rieder, 'The withdrawal clause of the Lisbon Treaty in the light of EU citizenship: between disintegration and integration', *Fordham Intern'l LJ*, 37 (2013), 147–174.

Constitutional Court, in its judgment on the Lisbon Treaty, clearly stated that 'whether these [national constitutional] requirements [referred to in Article 50 TEU] have been complied with in the individual case can, however, only be verified by the Member State itself, not by the European Union or the other Member States'.[36] The UK Court of Appeal, when deciding on the citizens entitled to vote in the 2016 withdrawal referendum, approvingly quoted the German decision which argued that Article 50 protected the conditions for the exercise of the right of withdrawal from EU level review: invoking provisions on EU citizenship to intervene to determine the constitutional requirements to be adopted by a Member State deciding whether to leave the EU would be contrary to Article 50.[37]

As mentioned, Article 50 releases the Union from the strictures of public international law and marks a stark contrast with the pre-Lisbon situation[38] when the absence of an explicit withdrawal clause meant the application of the Vienna Convention on the Law of the Treaties. Its Article 62 requires a 'fundamental change of circumstances' for legitimate unilateral withdrawal.[39] The International Law Commission indicated two conditions for interpreting what a 'fundamental change of circumstances' is: they should be central to the reasons for the state's acceptance to be bound by the treaty and/or the effects of the changes must radically change the extent of the obligations under the treaty. These two conditions resonate with the requirement of predictability of commitments as condition for membership which the German Constitutional Court inserted in its 1993 Maastricht ruling.[40] Article 50 does not contain any reference to changes of circumstances and/or obligations to ground a state's withdrawal, which releases the EU procedure from the (allegedly, very light) conditionality under international law. Even more worrisome from the perspective of the integrity of

[36] Judgment No 2 BvE 2/08, 30 June 2009, <http://www.bundesverfassungsgericht.de/entscheidungen/es20090630_2bve000208en.html>, accessed 27 February 2017.

[37] UK Court of Appeal: *Shindler & anr* v. *Chancellor of the Duchy of Lancaster & anr* [2016] EWCA Civ 469.

[38] For instance, Herbst (note 13), 1755: '[T]here exists no unlimited right of an EU Member State to withdraw from the EU; that is, without any further prerequisite and simply at the free discretion of the respective Member State, within the confines of its internal (constitutional) law provisions'.

[39] Scholars still dispute the meaning of the concepts behind Article 62 Vienna Convention. See Helfer (note 17), 1579.

[40] BVerfG, Judgement of the Second Senate of 12 October 1993, BVerfGE 89 Cases 2 BvR 2134/92, 2 BvR 2159/92 Re Maastricht Treaty [BVerfG 89,155]

EU law, the principle of loyalty/sincere cooperation do not impose any condition on withdrawing states,[41] although it may need to be taken into account.[42] In summary, although the neutralisation of the conditionality implicit in international law may be considered an autonomy enhancing tool for EU law, it may also affect some of its core principles.

- Non-immediate effect.[43] A unilateral right does not mean an immediate right and this is the sole limitation in the whole provision to the full exercise of sovereignty by the withdrawing state. Withdrawal enters into force two years after the formal official communication of a state willing to assert this right and the European Council, acting by unanimity, can prolong the two-year period with the agreement of the withdrawing state. The EU has not innovated institutionally with this provision: most international organisations require a 'preparation' or 'cooling off' period between the announcement of withdrawal and effective withdrawal and this period varies between ninety days (for instance, in the Korean Peninsula Energy Development Organization [KENDO]) and two years (for instance, in the Organization of American States [OAS]), with one year being the most common period.

Two possible interpretations may explain the function of this delay period. The first derives directly from Article 50: it permits the adaptation of the EU and the withdrawing state to the new circumstances and the changes required and specifically, the negotiation of the withdrawal agreement between the Union and the withdrawing state. The assumption is that some kind of legal relationship will still remain between the two and that the legal consequences of the withdrawal regarding the rights and obligations of natural persons and legal entities affected by the withdrawal need to be dealt with. In the absence of such an agreement, the specific legal consequences will remain in doubt.[44] The drafters adopted the longest period commonly provided in international organisations, but in practical terms, it remains still too short for negotiating any comprehensive agreement.[45] Perhaps because they conceived of withdrawal as an unrealistic possibility,

[41] Herbst (note 13), 1758.

[42] Hofmeister (note 14), 598. When interpreting Article 50, the principle of sincere cooperation enshrined in article 4(3) TEU needs to be taken into account.

[43] Hofmeister (note 14), 593.

[44] Herbst (note 13), 1757.

[45] Herbst (note 13), 1758. The UK Government and the House of Lords coincided in their estimation of not less than 10/9 years would be needed to negotiate a settlement. HM Government *The process of withdrawing from the European Union* (note 28).

the drafters did not properly think through how complex and lengthy the negotiations would need to be. In fact, the provision requires to negotiate but not to conclude a withdrawal agreement.

The second interpretation brings EU law in line with international law: in other international organisations, the delay between announcement and effective withdrawal serves as a 'cooling off' period allowing the withdrawing State to change its position. For instance, Spain decided not to withdraw from the League of Nations in 1928 shortly before its notice to do so would have taken effect. The question here is whether this general interpretation in international law can prevail when the aim of Article 50 has been precisely to create an autonomous withdrawal procedure. Crucially, Article 50 does not state anything about whether the decision is reversible and whether a state can backtrack once it has communicated its decision to withdraw. Because of this, the House of Lords (2016)[46] argued that 'nothing in Article 50 formally (prevents) a Member State from reversing its decision to withdraw in the course of the withdrawal negotiations'. Although this literal interpretation may fit the letter of the provision, *prima facie*, it seems contrary to the spirit of the provision (let alone with the political will asserted by the withdrawing state). To argue that a new government may change the decision of a previous one during this period to justify this interpretation places the interpretation of EU rules at the disposal of domestic political disputes. In any case, the ECJ remains the authoritative interpreter of the provision for any interpretative ambiguity.

In any case, the uncertainty on whether backtracking is possible, combined with the long and protracted negotiations on alternative agreements during the delay period, create a kind of *limbo membership*. Supposedly, the withdrawing state will be still bound by EU legislation and the principle of loyal cooperation (Article 4(3)). However, as the date of termination of legal obligations under the treaty approaches, domestic authorities may legitimately consider that they can exercise a policy of 'legal detachment'[47] (i.e. repealing EU law

46 House of Lords (note 18); Philip Syrpis 'What next? An analysis of the EU law questions surrounding Article 50 TEU: Part One' (2016) *eutopialaw*, <https://eutopialaw.com/2016/07/08/what-next-an-analysis-of-the-eu-law-questions-surrounding-article-50-teu-part-one/>, accessed 27 February 2017.

47 Adam Lazowski 'Inside but out? United Kingdom and EU', in Andras Jakab and Dimitry Kochenov (eds.), *The enforcement of EU law. Methods against Member States' defiance* (Oxford: OUP, 2017. The House of Lords (note 18) also indicated this as a probable position for the withdrawing state.

selectively, as well as the principles of direct effect, primacy and direct applicability). Furthermore, the withdrawing state will be in the awkward situation of being a full member of the Union but a third party to the effects of concluding the agreement.[48]

In summary, Article 50 has created an unilateral, unconditional albeit non immediate right to withdrawal. Having these characteristics in mind, the question is why would Member States seek exit from the EU? Section 5 discusses this but previously Section IV below lists and discusses the possible effects of having a formal explicit provision regulating exit.

## IV The Effects of the Exit Provision

An explicitly formalised withdrawal provision creates a wide panoply of possible effects since it stimulates both cooperation-diminishing and cooperation-enhancing dynamics.[49] While by no means an exhaustive list, the following effects can be listed:

### A. *Enlargement of the Possible Number of Members of an Organisation or Signatories of a Treaty*

Withdrawal provisions are perceived as guarantees for the broad membership of an organisation: they may encourage the ratification of a treaty by a larger number of states than those which would be prepared to ratify it in the absence of such a clause.[50] However, the positive value of this effect depends on the type of organisation: the number of participating Member States may in itself be of value for global organisations, which by definition aim to comprising all world states. However, this is not necessarily true for regional organisations which can have a maximum number of hypothetical participants (defined by geography). Restriction of membership to European states places the EU within this second interpretation.

Alternatively, withdrawal provisions (can) also enable states to negotiate deeper and/or broader commitments than would be attainable for treaties without unilateral exit clauses.[51] According to Helfer, governments often refrain from compelling their partners to accept the entire package of treaty commitments in order to facilitate the widespread adoption of multilateral agreements. Instead, they permit states to append reservations

[48] House of Lords (note 18): the UK would be treated as a non-EU State for the purpose of Article 50.

[49] Helfer (note 17), 1587.

[50] Helfer (note 17), 1599.

[51] Helfer (note 17), 1599.

before expressing their consent to be bound to an agreement.[52] The EU treaties do not permit reservations but they possess the functional equivalent: opt-outs which are often formulated in protocols. These opt-outs and the additional derogations and exceptional provisions for determined Member States are equivalent to a form of selective exits which permit Member States to tailor their membership in the Union. As will be discussed below, under such condition of selective exit, Member States may find it difficult to identify a clear rationale for full exit. In fact, selective exit serves to diminish the margin for full exit in theory, even though the UK case (a Member State with a significant number of selective exit mechanisms) has demonstrated that it did not function in this way.

### B. *Guarantee against Centralisation and Redistribution*

Exit provisions in trade- and economic-oriented organisations may fulfil specific functions: they may be thought as guarantees against centralisation processes and redistributive policies. Schäfer interprets exit provisions along these lines and he argues that exit, and partial exit, create a more efficient organisation. Specifically, granting Member States the right to withdraw partially or completely from central areas of policy in order to take on responsibility for these areas themselves encourages an accompanying process of finding the best solution to the problem of the institutional assignment of public tasks within the Community.[53] The right of secession therefore supports vertical institutional competition within the EU[54] and this finding supports Hirschman´s construction of the relationship between exit and voice. However, economists have argued in response that trade agreements are generally less effective where formal escape clauses are easily invoked.[55]

As for the effects on redistribution, Schäfer's opinion expresses an ideological preference for certain policies: an institutional right of secession in the EU corresponds completely with free trade trends caused by globalisation and the intentions of the institutions committed to free trade, such as the WTO.[56] Some economists have echoed a similar preference: thus, Alesina et al.[57] argue that for countries which primarily lose

[52] Helfer (note 17), 1640–1641. [53] Schäfer (note 30), 183. [54] Ibid.

[55] Suzanne Lechner and Renate Ohr, 'The Right Of Withdrawal In The Treaty Of Lisbon: A Game Theoretic Reflection On Different Decision Processes In The EU', *European Journal of Law and Economics*, 32 (2011), 357–375.

[56] Schäfer (n. 30), 184.

[57] A. Alesina and R. Perotti, 'Economic risk and political risk in fiscal unions', *Economic Journal*, 108 (1998), 989–1008; A. Alesina and R. Wacziarg, 'Openness country side and the government', *Journal of Public Economics*, 69 (1997), 305–321.

out in strategic redistribution games, the exit option – and even only threatening to use it – can work to reduce redistribution and therefore increase efficiency.[58] These economic analysis presuppose that utilitarian efficiency is the ultimate purpose of the EU and they neglect deeper and less graspable deontological issues.

### C. *Reputational Effects on the Withdrawing State*

Formalisation, however, also has important benefits for the withdrawing state: making the exit procedures formal, lawful and public, positively affects (in relation to not formalising them) the withdrawing state's reputation for compliance with international law.[59] Following an established procedure means complying with the norms even when breaking from an organisation and this sends positive signals as to the state's adherence to legal procedures, even in extreme situations such as withdrawal. Other states may take note and believe that the withdrawing state remains a reliable partner despite its abandoning the organisation.

### D. *Strategic Behaviour*

A significant number of scholars[60] agree that explicit withdrawal provisions provide a powerful tool for strategic bargaining. The authorities of a Member State can threaten withdrawal to obtain compensation in circumstances where a country's cost-benefit of membership calculation changes. In this situation, an affected state can try to persuade the EU to compensate it for such changes. Therefore, a Member State will make certain demands and threaten to withdraw if these demands are not met; that is, the threat of withdrawal can be used to obtain compensation for accepting decisions which are necessary to the integration process. And this can occur even if the EU perceives the threat as 'empty words': even in this case, the EU may choose to compensate in order to eliminate uncertainty.[61] Alternatively, a Member State may use the right to

[58] Schäfer (note 30), 184

[59] Helfer (note 17), 1590. See also the reasoning of the UK Government on the reputational costs of not following the EU rules (note 28)

[60] See among others, Lechner and Ohr (note 55); Tatham (note 8); Helfer (note 17); Sara Berglund, 'Prison or Voluntary Cooperation? The Possibility of Withdrawal from the European Union', *Scandinavian Political Studies*, 29 (2006), 147–167.

[61] Lechner and Ohr (note 55), 361 and 371

withdrawal as a potential right to veto, or as a potential threat, in order to prevent disadvantageous decisions.

The creation of a formal provision which permits the strategic negotiation of compensation explains the opposition of the Commission to the inclusion of a withdrawal clause in the 2004 Draft Constitution. The Commission argued that such provision would allow Member States to blackmail others by threatening to leave. These effects also explain why theorists have been concerned to find mechanisms to restrain the temptation of strategic gamesmanship. In fact, Helfer argues that the principal challenge facing treaty negotiators is to set optimal conditions for exit *ex ante* so as to deter opportunistic exploitation of exist clauses *ex post* after the treaty has entered into force.[62] As a result, scholars have suggested various mechanisms which could deter strategic behaviour such as extra-treaty sanctions or incentives;[63] including a referendum that requires the majority of citizens in the respective state to vote for withdrawal (sic);[64] or demand an exit fee to compensate the EU for losses caused by the departure of a Member State.[65]

Withdrawal provisions undeniably facilitate strategic bargaining behaviour. But is this option available equally to all members of an organisation? In fact, two factors condition the bargaining: the size and range of the costs in question, and the determination of the threatening government. For the first, the ability of a withdrawing actor to externalise the costs of its unilateral decision to the other members (and the limitation or non-existence of benefits for the remaining Member States) determines the size and range of such costs. Every type of cost becomes relevant in the equation: trading and economic costs in relation to the market, the feared impact on the dominant ideology within the Union, fears of triggering a domino effect, etc. Accordingly, to Lechnner and Ohr,[66] the effectiveness of the threat of withdrawal depends on three aspects: the benefit/loss the withdrawing state would experience following its decision, the relevance of the withdrawing member to the other members' integration benefits, the benefit loss the other members would suffer in case of withdrawal and the extent of the EU's benefit gains following the decision. Taking all the factors

[62] Helfer (note 17), 1600; Georg Ress, 'Ex ante safeguards against ex post opportunities in international treaties', *Journal of Institutional and theoretical economy*, (1994), 279.

[63] Helfer (note 17), 1601. [64] Lechnner and Ohr (note 55), 373

[65] Peter Kurrill-Klitgaard, 'Opting-out: the constitutional economics of exit', *American Journal of Economics and Society*, 61(1) (2002), 123–158.

[66] Lechnner and Ohr (note 55), 371.

together, this provision reinforces the conclusion that larger states are, by definition, best placed to gain the most from exit (i.e. large Member States have better chances of survival on their own and they can externalise more costs than smaller states). Also, larger Member States can cope better with the costs of withdrawal: the loss of investment and limiting effects as a result of previous Europeanisation can be assumed to be smaller for large Member States.[67]

The determination of the threatening actor contributes to establishing the credibility of the threat. The transformation of the negotiation into a two-level game in which a powerful domestic constituency can acquiesce to the results of a negotiation increases greatly the credibility of the threat. The paradoxical weakness of the government vis-à-vis this domestic constituency may also enhance the credibility of its threat and the readiness of other parties to negotiate.[68]

In summary, the provision has an anti-equality bias[69] which a counterfactual question elucidates: can the EU cope with the withdrawal of 'certain' Member States better than others? For instance, could the euro, the eurozone and even the EU withstand a hypothetical withdrawal of Germany? Accordingly, the provision has a different meaning depending on which state implements it and how this is done: even if withdrawal becomes legally feasible, political and economic considerations will nevertheless condition it as a realistic option.[70]

### E. *Spillover Effects*

The exercise of the right of withdrawal, even once, makes it more credible for other actors to activate the provision in future, thus lowering any cost associated with its activation. In fact, the Danish and Irish governments, both bounded by referendum traditions in EU matters, opposed the inclusion of the provision in the 2004 Draft Constitution since both governments feared that it would incentivise their domestic Eurosceptic groups.[71] On the occasion of the 2016 UK referendum, groups in other

[67] Following the reasoning on Europeanisation, Berglund argues that old Member States which have been shaped by membership for a larger period might find it more difficult to withdraw than more recent Member States (Berglund (n. 60), 157).

[68] Thomas Schelling, *The Strategy of Conflict*, (Harvard MA: Harvard University Press, 1960).

[69] Tatham (note 8), 152; Hofmeister (note 14), 598.

[70] Hofmeister (note 14); Berglund (note 60), 148.

[71] D. Spinant. 'Giscard Forum Set to Unveil Controversial EU "Exit clause"', *European Voice*, 9(2003).

Member States voiced their desire to hold similar referenda.[72] This has led to an inconclusive debate on spillover effects: some wonder whether Article 50 will lead to the gradual fragmentation of what was supposed to be an ever closer union,[73] warning of other alternative undesirable consequences such as cherry-picking, Europe *a la carte* or some sort of regressive, gradual disintegration.[74] Others in turn suggest that somewhat paradoxically, the withdrawal procedure may contribute to the EU's aim of an 'ever closer Union among the peoples of Europe', precisely by making it possible for states to withdraw if the integration process becomes untenable.[75]

## V The Rationale for Exit. Why Would a State Seek Exit?

The large state bias inherent to the exit provision anticipates a crucial question in discussing withdrawal: why would a Member State wish to withdraw? In more precise terms, what political and/or economic reasons would make a state wish to withdraw from the European Union? In utilitarian terms, decisions for withdrawal can emerge when exogenous or endogenous factors alter the cost-benefit calculation.[76] Rather than being separate, both factors act simultaneously.

a. Withdrawal as a response to a change of exogenous factors. The difference between EU membership and an external position is the decisive question of whether membership is purely and solely benefit-maximising.[77] In the early 1990s, Buchanan argued that economic integration areas cannot be definitive and flexible membership was therefore needed to accommodate market developments.[78] If there exist alternatives outside the organisation, states with good alternatives for trade beyond a given regional organisation can make demand on the other potential members. These other members must comply with the demands of the state with outside options to prevent

[72] Tara Palmeri and Kate Day, 'Brexit could lead to Czexit' (23 February, 2016) *Politico* <www.politico.eu/article/brexit-could-lead-czexit-tomas-prouza/>, accessed 5 June 2016.

[73] Hofmeister (note 14)

[74] See Brok et al. on behalf of the EPP Convention Group, 'Suggestion for amendment of Article I-59' <http://european-convention.europa.eu/docs/Treaty/pdf/46/46_Art%20I%2059%20Brok%20EN.pdf>, accessed 27 February 2017.

[75] Hillion (note 15). [76] Lechnner and Ohr (note 55), 360. [77] Ibid.

[78] James M. Buchanan, 'Europe's constitutional opportunity', in *Europe's constitutional future* (London: Institute of Economic Affairs, 1990)

it from exiting the agreement.[79] This option is asymmetrical for states depending on their size: exit options can create larger cost for smaller states. Once an agreement is created, it is often costlier for a small state to opt out, even if it would have preferred no agreement at all.

If exogenous factors trigger exit, then, formal exit provisions, in themselves, cannot be interpreted as triggers. Thus, Gray and Slapin question the extent to which these formal provisions can contain exit when confronting those exogenous pull factors. A significant body of literature argues that the existence of real incentives outside of the organisation (rather than formal provisions) explains changes in the internal dynamics.[80] On the one hand, when at least one state within a proposed organisation can make a credible threat of exit – or has reasonable prospects of trade beyond the organisation – the organisation may be less effective.[81] In contrast, if countries within a regional economic organisation have fewer options for world trade beyond the regional organisation, they will develop strong institutions and make substantial use of them.

b. A second utilitarian reason for withdrawal responds to endogenous factors and, specifically, losing voice (i.e. control on decision-making and its outcomes). Using a rational choice approach and drawing on the analogy with secession of marginalised regions,[82] Lechner and Ohr have interpreted the threat as an hypothetical response to qualified majority voting (QMV) losses: withdrawal is an alternative for

[79] Julia Gray and Jonathan Slapin 'Exit Options and the Effectiveness of Regional Economic Organizations', *Political Science Research and Methods*, 1(2) (2013), 281–303 at 285

[80] Ken Binmore, 'Bargaining and Coalitions', in Alvin E. Roth (ed.), *Game-Theoretic Models of Bargaining* (Cambridge: CUP, 1985) pp. 295–322; Abhinay Muthoo. 'On the Strategic Role of Outside Options in Bilateral Bargaining', *Operations Research*, 43(2) (1995), 292–297; Erik Voeten, 'Outside Options and the Logic of Security Council Action', *American Political Science Review*, 95(4) (2001), 845–858; Jonathan B. Slapin, 'Exit, Voice, and Cooperation: Bargaining Power in International Organization and Federal Systems', *Journal of Theoretical Politics*, 21(2) (2009), 187–211; Songying Fang and Kristopher W. Ramsey, 'Outside Options and Burden-sharing in Nonbinding Alliances', *Political Research Quarterly*, 63(2) (2010), 188–202.

[81] Jenna Bednar, 'Valuing Exit Options', *Publius: The Journal of Federalism*, 37(2) (2007), 190–208; John Odell and Barry Eichengreen, 'The United States, the ITO, and the WTO: Exit Options, Agent Slack, and Presidential Leadership', in Anne Krueger (ed.), *The WTO as an International Organization* (Chicago, IL: University of Chicago Press, 1989), pp. 189–209.

[82] Thus, Alesina et al. argue that regions whose preferences are not considered adequately by the central decision-making bodies may have an incentive to leave Alesina, Alberto, Enrico Spolaore, and Romain Wacziarg, 'Economic Integration and Political Disintegration', *American Economic Review*, 90(5) (2000), 1276–1296.

any state which perceives an accumulation of instances of being outvoted under QMV.[83] These authors elaborate on two scenarios in which withdrawal becomes meaningful: either the benefit of being sovereign outside the EU is regarded as more valuable than the alternative or membership in another regional area is regarded as potentially more beneficial than EU membership. Withdrawal can be considered an option in either scenario.[84] They conclude, optimistically, that the right of secession set out in the Lisbon Treaty is, all-in-all, a helpful institutional adaptation to meet the challenges besetting today's European Union.[85] However, as the evidence set out in the Section VI demonstrates, losses in terms of 'decisional-power' do not account rationally for dissatisfaction in the UK case.

c. Beyond these instrumental, utility-based considerations, identity has acquired enormous value in explaining satisfaction and/or dissatisfaction with the EU and, hence, it may also explain the push for exit. Hooghe and Marks have argued that citizens′ attitudes towards the EU must be understood, not only in terms of their economic interests, but primarily in terms of the perceived challenge to their identity that the EU can pose. The opening up of decisional arenas such as referendums permit citizens to be rearranged, away from their traditional alignments within the party system, to lines of conflict defined by support/rejection of the EU.[86] Decisions based on imperfect, incomplete or totally wrong information about the functioning of the EU and the costs and benefits for the UK were clearly in evidence in the 2016 UK referendum, making identity-based explanations a powerful alternative to understanding decisions.

## VI Enter Loyalty

The revision of the reasons for seeking exit, and the effects of the explicit withdrawal provision, pave the way to advancing beyond the binary relationship between exit and voice. Alongside these mechanisms, Hirschmann included a third, i.e. loyalty which he defined as 'the extent to which customer-members are willing to trade off the certainty of

83 Lechnner and Ohr (note 55), 360. 84 Lechnner and Ohr (note 55), 361.

85 Lechnner and Ohr (note 55), 373.

86 Liesbet Hooghe and Gary Marks, 'A postfunctionalist theory of European integration: from permissive consensus to constraining dissensus', *British Journal of Political Science*, 39 (2008), 1–23

exit against the uncertainties of an improvement in the deteriorated product'.[87] This definition connotes a utilitarian (rather than specifically moral) foundation for action. Loyalty is important in any organisation since, according to Hirschman, it fulfils a key function: it can neutralise, within certain limits, the tendency of the most quality-conscious customers or members to be the first to exit.[88] As a result of loyalty, these potentially most influential customers and members will stay on longer than they would ordinarily, in the hope or rather reasoned expectation that improvement or reform can be achieved 'from within'. Thus loyalty, far from being irrational, can serve the socially useful purpose of preventing deterioration from becoming cumulative, as it so often is when no barrier to exists.[89] For Hirschman, loyalty is a key concept in the battle between exit and voice because, as a result of it, members may be locked into their organisations a little longer and thus choose to use the voice option with greater determination and resourcefulness than they would otherwise have done.[90]

Hirschman presents a two-way relationship between voice and loyalty (i.e. loyalty increases the tendency to seek voice and having 'voice' increases loyalty). But he only shows a *one-way* relationship going from loyalty to exit. For him, loyalty or specific institutional barriers to exit are particularly functional whenever the effective use of voice requires a great deal of social inventiveness, while exit is an available, yet not wholly effective, option.[91] Note that exit being an available, and yet not a wholly effective option, is a good description of the situation of a Member State of the EU.

The second direction the relationship between exit and loyalty can take is important to extracting the meaning of withdrawal provisions. What happens when formalised and explicit exit enters the scene? What is the effect of increasing exit (i.e. making it less costly) on loyalty? My response is a straightforward one: easier exit options undermine loyalty. Taking the specific case of withdrawal provisions, they undermine loyalty in two ways: firstly, they grant legal certainty (next to facticity) to the full exit option and, because of this, also make it a more credible option. Those purely opposing EU membership can immediately argue that, with respect to the relative legal uncertainty of the previous situation, explicit withdrawal creates a clearly-defined legal outcome and the procedure to achieve it. This reduces the costs of the exit option even if only in the

[87] Hirschman (note 2), 77 [88] Hirschman (note 2), 79. [89] Ibid. [90] Ibid., 82.
[91] Ibid., 81.

sense that the ultimate legal case against it disappears (and citizens do not need to be convinced of the legality of this option and opposing constituencies cannot blame it as illegal). Making the provision explicit (perceptible beforehand as an implicit possibility) makes its use more credible as well as the threat of its use. The costs of activating the formerly purely political exit option decrease.

Second, an explicit and easier exit option permits a discursive construction of 'product deterioration' which may not be necessarily based on a loyal interpretation of the situation (and let us recall that loyalty is defined as the propensity to look for solutions to product deterioration *within* an organisation). A loyalist interpretation of product deterioration leads to demands for reform (i.e. voice) rather than to the exercise of exit. The Cecchini *Report on the Cost of non-Europe* (1988)[92] provides the archetype of a loyal diagnosis of product deterioration. Starting with the diagnosis of the problems in the functioning of the single market in the 1970s and 1980s, the Report valued the possible gains through common action at the EU level for achieving the single market. The SEA responded to this diagnosis by introducing the 1992 programme and a number of additional mechanisms, such as harmonisation and the extensive introduction of mutual recognition of standards, plus the adoption of qualified majority voting for market-related measures. The success of the strategy means that today, the Cost of Non-Europe Reports[93] follow the same approach of evaluating gains and/or the realisation of a public good through common action at the EU level. Note that the approach may also apply when the diagnosis recommends the suppression of EU competence: this is possible, for instance, with the CAP.

The existence of the exit option transforms diagnosis into an exercise in which changing preferences based on considerations such as identity can substitute the clear identification of 'product deterioration'. Thus, in the case of the UK process, examination of the hypothetical defects in the EU's economic constitution[94] have been found, in reality, ill-founded

[92] Paolo Cecchini, Michel Catinat and Alexis Jacquemin, *The European Challenge, 1992: The Benefits of a Single Market* (London: Gower, 1988).

[93] Joseph Dunne, 'Mapping the Cost of Non-Europe, 2014–19' (2014) European Added Value Unit European Parliamentary Research Service, <http://www.europarl.europa.eu/RegData/etudes/etudes/join/2014/563350/IPOL-EAVA_ET(2014)563350_EN.pdf>, accessed 27 February 2017.

[94] A CER Report summarised the standard critique of the UK's membership of the EU into the following arguments: 1. The EU does little to open markets on the continent, and so creates few opportunities for British exporters. It follows that leaving the EU would have little impact on Britain's European trade. 2. EU rules tie up the British economy in red

(and a poor rationale for leaving the Union).[95] Similarly, diagnosis of the EU's 'creeping competence' and its alleged attempt constantly to over-reach its powers are not confirmed by empirical scrutiny. This suspicion caused the Dutch and British 'review of competences': the British Government reviewed all the competences of the European Union on the basis of evidence submitted by independent stakeholders, producing reviews in thirty-two policy areas over the period 2013–2015. After two UK Government reports, the findings confirm that there is little or no case for a repatriation of EU competences.[96] Similarly, the Bank of England concluded that EU membership probably increased the dynamism of the UK economy and its ability to grow. It also noticed that flexibility in applying EU rules was respected for national regulators and

tape, and constrain the UK's ability to tap faster-growing markets outside Europe. A British exit would boost output by reducing the burden of regulation on business, and by freeing Britain to sign more free trade agreements with countries outside Europe. 3. If Britain left the EU, it would win back its net contribution to the EU's budget, which the Treasury estimates will be 0.5 per cent of GDP per year between 2014 and 2020. 4. Immigration from the EU diminishes Britons' employment prospects, and requires the British taxpayer to subsidise public services and provide welfare benefits for newcomers. 'The economic consequences of leaving the EU – The final report of the CER commission on the UK and the EU single market Centre for European Reform' (June 2014) <http://www.cer.org.uk/sites/default/files/publications/attachments/pdf/2014/report_smc_final_report_june2014-9013.pdf>, accessed 27 February 2017.

95 The same Report concludes that there are four reasons why these claims are ill-founded, and are a poor rationale for leaving the Union. First, the level of economic integration between the UK and the rest of the EU is very high, so healthy doses of competition and investment from elsewhere in the EU help to raise British productivity. Second, EU rules do not place large burdens on the British economy as a whole, or large constraints upon British exports to countries outside Europe: 'Brexit' would not be an economic liberation. Third, EU markets are of such importance to national prosperity that after a vote to leave, British negotiators would try to secure access to them. The experience of countries like Norway shows that this would involve accepting many of the rules of the single market, and a contribution to the EU's budget, but with little influence on EU decision-making. Fourth, there is little evidence that migrants from elsewhere in the EU reduce Britons' job prospects or their wages. A smaller proportion of EU immigrants receive benefits than do Britons, and EU migrants are net contributors to the public finances, helping to pay for the pensions and healthcare of an ageing society.

96 Michael Emerson, Steven Blockmans, Steve Peers and Michael Wriglesworth, 'British Balance of Competence Reviews, Part II: Again, a huge contradiction between the evidence and Eurosceptic populism' (June 2014) *EPIN* Paper No. 40. They argue, moreover, that for the UK in particular the EU has shown considerable flexibility in agreeing to special arrangements, such as in the policies they reviewed on asylum, non-EU immigration and civil judicial cooperation. In other areas reviewed, such as the single market for goods, external trade, transport, environment, climate change and research, they found a good fit between the EU's policies and UK priorities, with the EU being perceived by stakeholders as an 'amplifier' of British interests.

supervisors.[97] These examples refute the 'disloyal' construction of the product deterioration diagnosis.

Alternatively, how real is the loss of voice as the trigger for a withdrawal demand? In relation to the UK, Simon Hix and his collaborators have shown that the UK has not been marginalised on average in the making of EU laws. Moreover, the UK has been more closely aligned to the final outcomes more often than most other governments and this is true also for issues of greater salience for the UK Government. In fact, the UK Government's preferences were the fourth closest to the final policy outcomes.[98] When looking at the patterns of voting within the Council, records suggest that there has been a significant shift in the position of the UK Government when comparing 2004–2009 to 2009–2015, with the UK Government voting against the majority more often in the later period and being on the losing side more than any other state. Yet the UK was part of the wining majority 87 per cent of the cases (without neglecting the fact that most decisions are, in fact, adopted by consensus).[99] As for the EP, an analysis of MEP voting patterns (2009–2014) shows that British MEPs were less likely to be on the winning side than MEPs from any other Member State. But far from being evidence of marginalisation, the reason for these results is that the three main political groups dominated voting and the number of British MEPs in these groups declined as a result of the departure of British conservatives from the EPP and fewer British MEPs being elected from parties aligned to ALDE and the S&D.[100] Again, Hix et al. show that British MEPs did reasonably well in some policy areas the UK cares

97 Bank of England, 'EU membership and the Bank of England' (October 2015) <http://www.bankofengland.co.uk/publications/Documents/speeches/2015/euboe211015.pdf>, accessed 27 February 2017.

98 He uses data on approval of EU legislation between 1996 and 2008. Data do not cover international treaties nor legislative acts adopted after 2008. [Hix refers to Lord Lawson writing in the Times on May 2013: 'we are doomed to being consistently outvoted by the Eurozone bloc'] Simon Hix 'Is the UK marginalised in the EU?' (2015) <http://blogs.lse.ac.uk/europpblog/2015/10/20/is-the-uk-marginalised-in-the-eu/>, accessed 27 February 2017.

99 Hix and Hagemann include both 'no' and 'abstentions' as opposition votes. Caveat: the UK Government might be more willing than other governments publically to register its opposition to EU decisions [changes in patterns of opposition may also be related to change of government in the UK] 'Does the UK win or lose in the Council of Ministers?' (2015) <http://blogs.lse.ac.uk/europpblog/2015/11/02/does-the-uk-win-or-lose-in-the-council-of-ministers/>, accessed 27 February 2017.

100 Simon Hix, 'UK MEPs lose most in the European Parliament' (2015) <http://ukandeu.ac.uk/explainers/uk-meps-lose-most-in-the-european-parliament/>, accessed 27 February 2017.

about, such as the internal market, international trade and international development, but are most often marginalised in budgetary issues. This results largely from the British conservatives leaving the EPP (a move to placate euroskeptics within the Conservative party) and the increase in UKIP MEPs (who are almost always on the losing side).[101] But even in this situation, British MEPs have managed to capture a number of powerful agenda-setting positions; for instance, a Brit has chaired the powerful internal market committee since 2004.[102]

In summary, empirical evidence does not support the thesis of the 'declining influence' and, hence, the construction of the case for exit exhibit a 'disloyal' (in the Hirschmanian sense) position: rather than reacting to objective organization deterioration in terms of negative impacts, other less evidence driven factors seem to have activated exit in the UK case. As the authors of the Report[103] quoted above conclude, 'declining performance' may exist: at a more detailed level, there can be individual actions or laws which might be done better or not at all. In this context, voice represent a better mechanism for for correction of these issues. This form of declining performance is hardly a rationale for secession.

## VII The Change of the Voice Mechanism: Seeking Selective Exit

Section IV has outlined a typology of effects which connects with the discussion in Section V on the hypothetical reasons for withdrawal. This section in turn discusses how the interaction between the strategic effects and the dis-loyal construction of the diagnosis specifically affects how actors define 'voice' and the relationship between exit and voice. The explicit reference to exit ***changes the voice mechanism itself***. Weiler described the consolidation of EU secondary legislation and its attached principles in exchange for an increased participation of the Member States in decision-making.

[101] Simon Hix, 'UK influence in Europe series: The policy successes (and failures) of British MEPs' (2016) <http://blogs.lse.ac.uk/europpblog/2016/01/12/uk-influence-in-europe-series-the-policy-successes-and-failures-of-british-meps/>, accessed 27 February 2017.

[102] Simon Hix and Giacomo Benedetto, 'Do British MEPs get key positions of power in the Europe?' (2016) <www.theguardian.com/news/datablog/2016/feb/04/do-uk-meps-get-key-positions-of-power-in-europe>, accessed 27 February 2017.

[103] The economic consequences of leaving the EU (note 94).

The newly formalised exit constructs a different voice mechanism (let us recall that voice, for Hirschmann, was a messy and unclear mechanism in the domain of politics): 'voice' acquires the sense of acquiring some right for calling for the renegotiation (meaning *ex post* derogation) of the EU *acquis* and/or the terms of membership in the EU. In this respect, Article 50 can be read in connection with Article 48(2) which establishes that proposals for amending the treaties 'may, inter alia, serve either to increase or to reduce the competences conferred on the Union in the Treaties'. Article 48(2) was negotiated at the same time as the new withdrawal provisions. Voice then turns into demands to address the discursively constructed 'declining performance' through a reduction of the Union's scope of activity. And this marks a transformation of the relationship between exit and the closure of selective exit with which Weiler characterised the EU: while in Weiler's analysis voice remained a mechanism for guaranteeing intergovernmental control of decision-making, Article 50 allows states to gain voice by obtaining unilateral derogations and exemptions from previously unanimously agreed common policies.

For the moment, the rigidity of the Article 48 procedures protects the EU from unilateral de-constitutionalisation attempts. However, it does not discourage seeking alternative arrangements, as happened with the package negotiated and agreed with the UK Government in February 2016 (see above page 191). The threat of withdrawal thus forced the Union to enter into the negotiation of a 'reform' without using the Article 48 procedure (which implies *inter alia* a Convention). And a single Member State has been able to unilaterally establish the agenda.

Are there real prospects of these voice demands (equal to unilateral ex post derogations) being successful? The chances of this voice strategy succeeding are slim. The threat of exit matters if it is credible and if its exercise imposes costs onto the remaining members.[104] Certainly, a withdrawing state may gain some negotiating power through a strategy of 'defiance'[105] since the period between announcement and effective withdrawal creates opportunities for blackmail. The withdrawing state will remain part of the EU decision-making process and it may be tempted to use this as a tool to secure more beneficial terms in the withdrawal agreement. It may also be tempted to exercise some sort of legal detachment

104 I am grateful to Maraijke Kleine for drawing my attention to this point.

105 A. Łazowski, *Withdrawal from the European Union. A Legal Appraisal* (Edward Elgar Publishing 2016).

(see above). In this respect, the EU's responses (for instance, an infringement procedure) would be increasingly ineffective since the incentive of continued membership to comply disappears and, moreover, non-compliance feeds back into the dynamic of abandoning the EU legal order.

One potential cost for remaining members is the damage that an exit inflicts on the abandoned institutional structure (its credibility or its capacity).[106] The exit of the UK, however, would not undermine the EU's credibility, because there is substantial information about the benefits of EU membership (which contradicts and potentially disarms the Eurosceptic denunciation of the EU's decline in performance). Of course, Eurosceptics may conjure up a scenario in which the UK's exit causes the EU to plunge into a new age of protectionism. Nonetheless, it would appear that the advocates of a British exit grossly overestimate its impact on the remaining members, as well as their willingness to accommodate the British with substantial institutional reforms.

## VIII Conclusions

The introduction of Article 50 of the Treaty of Lisbon has subtly transformed the relationship between the voice and exit mechanisms that Weiler described in 1992. The explicit provision enables attempts to undermine loyalty by making it cheaper to level un-loyal criticism against the EU. But it has also allowed a transforming voice into demands for the degradation of the Union. Thus, the effects of the withdrawal provision in article 50 essentially mirrors the effects of the right to secede in state constitutions. Cass Sustein provided a number of adverse factors of such provisions:

> To place such a right in a founding document would increase the risks of ethnic and factional struggle; reduce the prospects for compromise and deliberation in government; raise dramatically the stakes of day-to-day political decisions; introduce irrelevant and illegitimate considerations into those decisions; create dangers of blackmail, strategic behaviour, and exploitation; and, most generally, endanger the prospects for long-term self-governance. Constitutionalism addresses precisely these kind of risks.[107]

[106] For a similar argument, see, for example, Mareike Kleine, *Informal Governance in the European Union. How Governments Make International Organizations Work* (Ithaca, NY: Cornell University Press, 2013), chapter 1.

[107] Cass R. Sunstein, 'Constitutionalism and Secession', *University of Chicago Law Review*, 58(2) (1991), pp 633–670.

Similarly, Hirschman also warned that 'once the exit mechanism is readily available, the contribution of voice' – that is of the political process – 'to such matters is likely to be and remain limited'.[108] The conclusions of these two scholars along with the analysis provided in this chapter and the lessons learned from the UK experience show that the withdrawal provision in Article 50 does not improve an inch EU constitutionalism and, rather, stimulate dynamics that may threaten the very basis of the European project: conditioning self interest to the fulfilment of the larger goal of achieving peace by sacrificing sovereignty in a joint project.

[108] Hirschman (note 5), 95

11

# This Way, Please! A Legal Appraisal of the EU Withdrawal Clause

CHRISTOPHE HILLION*

## I Introduction

The Treaty on European Union (TEU) explicitly foresees that a Member State may leave the EU. According to Article 50 TEU, the withdrawal process starts when, having 'decide[d] to withdraw from the Union in accordance with its own constitutional requirements', a Member notifies the European Council 'of its intention'. The latter then agrees on the guidelines for negotiating an EU agreement with the state concerned, which is to be concluded by the Council by a qualified majority with the consent of the European Parliament. In the event, the EU treaties would, in principle, cease to apply to the departing state once the agreement enters into force, or in the absence thereof, two years after the European Council has been notified. It is also foreseen that the former Member State would have to apply on the basis of Article 49 TEU, should it intend to rejoin the Union.

Article 50 TEU has generated considerable academic interest following its introduction in EU law,[1] but predominantly since the UK voted in favour of leaving the Union, a vote that has triggered its first ever

* Many thanks to Anne Myrjord, Steven Blockmans, Tony Arnull, Niamh Nic Shuibhne and Carlos Closa for their helpful comments on earlier versions. Any mistakes are mine.

1 For example, Raymond J. Friel, 'Providing a Constitutional framework for withdrawal from the EU: Article 59 of the Draft European Constitution', *ICLQ*, 53 (2004), 407; Laurent Grosclaude, 'La clause de retrait du Traité établissant une Constitution pour l'Europe: réflexions sur un possible marché de dupes', *Revue trimestrielle de droit européen*, 41 (2005), 533; Florentinas Harbo, 'Secession Right – An Anti-Federal Principle? Comparative Study of Federal States and the EU', *Journal of Politics and Law*, 1 (2008), 132; Jochen Herbst, 'Observations on the Right to Withdraw from the European Union: Who are the "Masters of the Treaties"?', *German Law Journal*, 6 (2005), 1755; Hannes Hofmeister, '"Should I Stay or Should I Go?" – A Critical Analysis of the Right to Withdraw From the EU' *ELJ*, 16 (2010), 589; Adam Łazowski, 'Withdrawal from the

activation. After a closer look at the terms of Article 50 TEU (Section I), this chapter discusses whether the Member States' ability to leave the Union as introduced by the Lisbon Treaty is entirely new (Section II), before questioning the rationale of its acknowledgement from the perspective of the EU legal order, and more specifically of the latter's central aim of an 'ever closer union amongst the peoples of Europe' (Section III).

It will hopefully become clear that the recent codification of the right to withdraw entails that it is now subject to EU rules rather than governed by the classic canons of public international law. Moreover, and somewhat paradoxically, the withdrawal procedure may contribute to the pursuit of an 'ever closer union among the peoples of Europe', precisely by making it possible for a state to step out of, rather than hold up, the integration process, and to participate in it in a different fashion.

## II A Closer Look at the EU Withdrawal Procedure

While Article 50 TEU acknowledges the possibility for any Member State to withdraw from the Union under its own constitutional rules, the

European Union and Alternatives to Membership', *ELRev*, 37 (2012), 523; Susanne Lechner and Renate Ohr, 'The Right Of Withdrawal In The Treaty Of Lisbon: A Game Theoretic Reflection On Different Decision Processes In The EU', *European Journal of Law and Economics*, 32 (2011), 357–375; Jean-Victor Louis, 'Le droit de retrait de l'Union Européenne', *Cahiers de droit européenne*, (2006), 293; Rostane Medhi, 'Brèves observations sur la consecration constitutionnelle d'un droit de retrait volontaire', in Paul Demaret, Inge Govaere and Dominik Hanf (eds.), *30 Years of European Legal Studies at the College of Europe/30 ans d'études juridiques européennes au Collège d'Europe: Liber Professorum 1973/74–2003/04* (Brussels: P.I.E.-Peter Lang, 2005); Phedon Nicolaides, 'Withdrawal from the European Union: A Typology of Effects', *Masstricht Journal of European and Comparative Law*, 20 (2013), 209; Jean Claude Piris, 'Should the UK withdraw from the EU: legal aspects and effects of possible options', (5 May 2015) *Robert Schuman Foundation/ European Issues* No 355; Clemens M. Rieder, 'The Withdrawal Clause of the Lisbon Treaty in the Light of EU Citizenship: Between Disintegration and Integration', *Fordham Inter'l LJ*, 37 (2013), 147; Jean-Luc Sauron, 'L'appartenance à l'Union européenne (article 7, 49 et 50 du Traité sur l'Union européenne)', *Gazette du Palais*, 171 (19 June 2008), 15; Allan Tatham, '"Don't Mention Divorce at the Wedding, Darling!" EU Accession and Withdrawal after Lisbon', in Andrea Biondi, Piet Eeckhout and Stefanie Ripley (eds.), *EU Law after Lisbon* (Oxford: OUP, 2012), p. 128; Alexis Vahlas, 'Souveraineté et droit de retrait au sein de l'Union européenne', *Revue du Droit Public*, 6 (2005), 1565; Carlos Closa, 'Troubled membership: dealing with secession from a member state and withdrawal from the EU' (2014) *EUI Working Paper* RSCAS 2014/91; Christian Calliess, 'Austritt aus der Union', in Christian Calliess and Matthias Ruffert (eds.), *EUV/AEUV* (Leiden: C.H. Beck, 2016); Carlos Closa, 'Interpreting Article 50: exit and voice and...what about loyalty?' (2016) RSCAS Working Paper No. 2016/71 http://cadmus.eui.eu/bitstream/handle/1814/44487/RSCAS_2016_71.pdf?sequence=1

formulation of the provision suggests that it is *not* an absolute and immediate power.[2] Only the *decision to depart* is taken in accordance with the state's domestic law, whereas *departure itself* is governed by EU law.[3] The EU exit procedure is thus not premised on a 'state primacy' conception of the power to secede.[4] Indeed, by speaking of '[a]ny Member State' instead of referring to the 'High Contracting Parties' of Article 1(1) TEU,[5] Article 50(1) TEU embeds the states' ability to withdraw within the EU legal order. The success of any exit initiative therefore depends not only on the member's intention but also on the fulfilment of the procedural and substantive requirements of Article 50 TEU specifically, and on its compliance, as regards the Member State, with the rules and principles underpinning the EU legal order more generally, under the control of the European Court of Justice.

In this respect, Article 50 TEU indicates that the *decision* to withdraw and its *notification* to the European Council are both subject to conditions.[6] The European Council, to which the decision has to be notified, should therefore be assured that the latter conforms to the state's internal 'constitutional requirements'.[7] If, for example, the decision to withdraw was challenged before a domestic court, and/or if the notification was communicated without adequate legal authority,[8] the European

[2] Friel (note 1), 425.

[3] Lazowski (note 1), 527. For another view, see the so-called 'Vote Leave Roadmap': <www.voteleavetakecontrol.org/a_framework_for_taking_back_control_and_establishing_a_new_uk_eu_deal_after_23_june>, accessed 25 June 2016.

[4] Friel (note 1), 422; Tatham (note 1) referring (at 17) to the proposal put forward by the 'Cambridge group': A. Dashwood, M. Dougan, C. Hillion, A. Johnson and E. Spaventa, 'Draft Constitutional Treaty of the European Union and Related Documents', *ELRev*, 28 (2003), 3.

[5] On the idea of Member States, see, for example, Christopher Bickerton, *European Integration: From Nation-States to Member States*, (Oxford: OUP, 2012).

[6] Referring to the literature on secession, and although EU law does not itself specifically require this, it has been suggested that the decision to withdraw from the EU ought to be subject to a stringent internal procedure in terms notably of requirements for democratic accountability, for instance in the form of a super qualified majority in the national parliament, or a referendum: for example, Tatham (note 1), 149.

[7] We could also examine what is meant in Article 50(1) TEU by a State *deciding* to leave; on the UK case see, for example, Mark Elliott, 'Can the EU force the UK to trigger the two-year Brexit process?' (2016) *Public Law for Everyone* <https://publiclawforeveryone.com/>, accessed 25 June 2016.

[8] On these questions, see, for example, Adam Tucker, 'Triggering Brexit: A Decision for the Government, but under Parliamentary Scrutiny', *UKCLA Blog*, <https://ukconstitutionallaw.org/>, accessed 29 June 2016; N. Barber, T. Hickman and J. King, 'Pulling the Article 50 "Trigger": Parliament's Indispensable Role', *UKCLA Blog*, <https://ukconstitutionallaw.org/>, accessed 27 June 2016 and the various reactions, also on the *UK Constitutional Law Association Blog*.

Council would arguably have to wait for that court's judgment and/or obtain clarification on the validity of that notification before formally acknowledging receipt. Indeed, it is only if this notification is considered as such that the withdrawal process begins, and in particular, that the clock starts ticking for the purpose of terminating the application of the EU treaties to the departing state, in accordance with Article 50(3) TEU.

Moreover, the *exclusive* authority of domestic constitutional requirements is predicated on the assumption, given that state's membership, that these conform to the general requirements of EU law and particularly to the values enshrined in Article 2 TEU.[9] Hence, *formal* compliance with domestic constitutional requirements might not suffice to validate the initial withdrawal decision under Article 50 TEU, if that decision was taken in the midst of internal constitutional turmoil, and consequently, if the appropriateness of such requirements was in doubt in relation to EU standards.[10] For instance, the European Council would have grounds to question the validity of a notification if the decision to withdraw was taken after significant modifications of the national constitution, for example curtailing the powers of the parliament and/or the judiciary, and reserving the power to make such a constitutional decision to the executive branch.

Arguably therefore, the domestic *decision to withdraw* is not entirely exempt from also having to conform, albeit implicitly, to EU requirements and notably the common values of Article 2 TEU.[11] Of course, the EU would have no interest in preventing a Member State's departure if the latter's constitutional evolution was increasingly at odds with the requirements of EU membership; on the contrary. However, based on Article 7 TEU, a state which seriously and persistently breached the values of Article 2 TEU could ultimately have its membership right to

[9] Recall that, according to Article 49 TEU, membership is based on the respect and promotion of the values of Art. 2 TEU.

[10] On EU oversight of the values enshrined in Article 2 TEU, particularly the Rule of Law, see, for example, the Commission's Communication, 'A new EU Framework to strengthen the Rule of Law' COM (2014)158 final. Also, Carlos Closa and Dimitry Kochenov, 'Reinforcing Rule of Law Oversight in the European Union' (2014) *EUI Working Paper* RSCAS 2014/25; Anthony Arnull, 'The Rule of Law in the European Union', in Anthony Arnull and Daniel Wincott (eds.), *Legitimacy and Accountability in the European Union* (Oxford: OUP, 2002), p. 239; Christophe Hillion, 'Overseeing the rule of law in the European Union: Legal mandate and means', (2016) *SIEPS European Policy Analysis* 1/2016.

[11] Tatham (note 1) is also of the view that the withdrawing state is 'still bound by Union values in the manner of its withdrawal. In particular, it could be argued that the values of democracy, the rule of law, freedom, solidarity and equality – Articles 2 and 49 TEU – are equally applicable to withdrawal'.

withdraw withheld, so as to protect the rights and interests of other Member States, and of the European citizens potentially affected by the putative withdrawal.[12] If the state intending to withdraw were to bypass the European Council's negative stance on the notification, or indeed ignore the EU rules of withdrawal more generally, it would not only risk damaging its international reputation at a time it would need it most, it could also open the possibility for natural or legal persons who have suffered damages as a result to claim compensation in the courts.[13]

Article 50 TEU merely stipulates that the *notification* has to come from the withdrawing state and be submitted to the European Council. Nothing in the clause specifies its *form*, nor its *timing*, thus seemingly leaving some discretion as regards these to the departing state. Given that it is the formal step which triggers the whole exit procedure, such notification should be unequivocal: there should be a clear message from the state concerned that it intends to leave the Union, following an internal decision to that effect. Therefore, as long as such a message has not been conveyed to the EU, and so long as the Member State continues to fulfil its membership obligations completely, the withdrawal process cannot be deemed to have been triggered.

These points should nevertheless be qualified. In particular, a state which has internally decided to leave should not be allowed use the exit threat to obtain bargaining leverage in the EU decision-making process,[14] and/or delay the notification to strengthen its future negotiating position, at the expense of the overall functioning of the Union. The discretion as to the timing for activating Article 50 TEU should therefore not be limitless, notably in view of the principle of sincere cooperation under Article 4(3) TEU. Though in more general terms, the Heads of State or Government of twenty-seven EU Member States made those points clear following the

[12] The 'all-affected' dimension of withdrawal has been underlined by Tatham (note 1); compare Herst (note 1) and Lazowski (note 1); see also Carlos Closa 'Reinforcing EU Monitoring of the Rule of Law: Normative Arguments, Institutional Proposals and the Procedural Limitations' and Jan-Werner Müller 'Protecting the Rule of Law (and Democracy!) in the EU - The Idea of a Copenhagen Commission' in Carlos Closa and Dimitry Kochenov (eds.), *Reinforcing Rule of Law Oversight in the European Union* (Cambridge: CUP, 2016).

[13] It has even been pointed out that since Article 50 TEU 'would be justiciable by the ECJ, this insertion [i.e. constitutional requirements] has catapulted that court into the role of final arbiter of a significant issue of national constitutional law'; Friel (note 1) 425.

[14] For example, A. Buchanan, 'Secession', in Edward N. Zalta (ed.), *The Stanford Encyclopedia of Philosophy* (Stanford, MA: The Metaphysics Research Lab, 2013); Andrew Shorten, 'Constitutional Secession Rights, Exit Threats and Multinational Democracy', *Political Studies*, 62 (2014), 99; Harbo (note 1).

UK 2016 referendum: while it is up to the British Government to notify the European Council of the UK's intention to withdraw from the Union, this 'should be done as quickly as possible [and] [t]here can *be no negotiations of any kind before this notification has taken place*' (emphasis added).[15] Indeed, if the domestic decision to leave is taken lawfully and deemed binding on the state's authorities, the latter's failure to take steps to implement that decision, including by triggering Article 50 TEU within a reasonable time, could fall foul of the rule of law requirement of Article 2 TEU, which could in turn prompt a European Council reaction under Article 7 TEU.

The question may be raised as to whether a notification could eventually be deduced on the basis of that state's actions and/or inactions. For instance, reduced participation in EU institution activities and/or meetings, particularly the Council and European Council, let alone deficient compliance with EU obligations, could not only form the basis of infringement proceedings against that state before the Court of Justice, those could also amount to tangible evidence that the state no longer intends to take part in the EU as a member, and thus to a deemed notification for the purpose of Article 50 TEU.[16]

The notification, or the absence thereof, has implications on the participation of the withdrawing state in the EU decision-making process. Notification does not, of itself, have a terminating effect.[17] As made clear by Article 50(3) TEU, the Treaties 'cease to apply' only when the withdrawal agreement enters into force, or 'failing that, two years after the notification [. . .] unless the European Council, in agreement with the Member State concerned, unanimously decides to extend the period'. However, the notification is not devoid of immediate legal implications: paragraph 4 of the same Article stipulates that for the purpose of Article 50(2) and (3) TEU, the member of the European Council or of the Council representing the withdrawing state will not participate in the discussions of these institutions, or 'in decisions concerning it'.

[15] Statement, Informal meeting at 27, Brussels, 29 June 2016.

[16] In the particular case of the UK, various elements could have been considered in that light, for example, the Council Decision establishing a revised order in which the Member States will hold the presidency of the Council of the EU until 2030 'Following the UK decision to relinquish the Council presidency in the second half of 2017', Council of the EU, press release 475/16, 26/07/2016, further: see Christophe Hillion, 'Leaving the European Union, the Union Way', *SIEPS European Policy Analysis* (Stockholm, 2016), and Christophe Hillion 'Le retrait de l'Union européenne. Une analyse juridique' (2016) *Revue Trimestrielle de Droit Européen*, 719.

[17] Herbst (note 1), 1756.

This suspension is logical in view of the significant involvement of the European Council and of the Council in the withdrawal process: the former determines the guidelines for negotiating the withdrawal agreement with the state concerned, while the latter concludes it. Conversely, the envisaged arrangement indicates that the withdrawing state's citizens who work for these institutions, even at administrative levels, or who are members of other EU institutions, such as the Commission (including the High Representative for Foreign Affairs and Security Policy, and the Vice-President of the European Commission), the European Parliament and the Court, not to mention the agencies, bodies and other working groups, would not in principle be immediately affected by this exclusion.[18] While this may be justified since they do not formally represent their state, some of these citizens might nevertheless be more prone to defending the state interests, if not their own, in the extraordinary context of withdrawal, and the job relocation that it would entail. They could therefore use their influence, for instance within the Commission, if and when, taking a legislative initiative which might be of significance to the withdrawing state.[19]

Indeed, if interpreted in reverse, Article 50(4) TEU indicates that the withdrawing state is allowed, somewhat paradoxically, to take part in all other Council and European Council discussions and decisions. While such participation may be defensible given that the state formally remains a 'Member State' until its effective withdrawal under the terms of paragraph 3, it is questionable whether, from the perspective of democratic legitimacy, it should nevertheless be entitled to influence EU decisions which might never apply to it, or indeed use its position to obtain concessions in the context of the withdrawal negotiations. While Article 50 TEU does not provide a legal foundation for the outright suspension of the withdrawing state's decision-making rights as soon as the exit process is formally initiated, paragraph 4 could nevertheless be construed broadly enough so as to limit its weight in the Council and European Council, and thus circumscribe its influence on the production of EU norms which would potentially not affect it. After all, the interests of that state's *people* would still be taken care of, notably in the European Parliament, where its MEPs would in principle still sit until formal

[18] Henry G Schermers and Niels Blokker, *International Institutional Law* (2003), at 93, footnote 193; Friel (note 1), 426; Herbst (note 1), 1747; Łazowski (note 1), 530.

[19] Tatham (note 1), 151.

withdrawal.[20] Should there be an interval between the end of the negotiations of the withdrawal agreement and its conclusion, for instance, if a referendum was organised by the withdrawing state on the draft agreement, or if there was a provision in the agreement stipulating its application after a certain time that pre-withdrawal phase could indeed, akin to the period following the signature of a treaty of accession, allow the state concerned a more limited 'observer' status – notably in the Council and European Council – rather than a fully-fledged voting right until the entry into force of the agreement.[21] Otherwise, the withdrawing state would paradoxically have more influence than a state about to become member.

That said, it could be argued that the suspensory effect of the notification should not be construed too broadly, so as not to make it too difficult for the state concerned to change its mind before completion of the process (e.g. following a new general election, or after another referendum) at least if it is accepted that, legally, the notification may be withdrawn, thereby stopping the exiting process. Article 50 TEU is ambiguous on this point. On the one hand, paragraph 3 foresees that 'the Treaties shall cease to apply to the State in question from the date of entry into force of the withdrawal agreement or, failing that, two years after the notification [. . .], unless the European Council, in agreement with the Member State concerned, unanimously decides to extend this period'. One reading of this provision is that once notification is given, there is no turning back: the treaties will cease to apply to the state concerned either upon the entry into force of the withdrawal agreement or at the end of the two-year period triggered by the notification; the only possible change in the process being that the European Council and the state concerned agree to alter the moment at which the treaties cease to apply, but not withdrawal as such. This would indeed prevent a Member State from abusing the procedure to gauge what exit terms it could get, while maintaining the assurance of full membership if unsatisfied with those terms. On the other hand, the remaining Member States might still

20 Arguably, withdrawal would concern not only MEPs of the nationality of and elected in the withdrawing state, as well as MEPs of a nationality of a different Member State elected in the withdrawing state, but also MEPs of the latter's nationality elected in another Member State. On the situation of MEPs linked to the departing state see 'British MEPs "in limbo" as Parliament considers their fate' (7 July 2016) *Politico* blog <www.politico.eu/article/european-parliament-considers-fate-of-its-british-european-parliament/>, accessed 17 July 2016.

21 Case C-413/04 *European Parliament v. Council* [2006] ECR I-11221; and Case C-414/04 *European Parliament v. Council* [2006] ECR I-11279; Case C-273/04 *Poland v. Council* [2007] ECR I-8925.

be open to hold up the withdrawal process following a genuine change of position of the state concerned. The European Council and the Member State could indeed extend the period long enough to establish a sufficient track record of tangible re-engagement with the integration process.[22]

The notification, once acknowledged by the European Council, triggers an obligation to negotiate an agreement with the departing state to set out the arrangements for its withdrawal. This obligation is only addressed to the Union. In contrast, paragraph 4 allows the candidate for withdrawal to wait until the end of the two-year period for its departure to become effective, even in the absence of an agreement. In other words, Article 50 TEU does not require a *negotiated* departure,[23] but only appears to establish a *best endeavours* obligation.[24] The negotiations only depend on the withdrawing state willingness to discuss, although as a Member State it remains bound by the obligation of sincere cooperation until effective departure, and therefore by the duty to help the Union carry out its tasks, including that of negotiating an agreement.

Whether such an obligation may have any actual bearing on the situation is moot. Indeed, in suggesting that the arrangements be set out with the withdrawing state 'taking account of the framework for its future relation with the EU' (paragraph 2), the procedure recognises that the terms and implications of withdrawal would heavily depend on the specific circumstances and the atmosphere in which a possible negotiation would take place. Ideally, the degree of interdependence created by membership could push both parties to address the complex implications of their separation, notably for EU citizens, cooperatively.[25] Indeed the absence of an agreed settlement might otherwise open the floodgates for legal claims, notably against the leaving state, and might also undermine the prospect of a mutually beneficial post-exit comprehensive agreement.

That a settlement should not be made exceedingly difficult is reflected by the procedural arrangements for the conclusion of the withdrawal agreement. First, in referring to Article 218(3) TFEU, Article 50 TEU

[22] Further on the possible revocation of the notification, see Christophe Hillion 'Le retrait de l'Union européenne. Une analyse juridique' (2016) *Revue Trimestrielle de Droit Européen* 719 at 729 and 'Editorial Comments: Withdrawing from the ever closer union?' (2016) 53 *Common Market Law Review*, 1491.

[23] It is thus considered by some as an '*unfettered* right to *unilateral* withdrawal': Hofmeister (note 1), 592; also: Tatham (note 1); Herbst (note 1).

[24] Medhi (note 1).

[25] As pointed out by David Edward, 'EU law and the Separation of Member States', *Fordham Inter'l LJ*, 36 (2013), 1151, also Lazowski (note 1); Medhi (note 1).

indicates that exit ought to be arranged by the EU institutions through an *EU agreement*, rather than through an inter-state process and treaty, as in the accession context of Article 49 TEU. Secondly, the Council has to conclude the ensuing agreement by a qualified majority vote (72 per cent of the remaining 27 Member States, representing 65 per cent of the population), irrespective of whether its content might suggest otherwise. No Member State is thus, in principle, able to veto the conclusion of the EU agreement, in contrast with an accession treaty. Given this particular arrangement, we could justifiably wonder whether the conclusion by the Council, and the absence of any reference to Member State ratification of the agreement also entails that recourse to a mixed agreement is in principle excluded.[26] Since EU treaties are rather explicit on where Member States must ratify specific agreements (e.g. accession treaties under Article 49 TEU, or an accession agreement to the ECHR, under Article 218(8) TFEU), the silence of Article 50 TEU could indeed be taken as precluding their participation, however surprising that may be in view of the possible broad scope of the agreement, and considering the law and case law on EU external competence.[27] That the Member States do not have to conclude the agreement would, however, be consistent with the apparent intention to facilitate its entry into force, and to prevent its ratification dragging on given the destabilising effects it would have on the functioning of the Union.[28] In short, once agreed, 'exit' will be procedurally easier than 'entry'.[29]

The procedure envisaged by Article 50(2) TEU could also mean that the agreement might not contain far-reaching EU commitments in terms of future cooperation with the withdrawing state, and be limited to setting out the technical 'arrangements for [the] withdrawal' (e.g. treatment of officials from the departing state working in EU institutions and bodies, transitional periods permitting some aspects of EU law to continue applying for a period, financial contributions and benefits) 'taking account of the framework for its future relationship with the Union'. Further articulation of this 'framework of its future relation' referred to in paragraph 2 would thus be left for a separate agreement, to be finalised and concluded at a later date, in a different legal

[26] Compare Lazowski (note 1).

[27] For example Allan Rosas 'Exclusive, Shared and National Competence in the Context of EU External Relations: Do such Distinctions Matter?', in Govaere et al. (note 1), p. 17.

[28] On the increasing difficulties to achieve ratification, see Carlos Closa, *The Politics of Ratification of EU Treaties*, (London: Routledge, 2013).

[29] Nicolaides (note 1).

framework, and when the withdrawing state would not be sitting on both sides of the negotiating table. That said, the arrangements for withdrawal, however technical, might still entail policy choices. A case in point would be the movement and treatment of citizens from the withdrawing state, and of citizens from other Member States resident in that state.[30] It is hardly imaginable that the borders would be shut completely as a result of separation.[31]

That a Member state's exit would entail further agreements also results from the fact that the withdrawal agreement, as an EU agreement, could not in itself modify EU primary law, though such modification would be necessary. For instance, the list of contracting parties included in the preambles to the treaties, Article 52 and possibly Article 55 TEU, the geographical references, for example, in Article 355 TFEU and the protocols to the treaties, where applicable, may all have to be amended and/or repealed. The amendments imposed by withdrawal would thus have to be introduced through, or in the context of another treaty based on Article 48 TEU, or possibly on Article 49 TEU,[32] as in a treaty of accession concluded with another state.

It remains the case that Article 50 TEU permits altering, in the sense of reducing, the legal borders and territory of the EU, as well as its state composition, without the formal approval of all its Member States. Indeed, if negotiated, the terms of withdrawal would in principle reflect the interests of the Union,[33] rather than those of the Member States as such. The reference to Article 218(3) TFEU indicates that, the Commission could be involved in drafting the negotiating mandate alongside the European Council,[34] and entrusted by the Council with the task of negotiating the withdrawal agreement, or, at the very least, be part of the negotiating team. For its part, the European Parliament, representing the interests of other EU peoples, would have to consent before the conclusion of the agreement, and could thus also influence its content. Incidentally, how possible institutional divergence regarding the content and nature of the agreement would be addressed can

[30] On the possible substance and shape of this agreement, see, for example, Łazowski (note 1), 528.

[31] Further: Edward (note 25), 1164.

[32] Bruno De Witte, 'Treaty Revision Procedures after Lisbon', in Biondi, Eeckhout and Ripley (note 1), p. 107 at p. 125.

[33] Compare Nicolaides (note 1).

[34] Although the participation of the High Representative should not be excluded at that stage, it is unlikely that she or he would negotiate the agreement as a whole, as it is unlikely to be considered as relating principally or exclusively to the CFSP.

also be questioned. The legal nature and basis of the agreement might also raise disputes. The *renvoi* in Article 50 TEU to Article 218 TFEU opens the possibility for the European Court of Justice to intervene, either by controlling the lawfulness of the decision to conclude it, through the annulment procedure (Article 263 TFEU) or indirectly through the preliminary ruling mechanism (Article 267 TFEU), or by way of an advisory opinion based on Article 218(11) TEU, to establish the agreement's compatibility with the Treaty.[35] Indeed, unlike an accession treaty based on Article 49 TEU, the jurisdiction of the Court over the withdrawal agreement does not seem to be in any way restricted.

The above discussion indicates that the TEU only sets out the basic elements of the withdrawal process. Much had indeed to be clarified once the process was activated by the United Kingdom. That the procedure is not more detailed may seem paradoxical. After all, its very insertion in EU law was meant to establish in advance the specific steps to be taken in the event of a separation, a context in which ad hoc procedural arrangements are perhaps less easy to agree upon.[36] That said, the imperfection of the procedure reflects the uncertainty of the implications of exit, and the need to leave room to cater for the particular needs of the situation. Perhaps the lack of clarity was also a way to avoid making the clause too user-friendly.

## III A New Right for EU Member States?

According to one view, leaving the Union had always been possible, both legally and practically, despite the pre-Lisbon treaties' silence on the matter. Like any other international treaty, the EU could be left by any of its contracting parties[37] on the basis of the application of public international law, such as the Vienna Convention on the Law of Treaties (VCLT), or of customary international norms for those states which have not ratified the Convention. To be sure, the absence of such a withdrawal clause in the statute of an international organisation does not, in itself,

35 There is however an ambiguity as to whether other paragraphs of Article 218 TFEU have relevance in the context of Article 50 TEU

36 Medhi (note 1).

37 While the Court of Justice had interpreted the EC treaty as constituting the Constitutional charter of the Community, it also consistently admitted that it remained an international agreement (notably in Case 6/64 *Costa v. ENEL* [1964] ECR 1251; and Opinion 1/91 *EEA I* [1991] ECR I-6079).

prevent withdrawal by its participating states,[38] and it is precisely because the EC/EU treaties lacked specific provisions to that effect that the above *lex generalis* would have applied. From that perspective, a Member State could always invoke, for example, a 'fundamental change of circumstances', i.e. the *rebus sic stantibus* clause (Art. 62 VCLT) to terminate its participation in the treaties, under the strict conditions of Articles 54 and 56 VCLT.[39]

Indeed, even if understood as the constitutional charter for the Union, muteness on withdrawal of the pre-Lisbon EU primary law would not necessarily preclude it either. After all, the absence in the Canadian constitution of the right of provincial secession did not prevent the Canadian Supreme Court from considering such secession conceivable, albeit under certain conditions and provided that it was negotiated with the rest of Canada.[40] Even the 'unlimited', 'indissoluble'[41] or 'perpetual'[42] characterisation of a Union may not in itself guarantee its everlasting existence. Hence, despite its Article 1 stipulating that 'the Two Kingdoms of Scotland and England shall upon the 1st May next ensuing the date hereof, *and forever after*, be United into One Kingdom by the name of Great Britain' (emphasis added), the 1706 Treaty of the Union between England and Scotland has been deemed reversible.

The notion that withdrawal from the Community/Union has always been plausible was epitomised by the nationwide referendum held in the

[38] As Łazowski aptly recalls, the absence such a clause in the UN Charter did not prevent Indonesia from withdrawing (note 1), 526; also Schermers and Blokker (note 18).

[39] This proposition is supported in the literature; for example, Mehdi (note 1) who recalls (at 6) that the Praesidium of the Convention made a link between the EU provision and the VCLT); Łazowski (note 1), 525; it was also the views of some of the *conventionnels* (e.g. proposal for amendment of Art I-59 by Mr Lopes and Mr Lobo Antunes), though criticised by, for example, Hofmeister (note 1) footnotes 12–14 (and literature mentioned).

[40] *Reference re Secession of Quebec* [1998] 2 S.C. 217; which led to the adoption of Bill C-20, 'An Act to give effect to the requirement for clarity as set out in the opinion of the Supreme Court of Canada in the Quebec Secession Reference', 2nd session, 36th Parliament, 1999 (first reading, 13 December, 1999).

[41] The term featured in the defunct Treaty establishing a European Political Community (<http://aei.pitt.edu/991/1/political_union_draft_treaty_1.pdf>).

[42] The notion featured in the *Articles of Confederation and Perpetual Union*, but not explicitly in the US constitution which replaced them. However see the US Supreme Court judgment in *Texas v. White*, 74 (1869) US 700. On the Articles, see, for example, Armin Cuyvers, *The EU as a Confederal Union of Sovereign Member Peoples – Exploring the Potential of American (Con)federalism and Popular Sovereignty for a Constitutional Theory of the EU* (Leiden: Leiden University, 2013).

UK in June 1975. Then, British voters were asked whether 'the UK should stay in the European Community (Common Market)', implying that there was no doubt, at least in the UK, that a Member State could always leave.[43] It has also been suggested that withdrawal partly occurred in the case of Greenland, though in the specific context of devolution within Denmark's constitutional system,[44] and when Algeria became independent from France, thereby leaving the Community's territory.[45]

In sum, the absence of an exit clause in the EU founding treaties, whether approached as international treaties or as the constitutional charter of the Union, did not make withdrawal impossible. It was even contended during the Convention which drafted the Constitutional Treaty that this addition might simply be superfluous.[46]

According to the contrary view, leaving the Union was inconceivable prior to the inclusion of Article 50 TEU, given the specific features of the EU legal order. The idea that the EC Treaty was concluded for 'unlimited duration',[47] 'creating a Community of [equally] unlimited duration', [48] aimed at 'an ever closer union', thus precluded Member States' unilateral withdrawal, including by means of international law. It has notably been wondered whether the strict conditions for termination based on a change of circumstances could ever be met by a Member State in view of the original 'ever closer union' purpose of the treaties to which all Member States had to subscribe, and considering that any modifications of the treaties require unanimous approval.[49] The supremacy of Union law, the enforceable rights it confers directly on Member States and individuals, its institutions endowed with sovereign rights and entitled to deal with economic, social and political issues, and its compulsory system for the judicial resolutions of disputes, have also been invoked to argue that, at the very least, 'Member States were not entitled *unqualifiedly* to revoke

43 Recall also the ambition of the Labour party to have Britain leave the EC without referendum in 1981 on the basis of international law; the PASOK party had similar intentions for Greece in 1981.

44 Interestingly, this was done by relying on Art. 48 TEU (OJ 1985 L29). Further: Friel (note 1), 409ff.

45 Tatham (note 1), 142ff.

46 Suggestion for amendment of Article I-59 Draft Constitutional Treaty by Mr Ernâni Lopes and Manuel Lobo Antunes; <http://european-convention.europa.eu/docs/Treaty/pdf/46/46_ArtI%2059%20Lopes%20EN.pdf>, accessed 5 July 2016.

47 Art. 53 TEU and Art. 356 TFEU.

48 Case 6/64 *Costa v. ENEL* [1964] ECR 1251, 1269–1271.

49 For more, see Herbst (note 1) 1755, Jean Paul Jacqué, *Droit institutionnel de l'Union européenne*, (Paris: Dalloz, 2015), p. 141.

their membership,[50] (emphasis added). The inclusion of an exit clause in the Treaty establishing a Constitution for Europe was thus regarded as contravening the commitment to an ever closer union that States take on when they become members,[51] and the underlying general principles of loyalty and solidarity to which they are thereby committed.[52]

## IV Withdrawal and the 'Ever Closer Union' Aims of the EU

While there is little doubt that Member States always had the possibility to leave the Union, the express inclusion of a withdrawal clause in the TEU does raise the question of its compatibility with the canons of the Union's legal order. In particular, how can it fit in with the system of the treaties, designed as it is to fulfil the EU's 'ever closer union' objective? The question is all the more acute since the withdrawal procedure involves EU institutions: how could they be empowered by the treaties to act against the Union's integration aim, in view of Article 13(1) TEU, according to which 'The Union shall have an institutional framework which shall aim to promote its values, *advance its objectives, serve its interests, those of its citizens* and those of the Member States, and *ensure the consistency, effectiveness and continuity of its policies and actions*' (emphasis added)? Certainly, such an exit right has a centrifugal force; it impedes the very functioning of the EU in that it becomes a bargaining chip with distorting effects on EU decision-making,[53] particularly in the hands of larger states.[54] Once used, it could also encourage other Member States to leave.

The broader (legal and political) context in which the clause was introduced is of key significance and should be carefully considered to comprehend its meaning and possible function. The clause finds its birthplace in the defunct Treaty establishing a Constitution for Europe (TCE). As such, it was an integral part of the EU constitution and constitutionalising package, rather than an element of the de-constitutionalisation course instigated by the 2007 Intergovernmental Conference, following the

[50] Koen Lenaerts and Piet van Nuffel, *Constitutional Law of the European Union*, (London: Sweet and Maxwell, 2005), p. 363.

[51] Friel (note 1); Harbo (note 1). [52] Compare Medhi (note 1), 3; Herbst (note 1), 1756.

[53] Friel then speaks of a 'system of delayed withdrawal [that] threatens both the withdrawing state and the stability of the Union'; (note 1), 427.

[54] As typified by the UK 'renegotiations' of the terms of its membership, prior the 'remain or leave' referendum. Further: Tatham (note 1), 151; Medhi (note 1), and literature on secession referred to above (note 14).

rejection of the Constitutional Treaty.[55] From this constitutional perspective, the inclusion of the clause in the TCE first reflects the intention to submit it to EU constitutional canons instead of leaving it to the vicissitudes of international law, should withdrawal ever occur.[56] As Article 50 TEU is the *lex specialis*, any withdrawal of a Member State would thenceforth have to occur within the framework of EU law, rather than outside it.[57]

Secondly, the *constituants'* intention to consolidate the dynamic of the 'ever closer union' may explain, at least partly, the acknowledgement of the right to withdraw. The latter was thus understood as a safety valve to reassure Member States[58] who would always be allowed to leave, should they be uncomfortable with the integration path envisaged by the Constitutional Treaty – which the Treaty of Lisbon did not fundamentally alter.[59] In the initial context of the constitutionalisation of the EU Treaties, and of the strengthened commitment to integration that it arguably entailed, the inclusion of the exit clause would therefore be a quid pro quo.[60] For the Member States' choice *not* to leave arguably entails a firm pledge to pursue the 'ever closer union' goal, in line with the principle of sincere cooperation now enshrined in Article 4(3) TEU. Conversely, the latter principle could be construed as inviting, though not obliging, a recalcitrant Member State to consider withdrawal to allow the Union to fulfil its tasks and pursue its integration objectives – instead of allowing that state to achieve the dilution, or deletion of its aim of ever closer union.[61]

55 Part 3 IGC, 2007 Mandate (11218/07, 26 June 2007). 56 Medhi (note 1).

57 The argument that Article 54 of the Vienna Convention on the Law of Treaties would make it possible for a state to withdraw from the EU outside the framework Article 50 TEU if Member States unanimously so decide, is questionable. The provision confers on the EU a competence to monitor the withdrawal process which it exercises through its institutions. The Member States would infringe that competence if they decided to allow withdrawal outside the EU framework. Either they would have to modify the EU treaties to withdraw that competence first, or arguably the EU would also have to approve withdrawal outside the EU exit clause.

58 For Shorten: 'a pressure valve that deflates full blown secessionist politics'? (note 14).

59 Jacqué (note 49); Medhi (note 1).

60 For example, Harbo (note 1), 42. Indeed, the then president of the European Convention considered that withdrawal should be open to those states which would not ratify the constitution, so as not to prevent the latter's ultimate entry into force.

61 'UK keen to delete "ever closer union" from EU treaty', <http://euobserver.com/political/121607>, accessed 5 July, 2016. See also the letter of 10 November 2015 of the then UK Prime Minister Cameron to European Council President Tusk, entitled 'A new settlement for the United Kingdom in a reformed European Union'; cp. Section C, pt. 1, of the Decision of the Heads of State or Government, meeting within the European Council,

The right to withdraw may thereby be interpreted as the ultimate elaboration of constitutional devices (e.g. the subsidiarity principle, enhanced cooperation, opt-outs, Article 4(2) TEU) conceived of to cater to the needs of less integrationist states. By the same token, it confirms that participation in the European integration process is essentially voluntary and that the continental vocation of an 'ever closer union' cannot trump its democratic foundations encapsulated in the idea expressed in the Preamble to the TFEU that only European peoples who 'share [this] ideal [. . .] join in [the Member States'] efforts'.[62] Indeed, the expressions of 'shar[ing] their ideal' and 'join[ing] in their efforts' may take several forms, of which membership is but only one, particularly in view of the changing conception of the accession-integration nexus.[63] Hence non-membership does not mechanically result in non-participation in, let alone rejection of, the European integration process. The network of EU association agreements with third European states *not* seeking membership, such as the EEA, or the EU bilateral arrangements with Switzerland, is a useful reminder of this point.[64]

The introduction of Article 8 TEU, by the Treaty of Lisbon, should also be considered in this context. Building upon the ad hoc European Neighbourhood Policy,[65] the provision establishes a specific mandate

concerning a new settlement for the United Kingdom within the European Union; Annex I of the Conclusions of the European Council of 18–19 February 2016.

62 See, in this respect, para. 27 to the Conclusions of the European Council of 27 June 2014, <www.consilium.europa.eu/uedocs/cms_Data/docs/pressdata/en/ec/143478.pdf>, accessed 5 July, 2016.

63 For more on this point, see C. Hillion, 'Accession and Withdrawal in the law of the European Union', in Anthony Arnull and Damian Chalmers (eds.), *Oxford Handbook of European Union Law* (Oxford: OUP, 2015).

64 Consider Norway's current position in relation to the EU, as thoroughly explored in Fredrik Sejersted et al., *Utenfor of innenfor – Norges avtaler med EU*, (Oslo: NOU, 2012); see also the contributions in Isabelle Bosse-Platière and Cécile Rapoport (eds.), *L'Etat tiers en droit de l'Union européenne* (Paris: Bruylant, 2014); as well as the status of 'associate membership' envisaged by The Spinelli Group, *A Fundamental Law of the European Union* (2013), <www.spinelligroup.eu/article/fundamental-law-european-union>, accessed on 5 July 2015, pp. 20 and 93; Adam Łazowski, 'Enhanced multilateralism and enhanced bilateralism: integration without membership', *CMLRev*, 45 (2008), 1433.

65 Steven Blockmans, 'Friend or Foe? Reviewing EU Relations with its Neighbours Post Lisbon', in Panos Koutrakos (ed.), *The European Union's External Relations A Year After Lisbon*, CLEER Working Papers 2011/3, 113; Marise Cremona and Christophe Hillion, 'L'Union fait la force? Potential and limits of the European Neighbourhood Policy as an integrated EU foreign and security policy' (2006) *European University Institute* Law Working Paper No 39/2006.

for the EU to develop a 'special relationship' with neighbouring states, aimed at establishing an area of prosperity and stability based on EU values and involving 'the possibility of undertaking activities jointly'.[66] Read in the light of Article 21(1) TEU, Article 8 suggests that the post-Lisbon integration goal transcends the legal boundaries of the Union, and of its constituent states.[67]

By definition, the withdrawing state would become a European neighbour of the Union, which would fall within the ambit of Article 8 TEU, and with which the EU would be bound to engage as a result.[68] This provision thus not only bolsters the normative basis for a *negotiated* withdrawal, it also points towards strong post-exit engagement by the Union with the former Member State. The withdrawing state's legal system might not be entirely shielded from the influence of EU law as a result. Indeed, while enlargement is an EU foreign policy aimed at transforming a third state into an operational member, withdrawal too is part of EU foreign policy.[69] It is a process whereby a member becomes a third state with which the Union is expected to entertain a special relationship.

Withdrawal thus entails the production of new post-membership external devices[70] which are all the more pressing given the degree of

[66] For more on Art. 8 TEU: Peter van Elsuwege and Roman Petrov, 'Article 8 TEU: Towards a New Generation of Agreements with the Countries of the European Union?', *ELRev*, (2011), 688; Dominik Hanf, 'The ENP in the light of the new "neighbourhood clause" (Article 8 TEU)', (2011) *College of Europe* Research Paper in Law – *Cahiers juridiques* No 2/2011; Christophe Hillion, 'The EU neighbourhood competence under Article 8 TEU', in Elvire Fabry (ed.), *Thinking Strategically about the EU's external action* (Paris: Jacques Delors Institute, 2013), p. 204.

[67] For example, Sandra Lavenex and Frank Schimmelfennig (eds.), *EU External Governance. Projecting EU Rules Beyond Membership* (London: Routledge, 2010); Anne Myrjord, 'Governance Beyond the Union: EU Boundaries in the Barents Euro-Arctic Region', *European Foreign Affairs Review*, 8 (2003), 239.

[68] Whether this provision was ever envisaged as a post-membership device is a moot point. Suffice to recall that in its initial formulation in the draft Treaty establishing a Constitution for Europe, the withdrawal clause was inserted in Title IX along with the accession and suspension clauses respectively, which followed Title VIII on the EU's relations with its neighbourhood.

[69] The two processes also have consequences for the rest of the world. Accession thus entails that the acceding states denounce agreements in areas where the EU is exclusively competent; conversely, the withdrawing state has to establish and re-establish agreements both with third states and the EU in those very areas, once outside the Union.

[70] For more, see Jean Claude Piris, 'Which Options Would Be Available to the United Kingdom in Case of a Withdrawal from the EU?' (2015) *CSF-SSSUP* Working Paper No 1/2015.

interaction and interdependence built into the context of membership.[71] Certainly, the concerns of Union citizens living and working in the withdrawing state ought to be addressed,[72] notably in view of the first EU mission which, according to Article 3(1) TEU, is to ensure the well-being of its peoples.

## V Concluding Remarks

The Treaty on European Union explicitly foresees that a Member State may leave the EU. This power is not entirely new, but its acknowledgement and partial articulation in EU primary law entail that the classic canons of public international law no longer exclusively govern its exercise. Moreover, and as paradoxical as it may seem, such a codification may ultimately serve the purpose of 'ever closer union' of the European integration process. In effect, it makes it possible for a member to step out of the EU in case its development becomes too disagreeable instead of obstructing it, and to envisage an alternative participation in the European integration process, alongside and with the Union.

[71] Edward (note 25), 1164; Adam Łazowski, 'How to Withdraw from the European Union? Confronting Hard Reality' (2013) *CEPS Commentary*, <www.ceps.eu/publications/how-withdraw-european-union-confronting-hard-reality>, accessed 5 July 2016.

[72] Herbst (note 1), 1755.

12

# Be Careful What You Wish for: Procedural Parameters of EU Withdrawal*

ADAM ŁAZOWSKI

## I Introduction

The ease with which political circles have talked about withdrawal from the European Union in the past years is rather surprising and proves that neither the legal parameters of an EU exit nor its consequences have been treated seriously enough.[1] This has changed in the wake of the Brexit referendum on 23 June 2016. Almost overnight Article 50 TEU, which regulates the withdrawal procedure, has become the centre of attention of political circles, policymakers and lawyers. In theoretical terms, Article 50 TEU permits unilateral exit as well as a consensual divorce. Arguably, the first is an interesting abstract proposition, which, however, in practical terms seems to be an unworkable solution. Alas, in the early days of 2017 it was under consideration of the British Government.[2] With this in mind, it is argued in this chapter that the only realistic option is a proper divorce based on a withdrawal agreement. As per Article 50 TEU, it would be negotiated by the European Union with the departing country and should cover the terms of withdrawal and 'take account of framework for future relations' between the EU and the divorcee. Arguably, in order to avoid a legal vacuum, this agreement should not only 'take account of future relations' but actually deal with them thoroughly. It would make the negotiations difficult and, most likely, time-consuming. This one of the reasons why in practice this option was rejected to the benefit of other scenarios considered for Brexit.

* This chapter was written in 2015, however it was subsequently updated to reflect the legal and political situation as it stood on 10 April 2017.

[1] For a textbook example, see Lord Lawson, 'It's time to quit EU', The Times, 7 May 2013.

[2] White Paper: The United Kingdom's exit from and new partnership with the European Union, <https://www.gov.uk/government/publications/the-united-kingdoms-exit-from-and-new-partnership-with-the-european-union-white-paper>

They include negotiations of two separate agreements, either in parallel or in sequence, regulating the terms of exit and future relations. Brexit aside, one must also envisage a scenario where a country leaving the European Union would join EFTA and become an EFTA-EU Member State of the European Economic Area. Should that happen, the scope of an EU withdrawal agreement would be limited to the terms of exit, while future relations between the divorcee and the European Union would mainly be covered by the EEA Agreement.[3]

This chapter unlocks the mechanics of Article 50 TEU and the withdrawal procedure it provides for. It covers the issues which should be attended to by the negotiators and provides an overview of dossiers likely to be covered in a withdrawal agreement.[4]

## II A (Theoretical) Option of Unilateral Withdrawal

Before we look at the legal parameters of consensual withdrawal it is fitting to verify whether unilateral exit is possible. Arguably, this is facilitated in theoretical terms by Article 50 TEU. However, the political, economic and legal consequences would be too profound to make it a realistic scenario. To put it differently, it should be avoided at all costs. Both the theoretical and the practical take on unilateral withdrawal are presented in turn.[5]

[3] Agreement on the European Economic Area [1994] OJ L1/1.

[4] For a more comprehensive coverage of legal aspects of EU withdrawal, see *inter alia*, A. Łazowski *Withdrawal from the European Union. A Legal Appraisal*, (London: Edward Elgar Publishing, 2017). See also P. Eeckhout, 695, E. Frantziou, 'Brexit and Article 50 TEU: A constitutional reading', CMLRev. 54 (2017), A. F. Tatham, '"Don't Mention Divorce at the Wedding, Darling!": EU Accession and Withdrawal after Lisbon', in A. Biondi, P. Eeckhout and S. Ripley (eds.), *EU Law after Lisbon* (Oxford: OUP, 2012), p. 128; H. Hofmeister, 'Should I stay or Should I Go? – A Critical Analysis of the Right to Withdraw from the EU' *ELJ*, 16 (2010), 589; C Hillion, 'Accession and Withdrawal in the Law of the European Union', in A. Arnull and D. Chalmers (eds.), *The Oxford Handbook of European Union Law* (Oxford: OUP, 2015), p. 126; A. Łazowski, 'Withdrawal from the European Union and Alternatives to Membership', *ELRev*, 37 (2012), 523; A. Łazowski, 'EU Withdrawal: Good Business for British Business?', *EPL*, 22 (2016), 115; P. Nicolaides, 'Withdrawal from the European Union: A Typology of Effects', *MJ*, 20 (2013), 209; C. M. Rieder, 'The Withdrawal Clause of the Lisbon Treaty in the Light of EU Citizenship: Between Disintegration and Integration', *Fordham Int'l LJ*, 37 (2013), 147. See also C. Hillion, 'This Way, Please! A Legal Appraisal of the EU Withdrawal Clause', Chapter 11 in this volume.

[5] See also A. Łazowski, 'Unilateral withdrawal from the EU: realistic scenario or a folly?', *Journal of European Public Policy*, 23 (2016), 1294.

Article 50(2) TEU requires a country seeking to leave the European Union to notify its other fellow Member States of its intentions. A decision on withdrawal, not a withdrawal *per se*, is taken in accordance with domestic constitutional requirements.[6] Hence a decision in this respect, depending on the domestic arrangement, may be taken by a national government with or without participation of parliament and other actors, voters included. The exact modalities are, of course, governed by national law. This, as the example of the UK proves, may not be a straightforward affair. The vote, on 23 June 2016, triggered an interesting constitutional debate whether, following the advisory plebiscite, the government can submit such a notification without prior approval of the Parliament.[7] The question was answered by the Supreme Court in the negative, hence the Prime Minister had to seek a clearance from the Parliament before submitting a notification to the European Council.

Once the notification is filed, the EU has a self-imposed obligation stemming from Article 50(2) TEU to negotiate a withdrawal agreement. This obligation, however, rests only on the shoulders of the EU and does not extend to a future divorce. To put it differently, according to Article 50 TEU, a country wishing to leave the European Union does not have an obligation to negotiate a withdrawal agreement. It is uncertain whether such an obligation could be deduced from the principle of loyal cooperation laid down in Article 4(3) TEU.

Article 50 TEU makes it clear that if an agreement is not reached within two years of the abovementioned notification, the Founding Treaties cease to apply to such a country and, by the same token, it stops being a Member State of the European Union and of Euratom.[8] As I have already argued elsewhere, the two-year deadline laid down in Article 50 TEU should not be perceived as an inflexible and non-negotiable time framework.[9] It may be considered as a tool to discipline the negotiators. To begin with, the European Council has the power to extend this deadline, should that be needed. In this respect, it is worth

6 See also C. Hillion, in this volume (note 4).

7 For the academic discussion, see UK Constitutional Law Association Blog, <https://ukconstitutionallaw.org/blog/>. See also judgment of the Supreme Court of the United Kingdom in Miller case: See https://www.supremecourt.uk/cases/docs/uksc-2016-0196-judgment.pdf.

8 By the same token, EU law *in toto* would stop applying to such a country.

9 A. Łazowski, 'Withdrawal from the European Union and Alternatives to Membership' (note 4), at p. 527.

noting that the scale of withdrawal negotiations can be, in a way, compared to the accession process. As explained later in this chapter, the negotiators may have to tackle a very long list of dossiers which will make the entire process time-consuming. Bearing in mind the possible contents of the withdrawal agreement, it may have to be concluded as a mixed agreement, requiring ratification by the withdrawing country as well as all remaining Member States of the European Union. Experience proves that it could take months to get all the ratifications in place.[10] Even such superficial analysis of the basic parameters of EU exit proves that if we were to consider the two-year period as an ultimate deadline for the conclusion of a comprehensive withdrawal agreement, this would be truly optimistic if not entirely groundless optimism. Alas, when this book went to print such an optimism was shared by some members of the UK Government.

However, the main argument against the possibility of unilateral withdrawal should be based on the levels of legal and economic integration between the Member States, even those covered by a plethora of opt-outs (the United Kingdom being a prime example). A unilateral exit from the European Union would create a legal vacuum and lead on the day of exit to an almost non-existent direct legal framework, comparable to contemporary EU political and institutional relations with such countries as Belarus, Libya or Syria. The main difference, when compared with the latter, would be the application between the two sides of the WTO framework, which – in the case of the United Kingdom – would have to be adjusted to reflect an EU withdrawal. Needless to say, that such an option would certainly lead to a political, legal,[11] and most probably, also economic turmoil. It is in the interest of both sides that an exit is handled in an orderly fashion and has a proper legal framework. This is explored in the Section III of this chapter.

## III Withdrawal Agreement: Procedure and Substance

### A. *Introduction*

Article 50 TEU provides the basic parameters for withdrawal from the European Union. Its wording is a product of political compromise dating

[10] See further C. Closa, *The politics of EU Treaties ratification*, (London: Routledge, 2013).

[11] For analysis of legal consequences of unilateral withdrawal, see A. Łazowski, *EU Withdrawal: Good Business for British Business?* (note 4).

back to the days of the European Constitution.[12] After the latter's early demise, it became part of the Treaty of Lisbon.[13] Alas, it cannot be considered as the treaty drafters' finest hour.[14] Not only does it lack precision but also, when combined with no relevant practice to rely on, leaves many questions unanswered.[15] This, in itself, creates a fair deal of uncertainty. The overall picture is that the very modest regulation of the exit procedure makes the European Union rather ill-equipped for Brexit.

The analysis that follows covers Article 50 TEU, Article 218(3) TFEU, to which it contains a cross-reference, as well as some of the unregulated aspects of EU exit which –when this book went to print – were being attended to by the European Union. The starting point is the legal character of a withdrawal agreement. This will lead to an elaboration of the mechanics of the exit negotiations, including preparation of a negotiation mandate, *modus operandi* for the withdrawal talks as well as the substance and conclusion of a withdrawal agreement.

### B. *Legal Character of a Withdrawal Agreement*

In accordance with Article 50 TEU a withdrawal agreement is concluded by the European Union with a departing country. Departure from the European Union also amounts to exit from Euratom, therefore a withdrawal agreement will have to be concluded with the European Atomic Energy Community as well. As already mentioned, a withdrawal agreement may take the form of a mixed agreement. If that were to happen, the parties would include the EU, Euratom and the remaining Member States on the one side, and the departing country

[12] Treaty establishing a Constitution for Europe [2004] OJ C310, p. 1. See further, J-C. Piris, *The Constitution for Europe: A Legal Analysis*, (Cambridge: CUP, 2006).

[13] Treaty of Lisbon amending the Treaty on European Union and the Treaty establishing the European Community [2007] OJ C306/1. For an academic appraisal, see *inter alia*, J-C. Piris, *The Lisbon Treaty. A Legal and Political Analysis* (Cambridge: CUP, 2010); P. Craig, *The Lisbon Treaty. Law, Politics, and Treaty Reform* (Oxford: OUP, 2010); A. Biondi, P. Eeckhout and S. Ripley (eds.), *EU Law after Lisbon* (Oxford: OUP, 2012); M. Trybus and L. Rubini (eds.), *The Treaty of Lisbon and the Future of European Law and Policy* (Cheltenham: Edward Elgar Publishing, 2012).

[14] See further on history of Article 50 TEU in R. Zbíral, 'Searching for an optimal withdrawal clause for the European Union', in M. Niedobitek and J. Zemanek (eds.), *The Constitutional Treaty – A Critical Appraisal* (Berlin: Duncker & Humblot, 2007), pp. 290–328.

[15] For criticism, see *inter alia*, Hofmeister, 'Should I stay or Should I Go?' (note 4).

on the other.[16] The procedure which will be followed will have idiosyncratic features, yet many elements of the standard procedure for conclusion of international treaties by the EU are likely to be followed. At the same time, however, the legal basis for conclusion of a withdrawal agreement is Article 50 TEU, though Article 218(3) TFEU will apply as well. This encapsulates the uniqueness of a withdrawal agreement. While these issues are explored further later in this chapter; for now, it is worth noting that there is a considerable difference between the legal framework for accession and for withdrawal.

In the case of the former, the terms of accession are traditionally included in a tailor-made treaty between the existing and future Member States.[17] It thus forms, along with the Founding Treaties, part of the primary law positioned at the apex of the legal order. In procedural terms, this means that the validity of an accession treaty can only be verified at the national level. In fact, the Court of Justice has no jurisdiction in this respect, though the legality of accession treaties may be scrutinised by the national constitutional courts.[18] A withdrawal agreement, however, is – from the point of EU law – merely an international treaty concluded with a departing country with all the consequences that result from that. The most obvious one is that it will not be part of the primary law of the European Union. This, among other things, translates into the Court of Justice's jurisdiction to scrutinise the competence of the EU and to conclude it in a particular shape and form,

[16] See further on mixed agreements C. Hillion, P. Koutrakos (eds.), *Mixed Agreements Revisited. The EU and its Member States in the World* (Oxford and Portland, Oregon: Hart Publishing, 2010).

[17] See, for instance, Treaty between the Kingdom of Belgium, the Kingdom of Denmark, the Federal Republic of Germany, the Hellenic Republic, the Kingdom of Spain, the French Republic, Ireland, the Italian Republic, the Grand Duchy of Luxembourg, the Kingdom of the Netherlands, the Republic of Austria, the Portuguese Republic, the Republic of Finland, the Kingdom of Sweden, the United Kingdom of Great Britain and Northern Ireland (Member States of the European Union) and the Czech Republic, the Republic of Estonia, the Republic of Cyprus, the Republic of Latvia, the Republic of Lithuania, the Republic of Hungary, the Republic of Malta, the Republic of Poland, the Republic of Slovenia, the Slovak Republic, concerning the accession of the Czech Republic, the Republic of Estonia, the Republic of Cyprus, the Republic of Latvia, the Republic of Lithuania, the Republic of Hungary, the Republic of Malta, the Republic of Poland, the Republic of Slovenia and the Slovak Republic to the European Union [2003] OJ L236/17.

[18] See, for instance, Constitutional Tribunal, 11 May 2005, Case K 18/04 (re Conformity of the Accession Treaty 2003 with the Polish Constitution) OTK Z.U. 2005/5A/49; an English summary of the judgment is available at the Constitutional Tribunal website <www.trybunal.gov.pl/eng/summaries/documents/K_18_04_GB.pdf>, accessed 5 June 2015.

as per Article 218(11) TFEU. Furthermore, the validity of decisions on the signature and conclusion adopted by the Council, may be verified in accordance with Article 263 TFEU.[19] Another consequence, although for the European Union alone, is the need to proceed with a formal treaty revision in order to modify or remove provisions, or even entire tailor-made protocols, from the text of the Founding Treaties covering a withdrawing country.[20]

### C. *Negotiation Mandate*

The starting point for negotiations of international agreements by the European Union is the preparation of a negotiation mandate. In terms of withdrawal this is where – a not necessarily clear – interplay between Article 50 TEU and Article 218 TFEU came to the fore in the wake of Brexit referendum. Article 50 TEU provides that the negotiations must be conducted 'in the light of guidelines provided by the European Council'. This is hardly surprising bearing in mind the political significance of withdrawal negotiations. However, since the European Council is empowered to adopt guidelines, the question emerged which institution was entrusted with approval of a negotiation mandate *per se* and, if necessary, the adoption of negotiation directives.[21] Would the guidelines serve as the negotiation mandate? That is what I argued in an earlier publication on this matter.[22] It should be noted, though, that Article 50 (2) TEU provides that also Article 218(3) TFEU applies to withdrawal negotiations. It would suggest involvement of the European Commission in preparation of the negotiation mandate. This is exactly how the situation evolved in the spring of 2017. To begin with, the European Council approved the Guidelines on 29 April 2017.[23] Although they

[19] Similarly, C. Hillion, Chapter 11 in this volume (note 4).

[20] In case of the United Kingdom this will include Protocol (No 15) on certain provisions relating to the United Kingdom of Great Britain and Northern Ireland; Protocol (No 20) on the application of certain aspects of Article 26 of the Treaty on the Functioning of the European Union to the United Kingdom and to Ireland; Protocol (No 21) on the position of the United Kingdom and Ireland in respect of the area of freedom, security and justice; Protocol (No 30) on the application of the Charter of Fundamental Rights of the European Union to Poland and to the United Kingdom.

[21] This is a departure from the traditional *modus operandi* where the bulk of work is solely in the hands of the European Commission and the Council.

[22] A. Łazowski, 'Withdrawal from the European Union and Alternatives to Membership' (note 4).

[23] Guideliness of the European Council following the United Kingdom's notification under Article 50 TEU.

clearly indicated the terms and conditions of the withdrawal negotiations, they were rather general. In turn it was the task of the European Commission to develop a draft negotiation mandate, which was then approved by the Council.

An interesting picture emerged from this exercise. Despite the fact that the United Kingdom remains a Member State of the EU until the actual date of withdrawal, it was already treated as a third country for the purposes of withdrawal negotiations.[24] The Recommendations of the European Council emphasised that the European Union will act as a unit and will aim to protect its own interests. Furthermore, at this early stage of withdrawal process, the European Parliament opted to be an active player, even though Article 50 TEU envisages its role only at the final stages of EU exit. Indeed, a consent of the European Parliament is required for approval by the European Union of the withdrawal agreement. Yet, *qua* a non-binding resolution the Parliament outlined its red lines for the forthcoming negotiations.[25] Here, too, the message was clear that the European Union should act to protect its own interests. As for the negotiations *per se*, it is the Council that authorised their opening (Article 218[3] TFEU) but, as discussed in the next section of this chapter, they were due to be conducted by the European Commission. Furthermore, it was the European Union that took the lead in determination of dossiers for negotiations and their sequencing. It was made clear in both, the Recommendations of the European Council and the Resolution of the European Parliament that negotiations of a framework for future relations between the European Union and the United Kingdom would commence only when sufficient progress was achieved in talks regarding the divorce.[26]

### D. *Modus Operandi for Withdrawal Negotiations*

Following a decision on the opening of withdrawal negotiations, which is explicitly provided for in Article 218(3) TFEU, the regulation of the negotiations *per se* is *terra incognita*. Neither Article 50 TEU, nor

[24] Apart from anything else, this puts EU staff holding the citizenship of a withdrawing country in a rather awkward position of conflicting loyalties, not to mention that their status after withdrawal would also have to be part of the withdrawal negotiations.

[25] European Parliament resolution of 5 April 2017 on negotiations with the United Kingdom following its notification that it intends to withdraw from the European Union, P8_TA-Prov (2017) 0102.

[26] See paras. 13–15 of the Resolution of the European Parliament.

Article 218(3) TFEU, determine which institution will be in charge of the negotiations and which other actors should be included in the process. It is notable that a cross-reference in Article 50 TEU provides for the application of Article 218(3) TFEU alone. At least formally, the other procedural rules laid down in Article 218 TFEU will not apply to the exit talks. This does not mean, however, that they cannot be employed *mutatis mutandis*, or at least serve as a point of reference for withdrawal negotiations. Arguably, the Treaty drafters decided to leave such issues unregulated in order to provide greater flexibility to the EU when the exit clause is triggered. This has become a source of controversy almost immediately after the Brexit referendum. It may well be that such details were simply not properly thought through, with Article 50 TEU having been assumed to remain a 'dead letter' of the Treaty. As argued by C. Hillion, we should not exclude that this was done on purpose to discourage the Member States from triggering the exit clause.[27]

The options were twofold. The first was to conduct the negotiations in accordance with the well-established rules on negotiation of international treaties by the European Union. The second was to introduce modifications partly modelled on the accession negotiations. The main difference laid in the institutional centre of gravity. In the first the key role is played by the European Commission. A cross reference to Article 218(3) TFEU suggests that this was the intention of treaty drafters.[28] In the second option the centre of gravity is on the Member States. As established in practice based on Article 49 TEU, in accession talks the key role is played by the Member States through the European Council, the Council and the Intergovernmental Conference which deals with the negotiations proper.[29] It is worth noting that for the purposes of accession negotiations, the EU *acquis* is divided into thirty-five chapters. As noted by this author elsewhere, because of the different character of withdrawal negotiations, the same classification cannot be employed here.[30] Yet it is quite obvious that the negotiations have to occur in

[27] C. Hillion, Chapter 11 in this volume (note 4).

[28] See Łazowski, 'Withdrawal from the European Union and Alternatives to Membership' ((note 4), p. 528), where I argued that the European Commission will conduct the negotiations.

[29] See further on the mechanics of membership talks in M. Vlašić Feketija and A. Łazowski, 'The Seventh EU Enlargement and Beyond: Pre-Accession Policy vis-à-vis the Western Balkans Revisited', *Croatian Yearbook of European Law and Policy*, 10 (2014), 1.

[30] Łazowski, 'Withdrawal from the European Union and Alternatives to Membership' (note 4), p. 532.

different thematic groups covering various aspects of withdrawal and, potentially, also the future relations between the divorcees or at least a framework for them. Of the two options mentioned here the first was eventually chosen by the European Union for the purposes of Brexit negotiations. When this book went to print, they were destined to be modelled on *modus operandi* applicable for negotiations of international treaties with the lead role assigned to the European Commission.

An interesting issue which merits attention is the status of the country pursuing EU exit during the withdrawal talks. This is only partially regulated in Article 50(4) TEU, which provides that it will have, neither the right to vote in the Council nor in the European Council, when withdrawal related matters are voted on. It extends well beyond the voting itself, as the provision in question also excludes representatives of the withdrawing country from discussions dealing with the withdrawal. What is not regulated, however, are the powers of the MEPs elected from the withdrawing country. We could argue, on the one hand, that Article 50(4) TEU should apply *mutatis mutandis* to the European Parliament, therefore UK MEPs should be excluded from the debates and votes dealing with the withdrawal. On the other hand, MEPs do not represent the Member States they are elected in, but rather all EU citizens[31] and therefore they should not be excluded after all. [32] The latter option was seemingly followed in the wake of Brexit referendum on 23 June 2016. The status of representatives of a departing country in a variety of the EU advisory bodies is not regulated either, though as things stood when this book went to print, it was likely to remain unchanged until the day of withdrawal.

The general status of the withdrawing country during the exit talks and, once they are completed, the ratification of a withdrawal agreement, are far more challenging. A crucial question that had to be attended to for the first time when the UK filed for divorce was to what extent such a departing state should be allowed to shape, or even block, pending proposals for EU legislation that it was unlikely to be bound by in the future. In this respect the experience with accession to the European Union proved to be of no use. In the latter case, a country aspiring to membership becomes an acceding country the moment it signs an accession treaty. As the ratification progresses, it is allowed to participate,

[31] As per Article 14(2) TEU.

[32] See *inter alia*, C. M. Rieder, *The Withdrawal Clause of the Lisbon Treaty in the Light of EU Citizenship: between Disintegration and Integration* (n. 3), at pp. 158–159.

among other things, in the work of the European Council, the Council and the European Parliament as an observer. It becomes a fully-fledged participant of the EU decision-making process on the day of accession to the European Union.[33] Such *modus operandi* cannot be employed, however, to leaving the EU. An acceding country is on the path to membership, hence its participation – as an observer – is completely justified. One should note that while its EU membership is still subject to the ratification of an accession treaty, an observer may attempt to shape EU legislation. Even if, for one reason or another, an acceding country does not join the European Union, a piece of EU *acquis* negotiated and adopted following the signature of an accession treaty will not apply to it. In the case of a withdrawal, we can imagine a situation where a country negotiating an exit decides to pull the plug either during the negotiations or even following the signature of a withdrawal agreement (but before its entry into force). This way it can remain bound by all EU legislation negotiated between the Member States during the period from the notification of its intention to withdraw, up to the point when the notification is withdrawn. This is why it has to remain as a fully-fledged Member State throughout the exit negotiations up to the date of entry into force of the withdrawal agreement. By the same token it remains bound by the principle of loyal co-operation laid down in Article 4(3) TEU. This is where the situation was heading following the referendum in the UK. The European Council in its communiqué following the informal meeting on 29 June 2016, made it clear that 'until the UK leaves the EU, EU law continues to apply to and within the UK, both when it comes to rights and obligations'.[34] This was confirmed in the already mentioned Recommendations of the European Council[35] as well as the Resolution of the European Parliament.[36] At the same time, no a phasing-out mode was developed at this stage of withdrawal.

[33] For a most recent example, see A. Łazowski, 'EU do not worry, Croatia is behind you: A Commentary on the Seventh Accession Treaty', *Croatian Yearbook of European Law and Policy*, 8 (2012), 1.

[34] European Council, Press information (2016) <www.consilium.europa.eu/en/meetings/european-council/2016/06/28–29/>, accessed 25 July 2016.

[35] See European Council guidelines following the United Kingdom's notification under Article 50 TEU, paras. 23–25.

[36] European Parliament resolution of 5 April 2017 on negotiations with the United Kingdom following its notification that it intends to withdraw from the European Union, point F.

### E. *Substance of a Withdrawal Agreement*

The substance of a withdrawal agreement is largely determined by the European Union. In case of Brexit, this happened with adoption of Recommendations of the European Council on 29 April 2017. Furthermore, the European Parliament in its Resolution also included a list of potential dossiers, demonstrating that the only democratically elected EU institution has no desire to remain a silent actor throughout the withdrawal of a Member State.[37] It is notable that in case of Brexit the European Union insisted on regulation of terms of withdrawal first before attending to a framework for future relations. The latter were due to be regulated in a separate treaty between the EU/Euratom (and potentially the Member States) and the United Kingdom. However, it should be noted that Article 50 TEU is flexible enough to accommodate other scenarios. They are analysed in turn.

It is clear that a crucial question is whether the negotiations should cover the terms of exit and future relations, or merely the divorce. The shape of future relations between the divorcee and the European Union matters too. Here, a rule of thumb emerges, the deeper the post-exit relations, the more complex and comprehensive the entire package has to be. The legal terms of withdrawal and the shape of the new regime largely depends on the desires of both sides and their ability to reach compromises. No doubts they will have their priorities or even red lines worth picking up a fight for. At the same time, a departing country is – by definition – in a weaker negotiating position with less room for manoeuvre.

As already noted, Article 50 TEU provides that a withdrawal agreement should deal with the terms of exit and take account of the framework for future relations. The question which has emerged after the Brexit referendum was how exactly this provision should be read. In my previous contributions to the debate I argued that the withdrawal treaty should regulate, comprehensively, the terms and conditions of the divorce as well as future relations.[38] This is dictated by the prerequisite of legal and economic certainty. Inclusion of both in a single agreement would guarantee the continuity of legal relations and provide some stability at the turbulent time of exit. By the same token, some of the unnecessary political shenanigans associated with ratification of treaties by the Member States would be largely avoided. This, as already noted,

[37] Resolution of the European Parliament, para. 17.

[38] For a different view on this matter, see C. Hillion, Chapter 11 in this volume (note 4).

was not a preferred *modus operandi* for Brexit. The withdrawal treaty was to be concluded on the basis of Article 50 TEU, while the future relations would be negotiated as per Article 218 TFEU, with an additional legal basis being used. When this book went to print, is was not yet known if post-divorce relations would take the form of an association agreement. From the perspective of EU external relations law, it would be the most natural step to take, demonstrating close links between the EU and its newly acquired neighbour. It would amount to an anomaly if, following a withdrawal of a Member State from the European Union, the latter had association agreements with, for instance, Ukraine,[39] Georgia[40] and Moldova,[41] but not with one of its former Member States. If that were the preferred option, the agreement could be concluded on a combined legal basis comprising Articles 217–218 TFEU or even Article 8 TEU. The latter provision regulates EU relations with neighbouring countries and, as Hillion argues, 'this provision [...] not only bolsters the normative basis for a negotiated withdrawal, it also points towards a strong post-withdrawal engagement by the Union with the former Member State'.[42]

The key question that had to be answered at the beginning of the withdrawal negotiations between the EU and the UK was whether these two agreements should be negotiated in parallel or in sequence. Again, legal certainty dictated that in order to secure a (relatively) smooth divorce, both agreements should be negotiated in one go and should enter into force simultaneously. Perhaps a guillotine clause *à la* the EU–Swiss bilateral I package could chain both of them.[43] Although this proposal seems *prima facie* sound, it was prone to procedural hurdles and was not to the liking of the European Union. Firstly, it required a creative interpretation of Article 218 TFEU, which governs the procedure for the

[39] Association Agreement between the European Union, the European Atomic Energy Community and their Member States, of the one part, and Ukraine, of the other part [2014] OJ L161, p. 3.

[40] Association Agreement between the European Union and the European Atomic Energy Community and their Member States, of the one part, and Georgia, of the other part [2014] OJ L261, p. 4.

[41] Association Agreement between the European Union and the European Atomic Energy Community and their Member States, of the one part, and the Republic of Moldova, of the other part [2014] OJ L260, p. 4.

[42] C. Hillion, *Accession and Withdrawal in the Law of the European Union*, (note 4) at pp. 150–151.

[43] The Bilateral I package contains a guillotine clause which provides that all the agreements it comprises of may enter into force only together and if one of them is terminated then all the other agreements are terminated too.

conclusion of international treaties with third countries. The challenge was whether it could be employed to negotiate a future deal with the EU's outgoing Member State. Secondly, to negotiate both agreements at the same time, and to have them approved by the EU and its Member States, would be a time-consuming exercise at a time when the divorcees clearly wished to proceed as quickly as possible. Thirdly, and most importantly, to opt for such a solution would require a political will on the EU side and that seemed to be in short supply when the UK filed its withdrawal notice. Thus, in the wake of Brexit referendum, the decision was made by the European Union to proceed with two agreements in sequence. As already noted, the European Council and the European Parliament opted for a caveat that the negotiations of future relations could only commence when sufficient progress was achieved in the withdrawal negotiations. Arguably, it was for the EU to decide when enough progress would be achieved. By any stretch of imagination this was not what was preferred by the United Kingdom. Arguably, it is the worst possible scenario, which is likely to create a lot of uncertainty and a legal void in the interim period which could last years or, it may force the parties to develop a transitional arrangement of sorts. That, in turn, would require considerable legal acrobatics to determine the status of the United Kingdom in such interim phase. Even if the withdrawal agreement were to contain such transitional regimes, it would be a complex and potentially dysfunctional solution.

Leaving Brexit aside, another solution, which should not be excluded in theory is if a withdrawing country pursued the option of staying in the European Economic Area as an EFTA country. Should that happen the future relations between the EU and the exiting state would be regulated by the EEA *acquis* and flanking agreements.[44]

[44] It should be noted that EU relations with the EEA-EFTA countries are not exclusively covered by the Agreement on European Economic Area. To begin with, two agreements were concluded by the EEA countries to facilitate establishing the EEA institutional structure (Agreement between the EFTA States on the Establishment of a Surveillance Authority and a Court of Justice [1994] OJ L344/1; Agreement on a Standing Committee of the EFTA States, <http://secretariat.efta.int/Web/legaldocuments/AgreementOnStandingCommittee.pdf>, accessed 25 July 2016). Furthermore, pre-existing free trade agreements between the EC and Norway, and the EC and Iceland remain in force in the areas not regulated by the EEA Agreement (Agreement between the European Economic Community and the Kingdom of Norway [1973] OJ L171/2; Agreement between the European Economic Community and the Republic of Iceland, [1972] OJ L301/2; see further E. P. Wellenstein, 'The free trade agreements between the enlarged European Communities and the EFTA countries' (1973) 10 CMLRev, 137). The main body of the EEA Agreement has not been revised since its entry into

Irrespective of discussed modalities, the key question is how far the de-integration process should go. There is no doubt that this deserves to be answered at the early stages of withdrawal talks when the negotiation positions are developed by the departing country and the EU. As a matter of principle, a departure from the European Union translates not only into an exit from all EU institutional structures, but also into a withdrawal from the internal market with all legal and economic consequences resulting from that. Furthermore, in case of Eurozone countries it would also amount to pulling out of the common currency. A short reminder is necessary that unless transitional arrangements are negotiated, as of the date of exit, the freedoms of the internal market cease to apply to the country leaving, thus the ex-Member State and its citizens no longer benefit from free movement of goods, persons, establishment, services and capital. One should also remember that the substantive law of the European Union is not limited merely to the internal market. Indeed, it has evolved tremendously over the years and the implications of withdrawal on a number of areas have to be thoroughly considered in withdrawal negotiations. This includes, among other things, the Area of Freedom, Security and Justice, competition, employment, consumer protection, transport and environmental policy. This, too, will have to be reflected in a withdrawal agreement. Furthermore, an important dossier to be attended to during the exit talks will be phasing out of various EU policies, in particular the Common Agriculture Policy (CAP) and the direct payments it provides for. Furthermore, highly contentious and potentially explosive dossiers: contributions to the EU budget and pulling out of the EU customs union should be on the agenda, too.[45]

force to extend the areas of cooperation between the EU and the EEA-EFTA countries. This materialised through agreements not falling within the EEA framework. See Agreement concluded by the Council of the European Union and the Republic of Iceland and the Kingdom of Norway concerning the latter the EEA countries to facilitate Wtion, application and development of the Schengen acquis [1999] OJ L176/36; Agreement between the European Community and the Republic of Iceland and the Kingdom of Norway concerning the criteria and mechanisms for establishing the State responsible for examining a request for asylum lodged in a Member State or in Iceland or Norway [2001] OJ L93/40. For an academic appraisal see, *inter alia*, H. Bull, 'The Schengen Cooperation and Norway', in P.-C. Müller-Graff and E. Selvig (eds.), *The European Economic Area – Norway's Basic Status in the Legal Construction of Europe* (Berlin: Berlin Verlag Arno Spitz, 1997), p. 141. See also S. Eiríkson, 'Deeply involved in the European project. Membership of Schengen', in B. Thorhallsson (ed.), *Iceland and European Integration. On the Edge* (London, New York: Routledge, 2004), p. 50.

45 See House of Lords: Brexit and the EU budget, <https://www.publications.parliament.uk/pa/ld201617/ldselect/ldeucom/125/125.pdf>

All these issues were discussed in the wake of Brexit referendum. A general position of the United Kingdom was outlined in a White Paper published by the UK Government in early 2017. [46] Seemingly a preferred option for future relations between the EU and the UK is a free trade area. However, one should not forget that a more ambitious deal could be on the cards, too. Should a more comprehensive agreement were to be opted for, one could expect a great deal of bargaining as it would require development of a model of integration without membership in the EU.[47] The off-the-shelf models of the European Economic Area, as well as the Swiss Confederation, could be a very good point of reference in this respect. They have one thing in common: even partial participation in the internal market requires the application of EU secondary legislation, which is traditionally listed in agreements between the Union and a third country, or a group of countries as in case of the EEA. The intensity of mutual relations traditionally translates into type of obligations resting on the neighbouring states. For instance, annexes to the EEA Agreement, listing all secondary legislation applicable to EEA-EFTA countries, are regularly and (largely) automatically updated. At the same time the EEA-EFTA states do not participate in the EU decision-making proper. Their involvement is limited to decision-shaping only.[48] Equally dynamic are a few of the Agreements signed by the European Union with Switzerland, while a large majority of Bilateral I[49] and

[46] White Paper: the United Kingdom's exit from and new partnership with the European Union, <https://www.gov.uk/government/publications/the-united-kingdoms-exit-from-and-new-partnership-with-the-european-union-white-paper>

[47] See, *inter alia*, A. Łazowski, 'Enhanced multilateralism and enhanced bilateralism: Integration without membership in the European Union', (2008) 45 *CMLRev*, 1433.

[48] See further, *inter alia*, A. Łazowski, 'EEA Countries (Iceland, Liechtenstein and Norway)', in S. Blockmans and A. Łazowski (eds.), *The European Union and Its Neighbours. A Legal Appraisal of the EU's policies of stabilisation, partnership and integration* (The Hague: TMC Asser Press, 2006), p. 95.

[49] Agreement between the European Community and its Member States, of the one part, and the Swiss Confederation, of the other, on the free movement of persons [2002] OJ L114/6; Agreement between the European Community and the Swiss Confederation on Air Transport [2002] OJ L114/73; Agreement between the European Community and the Swiss Confederation on the Carriage of Goods and Passengers by Rail and Road [2002] OJ L114/91; Agreement between the European Community and the Swiss Confederation on trade in agricultural products [2002] OJ L114/132; Agreement between the European Community and the Swiss Confederation on mutual recognition in relation to conformity assessment [2002] OJ L114/369; Agreement between the European Community and the Swiss Confederation on certain aspects of government procurement [2002] OJ L114/430; Agreement on scientific and technological co-operation between the

Bilateral II[50] agreements are static. To put it differently, the lists of the EU *acquis* which Switzerland applies in its relations with the European Union are not updated automatically and depend on the decisions of the Swiss authorities. This, however, comes at a price. Switzerland does not participate in the internal market to an extent comparable to the EEA countries.[51] Another example is a new generation of association agreements which the European Union has recently concluded with Ukraine, Georgia and Moldova. All three provide for deep and comprehensive free trade areas, which require extensive law approximation exercises covering dozens of pieces of EU secondary legislation under very tight time constraints.[52]

European Community and the European Atomic Energy Community, of the one part, and the Swiss Confederation, of the other part [2007] OJ L189/26.

50 Agreement between the European Union, the European Community and the Swiss Confederation on the Swiss Confederation's association with the implementation, application and development of Schengen acquis, [2008] OJ L53/52; Agreement between the European Community and the Swiss Confederation concerning the criteria and mechanisms for establishing the State responsible for examining a request for asylum lodged in a Member State or in Switzerland [2008] OJ L53/5; Agreement between the European Community and the Swiss Confederation providing for measures equivalent to those laid down in Council Directive 2003/48 on taxation of savings income in the form of interest payments [2004] OJ L385/30; Co-operation Agreement between the European Community and its Member States, of the one part, and the Swiss Confederation, of the other part, to counter fraud and all other illegal activities to the detriment of their financial interests [2009] OJ L46/8; Agreement between the European Community and the Swiss Confederation amending the Agreement between the European Economic Community and the Swiss Confederation of July 22, 1972 as regards the provisions applicable to processed agricultural products [2005] OJ L23/19; Agreement between the European Community and the Swiss Confederation concerning the participation of Switzerland in the European Environment Agency and the European Environment Information and Observation Network [2006] OJ L90/37; Agreement between the European Community and the Swiss Confederation on co-operation in the field of statistics [2006] OJ L90/2; Agreement between the European Community and the Swiss Confederation in the audiovisual field, establishing the terms and conditions for the participation of the Swiss Confederation in the Community Programmes Media Plus and Media Training [2006] OJ L90/23; Agreement between the Swiss Federal Council and the Commission of the European Communities with a view to avoiding the double taxation of retired officials of the institutions and agencies of the European Communities resident in Switzerland, nyp.

51 See further on the Swiss model, *inter alia*, L. Goetschel, 'Switzerland and European Integration: Change Through Distance', *EFARev*, 8 (2003), 313; S. Breitenmoser, 'Sectoral Agreements between the EC and Switzerland: Contents and Context', *CMLRev*, 40 (2003), 1137; F. Emmert, 'Switzerland and the EU: Partners, for Better or for Worse', *EFARev*, 3 (1998), 367.

52 See further G. Van der Loo, P. Van Elsuwege and R. Petrov, 'The EU-Ukraine Association Agreement: Assessment of an Innovative Legal Instrument' (2014) *EUI Working Papers* No 2014/09.

As noted earlier, the situation would be different were a withdrawing country to decide to join EFTA and subsequently the European Economic Area. In such a case the scope of the withdrawal agreement would be limited to the exit from the European Union, while the terms of withdrawal from the EEA, the accession to EFTA and then to the European Economic Area, would be determined in separate agreements negotiated by the country departing from the EU and the EFTA countries. This would require a lot of coordinated effort and additional negotiations to be conducted between all interested parties. Needless to say, it would be a resource-intensive and time-consuming exercise. As argued later in this chapter, all these agreements would have to enter into force on the same day to avoid any associated legal uncertainty.

There is one more major dossier that should be close to the heart of a withdrawing country, which, however, will not be covered by the withdrawal negotiations. As is well known, the European Union is party to hundreds of agreements with third countries, including over forty free trade agreements. All of these, will cease to apply to a withdrawing country as of the date of exit from the European Union. Those who believe that such agreements can be easily replicated through bilateral negotiations seem not to appreciate how complex and resource-intensive such an exercise would be.[53] Furthermore, as already noted, a withdrawing country remains a fully-fledged member of the European Union until the date of exit. Consequentially, without a tailor-made arrangement, it cannot commence negotiations of trade agreements with third countries until it leaves the European Union.[54]

### F. *Signature and Approval of a Withdrawal Agreement*

Basic rules on the conclusion of a withdrawal agreement are laid down in Article 50 TEU. A withdrawal agreement will be concluded by the European Union through a Council decision with the consent of the European Parliament.[55] For this purpose, a qualified majority will be required in the Council. It is worth remembering that a withdrawing country will not participate in this approval by the Council. A withdrawal

[53] For such an unrealistic view, see Lord Lawson (note 1).

[54] See A. Łazowski and R.A. Wessel, '*The External Dimension of Withdrawal from the European Union*', Revue des Affaires Européennes (2017), 623.

[55] As the European Parliament resolution of 5 April 2017 shows, this should not be taken for granted.

agreement, should it take the shape of a mixed agreement, will be then subject to ratification by all remaining EU Member States and the departing country.

As far as the internal EU procedure is concerned, a decision will have to be taken in respect of the *modus operandi* to be followed as well as a choice of legal basis for signing and concluding a withdrawal agreement. In the case of the former, there are two crucial provisions traditionally applied to international agreements, Articles 218(5) and 218(6) TFEU. They serve as the legal basis for the Council Decisions on the signing, and conclusion of, international agreements (respectively).[56] However neither of these provisions would formally apply to a withdrawal agreement. It is an open question whether, despite the lack of an explicit reference in Article 50 TEU, Articles 218 (5–6) TFEU, could be applied *mutatis mutandis*. If that were the case, decisions of the Council would be required for conclusion of a withdrawal agreement and for its signature. There is no doubt that the main provision on which conclusion and signature of a withdrawal agreement will be made is Article 50 TEU. Unless a departing country joins the EEA as an EFTA state and if the agreement covers the terms of exit and future relations, the legal bases could also include Article 217 TFEU and Article 8 TEU.

All the above are largely procedural matters which affect the European Union, but to a much lesser extent, a withdrawing country. This is true except for one crucial issue, which is the direct effect of a withdrawal agreement. If a tailor-made model is opted for, a withdrawal agreement will apply internally in the EU, like any other agreement concluded by the European Union with a third country. The doctrine of direct effect is one of the tenets of EU law, allowing individuals to invoke their EU law-based rights in national courts of the Member States. Following the famous Case 26/62 *Van Gend en Loos*[57] the doctrine in question has been extended to many provisions of the Treaty on the Functioning of the European Union,[58] secondary legislation adopted by the EU institutions,

[56] See, for instance, Council Decision 2014/295/EU of 17 March 2014 on the signing, on behalf of the European Union, and provisional application of the Association Agreement between the European Union and the European Atomic Energy Community and their Member States, of the one part, and Ukraine, of the other part, as regards the Preamble, Article 1, and Titles I, II and VII thereof [2014] OJ L161, p. 1.

[57] Case 26/62 *NV Algemene Transport- en Expeditie Onderneming van Gend & Loos* v. *Netherlands Inland Revenue Administration*, ECLI:EU:C:1963:1.

[58] Formerly EEC and EC Treaty.

including primarily regulations[59] and – most controversially – to directives.[60] The doctrine of direct effect has also been applied to international agreements concluded by the European Union with third countries, with an exception of some elements of the WTO package. The jurisprudence of the Court of Justice in this respect goes back to *Kupferberger*[61] and it is well established that the EU–Turkey Association *acquis*, the Partnership and Co-operation Agreements with the former Soviet Union countries or the Europe Agreements[62] are capable of producing the direct effect.[63] However, in recent years this well-established rule has suffered a reversal of fortune, with respect to the decisions of the Council on the conclusion and signing of international agreements.[64] The most recent examples are the decisions applicable to the Association Agreements with Ukraine, Georgia and Moldova. In all three cases the decisions of the Council on their signature explicitly precluded direct effect.[65] Furthermore, the

[59] See, for instance, Case C-253/00 *Antonio Muton y Cia SA and Superior Fruiticola SA* v. *Frumar Ltd and Redbridge Produce Marketing Ltd.*, ECLI:EU:C:2002:497.

[60] For the past forty years, this has been a hotly debated topic in the academic literature. See for instance, A. Dashwood, 'From Van Duyn to Mangold via Marshall: Reducing Direct Effect to Absurdity?', *Cambridge Yearbook of European Legal Studies*, 9 (2006–2007), 81; P. Craig, 'The Legal Effect of Directives: Policy, Rules and Exceptions', *ELRev*, 34 (2009), 349.

[61] Case 104/81 *Hauptzollamt Mainz* v. *C.A. Kupferberg & Cie KG a.A.*, ECLI:EU:C:1982:362.

[62] For the sake of clarity it should be noted that the Europe Agreements ceased to be in force ever since the Central and Eastern European countries joined the European Union in 2004 and 2007.

[63] See, for instance, Case C-192/89 *S. Z. Sevince* v. *Staatssecretaris van Justitie*, ECLI:EU:C:1990:322; Case C-63/99 *The Queen* v. *Secretary of State for the Home Department, ex parte Wieslaw Gloszczuk and Elzbieta Gloszczuk*, ECLI:EU:C:2001:488; Case C-265/03 *Igor Simutenkov* v. *Ministerio de Educación y Cultura and Real Federación Española de Fútbol*, ECLI:EU:C:2005:213.

[64] See, further F. Martines, 'Direct effect of international agreements of the EU', *EJIL*, 25 (2014), 129; A. Semertzi, 'The preclusion of direct effect in the recently concluded EU free trade agreements', *CMLRev*, 51 (2014), 1125.

[65] Council Decision of 16 June 2014 on the signing, on behalf of the European Union, and provisional application of the Association Agreement between the European Union and the European Atomic Energy Community and their Member States, of the one part, and Georgia, of the other part [2014] OJ L261, p. 1; Council Decision of 16 June 2014 on the signing, on behalf of the European Union, and provisional application of the Association Agreement between the European Union and the European Atomic Energy Community and their Member States, of the one part, and the Republic of Moldova, of the other part [2014] OJ L260, p. 1; Council Decision of 17 June 2014 on the signing, on behalf of the European Union, and provisional application of the Association Agreement between the European Union and the European Atomic Energy Community and their Member States, of the one part, and Ukraine, of the other part, as regards the Preamble, Article 1, and Titles I, II and VII thereof [2014] OJ L161, p. 1.

CETA Agreement itself precludes direct effect.[66] A detailed analysis would go beyond the limits of this chapter, yet two crucial points are worth noting. First, the same practice may also apply to a withdrawal agreement. Second, if direct effect is precluded only by decisions of the Council then they are unilateral acts of the European Union and they are not therefore formally negotiated with a third country. What has applied to the EU's neighbours may also apply to the EU's divorcees. To put it differently, when signing a withdrawal agreement the Council may, in its decision, introduce a provision precluding direct effect. Should that happen, it would put the citizens of a withdrawing country and its businesses, in a unique predicament. Not only would the EU exit take some of their rights away but it would also preclude the direct enforcement of the post-divorce settlement in the national courts of the EU Member States.

### G. *Ratification and Entry into Force of a Withdrawal Agreement*

Following the negotiations of a withdrawal agreement, it will be put for signature and ratification by the parties. This may not be as seamless as one would hope for and this is for a number of reasons. Firstly, the two-year period laid down in Article 50 TEU is very short if not unrealistic altogether. Secondly, if a withdrawal agreement has to be concluded by the EU and its Member States this would considerably add to the already tight timetable. When this volume went to print the assumption was that the Brexit Agreement would enter into force on 29 March 2019, that is exactly two years since the notification of intention to leave. However, as already noted, one should not exclude a decision of the European Council extending the deadline. In the same vein one should not exclude that a failure to reach such a decision could result in a unilateral Brexit. Furthermore, at the time when the United Kingdom formally triggered its withdrawal it was expected that some kind of temporary regime would be needed to guarantee smooth transition from membership to a new relationship with the European Union. However, the mechanics of it remained *terra incognita*.

The temporal aspects of EU exit may be of crucial importance and should be attended to during the exit talks. Similar to accession treaties, a

66 Article 30.(6)1 of Comprehensive Economic and Trade Agreement (CETA) between Canada, of the one part, and the European Union and its Member States, of the other part [2017] OJ L11, p. 23.

withdrawal agreement will require an intertemporal provision, this time, however, detaching a divorcee from the EU legal order as of the day of withdrawal or expiry of transitional regime.[67] Similar to the first years after accession, we should imagine the appearance in the national courts of a plethora of cases where such intertemporal issues would come to the fore. It is well established in the jurisprudence of the Court of Justice as well as in national jurisdictions that following accession, EU law only starts applying to facts which at least partly occurred after EU membership took effect.[68] To put it differently, EU law does not apply to purely pre-accession cases.

The situation in the case of an EU exit is even more complicated given the already discussed flanking agreements or treaties which would have to be concluded alongside a withdrawal agreement. Should a departing country and the European Union opt for a tailor-made post-divorce arrangement, a withdrawal agreement from the European Economic Area and an internal EU revision treaty should enter into force on the same day as the EU withdrawal agreement. If the EEA option is chosen as an alternative to EU membership, then switching sides within the EEA should also occur on the same day as the formal withdrawal from the European Union. In that case a separate EEA withdrawal agreement will likely be needed, followed by treaties regulating accession to EFTA and subsequently to the EEA. A similar *modus operandi* to that employed in 1995 for Sweden, Finland and Austria will not suffice. Back then, these countries were in EFTA and were merely switching sides within the European Economic Area.[69] For a country leaving the EU the situation is different as none of the EU Member States have EFTA membership. That would have to be acquired first in order to become an EFTA Member State of the European Economic Area.[70] Whichever option is chosen, legal certainty dictates that all necessary legal instruments enter into force on the same day or a transitional regime applies as of the day of exit.

[67] See Recommendations of the European Council.

[68] Case C-302/04 *Ynos kft.* v. *János Varga*, ECLI:EU:C:2006:9. See further, S. Kaleda, 'Intertemporal Legal Issues in the European Union Case Law Relating to the 2004 and 2007 Accessions', in A. Łazowski, *The Application of EU Law in Brave New World in the New Member States* (The Hague: TMC Asser, 2010), p. 99.

[69] See H. Tichy and L. Dedichen, 'Securing a smooth shift between the two EEA pillars: prolonged competence of EFTA institutions with respect to former EFTA States after their accession to the European Union', *CMLRev*, 32 (1995), 131.

[70] As per Article 128 of EEA Agreement, membership is open to EU and EFTA members only.

## IV Conclusions

A *cliche* it may be, but one cannot emphasise enough that withdrawal from the European Union will be a complicated affair with political, legal and economic strings attached. This chapter demonstrates how complex, and partly unknown, the mechanics of EU exit are. Such issues, along with alternatives to EU membership, are actively being considered following the Brexit referendum on 23 June 2016. This chapter also demonstrates that a plethora of procedural and institutional matters would had to be attended to in the early stages of the withdrawal process. Article 50 TEU only provides a skeleton framework which leaves a lot of questions unanswered. To put it differently, when the United Kingdom finally pulled the trigger on 29 March 2017, the European Union has stepped into unchartered territories, where a lot of strategic and creative thinking was in big demand. Those who argue that EU exit is an easy option for the United Kingdom should be careful what they wish for. EU withdrawal is by all means possible, yet the complexity of the process and its consequences are largely underestimated and were not objectively presented to the members of the public ahead of the referendum. It is as though the decision-makers believed, as Oscar Wilde said, that 'a little sincerity is a dangerous thing, a great deal of it is absolutely fatal'. The other, much worse option, is that those grouped in the Vote Leave camp were simply not aware what an exit from the European Union amounts to. Either way, an accidental EU exit should be avoided at all costs. As Article 50(5) TEU makes clear – a country which leaves the EU and decides to join again will have to go through the pains of pre-accession policy with no shortcuts or opt-outs available.

13

# EU Citizenship and Withdrawals from the Union: How Inevitable Is the Radical Downgrading of Rights?

DIMITRY KOCHENOV*

## I Introduction and Conclusion

This chapter is about EU citizenship and the eventual withdrawal of Member States from the European Union.[1] It thus does not concern itself with the issue of secessions of territories from the Member States as such,[2] which result in leaving a newly-formed state outside (or inside)[3] the European Union[4] – a matter meticulously analysed in the

* Chair in EU Constitutional Law, University of Groningen. I am overwhelmingly grateful to Carlos Closa for his patience and his help. Excellent assistance provided by Anna Gnap is gratefully acknowledged.

[1] Sionaidh Douglas-Scott, 'A UK Exit from the EU: The End of the United Kingdom or a New Constitutional Dawn?' (2015) *Oxford Legal Studies Research Paper* No. 25/2015; Michael Keating, 'The European Dimension to Scottish Constitutional Change', *The Political Quarterly*, 86 (2015), 208; Editorial Comments, 'Union Membership in Times of Crisis', *CMLRev*, 51 (2014), 1; Phedon Nicolaides, 'Withdrawal from the European Union: A Typology of Effects', *Maastricht Journal*, 20 (2013), 209; Nicholas Forwood, 'Chinese Curses, Lawyers' Dreams, Political Nightmares and New Dawns: Interesting Times for the UK's Relationship with the EU', *Cambridge Yearbook of European Legal Studies*, 83 (2012); Adam Łazowski, 'Withdrawal from the European Union and Alternatives to Membership', *ELRev*, 37 (2012), 52.

[2] For an analysis of the factors connecting secessions and withdrawals, see JHH Weiler 'Regional Secession as a Normative Dilemma in European Integration', Chapter 2 in this volume.

[3] Sionaidh Douglas-Scott, 'How Easily Could an Independent Scotland Join the EU?', *University of Oxford Legal Studies Research Paper*, No. 46 (2014); Dimitry Kochenov and Martijn van den Brink, 'Secessions from EU Member States: The Imperative of Union's Neutrality', *Edinburgh School of Law Research Paper* No. 2016/06 (2016).

[4] See in general, Carlos Closa (ed.), 'Troubled Membership: Dealing with Secession from a Member State and withdrawal from the EU' (2014) *EUI Working Paper* RSCAS 2014/91. For more complex scenarios, see, for example, Nikos Skoutaris, 'From Britain and Ireland to Cyprus: Accommodating "Divided Islands" in the EU Political and Legal Order' (2016) *EUI Working Paper* AEL 2016/02.

literature already.[5] A number of interesting issues arise, however, even when we look, as the editor has asked me to do, only at the citizenship issues related to the Member States planning to say goodbye to the journey towards an unknown destination.[6] This is particularly true when the interplay between the national and the supranational levels of citizenship is considered dynamically. This chapter uses one specific Member State as an example on a number of occasions: the United Kingdom. The discussion below, although written before 23 June 2016 and updated with a post scriptum following the Brexit referendum outcome, is thus as much connected to the UK specifically as it is of general application: the conclusions reached in this text are not at all country-specific. It is this possibility to extrapolate these to the situation in any other seceding Member State, while simultaneously nodding in the direction of the cause of the conversation about the withdrawals we are having, which makes me comfortable with the insistent use of the British example.

The key conclusion is very simple: the obvious loss of an overwhelming number of rights by the citizens of the withdrawing state or states (unless otherwise negotiated) notwithstanding, EU citizenship as such cannot possibly affect, legally speaking, the regulation of withdrawals: Article 50 TEU does not contain any EU citizenship-related conditions and reading them into the text would not be legally sound:[7] EU citizenship is the crucial part of the EU package, the 'fundamental status of the nationals of the Member States'[8] in EU law. To impose it – and all the supranational law which comes with it – on a people of a Member State, which has just voted precisely *to leave* the Union, would be an aberration

[5] See, most importantly, Daniel Kenealy and Stuart MacLennan, 'Sincere Cooperation, Respect for Democracy and EU Citizenship: Sufficient to Guarantee Scotland's Future in the European Union?', *European Law Journal*, 20 (2014), 591; Phoebus Athanassiou and Stéphanie Laulhé Shaelou, 'EU Accession from Within? – An Introduction' *Yearbook of European Law*, 33 (2014), 1; Phoebus Athanassiou and Stéphanie Laulhé Shaelou, 'EU Citizenship and Its Relevance for EU Exit and Secession', in Dimitry Kochenov (ed.), *EU Citizenship and Federalism: The Role of Rights* (Cambridge: CUP, 2017).

[6] J. H. H. Weiler, 'Journey to an Unknown Destination: A Retrospective and Prospective of the European Court of Justice in the Arena of Political Integration', *Journal of Common Market Studies*, 31 (1993), 417.

[7] Athanassiou and Shaelou, (note 5).

[8] *Rudy Grzelczyk* v *Centre public d'aide sociale d'Ottignies-Louvain-la-Neuve*: Case C-184/99 *Grzelczyk*, ECLI:EU:C:2001:458 [2001] ECR I-6193, para. 31. See also, for example, *Baumbast and R.* v *Secretary of State for the Home Department*: Case C-413/99 *Baumbast and R*, ECLI:EU:C:2002:493 [2002] ECR I-7091, para. 82; *Ruiz Zambrano:* Case C-34/09 *Ruiz Zambrano*, ECLI:EU:C:2011:124 [2011] ECR I-1177, para. 41.

of common sense since it will be a direct attack on the letter and purpose of Article 50 TEU, which ultimately leaves the precise conditions of withdrawal up to negotiators.

That said, the disapplication of EU citizenship to the nationals of the withdrawing Member State has very far-reaching implications in terms of rights which should not be underestimated: a 'full' withdrawal would put the nationals of the withdrawing state into a worse position than the citizens of third countries benefiting from non-discrimination clauses in the agreements with the EU.[9] This means that UK citizens in the EU would have a legal position inferior to Russians and Moroccans, in addition to losing all the well-known perks of EU citizenship, ranging from free movement in the EU, non-discrimination on the basis of nationality within the scope of application of EU law, political rights at local and at EP level in the country of residence, consular protection abroad through the representations of other EU Member States and others,[10] ultimately resulting in a reduction in the protection of the fundamental rights which are unquestionably connected to the status of EU citizenship.[11] Currently one of the top-quality nationalities in the world, UK citizenship will drop quite radically in quality after Brexit as a result of the loss of free movement rights in twenty-seven Member States.[12]

Such a situation is absolutely bound to have political implications, necessarily making the negotiators in charge of arranging the exact agreement behind leaving the Union mindful of the far-reaching nature of the losses in terms of rights that citizens are likely to experience in seceding Member States. It would appear too cynical for the negotiators of the withdrawing state to assume that reducing UK citizens residing (or importantly, wishing in the future to reside) in the other Member States to a status inferior to that of some third-country nationals with

[9] As we have seen in *Simutenkov*, such clauses can have direct effect: Case C-265/03 *Igor Simutenkov*, ECLI:EU:C:2005:213 [2005] ECR I-2579.

[10] See Part II TFEU.

[11] Eleanor Sharpston, 'Citizenship and Fundamental Rights – Pandora's Box or a Natural Step towards Maturity?', in Pascal Cardonnel, Allan Rosas and Nils Wahl (eds.), *Constitutionalising the EU Judicial System* (Oxford: Hart Publishing, 2012), p. 245; Dimitry Kochenov, 'On Tiles and Pillars: EU Citizenship as a Federal Denominator', in Dimitry Kochenov (ed.), *EU Citizenship and Federalism: The Role of Rights* (Cambridge: CUP, 2017), 1.

[12] See, for a meticulous methodology of measuring nationality quality applied to all the nationalities in the word, Dimitry Kochenov (ed.), *The Henley & Partners – Kochenov Quality of Nationality Index* (2nd ed. Zürich: Ideos, 2017).

unprivileged relationships with the EU would be acceptable, even if this would appear to have been the position of the British Government and the British courts all along. Judges have argued, quite astonishingly, that UK citizens residing elsewhere in the EU cannot challenge their disenfranchisement in the withdrawal referendum, since they will not be more affected by the outcome than UK citizens residing in the UK.[13]

In other words, EU citizenship, while not really a 'force' (legally speaking at least) in the withdrawal context, is thus bound to play an important role politically. The key reason why is very simple: leaving the Union without negotiating any arrangement in terms of citizenship rights which would be either bilateral with the individual Member States of the EU or EU-oriented, resembling for instance the current framework of free movement of persons with Switzerland or the EEA,[14] will definitely result in the almost instant and dramatic free-fall in the value of the nationality of the seceding state.[15] Post-secession citizenship will stop providing the holders with full access to the EU for work and residence, thus radically diminishing their horizon of opportunities, using Sen's language,[16] when compared to the pre-withdrawal period. EU citizenship's core value is

[13] *The Queen on the Application of Harry Shindler MBE and Jacquelin MacLennan* v. *Chancellor of the Duchy of Lancaster and the Secretary of State for Foreign and Commonwealth Affairs* [2016] EWCA Civ 469. The UK Supreme Court refused permission to appeal purely on the grounds of UK law, leaving all EU citizens of UK nationality residing outside the UK using their EU free movement rights for fifteen years or more disenfranchised in the Brexit referendum: UKSC 2016/0105.

[14] See the EEA Agreement (OJ 1997 L1/1); EC–Switzerland Agreement (OJ 2002 L114/6). On the EEA regime, Halvard H. Fredriksen, 'Bridging the Widening Gap Between the EU Treaties and the Agreement on the European Economic Area', *European Law Journal*, 18 (2012), 868; Maria Elvira Méndez-Pinedo, *EC and EEA Law: A Comparative Study of the Effectiveness of European Law* (Brussels: Europa Publishing 2009); Carl Baudenbacher (ed.), *Judicial Protection in the European Economic Area* (Stuttgart: German Law Publishers 2012); Adam Łazowski, 'Enhanced Multilateralism and Enhanced Bilateralism: Integration Without Membership in the European Union', *CMLRev*, 45 (2008), 1433; (on the EU-Swiss Agreement): Steve Peers, 'The EC-Switzerland Agreement on Free Movement of Persons: Overview and Analysis', *European Journal of Migration and Law*, 2 (2000), 127; Marius Vahl and Nina Grolimund, 'Integration Without Membership: Switzerland's Bilateral Agreements With the European Union', (Brussels: CEPS, 2006); Francesco Maiani, Roman Petrov and Ekatarina Mouliarova (eds.), 'European Integration Without EU Membership: Models, Experiences, Perspectives', (2009) *EUI Working Papers* RSCAS 2009/10, 103–135.

[15] See Figure 1 for a graphic representation of the value of the UK nationality before and after the possible Brexit based on the *Quality of Nationality Index* methodology (note 12).

[16] See, for the analysis of EU citizenship in such terms, Gianluigi Palombella, 'Whose Europe? After the Constitution: A Goal-Based Citizenship', *International Journal of Constitutional Law*, (2005), 3357. Compare, Amartya Sen, *Development as Freedom*, (Oxford: OUP, 1999).

precisely in the *scale* of rights which it provides, covering a number of states rather than one.[17]

Reducing the scale of rights is bound to derail the lives of many of those who relied on the pre-secession entitlements guaranteed by Part II TFEU, the citizenship Part, and EU law more broadly,[18] or who were likely to benefit from such entitlements in future. Crucially, while the comparison between the loss of rights experienced by the citizens of the withdrawing state on the one hand, and the citizens of the other Member States on the other (so long as free movement and other EU-level rights will cease being provided in the territory of the withdrawing state) could sound unjustified in terms of the sheer difference in scale between the two groups facing an unnecessary reduction of rights, we need to take the loss of rights by the remaining EU citizens following one state's withdrawal equally into account. From a purely pragmatic perspective it could be presented as a positive development, of course, that the loss of rights affects both sides, because when both parties are threatened with a loss, a more productive dialogue should be more likely. This increases the chances of an amicably negotiated solution leading to the minimisation of the loss of rights. The emphasis on rights is crucial in this respect, since the name of the legal status bringing the key rights is a contingency, of course: we can safely assume that the political logic of withdrawal under Article 50 TEU would demand dropping the pompous 'citizenship' label. Core EU citizenship rights, such as free movement and non-discrimination on the basis of nationality can easily be provided without membership, however, to which the current position of Switzerland and the EEA countries *vis-à-vis* the EU clearly testifies.[19]

At this point it should be easy to guess the answer that this contribution will offer with respect to the key question which looms large in the context of the interplay of withdrawals from the Union and EU citizenship. The question is, whether a dramatic loss of rights by citizens on both sides of the newly emerging EU border is an inevitable consequence of a withdrawal of a Member State from the Union, or whether some

[17] Dimitry Kochenov, 'Member State Nationalities and the Internal Market: Illusions and Reality', in Niamh Nic Shuibhne and Laurence W. Gormley (eds.), *From Single Market to Economic Union* (Oxford: OUP, 2012).

[18] Sharpston, (note 11), 245.

[19] Further, participation in local elections and the reciprocal consular protection of citizens abroad between the withdrawing state and the Member States remaining in the EU can be extended bilaterally. Only European Parliament elections definitely stay out of the picture.

legal-political tools can be found to avoid it. This question is obviously a tricky one. Any arrangement granting quasi-citizenship of the EU to the citizens of the Member State withdrawing from the Union will *de facto* negatively affect the core reasons behind wanting to withdraw – whatever those might be – thus openly acting *against* the objective which such a withdrawal is seeking to achieve. The resulting political balance here can be very complex: how much should the real and tangible rights of the withdrawing state's own citizens be cut in the name of the goals its withdrawal is aiming to achieve (however arcane these goals might seem)? This balance will be for the politicians of the withdrawing state to try to discern, bearing in mind that maintaining an EEA-like arrangement with the EU in the context of the free-movement of persons will obviously have a price at the negotiating table. This price will necessarily include reciprocal arrangements for EU citizens in the withdrawing Member State, or other important concessions, and will obviously limit the effects of the withdrawal from the Union. In addition, depending on the negotiating position of the other party, such balancing will be bound by the realisation that whatever outcome is reached, it will necessarily disappoint some part of the citizenry, should a 'true withdrawal' have been promised. It is useful in this regard that the negotiated solution is what Article 50 TEU precisely requires. It can thus be safely assumed that leaving the EU is not a yes/no question. Moreover, as will be shown below, the Union's legal history offers a broad palette of examples of a truly far-reaching recourse to flexibility, in terms of organising the territorial and substantive reach of its law, including within and outside the territory of the Member States.

Choosing a bilateral approach implies potentially significant costs in terms of the fragmentation of the current free movement space. Not a surprising outcome, you might argue, should a withdrawal decision be taken. While negotiating with the remaining Member States collectively will most likely make it impossible for the seceding state to discriminate between the nationals of the remaining Member States – indeed, they would be prevented from adopting such a position in the light of the core principles of EU law – bilateral negotiations are likely to be a totally different story. The wisest solution could easily imply maintaining full free-movement arrangements bilaterally only with the Member States where the majority of the expats of the withdrawing states reside, plus perhaps the most economically successful Member States of the EU, thus dropping all but a handful of the Member States, arguing that these are in any case of little interest for the citizens of the withdrawing Member State in terms of settlement and work opportunities. This approach is bound to be put on the table in any bilateral setting, given the clear mono-dimensionality of the flows of free movement of labour in the EU. It is not that UK citizens are all packing up to go to Slovakia or Bulgaria. The contrary is true. Dropping much of Eastern and some of Southern EU from the free movement arrangements under the withdrawal agreement could thus be presented by the negotiators as a reasonable way forward, to strike the right balance between the political goal of secession and the need to make sure that the citizens of the seceding state do not suffer a really serious blow to their rights.

The consequences for the Eastern European citizens now residing in the UK under EU law, should such an approach be chosen, could be drastic indeed, a valid reason to prefer a strictly multilateral approach and built-in legal guarantees in the final arrangement, over any such bilateral moves. Limiting free movement uniquely to the nationals of the richest Member States or to the Member States where British citizens are most represented is obviously a serious blow to the current regime, excluding the periphery at a much more dramatic scale than is currently the case in the context of EU law, which still tends to favour the centre both structurally and as applied.[20]

Lastly, the number and nature of the possible legal-political issues arising in the context of the organisation of withdrawals is so large and diverse, that this chapter can only aspire to touch upon the most important ones, unable to provide a truly encyclopaedic treatment of this important topic. It is my hope, however, that this sketch will nevertheless be helpful to your understanding of the core underlying factors influencing the interaction of secessions from the Union with EU citizenship.

The chapter proceeds as follows. It first briefly sketches the contours of the intimate relationship between citizenship and territory, looking both at the national and the supranational levels of this legal relationship. This

[20] In its current form the EU is persuasively criticised for not paying attention to the periphery: Damjan Kukovec, 'Taking Change Seriously: The Rhetoric of Justice and the Reproduction of the *Status Quo*', in Dimitry Kochenov, Gráinne de Búrca and Andrew Williams (eds.), *Europe's Justice Deficit?* (Oxford: Hart Publishing 2015), p. 319. The exodus of population from Lithuania or Latvia to the Western European Member States is thus not necessarily a success of the EU's policy, only revealing how harsh the effects of the economic disparities can be between the Member States and that not enough is being done to ensure the uniform development of all the Member States of the Union: Fernanda G. Nicola, 'Conceptions of Justice from Below', in Dimitry Kochenov, Gráinne de Búrca and Andrew Williams (eds.), *Europe's Justice Deficit?* (Oxford: Hart Publishing, 2015), 349.

relationship appears to be much less straightforward than what many politicians and tabloid writers would like to believe. The chapter moves to demonstrate that the issue of permutations of statehood among the Member States of the EU is not as exceptional and rare as the literature sometimes tends to assume.[21] The Union, however surprising this might seem to some, has always been overwhelmingly flexible in its essence. This flexibility is bound to manifest itself, at its strongest, in the context of the withdrawal negotiations under Article 50 TEU. Having tapped into the history and core building blocks of the existing tradition of flexibility, this chapter emphasises the consequences of various constitutional territorial permutations on the enjoyment of supranational rights in the Union.

The last section before the concluding question of how to organise the post-withdrawal free movement of citizens considers the political implications of the EU citizenship/EU membership story in the context of leaving the Union. This resides in the realm of political negotiations, not legal battles, as the UK Supreme Court has recently directly confirmed.[22] It is fundamental to realise, however, that for the reasons explained above, EU citizenship and the rights associated therewith, is likely to play the most important role in the context of withdrawals from the Union. In terms of the limits of the political possibilities the answer is quite simple: legally speaking, it would not be an exaggeration to state that virtually anything is possible, from the preservation of an EEA-like free movement regime between the EU and the withdrawing state to bilateral arrangements between the withdrawing state and the Member States of its choice following withdrawal. Restricting all forms of free movement is an extreme, and thus politically virtually unfeasible option. Allowing for a broad margin of appreciation is particularly sensible, given the general context of the flexibility of citizenship, nationality, territory and the rights arrangements that the EU has to offer in the context of constitutional change (including, necessarily, its own). A number of important factors are bound to be taken into account as leaving the Union is negotiated. A brief comparison will be made of the core (EU) citizenship options available to any newly formed states emerging as a result of secession from a Member State, eager to retain the status of EU citizenship for their populations. The post scriptum added

[21] The starting part of this section relies on Kochenov and van den Brink, (note 3).

[22] *Schindler*, hearing on application for appeal to UK Supreme Court, UKSC 1016/0105, 24 May 2016.

following the UK referendum contextualises the discussion presented in this chapter in the light of the plebiscite's outcome.

## II Citizenship and Territory: an Intimate Relationship

Citizenship, as 'an instrument and object of [. . .] closure,'[23] is naturally and intimately connected to territory. This connection is visible in particular through some modes of citizenship acquisition which are essentially territorial,[24] as well as a usual link between citizenship as a legal status of belonging or a mode of contestation,[25] and a particular public authority, which is usually territorial in essence.[26] Classical understandings of a state in the legal literature make both citizenship and territory indispensable elements of statehood, which necessarily connects the two. Any alteration to the legal status of a territory can thus naturally be expected to have consequences for the citizenship status of at least some of the inhabitants. Crucially, the core right of any citizenship relates to the ability to enter the territory the status is associated with, and remain there free of any border controls – a principle recognised in international and EU law.[27]

EU citizenship, although highly atypical compared with the nationalities at the Member State level,[28] is nevertheless informed by the same territorial logic.[29] Its core rights are enjoyed in the territory of the

[23] Rogers Brubaker, *Citizenship and Nationhood in France and Germany* (Cambridge MA: Harvard University Press, 1992), p. 23.

[24] See, for example, Iseult Honohan, 'The Theory and Politics of Ius Soli' (2010) *EUI RSCAS Paper* (EUDO Citizenship), <http://eudo-citizenship.eu/docs/IusSoli.pdf> accessed 5 June 2015. This crucial legal status is distributed in a manner akin to a lottery, where the place of birth and the nationality of parents are the two factors at play: Aylet Shachar, *Birthright Lottery: Citizenship and Global Inequality* (Cambridge, MA: Harvard University Press, 2009).

[25] For example, Engin Isin, 'Citizenship in Flux: The Figure of the Activist Citizen', *Subjectivity*, 29 (2009), 367.

[26] Charles Tilly, *Coercion, Capital and European States: AD 990–1992*, (2nd ed., London: Wiley Blackwell, 1992).

[27] Case C-434/09 *McCarthy*, ECLI:EU:C:2011:277 [2011] ECR I-3375.

[28] For overviews, see, for example, Jo Shaw, 'Citizenship: Contrasting Dynamics at the Interface of Integration and Constitutionalism', in Paul Craig and Gráinne de Búrca (eds.), *Evolution of EU Law* (2nd ed., Oxford: OUP, 2011), 578; Dimitry Kochenov, 'The Essence of EU Citizenship Emerging from the Last Ten Years of Academic Debate', *International and Comparative Law Quarterly*, 62 (2013), 97.

[29] Teresa Pullano, *La citoyenneté européenne: Un espace quasi étatique* (Paris: SciencesPo, 2014); Loïc Azoulai, 'Transfiguring European Citizenship: From Member State Territory to Union Territory', in Dimitry Kochenov (ed.), *EU Citizenship and Federalism: The Role of Rights* (Cambridge: CUP, 2017).

Union[30] and the fundamental rules for its acquisition are also frequently *de facto* territory-related: the *ius tractum* logic of becoming a European citizen – the derivative nature of its acquisition[31] – simply relies on the Member States' own determinations of who their nationals are,[32] with only minor derogations aiming at the protection of EU-level citizenship rights and the enjoyment of supranational personal legal status in full,[33] as well as the protection of citizens against discrimination on the basis of the mode of citizenship acquisition.[34] In essence, however, any citizenship, including the one of the EU, functions in exactly the same way, allowing the polity in charge of the status essentially to draw a line between those, who 'belong' and those who do not, thus using the status to take informed and predictable decisions about the individual entitlements of every person holding the status (or not) *vis-à-vis* the public authority.[35]

This picture is obviously too simplistic to reflect reality in full. While a notable connection between citizenship and territory is always there, the two function in radically different realms and frequently do not overlap in practice. In a metaphor effectively deployed by Rainer Bauböck, if the political maps of the world were drawn to show the citizenship of each individual in the territory of each of the states, rather than simply colouring state territory in a corresponding colour, the resulting picture would

30 Although the Treaty formulation actually points to this being the sum of the territories of the Member States, the concept of the Union territory is maturing very quickly in the case law of the ECJ, and plays an important role. Azoulai, (note 29).

31 Dimitry Kochenov, '*Ius Tractum* of Many Faces: European Citizenship and the Difficult Relationship between Status and Rights', *Columbia Journal of European Law*, 15 (2009), 169.

32 Art. 1 Convention Governing Certain Questions Relating to the Conflict of Nationalities (12 April, 1930), 179 LNTS, 89, 99. This position is also confirmed by the fact that the Court respects the Declarations made by the Member States in clarifying the meaning of their nationalities in the context of EU law. See Case C-192/99 *Kaur*, ECLI:EU:C:2001:106 [2001] ECR I-1237. Alice Sironi, 'Nationality of Individuals in Public International Law: A Functional Approach', in Alessandra Annoni and Serena Forlati (eds.), *The Changing Role of Nationality in International Law* (Abingdon: Routledge, 2014), 54.

33 Case C-135/08 *Rottmann*, ECLI:EU:C:2010:104 [2010] ECR I-1449. For an analysis see, Dimitry Kochenov, 'A Real European Citizenship: A New Jurisdiction Test; A Novel Chapter in the Development of the Union in Europe', *Columbia Journal of European Law*, 18 (2011), 56, 77.

34 Case C-214/94 *Boukhalfa*, ECLI:EU:C:1996:174 [1996] ECR I-2253. Similar logic applies to discrimination based on residence outside a particular territory outside the EU: Case C-300/4 *Eman and Sevinger*, ECLI:EU:C:2006:545 [2006] ECR I-8055. See Leonard F. M. Besselink, *Annotation of Case C-145/04* Spain v UK, *Case C-300/04* Eman and Sevinger, *and ECtHR Case* Sevinger and Eman v The Netherlands (2008) 45 CMLRev, 787.

35 Christian Joppke, *Citizenship and Immigration* (Oxford: Polity Press, 2010).

be a pixelated representation of an intricate reality which would show with clarity how citizenship and territory actually do not overlap.[36] This is an important point, which plenty of thinkers, including T. H. Marshal, have ignored: the world is much more interesting than what the official statist representations would like to make of it.[37]

When speaking about withdrawals, it is absolutely essential to have both pictures in mind. The dominant one, drawing a clear and idealistic line between citizenship and territoriality, on the one hand, and the less cleanly pixelated world which Bauböck had in mind, on the other. Importantly, both will inform our thinking about the potential influence of citizenship on the organisation and outcomes of Member State withdrawals from the Union. In other words, citizenship rights, including the core ones such as voting, can have a significant role to play outside the territory,[38] while plenty of those who are present in the territory will not enjoy the plenitude of rights enjoyed by the majority of citizens, even though the discrepancies here are thinning very quickly.[39]

Given that EU citizenship is not that different as a legal status, from the nationalities of the Member States from which it derives, it is similarly as non-territorial in essence, as it is connected to the territory. Crucially, while the majority of rights are then only available in the Union as such – including the rights to work, reside, etc. – possession of the status of citizenship as such is non-territorial. The intricate unsustainability of the arrangements related to the non-application of EU law in the Faroe Islands, particularly in terms of personal scope, could help to illustrate this basic point. When acceding to the Communities the Danish Government clarified that the 'Danish nationals in the Faroe Islands' would not be considered 'nationals for the purposes of Community law'.[40] Yet,

[36] Rainer Bauböck, 'Citizenship and National Identities in the European Union' *Jean Monnet Working Paper* (Harvard Law School) No. 97/04 (1997).

[37] T. H. Marshall, 'Citizenship and Social Class', in T. H. Marshall, *Citizenship and Social Class* (London: Pluto Press, 1992 [1950]).

[38] Heather Lardy, 'Citizenship and the Right to Vote', *Oxford Journal of Legal Studies*, 17 (1997), 75; Ruth Rubio-Marín, 'Transnational Politics and the Democratic Nation-State: Normative Challenges of Expatriate Voting and Nationality Retention of Emigrants', *New York University Law Review*, 81 (2006), 117.

[39] Christian Joppke, 'The Inevitable Lightening of Citizenship', *European Journal of Sociology*, 51 (2010), 37.

[40] Art. 4 Protocol No. 2 to the Act of Accession, Relating to Færoe Islands [1972] OJ L 73/163. The Islands are not part of the Union under Art. 355(5)(a) TFEU. See Niklas Fagerlund, 'Autonomous European Island Regions Enjoying a Special Relationship with the European Union', in Lise Lyck (ed.), *Constitutional and Economic Space of the Small Nordic Jurisdictions* (Copenhagen: NordREFO, 1996), 90–112

given that this limitation was merely territorial, there is no evidence that it has in any way affected the enjoyment of EU citizenship by the Faroe Islanders, as long as they do not travel on the green Faroe model of the Danish passport, which they can, but are not obliged to request.[41] Any territorial limitation of the status of citizenship clearly does not work. Moreover, EU law is clear that some EU citizenship rights which are not territorial *per se* and can thus be enjoyed outside EU territory, such as the general principle of non-discrimination, apply equally to all EU citizens of a particular nationality residing outside the territory of the EU.[42] The same cannot be said of the most important, territorial rights, which cannot be enjoyed by EU citizens outside the territory of the Union, be it in the Faroe Islands, Socotra, Aruba or Koh Samui.

In order to conclude which EU citizenship right will be operational outside the Union territory and which not, it is necessary to go right by right, conducting an individual analysis. It is clear that once a Member State withdraws, the majority of supranational rights enjoyed by EU citizens in its territory will by definition disappear into thin air, unless otherwise negotiated, since the national territory will no longer form part of the territory of the Union. EU law, as such, cannot possibly limit the principle of its own non-application in the territory of the withdrawing state, since there is no indication to this effect in Article 50 TEU. There is an important footnote to be made here, however: while Article 50 TEU does not make it impossible for the Member State seeking to withdraw to abandon all of the *acquis* of the Union – indeed, this is what 'withdrawal' means when approached purely linguistically – questions are bound to

[41] The Faroe Islands are not the only example of a Member State territory which never fell within the territorial scope of EU law. Other examples include Macao, Hong Kong ( Brian Hook and Miguel Santos Neves, 'The Role of Hong Kong and Macau in China's Relations with Europe', *The China Quarterly*, 169 (2002), 108), Suriname (which decided not to join the Communities when the Netherlands Antilles asked to be included as Overseas Countries or Territories (OJ 2413/64)), UK Sovereign Base Areas in Cyprus (SBAs) (Art. 355(5)(b) TFEU; Stéphanie Lauhlé-Shaelou, 'The Principle of Territorial Exclusion in the EU: SBAs in Cyprus – A Special Case of Sui Generis Territories in the EU'. in Dimitry Kochenov (ed.), *EU Law of the Overseas* (The Hague: Kluwer Law International, 2011), p. 153). Some did join at a point later than the ratification of the Treaties by their 'mother country'. The examples include the former Netherlands Antilles (See, de Overeenkomst tot wijziging van het Verdrag tot oprichting van de Europese Economische Gemeenschap ten einde de bijzondere associeatieregeling van het vierde deel van het Verdrag op de Nederlandse Antillen te doen zijn of 13 November 1962 [1964] OJ 2413/64) and Canary Islands (See, Council Regulation (EEC) 1911/91 of 26 June 1991 on the application of the provisions of Community law to the Canary Islands [1991] OJ L 171/1).

[42] C-300/4 *Eman and Sevinger*, ECLI:EU:C:2006:545 [2006] ECR I-8055.

arise, should the withdrawing state desire retroactively to terminate the rights enjoyed by EU citizens connected with other Member States in its own territory. The *ratione temporis* of the law will be of crucial importance. It is absolutely clear that an argument that their rights simply expire will not hold, since withdrawal cannot possibly amount to a retroactive annulment of all the EU law-inspired national legislation and regulations. In the case of the UK this means that the EU Citizens Free Movement Directive, as implemented in national law, will no doubt continue to apply until it is expressly overruled. Moreover, such overruling will have to comply with the national constitutional requirements of legal certainty, the protection of human rights and the Rule of Law. The same applies to countless other instruments. Arguing to the contrary would imply arguing for complete chaos supplanting the law, given the depth of the interpenetration of national and European law at this stage. In other words the drastic consequences of withdrawals for the rights of EU citizens, while absolute for those who have not used those rights yet, are in all likelihood somewhat tamed in the case of those who already reside across the newly-emerging EU border. Ultimately, however, this issue is bound to be one of the core aspects of the political negotiations under Article 50 TEU.

Unlike the non-application of EU law and rights to the territory of the seceding state post-secession, the contrary is true with regard to the status of EU citizenship: all those holding EU citizenship acquired on the basis of a connection with any of the Member States but the withdrawing one, will retain their status and will be able to enjoy the plenitude of rights connected to it, once returning to the territory of the Union (while being able to enjoy non-territorial rights in the withdrawing state itself). This very basic understanding is behind the rising numbers of UK citizens wishing to acquire an Irish nationality, to which many of them are entitled by law.[43]

## III The Tradition of EU Flexibility in Dealing with Territorial and Citizenship Changes

Recent European constitutional history teaches us the lesson of flexibility of the legal arrangements in many of the cases where the boundaries of territory and belonging have been redrawn and the status of citizenship,

[43] The Irish are not even foreigners in the UK, under UK law: s. 18(1)(b) Electoral Administration Act 2006, c. 22; s. 6(3)(e) Representation of People Act 2000, c. 2.

including the ability to benefit from supranational rights, has been affected. This flexibility definitely includes EU law and international law: from citizenship rules, where the EU simply follows pretty much *any* approach adopted nationally,[44] to adaptations to the unique circumstances of each particular case: Estonia and Latvia refusing to recognise large sections of their populations as citizens, triggering EU-level non-recognition of their EU-level rights claims,[45] just as the adaptations of the pre-accession regime to accept a divided Cyprus, in ephemeral control of the island, including full EU citizenship for the Turkish Cypriots qualifying for the status under the law of the Republic although residing in the occupied territories,[46] are the cases in point. When interpreting the limits of the Treaties in dealing with secessions, withdrawals and accessions, these lessons should be taken into account in full: both the understandings of 'citizenship' and that of 'territory of a Member State' are malleable.[47] In the context of withdrawals from the EU this would not amount

[44] EU law honours the Member States' determinations, for instance, of nationality for the purposes of EU law, which implies that non-nationals of the Member States could be considered EU citizens and vice versa, some nationals could be considered non-EU citizens. The German and the UK approaches to citizenship are particular cases in point, both tolerated by EU law: Case C-192/99 *The Queen* v *Secretary of State for the Home Department* ex parte *Manjit Kaur*, ECLI:EU:C:2001:106 [2001] ECR I-1237, para. 27.

[45] For a detailed analysis of this particular issue see, for example, Dimitry Kochenov and Aleksejs Dimitrovs, 'EU Citizenship for the Latvian "Non-Citizens": A Concrete Proposal', *Houston Journal of International Law*, 37 (2016), 1; Dimitry Kochenov, 'A Summary of Contradictions: An Outline of EU's Main Internal and External Approaches to Ethnic Minority Protection', *Boston College International and Comparative Law Review*, 31 (2008)

[46] Elena Basheska and Dimitry Kochenov, 'Thanking the Greeks: The Crisis of the Rule of Law in EU Enlargement Regulation', *Southeastern Europe*, 39 (2015), 392.

[47] Numerous other examples can be provided, ranging from the special treatment of the belonger status of the Åland Islands to Saami agriculture protocols and the limited EU citizenship rights of Manxmen and the Channel Islanders aimed at the preservation of their autonomy and specificity. See on the Isle of Man and Channel Islands UK citizenship status and EU rights: Documents Concerning the Accession to the European Communities of the Kingdom of Denmark, Ireland, the Kingdom of Norway and the United Kingdom of Great Britain and Northern Ireland, Protocol No. 3, 27 March, 1972 [1972] OJ L 73/164; see also Kenneth R. Simmonds, 'The British Islands and the Community: I–Jersey', *CMLRev*, 6 (1969), 156; Kenneth R. Simmonds, 'The British Islands and the Community: II—The Isle of Man', *CMLRev*, 7 (1970), 454; Kenneth R. Simmonds, 'The British Islands and the Community: III—Guernsey', *CMLRev*, 8 (1971), 475; On the Åland Islands belonger status: Dimitry Kochenov, 'Regional Citizenships and EU Law', *ELRev*, 35 (2010), 307; Niklas Fagerlund, 'The Special Status of the Åland Islands in the European Union', in Lauri Hannikainen and Frank Horn (eds.), *Autonomy and Demilitarisation in International Law: The Åland Islands in a Changing Europe* (The Hague: Kluwer Law International,

to much, however, besides having the EU tolerate a more extensive policy of naturalisation of the citizens of the withdrawing state by other Member States of the Union, like the Irish-British example referred to above.[48] A great deal can be done in terms of framing the national citizenship of a Member State and connecting, or eventually disconnecting it, from the EU citizenship status as the practice shows.[49] All in all, regrettably, more than twenty years of EU citizenship practice[50] have not altered the day-to-day reality of nationalism and the harmful and irrational citizenship regulation in Europe. Citizenship wars rage in the East of the continent – with the latest example coming from Slovakia, eager to deprive of its nationality its own citizens of Hungarian ethnicity willing to accept Hungarian nationality;[51] at a more general level, and notwithstanding the global trends,[52] multiple nationality is not yet accepted everywhere across the EU. Limitations can even apply to the cumulation of Member State nationalities.[53]

1997), 189. On the Saami territorial/legal status arrangements: Danielle Perrot and Franck Miatti, 'Les lapons et les îles Åland dans le quatrième élargissement', *Revue du marché commun et de l'Union européenne*, 413 (1997), 670.

48 There is a consensus in the literature that naturalising excessively large numbers of people at once could amount to a breach of EU law due to possible negative externalities for the other Member States. The exact threshold to understand when this rule is applicable is relatively high, however. Even naturalising 1,000,000 foreigners abroad over ten years, as Italy has done in Argentina, seems to be fully legal and has not attracted any criticism, while smaller-scale naturalisations in Bulgaria (as applied to Macedonians) and Romania (as applied to Moldovans) not infrequently receive negative press, supplying a clear example of the dual standards in the EU. Given that a million in ten years is clearly acceptable, however, we could still query whether Ireland, in one example, could naturalise *all* the willing population of the UK without breaching EU law. Important in this context is that the ECJ consistently ignores involuntary naturalisations: Case C-21/74 *Jeanne Airola* v *Commission*, ECLI:EU:C:1975:24 [1975] ECR I-221.

49 The ability to disconnect Member State nationality from EU citizenship, although confirmed in *Kaur*, is much more difficult for the Member States to use after *Rottmann*, which is a positive development, as it reduces the likelihood of invoking the right to bring unilateral declarations on the meaning of nationality for the purposes of EU law by the Member States wishing to deprive certain minority groups among their citizens of their rights.

50 Antje Wiener, 'Going Home? "European" Citizenship Practice Twenty Years after', in Dimitry Kochenov (ed.), *EU Citizenship and Federalism: The Role of Rights* (Cambridge: CUP, 2017).

51 Jose-Maria. Araiza, 'Good Neighbourliness as the Limit of Extra-Territorial Citizenship: The Case of Hungary and Slovakia', in Dimitry Kochenov and Elena Basheska (eds.), *Good Neighbourliness in the European Legal Context* (Leiden: Brill-Nijhoff, 2015).

52 Peter Spiro, *At Home in Two Countries: The Past and Future of Dual Citizenship*, (New York: New York University Press, 2016).

53 Dimitry Kochenov, 'Double Nationality in the EU: An Argument for Tolerance', *European Law Journal*, 17 (2011), 323.

Such negative examples notwithstanding, it is beyond any doubt that the EU's citizenship and territorial evolution has been particularly eventful over the last half a century. More than half of what used to be the founding Member States' territory has left their sovereignty since the creation of the European Communities.[54] Moreover, a significant number of the Member States of the EU are direct products of recent permutations of statehood, some of them gaining statehood with the clear support of the Union.[55] The same applies to some candidate countries.[56] Constitutional permutations of territory and, consequently, of citizenship, are thus quite common in the European context. The problems which secessions pose to citizenship at the national level[57] are very

[54] Besides of course Algeria, which was fully incorporated into the French Republic at the inception of the Communities, and the Netherlands East Indies and New Guinea, the Member States possessed a variety of territories around the world and it was not the intention of the Communities to let these territories go. Indeed, their incorporation into the internal market in the mid to long-term future was a crucial condition for French participation in the European integration project: Dominique Custos, 'Implications of the European Integration for the Overseas', in Dimitry Kochenov (ed.), *EU Law of the Overseas* (The Hague: Kluwer Law International 2011), 91. For a brilliant retelling of the complete background story, see Peo Hansen and Stefan Jonsson, *Eurafrica: The Untold History of European Integration and Colonialism* (London: Bloomsbury Academic, 2014). Following Ziller's helpful compilation, the Member States' territories then included: the Belgian territories of Congo and Rwanda-Burundi, the Italian protectorate of Somalia, New Guinea of the Netherlands, and French Equatorial Africa (Côte-d'Ivoire, Dahomey, Guinea, Mauritania, Niger, Senegal, Sudan and Upper Volta), French East Africa (Moyen-Congo (the future Central African Empire beloved by Giscard d'Estaing), Gabon, Oubangui-Chari and Chad), the protectorates Togo and Cameroon, the Comoros Islands (Mayotte, separated from them is now an outermost region of the EU), Madagascar, and Côte Française des Somalis. Following the UK's accession, the list of associated countries and territories became much longer, including (besides the countries and territories still on the previous list) the Bahamas, Brunei, the Caribbean Colonies and Associated States (Antigua, Dominica, Grenada, St. Kitts and Nevis, St. Lucia, St. Vincent and Anguilla, and British Honduras), Gilbert and Ellis Islands, Line Islands, the Anglo-French Condominium of the New Hebrides, the Solomon Islands, and the Seychelles. Jacques Ziller, 'L'Union européenne et l'outre-mer', *Pouvoirs*, 113 (2005), 145, 146–47.

[55] Which is attested, for instance, by the work of the Badinter Commission: Frank Hoffmeister, 'The Contribution of EU Practice to International Law', in Marise Cremona (ed.), *Developments in EU External Relations Law* (Oxford: OUP 2008).

[56] In one example, it was due to the EU's efforts that a deal laying down the rules of Montenegrin independence referendum was brokered between the pro and anti-independence movements. Following the EU's recommendations, it was decided that a 55% majority was required for independence to be gained. For a detailed analysis of the negotiations, see Karsten Friis, 'The Referendum in Montenegro: The EU's "Postmodern Diplomacy"', *European Foreign Affairs Review*, 12 (2007), 67.

[57] See Jo Shaw, 'Constituting Citizenship Regimes in Evolving Polities', Chapter 9 in this volume.

similar to the problems posed by withdrawals from the EU in the context of EU citizenship at the supranational level. Both levels clearly enjoy both elements of the citizenship/territory equation, even if the supranational level is somewhat more complex due to the constant reliance on the determinations of territoriality and also citizenship made by the constituent parts of the Union – the Member States – under their own laws. That said, the opposite could also be considered true: in the case of withdrawals from the EU the nationality of the population of the withdrawing entity is already clearly predetermined by its own constitutional law, which is not the case when states split. In other words, while the EU situation is relatively more complex when compared to the splitting of states, it is simultaneously also simpler, since there is no need, in the context of the secessions from the EU, to articulate an entirely new status of citizenship.

Since history knows no examples of withdrawals from the EU – and those who cite Greenland are obviously wrong, as Greenland never 'left' since it remains part of an EU Member State and Parts IV, II and many other provisions of the TFEU (to say nothing about secondary law) still apply there[58] – it is most logical to approach secessions from the Member States as a parallel to the story of possible withdrawals from the Union. After all, full secession – not a half-way devolution, as in the case of Greenland or St Pierre-et-Miquelon[59] – necessarily results in the full disapplication of supranational law to the territory in question, including the provisions on the personal legal status recognised at the supranational legal level. This is exactly the full extent of the outcome of any withdrawal under Article 50 TEU. In this sense, taking Article 50 TEU seriously – as a lawyer should – yields a result akin to Algeria's withdrawal from the EEC as a result of leaving France: all Algerians lost the

[58] Treaty amending, with regard to Greenland, the Treaties establishing the European Communities [1985] OJ L 29/1 (The Greenland Treaty); Friedl Weiß, 'Greenland's Withdrawal from the European Communities', *ELRev*, 10 (1985), 173. 'Leaving' is not a correct characterisation of this treaty's key legal effect: Greenland simply changed its status under the Treaties, becoming an Overseas Country or Territory in the sense of Annex II, which means that a lot of EU law applies there.

[59] France claimed to have changed the status of the territory unilaterally on a number of occasions. It is not entirely clear whether such unilateral change (which was entirely in line with the Treaty text at the time) actually resulted in a difference in treatment *vis-à-vis* the Communities. The Commission claimed it did: Written Question No. 400/76 by Mr. Lagorce to the Commission concerning the situation of the islands Saint-Pierre-and-Miquelon [1976] OJ C 294/16, para. 1.

status of Member State nationals for the purposes of Community law as a result of that move.[60]

The example of Algeria is both exceptional and not. Although not characterised as a colony in French law, legitimate claims can be made that *de facto* it *was* one, thus joining the chorus of other colonial possessions, leaving the sovereignty of their 'mother countries' and also cutting citizenship ties with the Member State in question and with the EEC. Remember the Eurafrican Union[61] and look at the contemporary maps: from Vanuatu to Congo, from Somalia and Suriname, European sovereignty has receded, bringing with it new, local citizenship statuses for the majority of the former colonial subjects of different kinds, some of them enjoying full citizenship of the European metropoles. The sovereign territories of the majority of the founding Member States of the Union have shrunk in the most radical fashion.[62]

Turning to Europe *proper*, a simple glance at the statehood of the current Member States suffices to make a basic point: changes in statehood are responsible for the creation/consolidation of a number of EU Member States, from the decolonization context, spurring Malta and Cyprus into existence as independent state entities, to the regaining of statehood by the Baltic States,[63] the split between the Czech and the

60 Algeria was fully incorporated first following the formation of the Second Republic (1848). Guy Pervillé, 'La politique algérienne de la France, de 1830 à 1962' *Le Genre humain*, 32 (1997), 27; Pierre Laffont, *Histoire de la France en Algérie* (Paris: Plon, 1979).

61 Peo Hansen and Stefan Jonsson, 'Building Eurafrica: Reviving Colonialism through European Integration, 1920–60', in Kalypso Nicolaidis, Berny Sebe and Gabrielle Maas (eds.), *Echoes of Empire: Identity, Memory, and Colonial Legacies* (London: I. B. Tauris, 2015); Hansen and Jonsson (note 54); Peo Hansen and Stefan Jonsson, 'Bringing Africa as a "Dowry to Europe": European Integration and the Eurafrican Project', *Interventions*, 13(2011) 443; Peo Hansen and Stefan Johnsson, 'Imperial Origins of European Integration and the Case of Eurafrica: A Reply to Gary Marks' "Europe and Its Empires"', *Journal of Common Market Studies*, 50 (2012), 1028; Custos, (note 54).

62 Germany, of course, is the most radical counter-example: Art. 1 Treaty on the Establishment of German Unity, 31 August, 1990, 30 ILM 457 (1991); Michael Bothe, 'The German Experience to Meet the Challenges of Reunification', in Alfred E. Kellerman et al. (eds.), *EU Enlargement: The Constitutional Impact at EU and National Level* (The Hague: TMC Asser, 2011); Eberhard Grabitz, 'L'unité allemande et l'intégration européenne', *Cahiers de Droit Européen*, 27 (1991), 3; Jean-Paul Jacqué, 'L'unification de l'Allemagne et la Communauté européenne', *Revue générale de droit internationale public*, 94 (1990), 997.

63 For a meticulous analysis, see Peter Van Elsuwege, *From Soviet Republics to EU Member States* (Leiden and Boston: Martinus Nijhoff, 2008). See also Ineta Ziemele, *State Continuity and Nationality: The Baltic States and Russia – Past, Present and Future as Defined by International Law* (Leiden: Brill-Nijhoff, 2005); Alekseijs Dimitrovs and Vadim Poleshchuk, 'Kontinuitet kak osnova gosudarstvennosti i ètnopolitiki v Latvii i

Slovak Republics,[64] the articulation of Slovenia and Croatia, as well as the unification of Germany following the incorporation of the German Democratic Republic (DDR) and Berlin (West) into the Federal Republic,[65] and France, with Algeria's departure. Crucially, the EU, as well as its individual Member States, played an important role in bringing about such changes in statehood, not only with regard to the entities which came to be Member States,[66] but also other countries, including the loose protectorates the EU has created.[67]

The splitting up of the colonial empires, besides triggering the creation of new states,[68] created large numbers of foreigners deprived of EU-level rights out of full citizens able to benefit from what European integration had to offer.[69] The developments here were not straightforward. Some of the newly-emerging foreigners lost EU citizenship[70] even without losing

Èstonii', in Vadim Poleshchuk and Valery Stepanov (eds.), *Ètnopolitika stran Baltii* (Moscow: Nauka, 2013).

64 For an overview of the legal implications of the dissolution of Czechoslovakia, see Martin Palous, 'Questions of Czech Citizenship', in André Liebich, Daniel Warner and Jasna Dragovic (eds.), *Citizenship East and West* (London: Routledge, 1995), p. 142. Specifically on the issues of citizenship: Dimitry Kochenov, 'EU Influence on the Citizenship Policies of the Candidate Countries: The Case of the Roma Exclusion in the Czech Republic', *Journal of Contemporary European Research*, 3 (2007), 124. For a general assessment of secessions in the context of the East-European eruption in state-making see Cass R. Sunstein, 'Constitutionalism and Secession', *University of Chicago Law Review*, 58 (1991), 633.

65 Ryszard W. Piotrowicz, 'The Status of Germany in International Law: Deutschland über Deutschland?', *International and Comparative Law Quarterly*, 38 (1989), 609.

66 Hoffmeister, (note 55).

67 On the role of the EU in Kosovo, see Wolfgang Koeth, 'State Building without a State: The EU's Dilemma in Defining Its Relations with Kosovo', *European Foreign Affairs Review*, 15 (2010), 227; Stephen Rozée, 'Order-Maintenance in Kosovo: The EU as an Increasingly Comprehensive Police Actor?', *European Foreign Affairs Review*, 20 (2015), 97; Spyros Economides and James Ker-Lindsay, 'Forging EU Policy Unity from Diversity: The "Unique Case" of the Kosovo Status Talks', *European Foreign Affairs Review*, 15 (2010), 495. For Bosnia see Anze Voh Bostic, 'The Role of the European Union's Expert Assistance in the Process of Peace-Building: The Case of Bosnia and Herzegovina', *European Foreign Affairs Review*, 15 (2010), 209; Milada Anna Vachudova, 'The Thieves of Bosnia: The Complicated Legacy of the Dayton Peace Accords', (2014) *Foreign Affairs* <www.foreignaffairs.com/articles/europe/2014-02-24/thieves-bosnia>, accessed 28 August, 2015.

68 Poul Kjær, *Constitutionalism in the Global Realm: A Sociological Approach* (London: Routledge 2014).

69 Similarly, but following a strictly territorial logic, former colonies graduating into statehood fell outwith the scope of European human rights instruments: Antenor Hallo de Wolf, 'The Application of Human Rights Treaties in Overseas Countries and Territories', in Dimitry Kochenov (ed.), *EU Law of the Overseas* (The Hague: Kluwer Law International, 2011).

70 Rather than EU citizenship *sensu stricto*, what was at stake was its precursor status, forming part of the 'informal resources of the *acquis*' Antje Wiener, *'European' Citizenship Practice – Building Institutions of a Non-State* (Boulder, CO: Westview

their Member State nationality *sensu lato*, as was the case with Mrs. Kaur, whose Member State nationality was considered by the Court as insufficient to consider her an EU citizen.[71] Others lost all their rights without losing their citizenship status due to the racist immigration policies adopted by the Member States of the EU,[72] or on the contrary, did not lose any EU rights at all, while *de jure* losing EU citizenship, as in the case of the Faroe islanders.

Numerous key EU citizenship cases deal with persons who, having enjoyed full entitlements to supranational rights since birth, lost those overnight, as 'their' country became independent of a Member State, thus depriving them of their 'legal heritage'[73] connection with the EU. While appearing neat in the legal literature, such cases often feed on human tragedy, separated families and sadness. *Morson and Jhanjan* is a case in point: a failed attempt to invoke EU law to secure family reunification between individuals who all used to be Member State nationals a short while before, thus free of border controls, their situation changing radically with the independence of Suriname.[74]

The ECJ's and ECtHR's approaches to the personal histories of EU citizenship (or a predecessor status) are drastically different.[75] For the ECtHR, your past lingers on at times as potentially legally relevant, such as the former Netherlands nationality of 'an illegal migrant' from

Press, 1998). This status was 'nationals of the Member States for the purposes of Community law' and predated the formal introduction of EU citizenship at Maastricht. The ECJ could distinguish between the two by making EU citizenship more inclusive by depriving the Member States of the possibility they enjoyed in the pre-citizenship legal context to limit its scope via unilateral declarations – a practice much criticised in the academic literature of the day: Richard Plender, 'An Incipient Form of European Citizenship', in Francis Jacobs (ed.), *EU Law and the Individual* (Amsterdam: North Holland, 1976). The ECJ has not done this, however, tacitly reaffirming the legality of the unilateral British declarations on the scope of UK nationality for the purposes of community law and potentially opening the door for further such limitations of the term 'nationals', in Article 9 TEU: Case C-192/99 *Manjit Kaur*, ECLI:EU:C:2001:106 [2001] ECR I-1237.

71 Case C-192/99 *Manjit Kaur*, ECLI:EU:C:2001:106 [2001] ECR I-1237. For a detailed discussion of this issue, see, for example, Kochenov, (note 31), 186–190.

72 Anthony Lester, Lord Lester of Herne Hill QC, 'East African Asians Versus the United Kingdom: The Inside Story' (23 October, 2003) Lecture, <www.blackstonechambers.com/document.rm?id=73>, accessed 5 June 2015.

73 Case C-26/62 *Van Gend en Loos*, ECLI:EU:C:1963:1 [1963] ECR I-1.

74 Joined cases 35 and 36/82 *Morson and Jhanjan*, ECLI:EU:C:1982:368 [1982] ECR I-3723.

75 Stanislas Adam and Peter Van Elsuwege, 'EU Citizenship and the European Federal Challenge through the Prism of Family Reunification', in Dimitry Kochenov (ed.), *EU Citizenship and Federalism, The Role of Rights* (Cambridge: CUP, 2017).

Suriname, residing with her Dutch family in the Netherlands in the case of *Jeunesse* v. *The Netherlands*.[76] The ECJ – just like the Member State courts – would usually ignore such a past, including past nationalities, entirely, declaring yesterday's citizens illegal aliens without a blink of an eye.[77] While legally correct, this approach is clearly problematic, especially in the context of the general move from 'the culture of authority' to the 'culture of justification'.[78] The global trend in law today is to see a *person* behind the impenetrable and simplistic legal façade of citizenship.[79] Seeing a person indispensably implies being capable of taking the personal history into account, not only the passport the person happens to be travelling on.

Two important lessons emerge from the above. Firstly, changes to statehood are not exceptional – secessions from states have been a day-to-day reality in twentieth-century Europe and the story continues into the twenty-first century. In this context withdrawal from the EU will be but one example among many. Indeed, many of the secession examples are sad ones, in essence, bringing about a decline in the quality of life and level of security to a level far below the time of the proclamation of statehood. In addition to the 'normality' of secessions and territorial fluctuations as testified to by their commonness and omnipresence, history also teaches us of the flexibility of the legal arrangements in many of these cases. This fully includes citizenship arrangements. Although examples of territories leaving the sovereign ambit of

[76] For example, *Jeunesse v The Netherlands* (App. No. 12738/10) ECtHR 3 October, 2014; *Beldjoudi v France* (App. No. 12083/86) ECtHR 26 March, 1992. For an insightful comment on *Jeunesse* in the context of EU law, see Adam and Van Elsuwege, (note 75).

[77] There is a consensus in the literature that the ECJ does not have the most enviable record in the protection of the rights of EU citizens, particularly those who are in a vulnerable position: Niamh Nic Shuibhne, '(Some of) The Kids Are All Right: Comment on McCarthy and Dereci', *CMLRev*, 49 (2012), 349; Elenor Spaventa, 'Earned Citizenship – Understanding Union Citizenship through Its Scope', in Dimitry Kochenov (ed.), *EU Citizenship and Federalism, The Role of Rights* (Cambridge: CUP, 2017); Charlotte O'Brien, 'Union Citizenship and Disability', in Dimitry Kochenov (ed.), *EU Citizenship and Federalism, The Role of Rights* (Cambridge: CUP, 2017).

[78] Moshe Cohen-Eliya and Iddo Porat, *Proportionality and Constitutional Culture*, (Cambridge: CUP, 2013). See also James Tully, *Strange Multiplicity: Constitutionalism in an Age of Diversity* (Cambridge: CUP, 1995) on the inherent problems of constitutionalism in the context of diversity.

[79] Linda Bosniak, 'Persons and Citizens in Constitutional Thought', *International Journal of Constitutional Law*, 8 (2010), 9; Loïc Azoulai, 'L'autonomie de l'individu européen et la question du statut' (2013) *EUI LAW Working Paper* 2013/14; Dimitry Kochenov, 'Citizenship of Personal Circumstances in Europe', in Daniel Thym (ed.), *Questioning Union Citizenship* (Hart Publishing, Oxford, forthcoming)

Member States and withdrawing from the realm of the potential or actual application of EU law are numerous, not a single clear-cut example of a state withdrawing from the Union has been recorded. It should be some consolation, however, that such an example is entirely unnecessary to definitively conclude on what will happen to the EU citizenship of the nationals of the withdrawing state. This status will simply expire and cease to exist for them. There is no persuasive argument which would permit this legal status to function as a legal pretext to deprive Article 50 TEU of its *effet utile* without depriving the people of the withdrawing Member State from the possibility of deciding, by democratic means, that no longer want EU membership. EU citizenship will go with the rest of the package. Withdrawal means leaving the ambit of the law of the Union and, in this sense, it will be no different from British Honduras leaving the UK or Java leaving the Netherlands.

## IV Political Dilemmas

Even though EU citizenship clearly cannot play a distinct role in the context of the practical application of Article 50 TEU, by providing legal argument against withdrawals resulting in the abolition of EU citizenship rights for the nationals of the withdrawing state, the considerations related to the supranational rights and status are bound to play an important role in the context of the withdrawal negotiations. While the EU's history of dealing with citizenship and territory issues, in the context of the deterioration of the colonial empires and the transformation of the Balkans and the Central and Eastern European countries, shows that the Union can be very flexible in trying to accommodate the specificity of the particular territories of its Member States; the context of the withdrawal negotiations could prove somewhat different from previous practice. This difference is due to the fact that EU citizenship is clearly *not* an autonomous status at the level of acquisition, numerous scholarly[80] and institutional[81] calls for change notwithstanding. Not

[80] For example, Dora Kostakopoulou, 'European Union Citizenship and Member State Nationality: Updating or Upgrading the Link', in Jo Shaw (ed.), Has the European Court of Justice Challenged the Member State Sovereignty in Nationality Law? (2011) *EUI Robert Schuman Centre for Advanced Studies* Paper No. 62.

[81] For example, most recently, European Economic and Social Committee (Rapporteur Pariza Castaños), 'Opinion on a More Inclusive Citizenship Open to Immigrants (own-initiative opinion)' (16 October, 2013) SOC/479: 'The Committee proposes that, in future, when the EU undertakes a new report of the Treaty (TFEU), it amends Article

being able to confer autonomous supranational level citizenship, the EU's room for manoeuvre in dealing with the wholesale loss of rights by the citizens of the withdrawing Member State is somewhat restrained, unless the Member States would be willing to change the Treaties to allow for an exceptional provision of full EU citizenship, or merely some rights associated therewith, for the nationals of the withdrawing state. The likelihood of this is nil, however, as the reasons for such an action on the part of the *Herren der Verträge* are not crystal clear. An alternative and more general reform, implying turning EU citizenship into a truly independent status at the level of acquisition and loss, is probably not politically viable at the moment, just as it has not been since the Treaty of Maastricht.

In a situation where such an independent supranational level status could be created, an array of legal options at hand would be significant, including, but not limited to four main options, tailored to ensure that the citizens of the withdrawing state do not lose supranational rights. This chapter is not the place to advocate for the creation of an autonomous status of supranational belonging. We should realise, however, that however improbable, it would be too much to say that it is legally or politically impossible. The following options come to mind:

1. Dual nationality of the EU and the withdrawing state. With the global rise of multiple nationality toleration, where dual nationality is not frowned upon in the majority of jurisdictions around the world, a combination of two nationalities could be the way forward, secured by a legal arrangement enabling independent EU citizenship not to expire for the nationals of a withdrawing Member State upon the departure of such a state from the Union.[82] Given that EU citizenship is not an independent status, however, this option is not achievable without serious reform to the law, unless one (or several) of the Member States wishes to naturalise all the citizens of the withdrawing state, which could be highly problematic from the perspective of EU law as discussed above.

20 so that third-country nationals who have stable, long-term resident status can also become EU citizens' (para. 1.11).

[82] In the sense that two distinct legal statuses are already available simultaneously to all the EU citizens, all the nationals of the Member States are unquestionably dual nationals, albeit holding the statuses which are not independent of each other, which is a common practice in federations: Christoph Schönberger, 'European Citizenship as Federal Citizenship', *European Review of Public Law* 19 (2007), 61.

2. Common nationality shared by the EU and the withdrawing state. This is an advanced variation on the previous option, the plausibility of which is weak for the same reason, though this does not make this option impossible. In fact, plenty of world entities share some variation of an arrangement of this kind. It is particularly favoured by semi-independent entities, which the UK will most likely end-up being as an outcome of the secession negotiations, given the high costs of complete secession leading to a total refusal to associate itself with the EU *acquis* and the internal market combined with the inability of the UK to influence EU-level law-making to the same degree of intensity as today, when it is still a Member State. All Arubans are in fact Dutch citizens, just as all Niueans are New Zealanders.
3. The elevation of the nationality of the withdrawing state to the rank of an associated nationality of the EU.[83] Examples of associated states offering their own nationality to their citizens in a legal context where that nationality in fact is equivalent, in a number of core respects, to the main nationality with which the state is associated are quite common. The Federated States of Micronesia nationality, in one example, entitles the bearer to home treatment and non-discrimination in the US, with which state the Federated States are associated.[84] Associated nationalities are usually acts of benevolence on the part of more potent states. In the context of the EU the recognition of the nationality of the withdrawing state as an associated nationality would most likely require Treaty change, or at least a common declaration by the remaining Member States. Given that the majority of the rights enjoyed by EU citizens, including most importantly free movement, are territorial in nature, and, knowing that the territory of the withdrawing state will not be part of EU territory for the purposes of such rights, it would be unclear why the Member States of the EU should take any such benevolent steps given that the territory of the withdrawing Member State will be off limits to EU citizens. This is a viable option, however, since the UK Government could always extend rights to EU nationals unilaterally, attaching its own conditions elaborated

[83] Seemingly a variation on this theme, albeit without legal elaboration, has been proposed by Guy Verhofstadt. See, *BBC*, 'Brexit: UK "Associate Citizensihp" to be Fasttracked' (9 Dec. 2016), www.bbc.com/news/world-europe-38264203 (last accessed: 25 Feb. 2017).

[84] Tung Lam Dang, 'Relation associative: les États Fédérés de Micronésie: les spécificités de l'association', in Jean-Yves Faberon et al. (eds.), *Destins des collectivités politiques d'Océanie*, Vol 1 (Marseille: Presses Universitaires d'Aix-Marseille, 2011).

under national law to the exercise of such rights, thus solving the mythical problem of 'unlimited free movement over which the UK has no control', which keeping free movement in place.

4. Lastly, and this option does not imply the creation of a truly independent EU citizenship status, an international agreement could be concluded between the withdrawing state and the EU and its Member States, aiming at ensuring that the free movement rights enjoyed by the nationals of all the parties involved continue beyond the point of the state's withdrawal. This option, which could be part of a larger EEA-like framework created by the parties, will however clearly undermine the effect of withdrawal and might therefore not be completely politically viable, unless the withdrawal is officially triggered by reasons unrelated to the issues of free movement and the management of the migration flows within the EU, which is not the case in the UK.

The four options above will most likely not be politically viable both in practice (as they will require Treaty change, or negotiating agreements *de facto* cancelling the effects of withdrawal from the EU) and in theory (as they assume that citizens voting for withdrawal want to remain EU citizens nevertheless – even if not in name). In other words, these options will, in all likelihood, not be acceptable to the parties, unless common sense prevails and the UK politicians start showing more responsibility for the future of their country.

This does not diminish the fact that plenty of outstanding problems caused by a Member State's withdrawal from the EU will need to be solved nevertheless. The solutions to such problems will necessarily need to imply taking the desire of the people of the withdrawing state precisely to withdraw seriously. The most viable among these could be the negotiation of bilateral free movement of persons agreements, between the withdrawing state and a handful of Member States. Such agreements will, however, address Member State nationals in their *national* status capacity and will thus not be concerned with EU citizenship as such.

## V Post-Secession Free Movement Bilateralism?

Any withdrawal from the EU offers its authors and their compatriots a disquieting dilemma. Any complete withdrawal automatically leads to a radical downgrade in the value of the nationality of the withdrawing state when viewed through the prism of the amount and the scale of rights such a nationality is associated with (see figure 13.1 below). The degree of difficulty

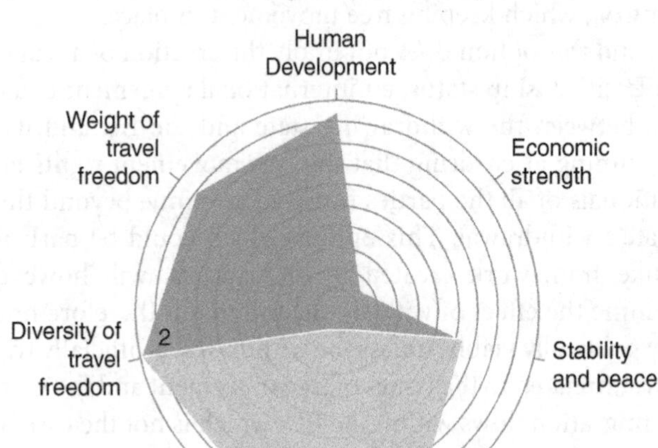

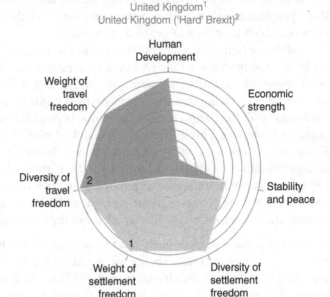

**Figure 13.1** The value of UK citizenship[85]

(and, possibly, human suffering) such an arrangement can cause is very difficult to ignore in the context of the negotiations. Yet no EU citizenship arguments as such could change the fate of the negotiating outcomes, as Article 50 TEU cannot be interpreted *contra legem*. Consequently, should Britain leave the EU, for instance, every British citizen in France, Poland, Spain and elsewhere in the Union (and there are hundreds of thousands of them) will instantly experience a rights downgrade to the level of Indian, Chilean or Russian citizens resident in the Union. Should the negotiations go well, such a downgrade could be mitigated somewhat, on a range from ensuring that UK citizens' standing in the EU is equal to Moroccans in the Union, to Turks in the Union, to the Swiss, and finally to the EEA nationals: Norwegians, Liechtensteiners and Icelanders.[86]

[85] The calculations used to produce the figure assume that the UK's withdrawal from the EU terminates UK nationals' supranational rights and follows the methodology of the *Quality of Nationality Index* (2016), (note 12).

[86] For an analysis of the exact rights of each of the privileged categories of foreigners in the EU, see, for example, Dimitry Kochenov and Martijn van den Brink, 'Pretending There Is No Union: Non-Derivative Quasi-Citizenship Rights of Third-Country Nationals in the EU', in Daniel Thym and Margarite Helena Zoetewij-Turhan (eds.), *Degrees of Free Movement and Citizenship* (Leiden: Brill-Nijhoff, 2015).

Only the latter two categories bring with them a right of free movement. Crucially, however, every additional grade on this scale means – and this is the dilemma – that the 'withdrawal' is increasingly illusory. Let us not forget that, in all likelihood, much more EU law applies in Iceland or Norway today than in the UK. In this context, the political price of securing privileges for its own citizens following withdrawal will most likely be very high. There is no reason at all to expect the Union to adopt an altruistic attitude towards former Member States busy ruining the European family as it stands today. That said, tailored mutually-beneficial bilateral free movement of persons arrangements, between the withdrawing state and the Union as a whole, or even a handful of other Member States, could provide a realistic way forward in an unfortunate context where a decision to withdraw is taken and cannot be rolled back.

## VI Post Scriptum

Once the outcome of the Brexit referendum was revealed on 24 June 2016, it became abundantly clear that this chapter would not be a purely hypothetical study of abstract possibilities. Following the decision of the UK, by a micro-majority of 51.9 per cent of those who took part in the referendum, to leave the Union, UK nationality will be seriously affected, bound *in fact* to lose political rights at the EP level and the local level elsewhere in the Union and, subject to the outcome of the Brexit negotiations, other EU citizenship rights.

In addition to affecting millions of people, this outcome is also a conceptual regression, detracting from the path towards European unity which has been characterised significantly by an ever-growing emphasis on rights,[87] providing an alternative to some national and nationalistic conceptualisations of the notion of citizenship, where duties rather than rights, at times tended to prevail. In this sense, if not in the nonsense sense of the UK debate – overflowing with absurd claims and with a hostile aversion to the facts – Brexit could be conceptualised as a knee-jerk reaction to precisely the values which the EU holds dear, as outlined in Article 2 TEU, thus implicitly disfavouring what Joppke characterised as the 'lightening of citizenship'[88] in favour of inclusion, non-discrimination and the protection of the rights of all residents. This would partially bring the UK

[87] Dimitry Kochenov, 'EU Citizenship without Duties', *European Law Journal*, 20 (2014), 482.

[88] Joppke, 'The Inevitable Lightening of Citizenship', (note 39); Joppke, Citizenship and Immigration, (note 39), 73–110.

in line with the general tendency of a 'grand return' of symbolic markers of 'thick' belonging in Europe, as exemplified by a rise in 'culture' and language testing.[89] In making this argument plausible, we should keep one fundamentally important difference in mind when comparing Brexit with 'ordinary' nationalism informed by anti-immigrant feelings: for the first time in recent history it is the actual citizens, *not* the naturalising newcomers or migrants, who are set to suffer the harsh consequences of a purely ideological andessentially, ill-informed decision.

While the role of the irrational in democratic politics is fundamental, and democratic institutions are usually designed to tame the blinding passions to a certain degree without silencing them entirely (which is probably a great explanation for democracy's success),[90] those who settle the cheques written by the outbursts of the irrational in citizenship and migration are almost never the citizens themselves. This is a pleasure always reserved to foreigners. The failure of the UK's institutions, which allowed for a 'democratic' decision[91] to opt for a 'plan B' when, firstly, there was no plan, and secondly, there was no correlation between the outstanding problems waiting for resolution and the democratic decision being taken, created this unique situation where the *citizens*, not so much the migrants, will now be asked to pay the hefty price of their own irrational fears.

Brexit could thus be presented as a triumph of a self-mutilating 'minimal human being',[92] if not the ruthless (or simply thoughtless?) behaviour of the British elites combined with the EU's own failure to distinguish between constitutionalism and the internal market,[93] leading

[89] Ricky van Oers, Eva Ersbøll and Dora Kostakopoulou (eds.), *A Re-definition of Belonging?* (Leiden: Brill-Nijhoff, 2010); Dimitry Kochenov, 'Mevrouw de Jong Gaat Eten: EU Citizenship and the Culture of Prejudice' (2011) *EUI Working Paper* RSCAS 2011/06.

[90] John Mueller, 'Democracy and Ralph's Pretty Good Grocery: Elections, Equality, and the Minimal Human Being', *American Journal of Political Science*, 36(1992), 983. The EU has been convincingly criticised for not paying enough attention to the irrational voices: Gareth Davies, 'Social Legitimacy and Purposive Power: The End, the Means and the Consent of the People', in Dimitry Kochenov, Gráinne de Búrca and Andrew Williams (eds.), *Europe's Justice Deficit?* (Oxford: Hart, 2015).

[91] For an analysis of the conceptual flaws in the thinking behind the referendum, which is as harsh as it is correct, see Kenneth Rogoff, 'Britain's Democratic Failure', *The Boston Globe* (25 June 2016), <www.bostonglobe.com/opinion/2016/06/24/britain-democratic-failure/Mx888Cle7t6OUyuWyX8n2M/story.html>, accessed 25 June 2016.

[92] Mueller, (note 90).

[93] Christian Joerges and Maria Weimer de Matta are absolutely right on this: 'The fictions upon which the project was based fostered its cause: integration is a good in itself which deserves to be promoted; and its promotion "through law" and legal institutions, in particular by a supranational court, is a reliable assurance of non-partisanship and

potentially to unjust regulation[94] which has undermined human lives, and constantly backed by expert claims selling a particular economic agenda as a science[95] of governance.[96] In truth, however, it would probably be unwise to criticise the Union for the self-mutilating inclinations of 'deep England'. Such arguments could gain credence if Greece were in Britain's place, probably;[97] in the case of Brexit – should we allow ourselves the dubious pleasure of passing judgment in terms of assigning the 'fault' – the cause of the problem seems to lie entirely with the political establishment of the country, all too ready to sacrifice the well-being of its citizens, if not the very existence of the state they are entrusted with, on the altar of short-term political convenience. Let us be fair: in the merry-go-round of *panem et circenses* that European politics is today, we know pretty well what to expect. In this respect the result of the referendum is *not* unexpected, all the pain it is likely to inflict notwithstanding.

The likely loss of free movement and political rights will hurt particularly. Once free movement is lost, UK nationals will only be able to work and reside in their country (including the Channel Islands, Gibraltar and the Island of Man, of course), not across the continent. This is an overwhelming cap to aspirations and possibilities: full sovereignty comes with its territory.

practical wisdom': Christian Joerges and Maria Weimer, 'A Crisis of Executive Managerialism in the EU: No Alternative?', in Gráinne de Búrca, Claire Kilptrick and Joanne Scott (eds.), *Critical Perspectives on Global Governance. Liber Amicorum David M. Trubek* (Oxford: Hart, 2014), 297; Kochenov, (note 11).

94 Editorial comments, 'The Critical Turn in EU Legal Studies', *CMLRev*, 52 (2015), 881 (and the literature cited therein). See Andrew Williams, *The Ethos of Europe* (Cambridge: CUP, 2009); Kochenov, de Búrca and Williams, (note 90); Floris de Witte, *Justice in the EU* (Oxford: OUP, 2015).

95 Marija Bartl, 'Internal Market Rationality, Private Law and the Direction of the Union: Resuscitating the Market as the Object of the Political', *European Law Journal*, 21 (2015), 572.

96 Gustav Peebles, '"A Very Eden of the Innate Rights of Man"? A Marxist Look at the European Union Treaties and Case Law', *Law and Social Inquiry*, 22(1997), 581, 605; Philip Allott, 'European Governance and the Re-branding of Democracy', *ELRev*, 27 (2002), 60; Dimitry Kochenov, 'The Citizenship Paradigm', *CYELS*, 15 (2013), 197; Charlotte O'Brien, 'I Trade Therefore I Am: Legal Personhood in the European Union', *CMLRev*, 50 (2013), 1643; Pedro Caro de Sousa, 'Quest for the Holy Grail – Is a Unified Approach to the Market Freedoms and European Citizenship Justified?', *European Law Journal*, 20 (2014), 499; Dimitry Kochenov, 'Neo-Mediaeval Permutations of Personhood in Europe', in Loïc Azoulai, Etienne Pataut and D. Barbou des Places (eds.), *Ideas of the Person and Personhood in European Union Law* (Oxford: Hart, 2016).

97 On the multi-layered crisis in Europe, see especially, Augustín J. Menéndez, 'The Existential Crisis of the European Union', *German Law Journal*, 14(5) (2013), 453.

Once political rights at the European level are lost, the citizens of the UK will not be able to influence the development of European law and policy, which will remain overwhelmingly important in the UK, as the Channel is unlikely to suddenly become a sea and the old trading (and other) ties will remain. Full sovereignty is only possible in the world of *Realpolitik*: as the EU's junior partner, the UK is bound to be a constant recipient of rules in a one-way relationship. Brexit, like 'full sovereignty', thus means less democracy and accountability. This is irrespective of what we think about the democratic nature of the EU itself, or the nitty-gritty behind the referendum, of course.

The loss of political rights at the municipal level for all the UK citizens residing in the EU will mean that Britons in Spain, France and Italy will not have a say at all in local politics, even in the municipalities where their interests are considerable, turned from equal members of the local communities into mere guests. No more British mayors in these outlying havens for retirees. Foreigners are outsiders.

In the grand scheme of things, the huge losses in terms of rights and the quality of nationality which the citizens of the UK are bound to experience now that they have spoken, are but the cherry on top of the Brexit pie, the recipe of which is so difficult for any intellectually honest person to understand. That the consequences of withdrawal will be harmful for many without solving the perceived but non-existent problems, such as 'welfare tourism' is as clear as day. In a unique feat of self-sacrifice of rights while asking for nothing in return and having no plan for the 'newly-regained' sovereignty – which will shrink the territory where the rights are enjoyed by British citizens as well as, most radically, their horizon of opportunities – the Brexit affair stands as a worrisome reminder that, in the absence of honest leadership and serious debate, the most absurd and harmful outcomes can certainly be produced by modern democracies. Britain awoke to a new, much less rational world of inexplicable mysticism and the self-inflicted mutilation of its citizenship.

# INDEX


*ab initio* citizenship, 164, 167
accession to EU, for newborn states, 95–96. *See also* Scotland
  bilateral issues for, 96–100
    economic operation factors, 100–102
    Euro as currency, 97–98
    military and defence issues, 99
    national boundary-setting, 98–99
    public debt and state property sharing, 99–100
  democratic principles, adherence to, 96
  economic governance factors for, 96, 232
  political stability as factor in, 96
  Rule of Law and, adherence to, 96
Accession Treaty, 80–81, 84–85, 87
accountability, democracy and, 20–22
Algeria, 78, 272, 273–274
Armstrong, Kenneth, 148
association agreements, 66

Baltic States. *See* Estonia; Latvia; Lithuania
Basque separatist movement, 71–72, 76
  cultural identity as factor in, 71–72
  economic interests as factor in, 72
  historical background for, 71
Bauböck, Rainer, 171, 181, 182–183, 266–267
Beary, Brian, 71
Belgium
  secessionist trends in, 76
  under Treaty of Lisbon, 58–59
Boyle, Alan, 117
British Exit (from EU) (Brexit)
  concretisation of withdrawal, 6
  Euroscepticism and, 13, 213
  free movement rights and, 156
  Gibraltar independence and, 7–8, 184
  international implications of, 283–285
  interpretation of votes for, 3
  MEPs and, 210–211
  Northern Ireland independence and, 7–8, 184
  Scotland and, 184
    independence from EU influenced by, 6–7
  Treaty of Lisbon and, 154–155
  votes for
    interpretation of, 3
    territorial disparities among, 158–159
Bulgaria, Schengen area and, 98

Cameron, David, 103, 137
Canada. *See also* Quebec, secession from Canada
  Clarity Act in, 62
CAP. *See* Common Agricultural Policy
Catalonia, secessionist movement in, 71–78, 136–144
  Catalan Parliament and, 139–141
    dissolution of, 141–142
  constitutional amendments for, 63
  Constitutional Court and, 139–141
  cultural identity as factor in, 71–72
  Declaration of Sovereignty in, 139–141
    draft resolution for, 143–144
  economic interests as factor in, 72
  EU citizenship issues in, 94
  EU neutrality on, 79
  Euroscepticism as factor in, 15–16

Catalonia (cont.)
historical background for, 71, 137–139
during Spanish Republic era, 138
from 1200–1930, 137–138
historical oppression in, 17
identity as predictor for support of, 3
illiberal democracy as factor in, 15–16
internal enlargement theatre of, 35
under international law, 88, 89–90, 91
international response against, 103
national citizenship in, 147–150
pro-independence parties in, 36, 49
provisional government in, 138
referendum on, informal presentation of, 73–76
regional elections for, 74, 75–76, 142–143
electoral results of, 142–143
under Socialist Government, 138–139
under Spanish Constitution, 62–63
Spanish Government response to, 72–73
as successor states, 92–93
unconstitutionality of, 62–63
change of voice mechanism, 211–213
Charter of Fundamental Rights, 146–147, 148–149
citizenship. *See also* EU citizenship
in iScotland, 159–171
*ab initio* model, 164, 167
under European Convention on Nationality, 164–165
identity politics and, 164–171
naturalisation criteria for, 167–168
new norms for, 164–171
laws for, legal purpose of, 159–160
national
EU citizenship compared to, 147–150
political citizenship in conflict with, 157–158
in Northern Ireland, 185–186
political, 157–158
territory and, 265–269
voting rights and, 183–186
citizenship rights
free movement rights, 156, 262–263, 281–283, 285
in iScotland, 175
after withdrawal from EU, 261–265
flexibility of, as EU tradition, 269–278
for free movement, 281–283, 285
free movement rights, 262–263
international agreements for, 281
naturalisation as part of, 271
political dilemmas as result of, 278–281
Clarity Act, 62
Common Agricultural Policy (CAP), 247
Conference on Security and Co-operation in Europe (CSCE), 69
Connolly, Christopher, 72
constitution without constitutionalism, in EU, 42
Constitutional Treaty, 52
Convention for the Protection of Human Rights and Fundamental Freedoms, 150
Convention on Future Europe, 192–193
Convention on Succession of States in Respect of State Property, 92
Convention on Succession of States in Respect to Treaties, 92
Copenhagen Criteria, for EU membership, 80, 90–91
Crawford, James, 117
Croatia, 70
Schengen area and, 98
CSCE. *See* Conference on Security and Co-operation in Europe
Cyprus, 91
Schengen area and, 98
Czech Republic, 79
Czechoslovakia. *See* Federation of Czechoslovakia

de Miguel Bárcena, Josu, 60–61, 81–82
Declaration of Sovereignty, for Catalonia, 139–141
  draft resolution for, 143–144
Declaration on Friendly Relations, 14
Dehousse, Renaud, 22–23
democracy. *See also* illiberal democracy
  accountability as part of, 20–22
  deficit of, in EU, 22–23, 24
  in EU, 5, 19–26
    accountability as part of, 20–22
    under Lisbon Treaty, 19
    *Panem et circenses* approach to, 25
    representation as part of, 20–22
  patterns of, 15
  public power through, 20
  representation as part of, 20–22
  in supranational organizations, desirable effects within, 5
democratic deficit, in EU, 22–23, 24

EC. *See* European Community
ECHR. *See* European Convention on Human Rights
ECJ. *See* European Court of Justice
ECtHR. *See* European Court of Human Rights
Edinburgh Agreement of 2012, 62, 154
  Political Parties, Elections and Referendum Act 2000 and, 112
  Scottish independence referendum under, 112, 117
Edward, Sir David, 44, 120
EEA. *See* European Economic Area
EEAS. *See* European External Action Service
EEC. *See* European Economic Community
EFTA. *See* European Free Trade Association
elections. *See also* referendums on independence; Scottish independence referendum
  for Brexit
    interpretation of votes, 3
    territorial vote disparities among, 158–159
  in Catalonia, for secession, 74, 75–76, 142–143
    electoral results of, 142–143
English Votes for English Laws (EVEL), 185
Estonia, 70
EU. *See* European Union
EU citizenship. *See also* political rights
  in Catalonia, after secession, 94
  in EU Member States, 127–131
  fundamental rights of
    under Charter of Fundamental Rights, 146–147, 148–149
    Member States' integrity and, 146–147
    right to secede as, 144–145
    Rule of Law and, 145
    secession as, 144–145
  inclusiveness for, 275–276
  national citizenship compared to, 147–150
  political citizenship in conflict with, 157–158
  political rights of, secession as, 134–135, 151–152
  *Rottmann* ruling and, 127–131
  in Scotland, after UK secession, 94–95, 127–131
  after secession from EU
    in Catalonia, 94
    political rights and, 134–135, 151–152
    in Scotland, 94–95, 127–131
    transitional rights for, 150–151
  state nationality as distinct from, 271
  territory and, 265–269
  in *Van Gend and Loos* case, 127–131
EU Court of Justice, 148–149
EU Member States. *See also* newborn EU Member States; partitions, of EU Member States; withdrawal, from EU
  citizenship in, 127–131
  Copenhagen Criteria for, 80, 90–91
  dissolution of, 91–93
    recognition of states after, 91–92
    successor states, 92–93

EU Member States (cont.)
new rights for, 191–199, 226–229
territorial organisation of, 51–60
EU Referendum Act 2015, 179
Euratom Treaty, 236, 238, 253
Euro as currency
in newborn EU Member States, 97
after Scottish secession from UK, 97
European Commission, 55–56, 57
European Community (EC), 48
Swiss Confederation and, 247–248
European Constitution, rejection of, 25–26
European Convention on Human Rights (ECHR), 114–115
European Convention on Nationality, 164–165
European Council, 219, 221, 236, 243
European Court of Human Rights (ECtHR), 94–95, 276–277
European Court of Justice (ECJ), 275–277
European Economic Area (EEA), 102, 246–248, 255
European Economic Community (EEC), 190
European External Action Service (EEAS), 102–103
European Free Trade Association (EFTA), 102, 234–235, 246–248, 255
European integration
Founding Fathers of, 17
independence movements as antithetical to, 18–19
referendums on independence and, 121–122
Schuman Plan and, 28–29
secession of EU Member States and, 65–66
withdrawal from EU and, conflicts with, 229–233
European Investment Bank, 93
European law
nationality under, 270
resources in, analysis of, 106–107
scholarship on Europeanisation and, 107
Scottish independence referendum under, 118–119, 132–133
international law in conflict with, 119–121
withdrawal from EU under, 217
European Neighbourhood Policy, 231–232
European Parliament
EU regionalism and, 55–56
UK MEPs and, 210–211
European Social Charter, 150
European Social Fund, 49
European Union (EU). *See also* exit options, from EU; partitions, of EU Member States; secession, of EU Member State; withdrawal, from EU
CAP in, 247
cohesion process for, 49
constitution without constitutionalism in, 42
Copenhagen Criteria for, 80, 90–91
democracy in, 5, 19–26
accountability as part of, 20–22
under Lisbon Treaty, 19
*Panem et circenses* approach to, 25
representation as part of, 20–22
democratic deficit in, 22–23, 24
derogations in, 2
'enlargement from within' for, 81–82
iScotland in, 177–181
legitimacy of, 24
MEPs and, 210–211, 222, 223
messianic narratives in, 15
modification of borders in, as taboo term, 69
neutrality of, towards Member State secession, 4, 36–41, 51–54, 61
'no demos' thesis and, 20
principles of, 6–8
Principles of International Law and, 69
public power through, 20
regionalism in
European Commission and, 55–56, 57
European Parliament and, 55–56
under treaties, 54–60

Scottish membership in, as independent nation, 7, 33–36, 122–127
legal mechanisms for, 124
long-term resonance of, 126–127
as negotiated membership, 124–125
under TEU, 123, 125–126
transition to, 123–126
Scottish withdrawal from, declaration of intent for, 126–127
secessionism in, as taboo term, 69
sub-state nations in, independence movements in, 32–36
successor states and, structured relationships between, 102–103
Swiss Confederation and, 248–249
UK withdrawal from, 1
voter participation in, decline in, 23–24
Europeanisation, scholarship on, 107
Euroscepticism, 12–13
Brexit and, 13, 213
in Catalonia, 15–16
iScotland and, 183–184
normalisation of, 12
Scottish secession from UK and, 15–16
EVEL. *See* English Votes for English Laws
*Exit, Voice and the State* (Hirschmann), 188
exit options, from EU. *See also* withdrawal, from EU
defined, 188
opt-outs, 2
product deterioration and, 208–210
selective, 211–213
voice and
change of voice mechanism and, 211–213
definition of, 188
during EU withdrawal, 188–191
loyalty and, 206–211
purpose of, 188

Færœ Islands, 267–268
Federation of Czechoslovakia, dissolution of, 70
Federation of Yugoslavia. *See also* Croatia; Slovenia
dissolution of, 70
Forcadell, Carme, 143
Frank, Anne, 29
free movement rights, 156, 262–263
in iScotland, 175
after withdrawal from EU, 281–283, 285
fundamental rights, of EU citizens
under Charter of Fundamental Rights, 146–147, 148–149
Member States' integrity and, 146–147
right to secede as, 144–145
under TEU, 145
Rule of Law and, 145

Gasperi, Alcide De, 29
Germany
Constitutional Court in, 150
National Socialism in, 29
under Treaty of Lisbon, 58–59
Gibraltar, independence movement for, Brexit as factor for, 7–8
González Bondía, Alfóns, 144
Greece, 91–92
Greenland, 78, 190, 273

Heidegger, Martin, 27
Herder's Community of Fate, 26–27
Hillion, C., 241–242
Hirschmann, Albert O., 187, 188
on loyalty, 206–211
on voice during EU withdrawal, 188–191
Hix, Simon, 210
Hollande, François, 103
Holy See, Euro as currency in, 97
Horowitz, D. L., 78
Human Rights Act 1998, 115
*Hungary v. Slovak Republic*, 136

ICCPR. *See* International Covenant on Civil and Political Rights
Iceland, 98

identity politics, 164–171
IGC. *See* Inter-Governmental Conference
illiberal democracy
  Catalonia secession movement and, 15–16
  Scotland secession movement and, 15–16
independence movements. *See also* Euroscepticism; referendums on independence; Scottish independence referendum
  European integration and, 18–19
  in Gibraltar, 7–8
  in Kosovo, 89
  in Montenegro, 60
  national citizenship and, 147–150
  in Northern Ireland, Brexit as factor for, 7–8
  in sub-state nations, 32–36
  in Veneto, Italy, 49, 50
    Italian Constitutional Court decisions on, 63–64
  Weiler on, 36–41, 121–122
independent Scotland (iScotland), 156
  citizenship in, 159–171
    *ab initio* model, 164, 167
    under European Convention on Nationality, 164–165
    identity politics and, 164–171
    naturalisation criteria for, 167–168
    new norms for, 164–171
  democratic policies in, 171–183
  electoral campaigns for, 162–163
  emigration history as influence in, 160–163
  in EU, 177–181
  Euroscepticism and, 183–184
  free movement rights in, 175
  putative *demos* in, 182–183
  rUK citizenship in, 169–170
  under Scottish Independence Referendum (Franchise) Act 2013, 112, 154, 173, 175
  state boundary issues for, 185–186
  under Thatcher, 161–162
  troubled membership in, 154–159, 183–186
  voting rights in, 172–178
  welfare state policies in, 162
Inter-Governmental Conference (IGC), 80–81
internal enlargement theatre
  of Catalonia, 35
  EU and, 81–82
International Covenant on Civil and Political Rights (ICCPR), 114–115
international law
  diplomatic rules of, 104–105
  EU withdrawal under, 198
  Principles of International Law, 69
  Quebec secession from Canada under, 88–89, 116
  Scottish independence referendum under, 116–118
    European law in conflict with, 119–121
  self-determination for sub-states under, 69
    in Catalonia, 88, 89–90, 91
    in Kosovo, 89
    in Quebec, 88–89
Ireland. *See* Northern Ireland; Republic of Ireland
iScotland. *See* independent Scotland
Italy. *See also* Veneto, independence movement for
  Constitutional Court decisions in, 63–64
  secessionist trends in, 76
  Veneto independence movement for, 49, 50

Joerges, Christian, 284–285
Juncker, Jean-Claude, 37–38, 81–82
Junqueras, Oriol, 142

Kokott, Julianne, 146
Kosovo
  Euro as currency in, 97
  independence movement for, under international law, 89
  international recognition of, 91

Latvia, 70
law. *See* European law; international law
Lenarcic, Janez, 19
Liechtenstein, 98
Lisbon Treaty, 8
  democracy under, 19
Lithuania, 70
loyalty, 206–211

Maastricht Treaty, 150
  EU regionalism under, 54–60
MacCormick, Neil, 81
Maier, Charles, 30
Marr, Andrew, 37–38
Marshal, T. H., 267
Mas, Artur, 75, 77, 142
May, Theresa, 184
Mazower, Mark, 15
Members of (EU) Parliament (MEPs), 210–211, 222, 223
Merkel, Angela, 103
messianic narratives, in EU
  in Catalonia secession movement, 15–16
  in Scotland secession movement, 15–16
Milward, Alan, 30
Mitchell, James, 184–185
modification of borders, as taboo term, 69
Monaco
  Euro as currency in, 97
  in Schengen area, 98
Monnet, Jean, 17
Montenegro
  Euro as currency in, 97
  independence movement in, 60

national citizenship
  EU citizenship compared to, 147–150
  political citizenship in conflict with, 157–158
National Socialism, 26–27, 29
nationalism
  referendums on independence influenced by, 121–122
  secession movements influenced by, 26–31
  SNP and, 160–161
nationality. *See also* citizenship
  EU citizenship as distinct from, 271
  under European Convention on Nationality, 164–165
  under European law, 270
  after withdrawal from EU
    common, 280
    dual, 279
naturalisation
  citizenship rights and, 271
  in iScotland, 167–168
newborn EU Member States, 77, 81–82. *See also* accession to EU, for newborn states; partitions, of EU Member States
  accession issues for, 95–96
    democratic principles, 96
    economic governance factors, 96
    political stability, 96
    Rule of Law as, 96
  bilateral issues for, economic operation factors, 100–102
  citizens in, 93–95
  EEA and, 102
  under EFTA, 102
  under EU treaties, 79–87
    legal procedures through, 80
    procedures arguments for, 82–87
    substance arguments for, 82–87
    TEU, 80–87
  Euro as currency in, 97
  right to work in, 101
  successor states as, 92–93
    citizens in, 93–95
    currency concerns in, 97–98
  under TEU, 80–87
    under Article 49, 82–87
    for EU admission procedures, 80–82
Nietzsche, Friedrich, 27
'no demos' thesis, 20
non-resident citizens, in Scotland, 157
Northern Ireland
  citizenship requests in, 185–186

Northern Ireland (cont.)
  independence movement for, Brexit as factor for, 7–8
  Referendums (Scotland and Wales) Act 1997 and, 110–111
Norway, 98

Obama, Barack, 103
OECS. *See* Organization for Eastern Caribbean States
O'Neill, Aidan, 134, 174–175
OPCW. *See* Organization for the Prohibition of Chemical Weapons
opt-outs, 2
Organization for Eastern Caribbean States (OECS), 191–192
Organization for the Prohibition of Chemical Weapons (OPCW), 191–192

*Panem et circenses* approach, to democracy, 25
partitions, of EU Member States
  under EU treaties, 79–87
    legal procedures through, 80
    procedures arguments for, 82–87
    substance arguments for, 82–87
    TEU, 80–87
  Rule of Law and, 79
  as taboo term, 69–70
  under TEU, 80–87
    under Article 49, 82–87
    for EU admission procedures, 80–82
political citizenship, 157–158
Political Parties, Elections and Referendum Act 2000, 111
  Edinburgh Agreement of 2012 and, 112
political rights, of EU citizens
  right to secede as, 134–135, 151–152
  after withdrawal from EU, 286
Primary Right or Choice theory, 38–39
principle of subsidiarity, 50, 56–57
Principles of International Law, 69
Prodi, Romano, 81–82
public power, 20
Puigdemont, Carles, 143–144
Pujol, Jordi, 138, 141

Quebec, secession from Canada, 14
  Canada Supreme Court ruling and, 62
  under Clarity Act, 62
  under international law, 88–89, 116
*Quebec Secession* case, 39

Referendums (Scotland and Wales) Act 1997, 110–111
referendums on independence. *See also* Scottish independence referendum
  in Catalonia, informal secessionist movement presentations, 73–76
  European integration and, 121–122
  European resources on, 108
  legality of, 109–122
  nationalism as factor in, 121–122
regional blindness, 48–51
  defined, 48–49
Remedial Right or Just Cause theory, 38–39
representation, democracy and, 20–22
Republic of Ireland, 98–99. *See also* Northern Ireland
rest of the UK (rUK), 156
  citizenship, 169–170
Ridao, Joan, 144
right to work, in newborn EU Member States, 101
rights. *See* fundamental rights
Romania, 91
  Schengen area and, 98
*Rottmann* ruling, 127–131
rUK. *See* rest of the UK
Rule of Law
  EU citizenship under, 145
  partitions of EU states and, 79
  secession of EU Member States under, 4, 65
  TEU and, 61–62
  withdrawal from EU and, 4

Salmond, Alex, 72, 134, 137
Saunders, Ben, 182

Schengen area, 98–99
Schuman Plan, 28–29
Scotland, secession from UK, 71–78. *See also* independent Scotland; Scottish independence referendum
 under Accession Treaty, 80–81
 bilateral issues for EU membership, 96–100
  economic operator issues, 100–102
  Euro as currency, 97–98
  military and defence issues, 99
  national boundary-setting, 98–99
  public debt and state property sharing, 99–100
 Brexit and, 184
  independence from EU influenced by, 6–7
 campaign length for, 33
 constitutional agreements in, 62
 constitutional issues, 122–127
  for continuity of governance, 123–126
 under Edinburgh Agreement of 2012, 62, 154
  Political Parties, Elections and Referendum Act 2000 and, 112
  Scottish independence referendum and, 112, 117
 electoral campaigns in, 162–163
 emigration history in, 160–163
 EU citizenship issues after, 94–95, 127–131, 154–159
 EU neutrality on, 79
 Euroscepticism as factor in, 15–16
 government structure in, 126–127
 historical background for, 72
 illiberal democracy as factor in, 15–16
 as independent EU member, 7, 33–36, 122–127
  legal mechanisms for, 124
  long-term resonance of, 126–127
  as negotiated membership, 124–125
  under TEU, 123, 125–126
  transition to, 123–126
 national citizenship in, 147–150
 non-resident citizens in, 157
 *Rottmann* ruling and, 127–131
 Scottish Independence Referendum Act 2013 and, 112, 154
 self-government in, historical development of, 160–163
 SNP and, 35–36, 72, 126
  as civic nationalist party, 160–161
 as successor states, 92–93
 under TEU, 33–36, 123, 125–126
 Thatcher government and, 161–162
 UK Government response to, 72–73
 *Van Gend and Loos* case and, 127–131
 welfare state policies in, 162
 withdrawal from EU and, declaration of intent for, 126–127
Scotland Act 1998, 112, 160–161
Scottish First, 65
Scottish independence referendum, 1, 49. *See also* independent Scotland
 Brexit as factor in, 6–7
 Edinburgh Agreement of 2012 and, 112, 117
 electoral votes against, 131–132
 under European law, 118–119, 132–133
  international law in conflict with, 119–121
 inclusiveness criteria as part of, 181–182
 interior perspective on, 106
 under international law, 116–118
  European law in conflict with, 119–121
 legality of, 109–122
  constitutional context for, 110–112
  external legal resources for, 113–115
  framework for, 112–113
  as process, 116–119
 legitimacy of, 117
 normative considerations for, 181–183
 organisation of, 73–76

Scottish (cont.)
political contestation of, 132
Political Parties, Elections and Referendum Act 2000 and, 111
Referendums (Scotland and Wales) Act 1997 and, 110–111
Scotland Act 1998, 112
triple-locks against future referendums, 127
*Van Gend and Loos* case and, 119–121
Scottish Independence Referendum (Franchise) Act 2013, 112, 154, 173, 175
Scottish National Party (SNP), 35–36, 72, 126
as civic nationalist party, 160–161
secession, of EU Member State. *See also* Catalonia; Euroscepticism; Scotland
contradictory trends in, 12–13, 25–26, 70–71
EU citizenship after
in Catalonia, 94
political rights and, 134–135, 151–152
in Scotland, 94–95, 127–131
transitional rights for, 150–151
EU neutrality towards, 4, 36–41, 51–54, 61
EU responsibility in, 76–78
European integration strategies and, 65–66
Euroscepticism and, 12–13
as fundamental right, of EU citizens, 144–145
historical development of, 16–19
international negative consequences of, 105
legal strategies for, 64–66
with *ad hoc* clauses, 66
with association agreements, 66
through consistent procedures, 67–68
through monitoring processes, 68
as moral paradox, 78–79
nationalism and, 26–31
political debate on, 41–46
on procedures, 42–45
reframing of political imagination in, 45–46
as political paradox, 78–79
as political right, of EU citizens, 134–135, 151–152
as process, 136–137
under domestic constitutional law, 137
under European law, 136
under international law, 136
reconfiguration of power as factor in, 2
under Rule of Law, 65
at state level, 2–3
constitutional requirements and, 4
Rule of Law and, 4
types of, distinctions between, 60–64
withdrawal from EU and
comparisons between, 2–6
EU principles as factor in, 6–8
secessionism, as taboo term, 69
selective exit, from EU, 211–213
separatist movements. *See also* secession, of EU Member State
among Basque, in Spain, 71–72, 76
cultural identity as factor in, 71–72
economic interests as factor in, 72
historical background for, 71
EU responsibility for, 76–78
Seubert, Sandra, 158
Single Act, 150
Slovakia, 79
Kosovo recognized by, 91
Slovenia, 70
SNP. *See* Scottish National Party
Socialist Government, in Catalonia, 138–139
Spain. *See also* Catalonia
Basque separatist movement in, 71–72, 76
cultural identity as factor in, 71–72
economic interests as factor in, 72
historical background for, 71
Constitution for, 62–63
Kosovo recognized by, 91
Spanish Republic era, 138
*Spitzenkandidaten* exercise, 21

Statutes of Minorities, 16
Sturgeon, Nicola, 65, 72, 112, 117, 184
Suárez, Adolfo, 138
successor states, 92–93
  citizens in, 93–95
  currency concerns for, 97–98
  EU and, structured relationships between, 102–103
Sunstein, Cass, 213
Swiss Confederation, 247–249
Switzerland, 102–103

Tarradellas, Josep, 138
TCE. *See* Treaty Establishing a Constitution for Europe
territory, citizenship and, 265–269
  in EU, 265–269
TEU. *See* Treaty on European Union
TFEU. *See* Treaty on Functioning of European Union
Thatcher, Margaret, 161–162
*Transformation of Europe* (Weiler), 189
treaties, EU. *See also* Maastricht Treaty; Treaty of Lisbon; Treaty on European Union; Treaty on Functioning of European Union
  partitions of EU states under, 79–87
    legal procedures through, 80
    procedures arguments for, 82–87
    substance arguments for, 82–87
    TEU, 80–87
Treaty Establishing a Constitution for Europe (TCE), 229–230
Treaty of Lisbon, 44, 53
  Belgium under, 58–59
  Brexit vote and, 154–155
  Committee of the Regions and, 59
  EU regionalism under, 54–60
  EU withdrawal under, 187
    under Article 50, 191–199
    formalisation procedures for, 191–199
    non-immediate effects of, 197–199
    unconditional criteria for, 191–192, 193–197
  Germany under, 58–59
  right to EU withdrawal under, 187, 226. *See also* withdrawal, from EU
    under Article 50, 191–199, 226–229
    formalisation procedures, 191–199
    non-immediate effects of, 197–199
Treaty of Maastricht. *See* Maastricht Treaty
Treaty on European Union (TEU). *See also* withdrawal, from EU
  partitions of EU nations under, 80–87
    under Article 49, 82–87
    for EU admission procedures, 80–82
  principle of subsidiarity in, 50, 56–57
  Rule of Law and, 61–62
  Scotland under, after secession from UK, 33–36, 123, 125–126
Treaty on Functioning of European Union (TFEU), 238, 239–244, 251
troubled membership, in iScotland, 154–159, 183–186

United Kingdom (UK). *See also* British Exit; rest of the UK; Scotland, secession from UK; Scottish independence referendum
  historical development of, 154–155
  MEPs in, 210–211
  Referendums (Scotland and Wales) Act 1997 and, 110–111
  Schengen area and, 98–99
  special economic considerations for, 209
  Thatcher government in, 161–162
USSR, dissolution of, 70

Valls, Manuel, 103
*Van Gend and Loos* case, 100
  EU citizenship in, 127–131
  *Vangendeology* and, 119–121, 131
Van Rompuy, Herman, 60–61, 82
*Vangendeology*, 119–121, 131

VCLT. *See* Vienna Convention on the Law of Treaties
Veneto, independence movement for, 49, 50
  Italian Constitutional Court decisions on, 63–64
Vienna Convention on the Law of Treaties (VCLT), 189, 226, 230
voice
  change of voice mechanism and, 211–213
  definition of, 188
  during EU withdrawal, 188–191
  loyalty and, 206–211
  purpose of, 188
vote totals, for Brexit, 3
  territorial disparities among, 158–159
voters, in EU, 23–24
voting rights
  citizenship and, 183–186
  in iScotland, 172–178

Weiler, Joseph H. H., 1, 32, 76, 187, 189
  on national independence movements, 36–41, 121–122
Weimer de Matta, Maria, 284–285
welfare state policies, as Scottish tradition, 162
White, Jonathan, 161
William of Ockham, 27
withdrawal, from EU. *See also* secession
  agreements for
    approval of, 250–252
    guillotine clause in, 246
    legal character of, 238–239
    negotiation mandates in, 239–241
    substance of, 244–250
  citizenship rights after, 261–265
    flexibility of, as EU tradition, 269–278
    for free movement, 281–283, 285
    international agreements for, 281
    naturalisation as part of, 271
    political dilemmas as result of, 278–281
  common nationality after, 280
  Convention on Future Europe and, 192–193
  dual nationality after, 279
  EEA and, 102, 246–248, 255
  EFTA and, 102, 234–235, 246–248, 255
  as elaboration of constitutional devices, 231
  enforcement of, 252–255
  entry into force for, 252–255
  EU integration and, conflicts with, 229–233
  under EU law, 217
  Euratom Treaty and, 236, 238, 253
  European Council and, 219, 221, 236, 243
  exit provisions in, 199–204
    economic centralisation and redistribution limitations in, 200–201
    organisation membership expansion and, 199–200
  under international law, 198
  length of EU membership and, 203
  loyalty and, 206–211
  MEPs and, 210–211, 222, 223
  nationality after
    common, 280
    dual, 279
  negotiated departure strategy in, 223
  political rationale for, 204–206
    endogenous factors in, 205–206
    exogenous factors in, 204–205
  political rights after, 286
  procedures for, 237–255
    modus operandi for, 241–244
    under TEU, 216–226
  ratification of, 252–255
  reconfiguration of power as factor in, 2
  reputational effects from, 201
  Rule of Law and, 4
  secession of EU Member State and
    comparisons between, 2–6
    EU principles as factor in, 6–8
  spill-over effects of, 203–204

at state level, 2–3
constitutional requirements and, 4
Rule of Law and, 4
strategic behaviour in, 201–203
under TEU, 215–216, 229–233
procedures for, 216–226
under TFEU, 238, 239–244, 251
under Treaty of Lisbon, 187, 226
under Article 50, 191–199, 226–229
formalisation procedures, 191–199
non-immediate effects of, 197–199
by UK. *See* British Exit
unconditional criteria for, 191–192, 193–197
as unilateral decision, 4
unilateral option for, 235–237
under VCLT, 189, 226, 230
voice during
change of voice mechanism and, 211–213
definition of, 188
during EU withdrawal, 188–191
loyalty and, 206–211
purpose of, 188

Yugoslavia. *See* Federation of Yugoslavia

Zapatera, Rodríguez, 138–139
Ziegler, Ruvi, 181